OUT OF PLACE

SUNY Series, INTERRUPTIONS:
Border Testimony(ies) and Critical Discourses
Henry A. Giroux, editor

OUT OF PLACE

Homeless Mobilizations, Subcities,
and Contested Landscapes

Talmadge Wright

State University of New York Press

Published by
State University of New York Press, Albany

©1997 State University of New York Press

For information, address State University of New York Press
State University Plaza, Albany, NY 12246

Production by Dana Foote
Marketing by Nancy Farrell

Library of Congress Cataloging-in-Publication Data

Wright, Talmadge.
    Out of place : homeless mobilizations, subcities, and contested
landscapes / Talmadge Wright.
        p.   cm. — (SUNY series, Interruptions — Border
testimony(ies) and critical discourses)
    Includes bibliographical references and index.
    ISBN 0-7914-3369-2 (hc : alk. paper). — ISBN 0-7914-3370-6 (pbk.
: alk. paper)
    1. Homelessness—United States. 2. Homeless persons—United
States—Political activity.   3. Public spaces—United States.   I. Series.
HV4505.W77   1997
362.5'8'0973—dc21
                                                                96-48447
                                                                CIP

In memory of my mother Laura Virginia Wright
and
my father Thomas J. Wright

And for all of those homeless men, women, and children
whose lives deserve the dignity and respect of all free people

Figures

Maps

ACKNOWLEDGMENTS

This book has emerged slowly over the past several years as a consequence of my involvement with homeless issues, social and cultural theory, urban studies, and social movements. Anchored in my concrete experiences with several different homeless communities and attempting to bridge the gap between the student community of the university and the street encampments and shelter spaces for many of the nation's poor, I have struggled to understand why homelessness has persisted in one of the wealthiest nations in the world. In particular, how were homeless persons and their supporters taking to the streets to effect change in a context of rapidly changing city economies and redevelopment strategies?

I owe a great deal to a great many people who have helped made this book possible through their support, encouragement, and critical comments at various stages. I would first like to thank Loyola University Chicago for their generous research grant support and media assistance, without which this book would not have been possible. The granting of a 1995 fall sabbatical by Loyola University was invaluable in enabling me to finish up large segments of the book and continue other research in the Chicago area on street homelessness. A special thanks also to the Chicago Coalition for the Homeless, who graciously provided me with primary source materials and verbal encouragement. And I would also like to thank the past and current members of the Student-Homeless Alliance and the former encampment members of Tranquility City in Chicago for granting me the necessary interviews and including me in their everyday lives. A special thanks to John Donahue, Les Brown, Calvin Gatewood, and Charles Nix for their assistance in helping me understand the world of one sector of Chicago's homeless.

I wish to thank the following colleagues of mine who have read early drafts or commented on various parts of the book at one stage or another: Kim Hopper, Peter Marcuse, Marc Gottdiener, Joe Feagin,

Ray Hutchinson, Sue Ruddick, Michael P. Smith, Roger Keil, David Wagner, Rob Rosenthal, Charles Hoch, Daniel Cress, Leon Anderson, Margory Robertson, William Spencer, Margit Meyer, Henri Giroux, Michael Robertson, Stephen and Maria-Videl Haymes, Phil Nyden, and Lauren Langman. I also wish to thank Michael Roberts, Suzanne Jones, Scott Wagers, and Nancy Nichols, whose explanations and continuing information about the progress of the Student-Homeless Alliance were most helpful. A special thanks is warranted to Scott and Nancy, who first introduced me to the street encampments in San Jose, California. I would also like to thank the Bay Area Homelessness Program based at San Francisco State University and the Sociology Department and the School of Social Work at San Jose State University for their support in assisting the internship program that facilitated my involvement with the Student-Homeless Alliance.

The following graduate research assistants have assisted in editing, reading, and in commenting on various parts of the manuscript over the past few years: Annette Prosterman, David Campbell, Edwina Jones, Mike Leachman, and Costas Spirou. In addition, my former undergraduate student Pat Baltazar deserves a special thanks for his work with the Tranquility City encampments and for his assistance in transcribing many of the ethnographic tapes. If I have left anyone out, the fault is mine and I apologize. Please be assured that your contributions were no less important to this project.

Early versions of several chapters were delivered as conference papers at the Midwest Sociological Association meetings, the 1994 International Sociological Association Conference (in Bielefeld, Germany), the American Sociological Association, and the Society for the Study of Social Problems. I would also like to thank the Chicago *Tribune* for permitting me to reproduce several important quotes concerning West Loop Shelters. I would also like to thank Oxford University Press for granting me permission to reproduce material from *Cultural Critique* by Linda Alcoff.

Finally, an early version of material from the Tranquility City hut encampments appeared in the 1995 *Comparative Urban and Regional Research,* Volume 5 series, *Marginal Spaces,* edited by Michael P. Smith, with the title "Tranquility City and Shelters: Homeless Placemaking, Protest, and Collective Gains within a Chicago Homeless Encampment" (pp. 37–68).

INTRODUCTION:
OUT OF PLACE

*One of the most powerful findings of recent research . . . is that there is no such group as "the homeless." . . .
Homelessness is not a characteristic of people, but rather a condition in which some people find themselves at some point in time.* (Blasi 1990, 208–9)

Might it not be more instructive to portray those who happen . . . to be homeless, as members of a larger class of the economically marginal. (Hopper 1991, 170).

In the contemporary United States, those identified by others as homeless act as stand-ins for "the poor," categories of people defined by their appearance and behavior rather than by their income or class. Visible homeless bodies, their comportment and appearance, have replaced invisible abstract notions of "poverty" as a key social concern. Poverty appears as too abstract and too overwhelming. This artificial separation between homelessness and poverty has direct implications for public policy and for the individuals who find themselves living on the streets. Those calling for the redistribution of wealth and income to address poverty are perceived as utopian dreamers, while others who build homeless shelters are rewarded for contributing to solving homelessness. Larger issues of power, property, and poverty are subordinated to technocratic considerations of funding patterns, grant writing, and shelter management.

The destitute who sleep in local parks, shelters, or motels, or spend nights on a friend's living room floor, with no fixed residence of their own, are people deemed out of place in the eyes of authority. And to be out of place means risking inspection by others, having one's identity defined by others as suspect, as "deviant," or "criminal," or as just "sick." Homeless bodies, poor bodies, visible to passersby, visible to the streets, are open to the public's gaze, to the gaze of authority. The policing of poor bodies by the cop on the beat, the social worker, the advocate, or the academic policy maker is informed by theoretical and ideological assumptions that presuppose normative notions of poverty, family, work, property, and power, of maintaining the status quo. As Wagner (1993) pointed out in his study of North City homeless residents, such normative notions provide an interpretive framework within which a homeless person's actions may be judged as "deviant," ignoring the fact that many, at least in the street camps he studied, "often fled family life, felt humiliated and oppressed by employers, and resisted government controls" (43). Normative notions of family and work are bound up with the equation that all families are places of nurture and that all work is healthy and good for one's soul. Homeless persons wander not only through the physical borders of our cities, but also through social borders, defined by moral, ethical, and normative interpretations of behavior. Resisting these normative interpretations is risky, but accomplished every day by members of street and shelter communities.

   This work explores the relationship between homeless social and political mobilization and urban social-physical spaces, the spaces of contested landscapes, the most visible terrain of the very poor. A comparative study of two distinct homeless communities and their attendant protests, one in a large midwestern city (Chicago), the other in California's San Francisco Bay region (San Jose), was conducted from 1989 through 1993. Both communities constituted microcase studies, bounded "cultural systems of action" (Snow and Anderson 1991), lending themselves to a combination of participant-observation, interviewing, and just "hanging out" (Rosenthal 1991), a method that gives a more accurate portrayal of homeless agency than simply conducting anonymous surveys. The mode of participant-observation chosen was a combination of what Snow, Benford, and Anderson (1986, 384–85) call the "buddy researcher" and the "ardent activist." The San Jose, California, homeless organization, called the Student-Homeless Alliance (SHA), involved the integration of students based at San Jose State University, homeless members, and community activists in a community that struggled to secure housing and dignity for its members from 1989 through 1993. I hesitate to say "organizations," because the groups studied had very little in the way of organizational structure, conforming more closely to the antisystemic movements found in fourteenth-century peasant rebellions. The term *affinity group* would be a more accurate description. SHA members set into motion a soup kitchen, direct advocacy for street homeless persons, public protests at local city council meetings, and finally militant planned housing takeovers in San Jose during November 1991. More than fifty persons were involved in the housing takeovers, including local homeless participants, students, church members and community activists. What began as a service-research ethnographic project evolved into a direct action group as students and homeless began to cope with the ramifications of their work.

As the initial advisor to SHA I facilitated relations between the homeless, the students and community activists, and municipal agencies placing me in an excellent position to observe the unfolding of group action over the course of a year and a half. My direct involvement with the group began informally by working with a student who had committed his time to assisting those people living under the bridges in downtown San Jose. This informal work developed into a formal commitment by June of 1990 continuing until my departure in June 1991. However, my involvement with group members has continued to this day from a distance, with occasional advice sought and given. During the formal research/activism period students acted as field researchers assisting homeless members, developed defensive strategies in coping with police harassment, assisted the homeless in accessing local social welfare agencies, and kept records of news clippings and television coverage of SHA events. Over twelve hours of video footage were recorded of SHA events, homeless camps, and interviews with homeless camp members. Student journals, field notes, and a chronology of events of the group were also developed. Documents generated by SHA were filed away for future reference. The intent was to conduct research while also being aware of how our involvement changed such research through our activist work. The object in all cases was to empower both the students and the homeless; to expand research, analysis, and action beyond the standard models of individual self-help into political and social change. Finally, systematic in-depth interviews were conducted in August and September 1992 with thirteen homeless and ex-homeless participants and ten student participants who were either still involved with SHA or had been involved in SHA sometime during the previous two years.

In Chicago, Illinois, between October 1991 and June 1992, I studied a set of homeless encampments on the Near West Side named "Tranquility City" by the encampment dwellers. These twenty-two huts were counted as home by over fifty people, according to hut dwellers, helping to generate a new homeless community. These organized homeless encampment members were able to establish extensive social networks with Chicago-area churches and local art galleries and enlist the assistance of community activists. In their active resistance to being moved, homeless participants were able to secure public housing for all of their encampment's members, without resorting to the indignities of the shelter system. The hut encampments in turn gave birth to a separate homeless organization called the People's Campaign for Jobs, Housing, and Food, which continued to organize homeless persons and the very poor from the confines of the Lathrop Homes public housing projects.

A product of several years of work with homeless people, students, and community activists, this work is an attempt, for me, to come to terms with what I saw as a nascent, presocial movement within the homeless communities I studied. In Chicago, I visited the homeless camps often, about once a week, sometimes twice, assisted by my students. Field observations were supplemented with thirteen in-depth interviews out of the initial thirty-six persons who I was told had lived in the camps (although later I was told that the number was closer to fifty) and seven with those who were indirectly involved. Interviews were conducted at a local homeless advocacy office and in the Chicago public housing projects, after the dismantling of the encampments. In both San Jose and Chicago, I was able to view longitudinally the development of two independent and quite different homeless groups. While I was in the field, my observation of how urban spaces were polarized into a multitude of different uses and meanings, and the manners in which both homeless and non-homeless used those spaces, called into question for me issues of social identity, social change, and the struggle over the meaning of urban space.

Urban spaces provide the immediate locales for both confirmation of and opposition to authoritative interpretations (normalizing) of one's ascribed status. The social identity one is charged with is closely bound up with both the social spaces (the networks of achieved and ascribed status distinctions imposed by others) and the physical spaces within which such status distinctions are grounded and through which one traverses. These spaces, what I term "social-physical spaces," are the fabric of urban, suburban, and rural landscapes. Urban, suburban, and rural spaces are endowed with interpretive, emotional meanings that create a social terrain, as well as a physical terrain, that must be navigated in order to preserve or alter one's identity; i.e. social-physical space. When I use the terms *space* and *urban space,* it is this concept of social-physical space to which I refer. Far from being separate from one's identity, social-physical space is intimately bound up with the constitution of identities, homeless or otherwise. It is easy enough to view this construction of identity in the particular characteristics of regional identities and what are often termed "cultural differences."

Identities require and acquire spaces within which they may be adopted. The relationship that one develops with surrounding spaces is a relationship predicated upon the acceptance or refusal of the defining of that space by others, either in authority or not in authority. For privileged consumers, the social and physical quality of the spaces through which they move—the shopping mall, the city park, the freeway, the office and restaurant complexes—present little challenge to their established identities insofar as such spaces are rendered consistent with previously established notions of a privileged identity. For homeless persons who move through these spaces, the negotiation of such spaces may call forth not only the way in which such spaces construct privileged identities, but also the manner in which those same spaces construct homeless identities. The refusal to be served, the sideways glance, the distance the privileged put between themselves and the homeless clearly communicate the informal meanings of such spaces and the worth of those homeless compelled to move through them. The direct reconstruction and redefining of urban spaces by homeless persons therefore constitutes a figurative and literal opposition to the conditions of homelessness, however small that opposition may be, and an active refusal to assume an ascribed social identity.

As active agents it is clear that poor people, like all people, attempt to reassert their "place" in society, to establish some "homeplace" in the midst of deprivation, humiliation, and degradation. The contesting of what constitutes a legitimate "place," both socially and physically, is often what social struggles are about. The battle over defining the legitimate purpose of particular locales is conducted both socially, in the attempt to define homelessness as distinct from poverty, and spatially, in the regulation of poor bodies by developing land, buildings, and resources for particular uses but not other uses. The defining and redefining of urban spaces are, in turn, affected by the types of *social imaginary significations* (Castoriadis 1987) particular to a given society. Briefly, social imaginary significations are the specific crystallizations of a wide variety of symbolic concepts available at any one time within a given society, concepts that order the world along very defined trajectories, that guide our understandings of race, class, gender, and natural phenomena. These imaginary significations are conveyed through symbolic devices (language, fantasy, plans, dreams) that work to normalize a particular vision and thereby justify particular social practices and discourage others. Dominant social imaginary significations, as we shall discuss in chapter 1, predate the creation of social identities. This concept of the social imaginary, in turn, requires developing a way of understanding urban social and physical space as active ingredients in both the creation of homelessness and the general process of identity formation, because the production of space is intimately connected to dominant social imaginary significations. The dominant social imaginary works through the city visions embraced by city planners and city officials, of what the "good" city should look like, who and what is to be included and/or excluded.

When the very poor redefine urban space in a manner that meets their needs, their actions are often explained by authorities as "survival" mechanisms or as creative "deviant" adaptations, not as resistance or opposition to a bleak situation. When the privileged redefine the meaning of urban space, it is considered to be good business sense, benefiting a particular community or city. The use of the terms *survival* and *adaptation* to describe homeless behaviors fits well with the dominant social imaginary where the urban poor are conceived as passive agents, merely reacting to their immediate situation; the reality is that homeless actions can include both survival and opposition, adaptation and resistance. These latter components we often forget when talking about the very poor. The choice of focusing on survival-adaptation versus resistance-opposition demonstrates the manner in which the dominant social imaginary held by the privileged of the very poor, the homeless, allows for the avoidance of larger questions of power and domination. This is possible, in part, because the definition and use of urban space remains unproblematic for the privileged; established and authoritative definitions of urban space are sufficient for negotiating such spaces. Unfortunately, the few times when active agency is ascribed to the behavior of poor and homeless people, discussions are centered on civil disorders or crime. Those who have the power to define who is and who is not legitimately poor, who is and who is not homeless, often equate active agency with criminal activity, and passive agency with knowing your place and following institutional rules. Defined in history as the "dangerous classes," the urban poor have always received either the boot or the stick. Once consigned spatially to the back wards of hospitals and poor houses at the turn of the century, America's poor now walk our city streets in endless amblings, a bleak testimony to the failings of private housing markets.

Urban spaces are not "neutral" backdrops to individual actions of the poor, but socially produced disciplinary spaces within which one is expected to act according to a status defined by others, a status communicated by specific appearances and locations, by the *visual* comportment of bodies. Homeless street identities are not simply the product of a deranged mind or an amoral character. Rather, they emerge from the complex negotiations over the meanings of urban space within which homeless persons find themselves. These meanings are generated in the making of a city, the provision of services, the behavior of those who have power over the powerless. Hence, conceptualizing urban space as an active relationship between city authoritative power and individuals is crucial for understanding how homeless street identities are constructed, resisted, and reconstructed. At the same time, it is important to understand how policy makers, advocates, and researchers define a particular sector of the poor as "homeless" and not "poor," in order to understand how the concept of homelessness is constructed for and by middle-class activists, researchers, policy makers, and social workers. Negotiations are conducted not merely over the definitions and redefinitions of urban space, but also over the meaning of distinctions created between different races, classes, and genders.

The ebb and flow of negotiations over the complex meanings of urban space can generate the conditions for the emergence of homeless social movements, and indeed for other social movements. Negotiations among researchers and advocates, over the meaning of what homelessness is, and who the homeless are, reflect the disciplinary border work that either attempt to establish new meanings of homelessness— challenging established definitions, integrating homeless persons as both actors and objects—or seeks to preserve disciplinary boundaries by reinforcing the isolation of homeless persons, "objects" for an authoritative gaze. The fluid nature of definitions is fixed in the social practices of academic researchers, policy makers, police, social workers, city officials, planners, business owners, and the homeless themselves. The power and efficicacy afforded these practices will determine the shape of such negotiations over identity and urban space.

Social networks emerging out of frequent contact and shared activities of the very poor are initiated within those urban spaces that often remain marginal in the imaginations of dominant elites, and spatially segregated from middle-class landscapes. In such a context, where researchers, advocates, and homeless persons often come from quite different racial and class backgrounds, it is all too easy to adhere to set interpretations of, and normative assumptions about the very poor-associated with one's race, class, and gender position. Simply employing correct "scientific" methodology will not address this difference in social power; such a positivistic notion of realist truth masks a much deeper reality: What is and what shall be our relationship to the perceived "Other," to those most often defined as "outside" of mainstream society?

The struggle over the definitions of and use of urban space may be clearly viewed in city policies that actively disperse homeless street populations for being "out of place" and simultaneously attempt to contain them in institutional settings (shelters, rehabilitation clinics, armories, prisons). Such dispersions and containments can have the drama of a police raid or the subtlety of gentrified redevelopment. Unlike middle-class protest movements conducted by housed persons, homeless street protests and homeless communities occupy a social space of constant movement. Nomadic identities, imposed upon street populations by city and state officials practicing authoritative strategies of containment and dispersion, are resisted by the creation of homeless communities in specific places, often in marginal, or what I shall call "refuse," spaces. These places are themselves subjected to constant surveillance, a policing of the boundaries between the homeless and the housed community.

In the remainder of this introduction, I will highlight the key points of the following chapters and discuss two controversial points in understanding the relationships among contested urban spaces, homeless populations, and social movement formation. The first point is the manner in which homelessness is socially constructed to displace concerns about relative power and the "poor," through reifying a sub-category of very poor people. Typically this involves using classification schemas to develop ever more elaborate policy guidelines for subsets of poor people, without examining the political, social, and economic preconditions for such classifications. Classification schemes may help elucidate the specific differences between "types" of homelessness, while at the same time obscuring the power involved in generating such classifications, the power to define and thereby control a poor population. In particular, I discuss how homelessness came to be defined as a problem, socially constructed by both advocates and academics.

Second, I examine the boundary work accomplished by researchers studying homelessness, and the problematic nature of "speaking for" the homeless. A brief illustrative case is provided by examining Charles Hoch's debate with Peter Rossi over the differences in defining homelessness (Hoch 1990; Rossi; 1991). This difference is highlighted by contrasting the work of Michael Sosin (Sosin, Colson, and Grossman 1988) at the University of Chicago and that of Rossi (1989) at MIT. The boundary work that sets and defines distinctions between "homelessness" and "poverty" is informed by a deeper social imaginary that informs how "the Other," "the stranger," "the outsider," is to be approached in contemporary America.

Chapter 1 examines the application of the concept of the social imaginary to the gendered, race, and classed notions of poverty and homelessness. The question is raised of where people without homes are "located," both in theory and in practice. The body, as the working site for the social imaginary, acts somewhere. This somewhere I define as social-physical space. Discussing a variety of perspectives on social-physical space, I link the concept of social-physical space and the homeless with a particular configuration of the hypermodern city, which is examined in more detail in chapter 2. This raises the question of how we define "urban" in the 1990s and what relationship that definition has to the lives of the very poor, the homeless.

Although discussions in this introduction center around the borders of homeless research, these theoretical and practical actions must be considered as occurring within the context of changing city and suburban life. Rather than being a definitive break with the modern city (i.e., the postmodern city), the contemporary city is, I believe, a city of intensified patterns, schemas, flows, pleasures, and oppressions—more characteristic of the hypermodern, an accelerated version of the modern city, than of anything postmodern. The expansion of finance, insurance, real estate (FIRE), and other service sector industries within regional labor markets, combined with the spreading of global mass media and marketing culture, entertainment complexes, the conservative emphasis on ending the social wage, and the expansion of global capital with an attendant influence on local city decision making, spell less an advance into something "postmodern," or a "break" with the modern, and more a "back to the future" retreat into capitalist city forms present during the late 1800s. The hypermodern city is a reconstruction of the Social Darwinian landscape, with the addition of expanded high-technology surveillance and increasingly integrated multinational corporate relations.

Chapter 2 extends the discussions concerning the relationships among social imaginaries, social-physical space, and homelessness, and examines the role of contemporary urban redevelopment in the dispersion and containment of the very poor. I maintain that the dispersion of the poor and homeless from downtown shopping areas, and containment of them in marginalized areas of the city, results from using an *exclusive* redevelopment vision rather then an *inclusive* vision. City redevelopment as a strategy to recoup financial losses is interconnected with the expanding role of visual aesthetics in prompting consumption of social-physical spaces, and of global capital and the increasing domination of financial and real-estate institutions in restructuring the hypermodern city.

Redevelopment followed by gentrification is the traditional way in which poor marginally housed populations have been displaced. However, mobilization of resistance from those without homes is often ignored in the literature in favor of renter or homeowner resistance. Differences between working- and middle-class housed citizens and homeless street people are often observed in the active refusal of homeowners to accept low-income housing or shelters in their neighborhood. Chapter 2 discusses how redevelopment in downtown areas generates "refuse" spaces through exclusion and dispersion of the very poor and homeless, and the concentration of capital within spaces of "pleasure" for the middle classes. These "refuse" and "pleasure" spaces, shaped by a dominant social imaginary that produces specific dreams of what constitutes pleasure and refuse, alternate in a complex polarized topography of city spaces. These pleasure and refuse spaces intersect with intentionally designed urban spaces, "functional" single-purpose spaces. Negotiating these topographies is problematic for the very poor, because they have few resources to redefine the use of city space on their own. Homeless persons are expected to occupy and act within those urban spaces commensurate with their status. Insofar as those defined as homeless have no set place, they are constantly at risk of violating, simply by their presence, the boundaries between pleasure, refuse, and functional space set by authoritative others.

Chapter 3 extends the concepts discussed in chapters 1 and 2 by examining two specific cases of urban spaces in the context of the particular homeless struggles that were investigated in, Chicago, and San Jose, California. Both cities allocated a tremendous amount of capital into downtown redevelopment projects in the 1980s and 1990s. These developments impacted the very poor, contributing to what I have called *polarized topographies*, geographic areas with extreme examples of wealth and poverty closely interconnected. Both cities present good examples of how the envisioning of city development by city officials and planners works to reproduce a version of the city which excludes the very poor, and that racially acts to exclude poor African Americans and poor Latinos. Specifically, four census tracts in the South Loop area of Chicago are examined, revealing the dynamics of city redevelopment on racial and class displacement, the displacement of single-room-occupancy hotels and shelter housing in favor of residential pleasure spaces, the luxury housing of Dearborn Park and Central Station, and expanded consumption centers. Also the pleasure spaces on the Near West Side are briefly examined, focusing on the United Center sports stadium and the luxury residential complex Presidential Towers, along with the tentative position of West Side city shelters. The City of San Jose's redevelopment policies and city visions are examined with reference to their impact on the local homeless population. It is argued that redevelopment policies that act to reproduce a particular image of the city are not the result of a natural processes, but rather are the direct result of strategies and tactics used by city officials to secure a particular vision of the city.

In chapter 4 I demonstrate how the above population dispersions and containments are a result of authoritative strategies of power. These strategies involve spatial practices of exclusion, displacement, repression, and assimilation, and they work to contain and or disperse homeless persons. These strategies are illustrated with examples from Chicago and San Jose, and other examples noted. Chapter 4 also discusses the struggles over police sweeps and the policing of homeless bodies, and tactical resistances of the homeless to those authoritative strategies which attempt to contain or disperse them. Finally, chapter 4 examines how media representations "frame" homelessness and homeless encampments. Media productions, both movies and television news, are critical in understanding the relationship between social-physical space, identity formation, and city redevelopment, because they assist in guiding interpretations of events by "framing" specific news stories and presenting images of homelessness in movies that reconfirm dominant social imaginaries about the very poor.

To assume that city policies work on homeless bodies simply through overt manipulation without resistance is to deny the active agency of homeless and poor people. Detailed examples, supporting a concept of active homeless agency, are given in chapter 5 through a close examination of the birth and development of the Student-Homeless Alliance in San Jose and the development and operation of Tranquility City in Chicago. These two comparative cases provide contrasting examples of homeless organizing, an important counterpoint to the apparently seamless nature of authoritative strategies of power.

Chapter 6 focuses specifically on the relationship between homeless resistance and the formation of collective identities and social space. Homeless placemaking, collective identity formation, and the potential for collective action are examined using the conceptual tools provided by the work of Alberto Melucci (1988, 1989, 1985) and Alain Touraine (1981, 1985). Using the data gathered from Chicago and San Jose, I examine the gains made by involvement in homeless protests, perceptions of urban spaces, and differences among homeless participants. By revealing the relationships among homeless placemaking, collective identity formation, and collective action, I hope to indicate a possible direction for a theory of social movements, incorporating physical space and active resistances by the very poor.

Finally, chapter 7 examines possibilities for teaching students about homelessness and city redevelopment issues, the problems and the rewards based on the data gathered from San Jose and Chicago, supplemented with material from other service learning programs. How can we educate our students to move from charity to social justice?, How do homeless encampment participants perceive this change?, These are important questions in judging the ability to speak with a perceived "Other."

Talking Homeless, Walking Poor

In popular and academic literature, personal alienation from mainstream institutions and family, disaffiliation (Bogue 1963; Bahr 1973, 1970; Baum and Burnes 1993; Rossi 1989; Ropers 1988), and non-normative behavior and values are often presented as leading causes of homelessness. This individualistic perspective contrasts with the volunteerist perspective, which assumes that homeless people are on the streets because they "choose" to live in their own "subculture." These early perspectives, steeped in "blame the victim" rhetoric, emerged from the studies of Skid Row residents and transients, which predominantly examined white, middle-aged and older men (Bogue 1963) and "hobos," "bums," and "tramps" (Anderson 1923). African Americans were conspicuously absent in discussions of Skid Row, even though studies revealed that they constituted "22.3 percent of the 'skid row case load' in New York City in 1955" (Hopper 1995, 12). While not in the majority, African Americans on Skid Row were ignored in popular accounts even as research pointed out their significant presence.

Thinking of homelessness as primarily an individual problem, to be solved by clinically based therapies, displaces the concern over structural social inequalities onto concerns over "proper" comportment and individual responsibility. Social failures are treated as either moral failures or as medically based failures—failures to adjust. As in the current debates over the "underclass," discourse on the homeless remains trapped in distinctions that ideologically divide homeless bodies into the "deserving" versus the "undeserving" poor (Katz 1989; Himmelfarb 1984; Handler 1992), as degrees of individual responsibility are assigned, by policy makers, researchers, advocates, and politicians. This makes it difficult to see how homelessness is intrinsically linked with city, region, and national underdevelopment.

The liberal-structuralist perspective, by way of contrast, discusses poverty and homelessness as if they were mere aberrations of a market economy, soon to be rectified upon application of the appropriate technocratic solution, better housing, more rehabilitation, extensive job training. In today's social climate, however, even this technocratic perspective is gradually being abandoned for a return to the nineteenth-century legacy of Social Darwinism and the poorhouse. A "liberal" perspective acknowledges the objective structural features of homelessness, lack of housing and jobs, deinstitutionalization of the mentally ill, and other macro factors. Inadequate provision of affordable housing and low wages have been cited numerous times as causes for widespread homelessness (Blau 1992; Hopper and Hamburg 1986; Hoch and Slayton 1989; Jencks 1994; Fabricant and Kelly 1986; Lang 1989; Marcuse 1988, 1989; Ringham 1990; Barak 1992). Wages for working people have experienced a net decline since the early 1980s and families race to keep ahead. The expansion of union-busting techniques and a lack of federal support for working people have amplified inequality trends established during the mid-70s. Indeed, the rich are getting richer and the poor are getting poorer as the ratio of family income of the top 5 percent of the population to the lowest 20 percent of the population grew from 11.3 percent in 1973 to 18.2 percent in 1993 (Mishel and Bernstein 1994, 36). This historic increase in inequality affected different social groups unevenly, with poor single mothers and African American males experiencing some of the largest declines in income. People of color and poor single mothers are represented disproportionately in the national homeless population. The 1980s were a time of unprecedented transfers of wealth from the middle, working, and poor classes to the very wealthy and a squandering of capital on misplaced investments, such as the Savings and Loans debacle.

It is generally acknowledged that in the 1980s and 1990s there was a net drop in the number of affordable housing units available to the poor and a significant decline in the commitment of federal dollars to rectify this decline. Advocates often cite federal housing aid reductions of 60 to 80 percent as one of the prime causes for the lack of adequate housing. However, Christopher Jencks, in his book *The Homeless* (1994), contests these figures as misleading, arguing that federal aid for low-income housing actually increased during this period. Jencks argues that the so-called reductions in federal aid for housing were actually reductions in federal appropriations and that real outlays increased in the 1970s through the 1980s. He argues that "[actual outlays] rose from $9 billion in 1980 to $18 billion in 1992, and the number of federally subsidized rental units grew from 2.9 to 4.7 million" (97). While he acknowledges that the 60 percent growth in federal programs for low-income tenants between 1980 and 1992 was less than during the 1970s, he states that "it was still growth, not shrinkage." What is ignored is that the majority of subsidized units were for Section 8 certificates, negotiated through private landlords, not for actual public housing, whose available units did shrink in relationship to growing need (Barak 1992, 69). What is not discussed is how much of outlays for public housing went to administrative costs as opposed to actual construction and maintenance. By using aggregate housing figures from the *American Housing Survey*, Jencks (1994, 82–94) also ignores the regional distribution and cost differential for rents, which makes it difficult to find federally subsidized housing within a given region. Finally, the 1986 Tax Reform Act (H.R. 3838) severely cut private-sector investment in low-income housing further reducing the amount of private housing, available to the poor (Barak 1992, 69).

Given the debates over the extent of housing availability and the inability to live on minimum wage jobs, one would expect a more radical analysis, an analysis that would lead to substantial changes in the ways wealth and income are distributed and priorities of investment are established. However, such acknowledgments of housing and employment inadequacies have rarely moved beyond reform-minded programs to ask the deeper question about the relationship between social inequality and property. In housing markets that privilege luxury condos and subminimum wages, liberals call for special programs to fund a miserly scattering of low-income units and employment training for those whose career paths will most likely lead them into dead-end jobs. The larger structural issues of inequality are not, and I maintain will not be, addressed, because large segments of the privileged classes benefit from the existence of inequality.

"Homelessness" emerged as a social problem during the early 1980s as an attractive research topic and as an objective phenomenon, a result of the deteriorating conditions of vast numbers of poor Americans. However, unlike previous periods when such conditions would evoke a rhetoric of civic and corporate responsibility, the conservative political entrenchment of the 1980s replaced the debates about structural poverty and inequality with rhetoric about individual responsibility and success. The brief flirtation with ending structural poverty, expressed in Lyndon Johnson's War on Poverty, now came to a close. In this cultural milieu, talk concerning the very poor assumed a conservative tone. Those structural inequalities that generated homelessness were rarely addressed. Policy makers and politicians focused instead on individual *visible* dysfunctions in behavior and appearance.

Homelessness emerged, then, as both a rhetorical device and a real, objective situation. Within this changing cultural milieu the adoption of the label *homeless* had both negative and positive effects. Positive, because it allowed for a way to talk about a special segment of the very poor in a manner that would capture public sympathy, and negative, because it displaced concerns over the unequal distribution of power, property, and privilege. Whether deserving or undeserving, homeless bodies, like the poor in general, were perceived as out of place and therefore out of control. Homeless street people were criminalized, treated academically and popularly as submembers of the "underclass" if they talked back, or presented as charitable victims worthy of middle class affection if they stayed in their place. In either case homeless street persons were and still are treated with little respect, rendered as either passive victims of circumstances or as possible threats, as members of the "dangerous classes."

Homelessness, therefore, is an ideological term that serves to maintain the borders between the cultural capitals of middle-class society and the poor. What the above distinctions illustrate is the manner in which "homelessness" and policies developed to combat homelessness are socially constructed to express dominant values and communicate a poor person's status to others. Homeless policy, like welfare policy, is organized around programs that act both expressively and symbolically (Handler and Hasenfeld 1991, 15). As Handler and Hasenfeld (1991) illustrate:

> Conditions become social problems, enter political language, not because they suddenly materialize or change in character; usually they have always been present. Rather, conditions become social problems for ideological purposes. Social problems are constructed. They serve the interests of those who define them. The distinction between "deserving" poor and the "undeserving" poor is a moral issue; it affirms the values of the dominant society by stigmatizing the outcasts. (15–16)

The risk in using the term *homelessness* in academic discourse is the way it unwittingly serves to reduce people who are without a home to passive victims, stigmatized as "unworthy," through the imposition of a "medical," "social work," and or "criminal" model of treatment. Restoring a sense of active agency requires us to ask questions like these: How do the homeless understand their condition? When we listen, which stories do we hear and which do we ignore? How does academic and policy discourse on homelessness normalize middle-class family and work relations?

Procacci's (1991) analysis of the development of distinctions between poverty and *pauperism* is instructive in answering the questions of why and how homelessness was separated from poverty. Examining the discourse of social economy, beginning with Sismondi in France and Malthus in Britain, Procacci reveals how the social was turned against the economic through an analysis of pauperism. According to Procacci this was accomplished by the use of a double meaning of poverty present during the first half of the nineteenth century. Poverty provided both the "limit to economic discourse and the key to economic conquest of a new continent" (154). Unlike political economy, where poverty was viewed as the downside of wealth, social economy broke with this conception of a division between wealth and poverty, privileging instead technocratic attempts to organize, manage, and systematize social situations, linking philanthropy with the reformation of pauper behavior. The pauper, then, became a scientific object for social economists like Sismondi. What occurred was, in Procacci's borrowing of Jacques Donzelot's phrase, a "'systematic grafting of morality on to economics', the techno-discursive instrument that makes possible the conquest of pauperism and the invention of a politics of poverty" (157). Hence, the issues shifted from accumulating wealth and policing poverty, to policing a moral order—focusing on the individual behaviors of the poor. Now a signifier for a larger set of moral acts, pauperism became a trope for all that was "dangerous" in society, the very representation of disorder and unruliness. Pauperism, like contemporary homelessness, became that which was thought to be beyond control, "hidden from the scrutinizing gaze of any governing instance" (Procacci 1991, 158). Inequality was taken as a natural fact by political economists such as Ricardo and Adam Smith; therefore social economy, because of its technocratic concern with improving moral behavior, focused on personal happiness, not on justice or inequality. The pauper (the correlate of contemporary society's homeless) was perceived as a subject quite different from the laborer. The pauper assumed the mantle of "difference," carrying behaviors that were subject to moral scrutiny, whereas the laborer was perceived to be caught in the "stigma of inequality." Therefore solutions evolved in radically different directions: for the laborer, higher wages and benefits, control over the means of production; for the pauper, hygiene, reinforcment of the family, attendance of religious services, education, and other avenues of moral education.

Constructing the "Homeless," Deconstructing the "Poor"

Since the 1980s, a vast body of literature has developed that examines the conditions, lifestyle, psychology, and economics of this subset of the very poor, the homeless. Homelessness as socially constructed (Stern 1984), or as a political spectacle (Edelman 1987), depends on the formation of a socially shared image of the absolute poor put forth by claims-making actors (Spector and Kitsuse 1977; Schneider 1985). This socially shared image contains other images that convey social distinctions between housed and unhoused people, and judgments about who is deserving of receiving benefits and who is undeserving. The preoccupation by researchers and policy makers with defining the numbers of homeless and their behavioral characteristics acts to displace concerns regarding uneven development within market economies, in favor of ameliorative reforms and/or proper comportment within urban settings. Policy makers, researchers, and the general public exercise the dominant social imaginary of homelessness when they act, often unintentionally, to reproduce the distinctions between the "undeserving" and the "deserving" homeless, displacing questions about the impact on the very poor of city redevelopment policies and land-use decisions.

Social science research, applied to the counting of how many homeless there are in a given city, occurs within a politically charged setting, relying upon specific social imaginaries of who and what the homeless are. The question of what constitutes legitimate talk or legitimate knowledge about the homeless, and who talks either "for" or "with" them, is a major problem implicit in contemporary debates.

Often divisions are created between those who take a stance in defense of homeless populations (advocates) and those who attempt to use "scientific detachment" and the measures of "bias" as a way to gain legitimate knowledge about the abject poor. I would maintain that the latter perspective, like that of British anthropology in the nineteenth century, is a discourse and method that masks the inherent colonizing feature of its gaze, treating the homeless as objects of power to be worked upon, fought over, discussed.

How easy it is to forget the invisible families in poverty while focusing on the visible bodies of the street homeless. Early public media images portrayed a destitute population wandering the streets in rags, with excessive body odor and tangled hair, often talking to invisible companions; the contemporary "homeless" were equated with a small portion of the mentally ill who had been cast into the streets as a result of deinstitutionalization and the failed funding of community mental health centers during the mid 1970s. Their visibility guaranteed their status as a trope for "the homeless." This equation of the visible homeless with all homeless meant that those with the most aberrant behavior would assume the mantle of representative homeless person for the general public. Hence, it is not surprising that the general public assumed that mental illness was the main cause of homelessness, a myth that has been effectively contested by Snow, Anderson, and Martin (1986), Ropers (1988), Belcher and DiBlasio (1990, 105–23), and others. This does not mean that mental illness or substance abuse is not a problem. A reasonable estimate is that close to 30 percent of those defined as homeless suffer from some combination of these problems. However, observing symptoms and ascribing causation are two different things. Given the evidence from recent studies, the question of causation cannot be laid to rest at this doorstep. Indeed, as Koegel and Burnam (1992, 80) state, "homelessness, then, inflicts environmental stress on individuals that might produce symptoms of mental illness—symptoms that might well disappear if individuals were fed, clothed, sheltered, cared for, and assured that they could count on a more stable future." Of course, one can easily extend this beyond homelessness to the poor in general.

Other images of the late 1970s and early 1980s focused on home-less women carrying their possessions in shopping bags and carts (Golden 1992, Rousseau 1981). This segment of the homeless population, labeled "shopping-bag ladies" by the media, were counterposed to homeless men, who more often than not were still equated with "bums," tainted by their prior association with Skid Row. The negative references surrounding homeless women (Merves 1992) reproduced gender stereotypes of women as supposedly preoccupied with "alleged attention to minute details." As Merves (1992) points out, the image of the "bag lady" came to be exploited in places like Bloomingdale's department store, which "featured a 'bag lady look' emphasizing lay-ered, oversize clothes, and recently Tiffany's presented an image of a homeless woman next to an expensive piece of jewelry"; homeless women with children, conspicuous by their prior absence in the overly patriarchal world of Skid Row, were, however, embraced as the new "deserving poor" (230).

As research and protests advanced in the early 1980s, housing scholars and activists, such as Kim Hopper (1981, 1982; Hopper and Hamburg 1986), Ellen Baxter (Baxter and Hopper 1981), Mary Hombs (Hombs and Snyder, 1983),[1] Mitch Snyder of the Community for Creative Non-Violence (CCNV) (Rader 1986), and Robert Hayes (Blau 1992, 98–100), of the Coalition for the Homeless, began to actively challenge popular stereotypical perceptions (a subcategory of the dominant social imaginary) of the very poor as "bag ladies," "bums," "winos," "transients," and "vagabonds" by redefining our understanding of poverty. *Homelessness* and *the homeless* now signified a special population in need, the deserving poor, separated from "the unworthy poor."[2] Segments of the very poor were successfully redefined as deserving, as victims of larger social-structural forces, although in more recent times Baum and Burnes (1993) have attempted to resurrect the language of disaffiliation, reducing homelessness again to individual pathologies. These redefinitions were reinforced by the empirical reality of reductions in federal spending on public housing, rapidly increasing urban rental rates, lower wages, city redevelopment projects that forced the poor from low-rent areas, and a substantial change in the composition of the "homeless"—including larger numbers of women, people of color, and children. This redefinition of the very poor, useful to advocates in developing active resistance movements, was also useful to local and regional governments in developing new programs and institutions, such as "homeless shelters." By separating the "poor" from the homeless, policy research, which could have addressed issues of structural inequality in order to end poverty, shifted into the containment of a subset of the poor via the construction of shelters and the promotion of job training. Containment of homelessness, not ending poverty became the new goal of policy makers and politicians, and ending poverty faded from the political agenda. Concepts of "homelessness," in turn, were adopted by the directors and staff of newly emerging shelters and by social welfare agencies as ways of understanding how this population differed from previous destitute populations of predominantly white, middle-aged males (Miller 1991) associated with Skid Row (Hopper and Hamburg 1986). This created difference worked to separate the former Skid Row inhabitants, often labeled as "undeserving," from the new "homeless" found in shelters, the "deserving." Antipoverty agendas directed at issues of economic and political redistribution were diverted into developing ever finer discriminations between types of the poor and into ameliorative policies that overlooked issues of power and property.

The change in characteristics of this newer population, which contained a higher percentage of females, families, young children, and African Americans, gave rise to the perception that the "new" homeless were different from the "old" homeless, that the "new" homeless were related somehow to larger social-economic trends. Most homeless, though, continued to be poor, single, unmarried, males. Even with the development of distinctions based on the "new" homeless, race as a factor in homelessness remained invisible in both the academic and the public discourse. As Blasi (1994, 577) points out in his NEXIS search of 10,663 popular and academic articles containing the word *homeless* during the first nine months of 1993, "only 24 contained the same word in a phrase with the modifier 'Black' or 'African-American.' Neither advocates nor civil rights leaders hammered home the race question with regard to homelessness. For advocates, as Blasi points out, the desire was to distance the "new" homeless from Skid Row images of male, white alcoholics, and for civil rights leaders issues of success in mainstream society became more important than images of failure. No major established civil rights body, not even the NAACP, picked up on homelessness as a dominant theme. The exception was Jesse Jackson's organization, PUSH. As Blasi (1994) comments, this was most likely due to tactical considerations on the part of the civil rights groups. Still, social science bears responsibility for the invisibility of race and homelessness in public discourse. According to Blasi, "although social scientists have documented the high proportions of minority persons on the streets, social science has done little to alter the more general invisibility of this aspect of the problem" (577). It is not surprising that a disproportionate share of the urban homeless are African Americans, given the high poverty rates within the inner cities. According to Burt and Cohen (1989), a little over one half of the homeless are members of minority groups. Only recently has research on race and homelessness advanced, with the work of Blasi (1994), Belcher (1992), Baker (1994), Hopper (1995), and Roth, Toomey, and First (1992). Integrating issues of race and gender into discussions of homelessness and the larger debates over poverty promises a more fruitful line of research than those of previous years.

Academic Segmentation of Homeless Bodies

As granting agencies, such as the *National Institute of Mental Health*, the *National Institute of Health,* and the *National Institute of Alcohol Abuse and Alcoholism*, established research lines, the homeless were further subdivided into "homeless teenagers," "homeless mentally ill," "homeless veterans," "homeless women with children," and so on. Granting agencies reinforced mediated images of homelessness by focusing on their particular areas of expertise and the claims to special knowledge as a product of their different professions. For example, the National Institute of Alcohol Abuse and Alcoholism allocated large grants for research that would document alcohol problems within any particular segment of the homeless population. However, larger issues, such as land-use policy, would not fall under their granting category. The normalizing feature of alcohol and mental illness research leads to answers that connect homeless solutions to detoxification or drug treatment programs and or transitional housing. The "answers" that such research can come up with might then be used to justify and rationalize a given policy perspective. For example, Baum and Burnes (1993), one an executive director of a homeless service program and the other a substance-abuse counselor in the Washington, D.C., area, maintain that advocates and the broader public are in denial about the real causes of homelessness, which they identify as mental illness, substance abuse, and bad values. Broader questions about the distribution of power, property, and social inequality are not considered as valid subjects in studying homelessness, because for them the apparent visual comportment of individuals is overwhelming testimony to causality. What appears is true, and what is true appears.

The proliferation of research focusing on the "pathologies" of homeless behavior, a reinvention of the "culture of poverty" thesis, further reinforced researcher perceptions that these pathologies where in fact the main issues to be addressed. The rapid proliferation of medical, psychological, and psychiatric studies of homelessness provided a self-fulfilling prophecy in demonstrating the importance of these research lines, simply because they were the lines where most of the research was being done. Doing research along the lines wanted by granting agencies was understood not only as financially lucrative, but also safe, insofar as research would be accepted within the parameters set by the granting institution. For many researchers, this transformation of a growing, destitute population into "the homeless" and then its attendant dispersion into segmented social categories moved the political agenda away from issues of poverty, redevelopment, displacement, land use policies, job loss and other structural features of capital to those agendas generated by perceivable behavioral differences within a destitute population (van Vliet 1989) and the problems associated with creating better service networks (Fabricant 1986). These differences, while drawing attention to the diversity and needs of the homeless population, also worked to separate poor populations from each other in terms of priority research funding, policy making, and social activism. The categorization of the poor in terms of visible behavioral differences encouraged the reduction of "homelessness" to problems of either individual behavior or deficient structural features special for each population (e.g., "mentally ill homeless" require greater funding for community mental health clinics or transitional housing). In analyzing the listings of research articles related to homelessness, Blasi (1994)[3] discovered that the greatest number of studies were conducted in psychiatry and psychology (27.4 percent); and medicine (36.7 percent); 10.4 percent of the articles were in social work and only 9.9 percent were in sociology. Using the article title as an identifier for a particular subgroup, Blasi (1994, 580) noted that 36 percent of the articles focused on homeless persons with chronic mental disorders or substance abuse problems. The remaining identifiable subgroup consisted of homeless families. Most articles examined the individual behaviors and characteristics of homeless persons and ignored the larger structural, political, and economic issues involved in producing homelessness.

Within the liberal/conservative framework, a framework that promotes the ideology of opportunity versus the realization of equity, individual behavior and "proper" attitudes are considered legitimate properties to study. Proper individual behavior is thought to lead to increased social mobility by placing one in a better competitive position in the struggle over scarce resources. However, why those resources are scarce is rarely questioned; when it is questioned, the explanation is usually in terms of the dominant ideological framework of property rights and pluralist politics. This is not unusual given the pattern of funding homeless research. The direction of homeless research is intimately affected by granting agencies and funding patterns. As Blasi points out, there is more grant money available from such agencies as the National Institute of Mental Health than from the Department of Housing and Urban Development (HUD). Combined with the ideological predispositions of both the general public and academic researchers to view poverty as the result of individual personal failings or pathology ("blaming the victim"), these types of distributions should not be surprising. Only a handful of researchers engage in giving structural explanations for homelessness, and still fewer understand the issue as one of the control and ownership of property, of land use and the distribution of resources, of poverty and city redevelopment. The homeless social imaginary still remains disaffiliated, alienated, pathological, and isolated, a "transient."

The preoccupation of researchers with endless classificatory schemas and counting wars distorts the understanding of how poor people find themselves in a homeless condition. Developing ever finer discriminations of individual "types" may help the shelter provider understand how to develop tailored services for the very poor, but it does little to increase our understanding of homelessness. Invariably, such categorizations work to replace broader understandings of homelessness and poverty with narrow definitions that allow discriminations based on normative mainstream values which are race, class, and gender specific. For example, Baum and Burns (1993) level accusations at housing and homeless advocates for denying (what they believe is a fact) that "85 percent of all homeless adults suffered from chronic alcoholism, drug addiction, mental illness, or some combination of the three" (3). In other words the homeless are all crazy drug addicts who need extensive drug treatment and rehabilitation—a corrective in their minds to the preoccupation of homeless activists with housing issues. While there is some truth in their claims, as there is in all claims, Baum and Burnes go on to blame the baby boomers "who 'lost their inner maps' to drugs in the 1960s and who suffer from serious and persistent mental illness" (55) and members of the urban "underclass." Blaming the 1960s counterculture and the urban poor for homelessness is a socially acceptable way to reify normative concepts of home (suburban detached), family (patriarchal), politics (Republican) and morality (conservative Christian). Little is gained from such pseudo-explanations. They constitute distorted observations masquerading as explanations.

One can also see this preoccupation with "moral" behavior in the early classificatory schemas of Sutherland and Locke (1936), Robert Hunter (1912), and Kelly (1908). Edmond Kelly, in *The Elimination of the Tramp* (1908), called for the setting up of forced labor colonies for the very poor. He based his argument on a classification schema that separated the population into able-bodied men and non-able-bodied men (vagabonds and miscreants). In such schemas, variants of the slogan *Work Shall Make You Free*, homeless poor bodies became objects of overt abuse. Robert Hunter, in *Poverty* (1912), attempted to distinguish between the "pauper," the "vagrant," the "sick," the "child," and the "immigrant," reaching back to the early English Poor Laws. And finally, Sutherland and Locke, in *Twenty-Thousand Homeless Men: A Study of Unemployed Men in the Chicago Shelters* (1936), attempted to divide those who use shelter services into such types as "home guard casual," "migratory laborer," "steady unskilled," "skilled tradesman," and "white collar worker," with individual behaviors ascribed to each classification. However, as in previous classification schemas, Sutherland and Locke reduced explanations for homelessness, and indeed for the variance of individual behaviors, to four vices: gambling, drinking, "irregular" sexual behavior, and begging. Classification schemas masquerading as explanations are deployed to regulate and control the boundaries of debate surrounding the relationship of poverty to wealth and property. Indeed, in 1834, during the period of the adoption of the Laws of Relief of the Poor in England and Wales, the Royal Commission Reports, whose recommendations enabled the enactment of the Poor Laws Amendment Act, took great pains to achieve taxonomic clarity in separating the working poor from the indigent (Green 1983, 121). During the debates over the English Poor Laws, the terms *deserving* and *undeserving* were used to separate those with supposedly identifiable moral character from those who were perceived to have flawed character. Although Herbert Gans (1995, 14) identifies the distinction between unworthy and worthy as originating from the period when responsibility for the poor was handed over by the churches to local parishes during the fourteenth century, the regular usage of the terms *deserving* and *undeserving* did not begin until the early 1800s. The concern with taxonomic clarity in this period constituted both a fear of releasing unwanted desires and expectations (a fear of being unable to distinguish between the "monstrous" and the virtuous) and a way to justify "the moral sentiments of punitive indignation and charity" (Green 1983, 122). The elaborate deployment of classification schemas to discipline poor bodies continues in the contemporary debate over the politics of welfare reform (Handler and Hasenfeld 1991; Quadagno 1994; Pivan and Cloward 1971), a debate that now includes the subsets "underclass" and "homeless."

As Marks (1991, 1989), Collins (1989), Morris (1994), Harris (1992), Lawson (1992), and West (1992) have pointed out, the creation and deployment of categories of the poor, in particular "underclass," have displaced considerations of economic and political equity in favor of individual "moral" behavior and the resurrection of the culture-of-poverty debates derived from the early works of Edward Banfield, Patrick Moynihan (1965), Gunnar Myrdal, and Oscar Lewis. When the term *underclass* was used by Gunnar Myrdal to describe isolated rural peasants in third-world countries and marginalized poor in urban areas removed from the possibilities of social advancement, the underclass included people of all races, ethnic groups, and genders who were poor. The key problem was how to address the economic and political inequalities that shoved the poor to the margins.

As the term *underclass* gained political and social acceptance during the 1980s other categorizations were added, including gender distinctions, (Glasglow 1981; Rossi and Wright 1989)[4] and characteristics that the dominant social imaginary associated with poverty—such as crime, poor education, and teenage out-of-wedlock births (Lemann 1986, 1988). Marks (1991, 446), in examining the way definitions of the poor are developed, noted Ken Auletta's (1982) characterizations of the underclass as street criminals, underground entrepreneurs, the traumatized and "passive victims" of government support. Lost in the endless associations of pathologies with the poor was the recognition of just how these created associations took on a life of their own, demonizing African American men and women and reasserting by default "normal" qualities and cultural assumptions of goodness associated with the dominant imaginaries of whiteness and middle-class comportment. What started out as an attempt to explain the poverty of Latino, white, Native American, black, and other racial/ethnic groupings in an unequal capitalist market economy was refracted over time and reduced to the problems of inner-city black behavior (Collins, 1989, 80).[5] The poor during the Reagan-Bush era, and particularly the African American and Latino poor, became the repositories for social fantasies of disorder, darkness, decay, and general waste, social representations that have been commonly applied to minority groupings at key historical periods in American history. The shift from economic justice and the problems of opportunity and inequality to one of negative values was completed. During the 1980s, as Marks (1991) points out, debates around poverty and the "underclass" alternated between cultural-determinist models (culture-of-poverty), structural models, and, later, the ethnographic models that helped illustrate the complexity of poor behaviors by describing the diverse forms they occupied. But all of these models avoided seriously grappling with the issues of economic and political justice.

As in the debate about homelessness, these debates ended up downplaying, if not outright denying, that the poor exercised active agency; ignoring the nature of communities in the inner cities; and concealing the complexity of the poor by stigmatizing an entire class of people as an underclass. Active agency, which is a product of the interrelationship between personal experience and structural social, economic, and political relationships, is reduced to surface differences of comportment within a given population, to fashion. Absent from the discussion are considerations of global economic trends and economic polarizations, elite involvement in displacing the poor, and the conflation of actions by particular members of a group to the actions of an entire class, considerations which, when they were raised in the 1970s, were immediately displaced into traditional "culture-of-poverty" arguments.

This displacement, therefore, worked as a strategy to control the discourse over poverty, a strategy to control poor Black bodies.

Unwittingly, William J. Wilson's initial use of *underclass*, in *The Declining Significance of Race* (1978) and later in *The Truly Disadvantaged* (1987) had the effect of reaffirming a conservative political agenda that took hold in the 1980s by splitting off discourse about equity, justice, structural inequalities, and elite behavior from discourse about the newly created subcategory of the population, the underclass. Wilson's sole reliance on a structuralist perspective, using quantitative data at the expense of qualitative studies, suffered from assumptions about the pathology of poor African American families. As Jarrett (1992), Stack (1974), and Newman (1992) point out, the variety of lifestyles of black families should give pause to any schema that attempts to paint a general picture of pathology among poor black families. Provided with an opening, conservative writers, such as Charles Murray in *Losing Ground* (1984), could make outrageous statements about the poor that acted to reconfirm white fears of African Americans. In response, Wilson, not unlike Oscar Lewis and Gunnar Myrdal before him, argued that individual behaviors, that appear pathological among the poor have structural origins. However, in a conservative period of budget tightening and the mythical invocation of "family values," assertions of individual culpability look more attractive than spending the required funds to challenge deeply rooted structural inequalities. Responding to his critics, Wilson (1989) refuted the "welfare ethics" promoted by Charles Murray and reasserted the domination of structural economic trends and racially shaped public policies that marginalize poor urban African Americans. This, of course, does not mean that individuals do not have problems or behavior patterns that make it difficult to become successful in mainstream society. Many individuals have serious problems, but, due to privileges allocated to specific race, gender, and class distinctions, some individuals have greater access than others to resources that allow them to cope more effectively. When individual behavior is made the prime focus for research and policy, deeper questions of structure, agency, and access to power are sacrificed to political expediency.

A similar process of demonizing the poor was repeated during the late 1980s and early 1990s in discussions over the causes of homelessness. On the one hand, the rapidly developing categorizations of homelessness illustrated the diversity of the marginally poor. On the other hand, such categorizations, besides displacing the debates over equity and justice, also served to reconfirm the general category of "underclass," or "homeless," through the very proliferation and repetition of their subdivisions. The generalizable category "underclass" or "homeless" was reinforced by showing all of the possible combinations such a category could assume. The whole became known by the combinatory sum of its parts.

The splitting of explanations of homelessness into either individualistic models or structuralist models, with no attempt to link the two, made it difficult for researchers and policy makers to establish a connection between theoretical concepts and practical actions related to "homelessness" and the operations of gender, race, and class within a market economy. Issues of agency were ignored in favor of a "language of disability" (Snow, Anderson, and Koegel 1994, 467).[6] Possibilities for active social change outside of acceptable channels were obscured insofar as "homeless" persons were treated as passive subjects, subordinate to the intentions of researchers, policy analysts, advocates, and shelter providers, not unlike in previous debates over the "underclass."

"Languages of disability" have been accompanied by what Hoch and Slayton (1989) term the "politics of compassion" (203). This form of politics works on the basis of personal and or corporate charity to relieve private suffering. As Hoch and Slayton exclaim, "the politics of compassion favored assigning moral priority to the treatment of those homeless who were most vulnerable," those deemed the deserving homeless (203). Unfortunately, those who *appear* to be the most vulnerable are those with the most identifiable physical and mental problems. Hence, it is quite easy to make the logical jump of assuming that homelessness was "caused" by mental illness, or by the prior release of the mentally ill from state institutions. With the exception of the work of Michael Dear and Jennifer Wolch (1987), who examined San Jose's land-use policies, and their impact on service provision for the homeless, the politics of compassion relegated homeless investigations to the realm of clinical psychology, medical treatment, and charity. On the other hand, what Hoch and Slayton termed the "politics of entitlements," embracing a structuralist analysis of the problems of homelessness, emphasizing rights instead of personal deficiencies, also remained problematic by emphasizing a specific class of rights rather than universal rights for all poor persons.

The "politics of compassion" enabled policy makers to understand homelessness through a client model that portrayed homeless persons as passive victims deserving of charity. This perspective is far different from recognizing homeless persons as active subjects who, if given the resources, could actively organize on their own behalf. On the other hand, a "politics of entitlement" understood homelessness as a problem of inadequate housing, low wages, and a host of other structural social problems, deploying the language of rights in order to secure shelter and food, while marginalizing involvement of the homeless. However, in the struggle over defining the issues of homelessness, as Hoch and Slayton (1989) point out, the "politics of compassion tends to displace the politics of entitlement" (210). Homelessness still remains a moral issue subject to charity in the eyes of the public, not one requiring systematic institutional reform. One difficulty of advocating a rights-based program (e.g., the right to shelter) is the possibility that shelters will be institutionalized as the late twentieth century's new poorhouse. In addition, the weak political power exerted by homeless organizations makes a platform of specialized rights for the homeless a self-defeating prospect. Connecting with larger rights-based issues, working with other groups on broad-based coalitions, and advocating universal entitlements would be a more productive strategy. Reintegrating discussions of homelessness into a critical poverty discourse would be far more effective at raising the issues of wealth redistribution and would reduce the tendency to see the homeless as a specialized charitable subcategory of the poor.

Early solutions proposed by policy makers remained within the orbit of individualistic solutions—more shelters, more soup kitchens, and more job training—or structuralist solutions of more affordable housing. Both sets of solutions were dependent upon charitable reform efforts and/or legislative activity to resolve the "problem of homelessness" (Fabricant and Epstein 1984; Blasi 1987; Simon 1992; Barak 1992, 145–71). The Stewart B. McKinney Homeless Assistance Act of 1987, allocating federal money to cities to alleviate the plight of the homeless, is typical of the legislative response to this problem. Collective efforts by the homeless themselves in conjunction with political militancy were rarely addressed.[7] Social constructions of homeless persons still revolved around either micro models of disaffiliation or macro models of structural economic inequality. Now that such ameliorative reforms are clearly not working, the stick is replacing the carrot, punitive measures are being adopted by many cities to rid themselves of homeless persons and make downtowns more attractive.

Those advocacy groups that did emerge and incorporated the homeless, such as the Coalition for the Homeless and the Union of the Homeless, drew attention to the loss of low-income housing and the moral question of deprivation in a wealthy country. However, they failed to effectively develop the connections between the loss of housing, the destitution of the poor, and the larger issues of capital accumulation and economic polarization that operated locally through corporate downsizing, gentrification, and redevelopment. Effective critiques were developed around housing and national policy, but critiques of local policy were weaker, especially in regard to land use and employment issues. Exceptions to this were the work of Kim Hopper (Hopper, Susser, and Conover 1985), Michael Fabricant (1987), Michael Dear and Jennifer Wolch (1987), and Peter Marcuse (1988, 1989), all of whom examined the larger issues of homelessness, regional political economy, and land use.

During the early 1990s, some advocate groups, marginal to "mainstream" organizations, such as the Up and Out of Poverty Campaign and Empty the Shelters, developed a more expansive political and economic critique and were able to organize national campaigns. Up and Out of Poverty, for example, was able to mobilize squatting actions in a variety of U.S. cities over Thanksgiving in 1991. The Student-Homeless Alliance (SHA) participated in this event, squatting several vacant houses in San Jose, California. The SHA also maintained a clearly developed analysis that examined how homelessness is connected to both the political policies of city redevelopment agencies and larger economic issues of privileging market-based consumers over the unemployed and homeless. Members of leftist political groups, such as the Communist Labor Party and the Committees of Correspondence, worked closely with homeless activists, lending organizational support. Leftist activists worked in the Student-Homeless Alliance and supported Chicago's "Tranquility City," adding an important critical dimension to homeless activism.

In the academic world, Blau (1992), Lang (1989), and Barak (1992) drew attention to the political economy of homelessness. However, the popular strength of most homeless activist groups and shelters still resided with their moral appeal, especially during the holidays. They did not directly challenge the distribution of social control, power, and property, and they remained within a local reformist framework. While local state agencies operated on the conception of "homelessness" as a problem of individuals, as a problem for social welfare agencies to address, advocacy groups organized around liberal reform goals of more low-cost housing—developing alliances with quasi-governmental commissions, legislators, and support groups, who carefully avoided issues of private property distribution, power, and social inequality. Land-use issues, which involved direct struggle over property ownership, wealth, income, and city development, were rarely addressed by

homeless advocacy groups in the early stages of homeless organizing.
Collective organizing among the destitute was used as a method toward
a reformist goal of ultimately integrating "the homeless" into mainstream society—not transforming that society; an admirable goal, but
insufficient for getting at the root of the problem.[8]

When, during the mid to late 1980s, advocates emphasized mainstream integration, seeking more funds for shelters and low-income
housing, public attitudes remained supportive. Individual empowerment was equated with personal success. However, though it is indeed
true that many of the homeless want to be integrated into the mainstream, it is also clear that their desire conflicts with the demands of
a global economy that has increasingly little use for their labor or
presence. At the beginning of the 1990s, elite attitudes hardened toward
the homeless, a shift trumpeted in the media as "compassion fatigue."
Homeless advocates moved from protest marches and demonstrations
to national campaigns of housing takeovers. Protest marches, perceived
as legitimate actions within a democratic society, engendered elite
support, but squatting takeovers and civil disobedience were frowned
upon. Interestingly, the general public, unlike elite groups, remained
supportive of homeless persons, contrary to many media reports. In a
Gallup Survey conducted between 9 October and 13 November, 1995
(Gallup Organization 1995), 58 percent of those surveyed indicated that
their levels of sympathy toward the homeless had not changed over the
last five years, and, in fact, one in three reported that they were even
more sympathetic than five years previously (3). Respondents who
indicated increased sympathy for the homeless "all felt they had a
'better understanding of the problems of being homeless' " (3). For elite
decision makers, however, homeless groups changed in status from
charity-deserving victims to rebellious squatters who did not know their
place. They were acting out of place. For segments of the public and
early advocates engaged in charitable action, giving the homeless a
"voice" was fine as long they didn't talk too loud or act too bold, in
a way which would embarrass the advocate. Acceptable activism was
"respectable" activism.

Research that involved the voices of the homeless themselves,
integrated with a critical analysis of market economies and the uses and
meanings of social-physical space, did not begin to fully emerge until
the 1990s, in the works of Ruddick (1995, 1990), Wagner (1993), Wagner
and Cohen (1991), Yeich (1994), and Rosenthal (1994). Only now is a
critical perspective on homelessness beginning to develop with material
from homeless members themselves. This new line of research calls

into question the manner in which academics speak "with," "for," "about," or "to" the homeless. This developing historical context must be included in the debates over how homeless research should be conducted and over how homelessness is constructed as a social object. Each "with," "for," "about," and "to" involves different subject positions that can have serious consequences for the population studied and for the researcher.

Boundary Work and "Speaking for Others"

Linda Alcoff (1991), following Spivak (1988), outlines the problem of speaking for others as resulting from two positions. The first concerns a "growing recognition that where one speaks from affects the meaning and truth of what one says" (6). As she points out, one's social location is important in determining the meaning of what is said. Her second point, that "certain privileged locations are discursively dangerous . . . In particular, the practice of privileged persons speaking for or on behalf of less privileged persons" (7) is easily applicable to discourses surrounding both homeless research and homeless advocacy. Of course, one could say that to speak "for" the homeless is advantageous if the homeless have no voice at all. But this begs the question. In what manner does speaking "for" the homeless disempower or increase the oppression of the poor? This is not to say that one should not speak "for" the homeless, only to question one's relationship to the homeless, a relationship about which one speaks. Who is doing the speaking and why?⁹

The methodological traps often contained within the first position are easily folded over into the second. How often does homeless research, which proposes to study the disadvantaged with the latest methodological tools, to maintain an "objective" and social scientific stance, mask the domination of less privileged speakers? In this instance, does "just doing science" become a rationale for avoiding responsibility for the "why" and the "how" with which one speaks? Clearly, either retreating from the issues of poverty, social inequality, and homelessness or advancing by speaking authoritatively about "those" people is untenable. What is one to do? Alcoff says, "I would maintain that if the practice of speaking for others is problematic, so too must be the practice of speaking about others, since it is difficult to distinguish speaking about from speaking for in all cases" (9). Since our speaking is mediated through our socially imagined vision of the less privileged, and that imagination is highly contingent upon our own relationship to the less privileged, then the types of speaking "for" or "with" we undertake will be dependent upon what kind of social imaginary we have constructed. However, invoking an inability to "speak for" can also be a concealment of one's privileged location and unwillingness to act politically when confronted with deprivation.[10] One cannot avoid the fact that "the discursive context, is a political arena" (Alcoff 1991, 15). Rather than reject outright speaking for others, speaking for the homeless, it would be helpful to ask in what way can "speaking for" be assisted by "speaking with" the homeless.

The notion that those who experience homelessness have the unvarnished truth about the meaning of their experience can only be partially true. Homeless persons have to contend with the same systems of oppression and discrimination that both privilege those who profess to speak for them and repress those who speak with them. Homeless persons, like advocates and academics, are caught up in systems of interpretation, refracted through the dominant social imaginary, conditioned by the differential social locations of each, by their race, class, and gender positions, and existing in specific social-physical spaces. The degree to which researchers and advocates remain unaware of the privilege of their talk and how that privilege is connected to their own race, class, and gender positions is the degree to which talk "about" or "for" the homeless will be distorted talk. In this hierarchical system of social inequality, it is all too easy for the most powerful voices to drown out the less powerful. It is also true that the voices of either may be wrong or right. Social location doesn't necessarily guarantee truth.

The solution of how to escape this morass involves conducting ourselves in a *dialogue*, both listening and speaking with and to those we work with. As Alcoff (1991) puts it, "We should strive to create wherever possible the conditions for dialogue and the practice of speaking with and to rather than speaking for others" (23). Through dialogue we come to understand how our research on, with, for, by, and to the homeless can become either a dangerous or a liberatory enterprise for those we work with. The basis for our obligation to engage in dialogue rests upon the fundamental assumption that those we work with or study should be respected as we respect ourselves. Clearly, spaces for dialogue must be created in the study of homelessness. Social-physical spaces on the street, in shelters, in parks, in classrooms should be spaces to begin a dialogue on the factors that create the conditions for degradation and alienation. Understanding the impact our research has on the populations we study often is eclipsed in methodological debates and concerns for the correct "numbers" to satisfy policy agendas and narrow political concerns. Ethnographic accounts, while closer to speaking "with and to" the homeless, still suffer from accounts that speak "about" the homeless. What are often excluded are questions of how we construct the poor as "homeless," and what "social imaginary" homeless persons occupy for the researcher—how are poor people constructed as "Other"? An even more poignant question is how that "Other" a metaphor for race and gender relations, marginalizes people of color and women? In what manner does the term *homeless* substitute for African American—a skillful avoidance of America's race question? Is research on homelessness simply another way to avoid the issues of poverty and social inequality, much as the term *underclass* is used to marginalize debates over power between white and black communities?

Often these debates (homeless research is just one of them) take the form of "boundary work" (Gieryn 1983) in which battles are waged over the correct way to represent a subject, over which method works to capture the ultimate truth of the object under study, and how that truth is guarded through border work within "disciplines" (Klein 1990, 104–17). This boundary work is an attempt "by scientists to distinguish their work and its products from non-scientific intellectual activities" (Gieryn 1983, 782; Latour 1987).[11] The ideological splits of "value-free" Weberian social science, free of emotions, private interests, and bias, in contrast to the subjective and emotional nature of religion, can still be viewed in the way poverty and homeless research is conducted. The ambiguous boundaries of science and the boundary work that goes into policing those established disciplinary boundaries make the battles over methods, of ways of "speaking for and about," the homeless and poor more than mere rituals. And it is quite often the disciplines that cross borders, such as applied sociology, that run the greatest risk of incurring the wrath of intellectual border police.

In the 1990–91 issues of the *Journal of Applied Sociology* (Hoch 1990; Rossi 1991), an exchange occurred between Charles Hoch, coauthor of *New Homeless and Old* (Hoch and Slayton 1989), and Peter Rossi, who conducted a survey of homeless street people in Chicago, 1985–86, and who authored *Down and Out in America* (1989). The exchange between Hoch and Rossi is both illustrative of the boundary work with regard to representing the state of homeless research, the problems pointed to by Alcoff and Spivak, and instructive in how the poor are often treated by those with privilege. Hoch opens his critique of Rossi's homeless research by comparing Rossi's research, which began in April 1985, with the research of Michael Sosin at the University of Chicago, who began his study in January 1986. Although both researchers arrived at similar conclusions regarding the state of homelessness in Chicago, Rossi's work was the more politically explosive. Sosin and Rossi used quite different methods and had quite different goals. The difference in these methods and goals led to differing degrees of emphasis, what Hoch termed "scientific objectivity" and "practical objectivity." What were Rossi's goals and how did these goals determine how Rossi as an academic "spoke about or for" homeless persons? Likewise, what were Sosin's methods and goals, and how did they influence his "speaking about and for" homeless persons, and why did his conclusions, not that dissimilar from Rossi's, produce so little controversy? We shall come back to this shortly.

Rossi was perceived to have privileged the use of "scientific objectivity" over "practical objectivity." Said Hoch (1990, 12), "One analyst used the rhetoric of scientific objectivity in the public domain to justify his research. In contrast, the other analyst adopted a strategy that combined scientific and practical objectivity in both design and implementation of his research. The analyst relying on scientific criteria alone profoundly undermined the public credibility of his research and inspired distrust and antagonism among those most prepared to put the results of his research to practical use." A researcher who is preoccupied with scientific measuring, with methodology at the expense of the practical context in which such research is conducted, ignores practical objective concerns of audience and rhetorics of power within a system based on social inequality. One does so at one's own peril. Practical objectivity requires that the purposes of research be legitimate to the community in question, providing an explanation of why particular research adopts some interests and not other interests. That is, practical objectivity understands the context of power within which research operates, whereas scientific objectivity, as that term is used here, remains limited to what Weber termed "instrumental rationality," quite often taking the form of a preoccupation with carefully applied rules and methods but ignoring the political and social context within which they are implemented. Practical objectivity also understands that "the authority of legitimate research attracts attention not only because it contributes to the understanding of social problems, but because it shapes what counts as a legitimate object of practical concern in the public domain" (Hoch 1990, 12).

Without recounting the policy struggles of the mid 1980s, suffice it to say that Rossi's and Sosin's research occurred within the context of an expanding conservative agenda at the federal level and followed closely the release in 1984 of a report by the U. S. Department of

Housing and Urban Development (HUD) (1984) that estimated the number of the nation's homeless at between 250,000 and 350,000, far below the estimate of 3 million often used by advocates at the time. The political and social context created in advocates a quite reasonable fear that lowering the figures would result in a loss of political commitment in Washington to ending homelessness. This "numbers game" reappeared in the controversy over the 1990 U.S. census count of the nation's homeless, figures promptly discounted by most city mayors. Rossi's study revealed a total street population for Chicago of only 2,700 individuals on any given night of the year, far below either the original 1983 HUD estimates of 17,000 to 36,000 for the Standard Metropolitan Statistical Area or the Chicago Coalition for the Homeless estimates of 25,000 homeless in 1983. Of course, much of this difference can be traced to the differing definitions of what constitutes homelessness; Rossi chose the more restrictive definition, "literal" homelessness.

It is clear that the primary issue in the acceptance of Sosin's work and the rejection of Rossi's revolved around who would be counted. Contrary to Sosin's study, which used an inclusive definition of homelessness, taking into account those living on the streets, those at treatment centers less than 90 days, those living with friends or relatives, and women in battered women's shelters; Rossi was interested only in those who were "physically" homeless, those on the streets and in homeless shelters. Since Sosin was not concerned with measuring the actual numbers of homeless persons, he was able to explore the causes of homelessness in greater detail.

For Rossi, establishing viable numerical estimates remained the primary goal of his study. He rejected with hubris advocates' claims that his focus was too narrow and should be broadened; Advocates had good reason to believe that a report that focused on only the most visible homeless would seriously distort the extent of homelessness in Chicago. If Rossi had qualified his study by claiming that his sample was very narrow and not representative of the general population of homeless persons, most probably the uproar within the community would have quietly dissipated. Rossi protested that he included in press reports "the limits of our estimates," adding, "I could not make promises for the media and cannot be held responsible for their neglecting the qualifications we clearly placed on our estimates" (Rossi 1991, 79), a good example of ignoring practical objectivity.

Rossi and Sosin both understood the political context within which their respective studies would be received. They chose different approaches to that context and thereby constructed different versions of "speaking about and for" the homeless. Again Hoch (1990): "scientific objectivity attempts to control for bias, while practical objectivity seeks to anticipate, account for, and respond to relevant sources of bias" (21); what and who counts as homeless is clearly a "political decision reflecting the ideas and purposes of those fixing the boundaries" (4). Rossi's (1991) response to this critique was understandably defensive; he claimed, "Our study had as a major goal to estimate the size of the literal homeless population of Chicago . . . . Sosin made no like attempt nor did he have any such objective" (78). Rossi then claimed that had Sosin started out to do numerical estimates, that he would have found himself in the same dilemma. This is most probably true. But this begs the question. The point is, what was the purpose of Rossi's study and how did that purpose, in the final analysis, assist in constructing the social imaginary of homelessness? How did Rossi's study "speak about or for" the homeless? As Rossi himself said, "the central purpose was to test out an innovative modification of sample survey methods that could be used to estimate the potential client bases and direct medical needs for the program of medical clinics for the homeless being set up in numerous cities throughout the country by the Robert Wood Johnson Foundation and the Pew Memorial Trust" (78). Rossi then attempted to counterpose scientific truth to myth in discussing the inflated homeless figures used by advocates. Even while acknowledging that advocates used such figures for fear of losing funding and political support, Rossi attacked advocates for parochial interests, of being self-interested: "The advocates may represent the interests of the homeless, yet the likelihood is that they represent the interests of their organizations more strongly" (78).

This type of intellectual mud-slinging is characteristic of many border disputes and boundary work. The question again is, who shall "speak about or for" the homeless? The notion of the social scientist holding forth against the powers of political unreason, of myth, is simply untenable. What is lacking is a critical self-evaluation that calls into question the agenda of "science objectivity" and its relationship to the issues of social justice, power, and community—or practical objectivity. Who is going to control the agenda? Rossi was afraid that advocates would spoil his research by controlling his research agenda; advocates feared Rossi would spoil their work by controlling the political agenda through distorting what they thought was the definable homeless population. The advocates perceived Rossi as ultimately "speaking for" himself and not for the homeless, and themselves as "speaking for" the homeless. Rossi perceived the advocates as "speaking for" themselves and not for the homeless, and himself for scientific truth.[12]

While it is true that advocates exaggerated the size of the homeless population and many estimates were simply guesswork, it is also true that without playing the "numbers game" it is doubtful if homelessness would have attracted the support from politicians that it did. At the very least such exaggerations, even while ultimately self-defeating, did draw attention to the problem. In a society where social policy is driven by numerical estimates combined with spectacular media reportage, questions of why problems are problems in the first place and how those problems are connected to larger political issues involving the distribution of power and wealth are often shunted aside in favor of the expediency of simple dramatization. In addition, the developing conservative politics of the Reagan-Bush era made debates over poverty less politically tenable than debates over homelessness. In this situation the "truth" of homelessness is not simply a neutral object for research, as perhaps is implied in Rossi's research agenda, but rather is a social construction involving political actors with specific interests and real effects on outcomes. Homelessness and the "truth" about those who are homeless remain political footballs tossed to and fro by policy makers, politicians, and advocates, all with their own set of interests.

The boundary work being accomplished here illustrates that our methods and cognitive constructs of "doing social science" (e.g., examining the issue of homelessness) can lead to serious misunderstandings between the researcher and the community with which that researcher works. This singular example speaks to the question of the methods, purposes, goals, and ways we profess to "speak about and for" the homeless and invites the question of how we "speak with and to" the homeless.[13]

To do research that respects its subjects to "speak with and to" the homeless, requires changes in methods, goals, and analysis. Traditionally the ethnographic literature has favored painting a broad picture of homeless life—from the romanticized picture of "hobos" presented by Nels Anderson in *The Hobo* (1923) to contemporary reports about New York subway dwellers (Toth 1993), Los Angeles "Bridge" people (Underwood 1993), and homeless women in shelters (Liebow 1993). However, ethnographic reports often suppress mention of the structural features that generate the conditions for homelessness, or at the very least fail to integrate the ethnographic findings with larger structuralist concerns of politics, culture, and economy.

Conversely, structuralist accounts often ignore the voices of the homeless themselves. Attempts to bridge this gap are evident in new work emerging by Ruddick (1995, 1990), Wagner (1993), Rosenthal (1994), Golden (1992), Snow and Anderson (1993), Wright (1995), and Wright and Vermund (forthcoming), who have attempted to bridge the structural/individualist gap by incorporating ethnographic and structural materials within a critical sociological analysis. Ruddick's analysis of homeless youth incorporates a concept of strategy and tactics to explain how Los Angeles homeless youth make sense of their social-physical space within a city undergoing extensive downtown redevelopment. Wagner examines the protests of homeless encampments in North City, employing their voices to speak about the non-normative conditions of family and work.

The next steps in analysis should be to closely examine the ways social imaginary significations display themselves through the concepts and practices of city planners and officals, to examine the promotion of redevelopment policies that act to disperse and contain the poor, and to investigate the labor market changes that diminish the ability of the very poor to advance in society. This analysis should also be connected with ethnographic accounts to examine the interplay between the context of urban spaces and the real, everyday actions of homeless populations. Any analysis should also contest normative notions of family, work, and comportment, with an eye toward understanding homeless resistance as a response to situational deprivation. To facilitate this understanding I will begin by presenting a theoretical model that draws upon Castoriadis's theory of the social imaginary and Lefebvre's theory of the production of urban space, wedded to a concept of the city that recognizes the contested nature of urban space. This will allow us to see how the very poor and homeless exist as both subjected and as active subjects in a landscape undergoing constant change.

Chapters 1–3 are designed to provide theoretical tools to situate the organization of ethnographic data presented later in chapters 4 through 7. Taking the time to assimilate the theory will help in understanding how the homeless populations I studied were connected quite intimately within the web of power relationships that make up the context of city space. However, those who would like to jump right into the ethnographic material might skip ahead to chapter 4 and examine the various authoritative strategies and local resistances employed by those in the Student-Homeless Alliance and in Chicago's "Tranquility City."

Social-Physical Space, Social Imaginaries, and Homeless Identities

The construction of its own world by each and every society is, in essence, the creation of a world of meanings, its social imaginary significations, which organize the (presocial, "biologically given") natural world, instaturate a social world proper to each society (with its articulations, rules, purposes, etc.), establish the ways in which socialized and humanized individuals are to be fabricated, and institute the motives, values, and hierarchies of social (human) life. (Castoriadis 1991, 41)

Space is not a scientific object removed from ideology or politics; it has always been political and strategic. (Lefebvre 1976b, 31)

The intellectual struggles over the boundaries of homeless discourse and the material struggles over housing, wages, and city displacement and gentrification raise questions about the theoretical and practical location of homeless persons within a society of expanding social inequality. What does that location mean for housed versus nonhoused people? How are these "locations" created? Homeless persons, like all persons, exist, move, thrive, and die within urban, suburban, and rural spaces, acting and reacting to imposed practices that seek to regulate their bodies. A homeless person is not simply an object for investigation, a "problem," but real breathing, bleeding flesh, a present humanness that is often stripped bare by the authoritatively imposed categories of others. Living with "spoiled identities," the very poor are categorized, inspected, dissected, and rendered mute in the public discourse about their future by those who have the power to enforce those categorical distinctions discussed in the introduction. Such distinctions are present not only in the verbal and textual discourses of researchers and policy makers, but also in the imagined distinctions of city life promoted by city officials, planners, and other agents of authority. Understanding this requires a theory that can link how city officials imagine urban spaces, carry out their conceptions, and rationalize their creations by the invoking of the rhetoric of "progress" or conversely the rhetoric of "safety." While this will be discussed in more empirical detail in chapters 2 and 3, here I would like to outline a theory that can account for the categorization of homeless bodies and their regulation in urban space.

Social Imaginary Significations and Everyday Life

Perceived as outside the boundaries of middle-class comportment and respectability,[1] homeless persons are kept at both an ideological distance and a physical distance. Homeless populations, "framed" and contained in academic and policy discourse as passive apolitical subjects, are also subjected to a physical isolation through containment in shelters and segregation in marginal industrial areas. These actions require the active production and policing of city social space by local institutions. Therefore the contesting of social alienation and oppression occurs not only on the factory floor but in the realm of everyday life, in and through the very spaces we so often take for granted. The simple act of occupying particular urban spaces, of choosing a spot to place one's head at night, may conflict with what city officials define as the "proper" place for homeless persons. Such actions, as simple survival mechanisms for homeless persons, may be viewed as contesting city authority, especially if accompanied by any attempt of homeless persons to organize themselves. The mere presence of homeless persons in city areas, unofficially designated "off limits," will often be met with active city responses, from police sweeps to arrests. By their very presence homeless persons communicate their "out of place" status. This control of urban space, a highly political creation, is a means by which the privileged render the very poor "invisible." For local governments, people without an established home are to be installed in shelters, "in their place," out of sight.

Cornelias Castoriadis, a former editor of *Socialisme ou Barbarie* and an advocate for worker self-management and the revolutionary praxis of autonomy, and Henri Lefebvre, a contributor to the *Arguments* group and a writer on theories of urban space and consumption, both contributors to the Paris uprisings of 1968, offer an understanding of both the social imaginary and urban space. An integration of these concepts provides a context within which to understand the "out of place" character of homeless persons. Taking an active stance to oppose traditional Marxian theory and bureaucratic careerism, Castoriadis and Lefebvre extended the understanding of alienation and oppression from the factory floor to the world of everyday life, and in particular to struggles over city space, racism, and sexism. The conditions of everyday life, and a concern with how everyday life is the battleground for extended deprivation, offer a way to understand what it means to be "out of place" and homeless.

Homeless persons, working at marginal jobs or struggling on the streets with handouts, exist outside of the formal labor economy; they do not fit within the Marxian model as active subjects in any category other than a derogatory "lumpen." Hence, the emphasis upon the conditions of everyday life, combined with concepts of authoritative strategies and tactical resistances, offers a better model with which to analyze my ethnographic data. This will be discussed in detail in chapter 4. Struggles against alienated labor extend from the factory to the gendered, racial, and class segmentations fostered by the market economy, to the *conditions of everyday life*.

Our principal human activity, according to Castoriadis, is not merely to produce and consume, but also to give meaning to the world, to make sense of the world around us. And the giving of meaning to the world around us, as an area of human action that involves both discourse and embodied praxis, is the province of a deep legitimated collective representation of that world, the *social imaginary* (Howard 1977, 265; Castoriadis 1987; Laclau, 1990 Hesse 1993).[2] The giving of meaning to the world, the province of the imaginary, the realm of dreams and fantasies, is itself conceived of as a material force, every bit as legitimate as the production of commodities. Castoriadis argues for an ontology that unites both discourse and body, that attempts to conceive of a dynamic relationship between the interpretive strategies we deploy in the world and the material basis of that world. How can we understand the forced social inequalities of market economies, the deprivation of homeless populations, "except in relation to intentions, orientations, chains of significations" (Castoriadis 1987, 136) and their referents? Whose intentions, whose orientations? These questions always bring us back to material explanations, which call forth an examination of the material practices of planners, city officials, police, and social workers. Explanations of material exploitation and oppression as a result of the industrial division of labor, the extraction of surplus labor value, and the varieties of uneven development must be supplemented with an understanding of how our very dreams and fantasies, our imaginations, are constituted through our social relationships with each other and with the social institutions we come in contact with. In and of themselves economistic explanations cannot answer the question of why the poor have been partitioned into "teenage welfare mothers," "homeless veterans," "homeless teenagers," or why they are shunted into institutionally controlled settings, such as shelters.

For those living on the streets or confined to shelters, as indeed for the rest of us, alienation and deprivation are expressed in the most intimate way possible—through language and the body. It is at this concrete level of everyday life that such exploitation makes itself felt in the very manner in which homeless experiences are discussed, reflected upon, imagined, and acted out by the homeless themselves, by researchers, policy makers, planners, and law enforcement. Paying attention to these microactions of everyday adjustments reveals the horrendous disguise assumed by alienation. And these microactions are informed at the most basic bodily level by networks of meanings established through the production of symbols, networks of meanings composed as constellations of signs arranged in patterns that give coherence—symbolic meaning and symbolic networks—to one's thoughts as well as one's actions. Social institutions—the police, the courts, families, schools, and hospitals—all exist within these symbolic networks of social power connected together through those routine practices participants train for and are rewarded for exercising, practices guided by specific constellations of meaning established to control others.

These symbolic networks raise the question of meanings. In particular, as Castoriadis (1987) exclaims, "What are the meanings conveyed by the symbols, the system of signifieds to which the system of signifiers refers?" (136). Understanding these meanings is a matter of empirical investigation, the examination of texts, plans, discourse, and designs, which we shall do in the following chapters. However, the search for any well-established or fixed meaning is futile. Meaning is not arbitrary, except in an ideal sense, but "fixed" through *social practice*, practices that reinforce the distinctions created within and between the relations of economic, political, and cultural power operating through everyday life. These practices may exist in the generation of symbolic combinatory associations that employ binary either/or or us/them orientations, or in more complicated sequences that express a more sophisticated relationship of power. Simple combinatory relationships do not equal meaning, however; they merely provide the basis from which meaning is constructed.

The social practices of homeless rebellion and resistance, of defiance toward established authoritative practices, can work to shake the very foundations of the dominant social imaginary. Social practices are, therefore, generated by the workings of social imaginary significations through symbolic networks. These networks are contained within social-physical space, by actors responding to, interpreting, resisting, and acting on their everyday life, through their bodies and on the bodies of others, whether they are city officials or homeless encampment members.

Signification is complex and polysemic, both negotiated and routinized. Symbols can carry signification only if they can be organized systematically, into an "intersecting unity," a network of meanings. This, in turn, points to the ways such symbols can extend, reproduce, and modify further significations, developing new symbolic networks. This "signification, which is neither something perceived (real) nor something thought (rational), is an imaginary signification" (Castoriadis 1987, 140) which can only be approached indirectly.[3] The fact that symbolic networks can be produced by combinatory relationships, that signification is a result of created distinctions, does not address why or how, for example, social practices that generate relationships of domination and submission are accepted as a "natural" within capitalist societies; why, for example, "shelters" are thought of as "natural" places for homeless persons. These practices depend upon social imaginary significations,[4] which find their most immediate expression through the production of symbols and signs and, in particular, in the development of categorical social and physical spatial and temporal distinctions that serve as intimate maps of power within a society; who is to be accepted, who is to be rejected, and where, in what location, are such distinctions performed? At the level of social-physical space, what are the "proper" places within which rejected and accepted bodies are to be placed by those who have the power to do so?

The social imaginary exists prior to logical reason; reason emerges out of the social imaginary. And yet the social imaginary is also deeply altered by the forms of reason and practice employed within a given social world. According to Castoriadis (1987):

This element—which gives a specific orientation to every institutional system, which overdetermines the choice and the connections of symbolic networks, which is the creation of each historical period, its singular manner of living, of seeing and of conducting its own existence, its world, and its relations with this world, this originary structuring component, this central signifying-signified, the source of that which presents itself in every instance

as an indisputable and undisputed meaning, the basis for articulating what does matter and what does not, the origin of the
surplus of being of the objects of practical, affective and intellectual investment, whether individual or collective—is nothing other
than the imaginary of the society or of the period considered.
(145)

Therefore the organization of societies, of race, ethnic, gender, and class
configurations, of social-physical space and temporal organization, is not
conducted strictly along biological or chemical lines, or by the logic of
reason, or by a materialist logic of capital development, but are the by-
products of the organization of fantasies, of the working of the social
imaginary in a dialectical relationship with the material world. A social
world comprised of vast social inequalities will produce different fantasies of "normality," struggle, resistance, and domination than a world in
which social inequality is abolished. The social imaginary does indicate
its presence in the construction of particular types of reasoning, reasoning that shapes intellectual and physical practices. Such *logics*, technical
or otherwise, work to reshape the dominant social imaginary by their
expression through social practice. Therefore the social imaginary works
through the social and economic relations of a society, expressed along
particular cultural dimensions and refracted through the race, ethnicity,
class, and gender aspects of populations.[5] Constructed images of the
homeless are readily visible in Hollywood films, as we shall see in the
forthcoming chapters, and in the procedures of Departments of Public
Aid, and the practices of local police departments.

　　The social world, then, is a product of the organization of systems
of signification, networks of meaning, informed by dominant social
imaginary significations. Symbols and icons arise as a result of the
historical playing out of conflicting systems of significations expressed
materially in political, cultural, and economic struggles, often in and
through urban spaces. Old social imaginaries are transformed through
human struggles in everyday life, struggles over the meanings of social
practices that have been shaped by dominant social imaginaries. And
these struggles will be indicated by changing social practices, often
violations of routine or traditional ways of accomplishing something.
Not all symbols end up as social representatives, not all systems of
reason or expression end up constituting a society. Through the operations of the dominant social imaginary on symbolic networks, answers
to the questions—Who are we? Who are they?—are produced and
reproduced, answers that often remain unconscious to the participants.

Social imaginaries, therefore, are deeply implicated in the very formation of homeless social identities, identities that are contained and expressed through specific intellectual and material practices. The indirect grasping of the material limits of an expressed social imaginary might be possible only during times of revolutionary change, when the very foundations of everyday life, and hence social identities, are radically altered, providing an opportunity for a brief glimpse of what is possible beyond the status quo. This is not to negate the very real role of material production, merely to understand that material production, exploitation, and alienation constitute a larger world than that of the factory, the commodity, or of the relationships of use to exchange value.

The Production of Space and the Location of Identity in Everyday Life

The constitution of identity as defining what is "us" and what is "them" is fundamental to any society. When we examine the issue of class in North American society, the particular social imaginary that informs the construction of identities is the imagined distinctions generated between the "deserving" and the "undeserving" poor, key elements of a deeper fantasy that operates to create a particular identity of what a "good" American is, of what a "good" person is. The American frontier myth of self-reliance, combined with a possessive individualism, works to maintain distinctions between the deserving and the undeserving poor, explaining homelessness by invoking descriptions of personal failure.

Performances of success or personal failure are judged according to standards of worth that are made possible by prior discriminations of who is and who is not worthy. These distinctions are established by the dominant social imaginary working within real material interests. Because social imaginary significations operate by establishing distinctions, they also create hierarchies of worth, both socially and physically, allowing for the assembling and disassembling of material objects, groups of people, and urban spaces, creating vast areas of contested land. The very creation of social and physical spaces indirectly points to the workings of dominant social imaginaries in the very distinctiveness, in the manifold uses, with which land is developed.

Lefebvre (1976a, 1979, 1990, 1991) understands social and physical space as something more than a mere container for human action.[6] Space is active, creating and recreating the social relationships of everyday life in a dialectical manner that is both *utopian* and *strategic*.[7] Dominant social imaginaries work through these utopian and strategic manifestations of space to produce specific city landscapes that are essential to the formation of social identities. Active human agents strategically maneuver within social spaces but have the potential of actively exploring alternative, liberatory forms of social space; the homeless encampments of Chicago are merely one form of these liberatory spaces.

Placing human agency at the forefront, Lefebvre extends the understanding of social and physical space beyond the realm simply of domination, beyond Michel Foucault's "networks of power" and microresistances, to a general concern with everyday life as a locus for emancipatory practices in the midst of an economically, culturally, and politically polarized landscape.[8] Spatial hierarchies of worth, generated by the social imaginary working through social practices, both produce and maintain an increasingly fragmented and socially polarized city topography. Therefore, space is not simply a reflection of economic contradictions produced by the production process, but rather a fundamental aspect of the production process itself; *space, labor, capital.* This is because, as Gottdiener (1985) puts it, "the social relations governing the activities associated with space need to conform to the way in which space is used to acquire wealth. This relationship is contradictory since the uses of space to make money are continually coming into conflict with the institution of private property" (125). Space is produced and space is consumed. Space facilitates or retards production, consumption and distribution, not only of products but also of the worth of human actors.

Downtown spaces are produced to facilitate financial exchanges, light manufacturing, and the reproduction of middle-class lifestyles, while an adjacent space is consumed in the form of visiting museums, art galleries, sports games, and the like. Insofar as urban spaces are imagined as playgrounds for tourists, those people who conflict with the imagined realm of tourism will be effectively locked out of such spaces through police practices designed to restrict the movements of those thought of as "out of place." Other urban spaces become repositories for throwaway populations. Still others, for segments of the privileged and well heeled. The organization of these differences in social-physical space is not natural, but the result of social imaginaries working through the social practices of developers, bankers, designers, architects, politicians, policy makers, and police enforcers.

Lefebvre encourages us to think about space as an instrument of social control via the state and also an instrument for liberation from the alienation of everyday life under capital. Space can be viewed as "administratively controlled," a policed space that acts to reconfirm the dominant social-spatial hierarchical organization, to ensure that everyone is in their proper place. Clearly, this is the form of space most frequently encountered by those who find themselves poor or homeless. City, county, and state political divisions serve to establish administrative districts that provide for the control of land-use development and the regulation of police, health, and social services by location. These administrative distinctions are shaped by the dominant social imaginaries within a given society.

The social space of status distinctions associated with moral worth and the physical spaces of differentiated activities are the major vehicles for reproducing a Gramscian cultural hegemony; such a hegemony is established through an underlying logic working through the actions of knowledge and technical experts who generate necessary "systems" of control, spatial control. Understandably, such hegemonic attempts to systematize space, to establish a particular reasonable logic throughout everyday life, informed by the dominant social imaginary, is fraught with contradictions and conflicts that must be negotiated. These negotiations occur through our coded understandings of social-physical space. Lefebvre understands that space can be decoded, or read, because social-physical space is an aspect, a "process of signification," organized as a spatial code that is historically constituted. However, unlike those who are willing to reduce decoding to formal plays of sign systems, to readable formal codes, Lefebvre (1991) is more interested in looking at the dialectical nature of spatial codes as "part of a practical relationship, as part of an interaction between 'subjects' and their space and surroundings" (18). In this sense, then, social-physical space may be viewed as the product of social practices that create specific coded contents, whether it is the construction of sports stadiums or the establishment of shelter facilities in specified parts of the city.

Briefly, Lefebvre (1991, 33) specifies that we can examine space in terms of (1) spatial practices, (2) representations of space, and (3) representational spaces. *Spatial practices*, which involve the creation and re-creation of social formations within given locations and sites, assists in generating a degree of social cohesion and continuity within a society. In modern capitalist society, spatial practices may take the form of the daily life of suburban commuters or the wanderings of those living on the street. Each individual actively engaged in everyday life gives form to urban and suburban spaces, generating an apparent "structure" of everyday life, a minimal sense of cohesion, in which the very actions of oneself and others create the illusion that space is merely a container for those actions. What is often not recognized is the manner in which everyday life, as a spatial practice, is subverted by those perceptions, or dualisms, discussed earlier, that separate out persons from spaces, individuals from the social, the cognitive from the somatic, and thought from action. And as Bourdieu (1984) has pointed out in *Distinctions*, spatial practices have a strong class component to them in the realm of consumption, as well as in production. It is also clear that spatial practices can also be oriented along racial, ethnic, and gender lines, as we shall see.

Representations of space, what Lefebvre associates with the space of engineers and planners of all kinds, is space conceptualized abstractly and conveyed through different expert discourses. Technical conceptions about how people live and should live are equated with what can be thought about, organized within verbal and visual sign systems (Lefebvre 1991, 39). Representations of space may be viewed in the plans of engineers, the schemas of politicians, the zoning discussions of land-use planners, and many other professional areas of expertise, the dominant social-physical space of any given society. For example, Liggett (1995) discusses the planning documents included in the City of Cleveland's *Cleveland Civic Vision 2000 Citywide Plan* as an institutionalized representation of space, designed to convey how Cleveland should be understood and perceived. City and suburban planning documents, especially those directed at downtown redevelopment schemes, constitute representations of space, which guide us in understanding who is to be legitimately included within the dominant vision of the city and who is to be excluded. The City of San Jose holds a particular concept of downtown space as a "recreational" space that excludes homeless persons, unless they are "contained" within established institutional settings. It is this category of space that we shall look at in more detail in the next two chapters.

Representational space, however, is space that is "directly lived through its associated images and symbols" (Lefebvre 1991, 39), often the realm of artists, philosophers, writers. Lefebvre understands this form of space as one that is often dominated within a given society, but also a space through which the imaginary attempts change. One can easily think of the production of public monuments, historic fountains, market squares, public parks such as Central Park in New York or Golden Gate Park in San Francisco, historic Greenwich Village or North Beach, and a host of other spaces too numerous to mention.

Representational space can provide the utopic dreams within which dominant social imaginaries may be challenged.

These three ways of examining "space" move the debate about urban and suburban space beyond the inherent dualisms visible in both Erving Goffman's front and back "regions" and Anthony Giddens's "structuration," to understanding social-physical space as a complex set of relationships with many historically produced contradictions and distinctions. What anchors these distinctions is the work of the body within social-physical space.

Goffman's analysis of back-region behaviors reads like a list of disrespectful actions: using profanity, "sloppy" sitting and standing, smoking, and elaborate belching and flatulence. For homeless people living on the streets, performing in front regions is a constant task, with little space or time to relax. According to Duncan (1979), the "moral order" of the "landscape" through which homeless persons must move is populated by distinctions between "prime" and "marginal" spaces that serve to confirm a degraded status identity in the eyes of others. Nonetheless, Duncan outlines how those labeled as "tramps" use the landscape as cover for their activities, as a strategy for survival, to negotiate the differences between how spaces should be used according to authorities and how they are actually used by people who are homeless.

Duncan, like Goffman understands urban space as the realm within which people act and negotiate their identities, making adjustments to meet the demands of the moment. Therefore, the desire to "get off the streets" is not simply an issue of solitude or individual "privacy" but, as Giddens (1984) understands, a place where one can engage in "the expression of 'regressive behavior' in situations of co-presence" (129), where one can be free of those who would judge one's behavior. For example, being forced into shelters, as "total" institutions, means that such "regressive" behaviors will be discouraged, that one will be expected to engage in front-region behaviors. Without the ability to "let off steam," shelter rules that demand a front-region performance to prove one's credibility might produce further frustration and anger among homeless patrons. Often interpreted by homeless encampment members as forcing a "loss of privacy," shelters were avoided in favor of the camps because the camps offered the possibility of back-region behavior and security. The advantage of homeless encampments over shelters was their ability to generate a back region of one's own, often within another back region of housed society.

Giddens advances Goffman's (1959) dramaturgical theory by examining "the situated character of action in time-space, the routinization of activity and the repetitive nature of day-to-day life" (Giddens 1984, xxiv). While Giddens understands Goffman's observations of face work, gestures, and reflexive control of the body, the positioning of individuals in everyday life, Giddens also realizes that "positioning" must be understood through the encounters one engages in, one after the other, across time and space, conducted within specific places or locales.[9] People are positioned in multiple ways attached to specific and assumed social identities. The body must mediate these multiple positionings. To the degree that positionings are contradictory, the body will have to work harder to integrate them into some type of order.[10] If the body/subject is not successful in this task, increased stress is the result. Although Goffman pointed out how daily social interactions occur and how institutions could perform their functions through routine practices, Giddens contributes a sense of history that gives such actions shape and meaning. Giddens attempts to restore a sense of intention and motivation to social action. He attempts to break with the dualisms of individual/social, micro/macro, subjective/objective by positing a theory of structuration that integrates human action within a temporal and spatial flow influenced by historical developments, a theory that privileges the examination of social and system integration (142).

Routinization is the means by which place, or locale, and space are integrated, a means by which we come to see the world as "whole." In integrating Castoriadis's theory of the social imaginary with Giddens's concept of body routinization, we can note that the "fixing" of signification occurs at multiple levels on and through the body, a body subjected to routinization on a daily basis, a body acting to configure the specific manner in which practical consciousness[11] operates in the understanding of the world.[12] It is this practical consciousness, often conducted within institutions, that is most influenced by routinization. An obvious problem with this schema, however, is the disallowance of conflict and change as integral elements of identity. Cannot identity also be produced through nonroutinized forms of action, through conflict and struggle?

Giddens (1990) argues that the separation of space from place, where place is represented by locale referring to "the physical settings of social activity as situated geographically" (18), is the main characteristic of modernity since the Enlightenment. "Empty spaces" are the end products. This separation of space from place assumes that time and space can be recombined in the "time-space 'zoning'" of everyday life where local actions and knowledges are now structured by distant social influences, whether regional or state planning associations or corporate boards of multinational companies. Extended travel and the expansion of interconnected information and communication systems mean that local places are increasingly dominated by regional and global organizations of space and time.[13] Culturally, one has merely to look at the rapid expansion of all forms of national and international media into the home and on the street, including advertising and marketing. And yet such an organization of space merely increases personal and social isolation of homeless persons who are not connected directly to the market. Unfortunately, Giddens's concept of social and physical space remains relatively immobile; it does not specify how particular forms of time-space regionalizations, spatial organizations, are supposed to change, except through the introduction of new technological developments.[14]

Avoiding these problems, Michel Foucault's (1980) concept of space as an intrinsic and active aspect of understanding (70) adopts spatial metaphors of territory, field, displacement, domain, region, soil, horizon, and site in order to describe the deployment of knowledge/ power throughout society (68).[15] Foucault's spatial concept, however, remains wedded to a concept of space that, while performing an excellent job of explaining the deployment of administrative power throughout urban landscapes, is less useful in understanding the possibility of resistance as it emerges from utopian dreams of liberation. Resistance remains local.

Still, Foucault's concepts can be useful in examining the application of "truth regimes" to specific organizations of administrative spaces and the spaces of local resistances to such power. Foucault's concept of heterotopias is useful as a descriptive term for categorizing the various types of administrative spaces within a city. For example, those who find themselves homeless often float between city spaces defined as *heterotopias of deviation* (Foucault 1986), the world of rest homes, prisons, and psychiatric hospitals, spaces where deviation from constructed norms is expected, and a declining set of *crisis heterotopic* sites, which, in contrast, are "privileged or sacred or forbidden places, reserved for individuals who are in a state of crisis" (24). Homeless shelters would constitute a heterotopic space somewhere between these two types of social spaces, although, according to Timmer (1988), in management ideology and function, as we shall see in chapter 4, shelters closely resemble correctional facilities. Ruddick (1990, 188; 1995) applies Foucault's spatial perspective in her examination of the homeless geography of Los Angeles. She identified a series of heterotopias occupied by homeless families and individuals, such as the Ocean

Front Walk in Venice, along Rose Avenue in Santa Monica, and Plummer Park in Hollywood. In my work in San Jose, California, homeless heterotopic spaces consisted of McKinley Park, the Guadalupe River, a doughnut shop on San Carlos Avenue next to Fifth Street, St. James Park, and the southern reaches of Coyote Creek. More often than not these heterotopic spaces weave themselves through the fabric of the city and are often adjacent to fashionable areas. When the very poor who occupy such spaces begin to move, organize, or demonstrate, such spaces cease being simple heterotopias of "difference" and instead become what I would term *resistant heterotopias.* The risk of the very poor transforming heterotopias of deviation into resistant heterotopias calls forth constant policing from city officials—social practices (such as police sweeps) that work to break up organized groups before they begin to form, through the enforcement of "public" space rules (Murray 1995).

The deployment of truth regimes, as administrative knowledges working through specific heterotopias, is evident in the panoptic regulation of homeless bodies through the integration of shelter services and rules, police surveillance practices, and arrest procedures that convert those who find themselves homeless into statistical data that can then be integrated with other service and or work opportunities. The dispersal of this type of network of power often remains invisible to housed persons in middle-class society but is quite obvious to those living on the streets. The nationwide deployment of shelters as homeless "barracks" speaks to the understanding of power and poverty through a militarization of schemes of control. In refusing to use shelters, the homeless encampment members of SHA and "Tranquility City" refused a place that reconfirmed their status as "spoiled identities." These identities were reinforced by the elaborate rule systems and punitive measures employed by many city shelters. Shelters were used only as a last resort when street locations became too precarious due to police activity in the area.

In applying Foucault's theory of power/knowledge to understanding the actions of those working in inner-city human service agencies, Dear and Wolch (1987) uncovered how "surveillance and disciplinary procedures of the Welfare State were articulated by and penetrated the routines" of professional social workers and community workers (12). With the move to deinstitutionalization of the mentally ill during the 1970s and 1980s, professional social workers faced a contradiction between caring for their patients and being forced to refer them to community workers out of their control as a result of state political changes. Struggles over the decline of the welfare state, (e.g. the rise of Proposition 13 antitax legislation in California and the decline of state and federal welfare budgets) affected the ability of cities to take care of their very poor. These overt political struggles directly affected the spatial expression of power within cities, leading to what Dear and Wolch (1987) termed "service-dependent ghettos" that concentrated shelters, halfway houses, and group areas within a small, confined area of the city.[16]

The term *service-dependent ghetto* implies that the type of space produced concentrates and controls in a "total" manner those who receive services there. In fact service-dependent ghettos may be thought of not as a homogeneous terrain of surveillance and discipline, but rather as a terrain that is fractured, open to the possibility of resistance. The manner in which Dear and Wolch (1987) chose to analyze the treatment of service-dependent populations privileges a view of spatial power as overwhelmingly dominant and powerful, with little, if any, room for local resistances, fractures, or alternative spacings. On the other hand, Foucault does offer a model of local resistance through microactions. For Foucault, however, resistance remains localized and spatially distinct. Is this reduced version of resistance a product of Foucault's theory, or is it an empirical phenomenon? Perhaps a little of both. Current political forces have made it difficult to sustain any broad utopian resistance movements that could challenge the imposition of dominated space. Resistance is confined to perfunctory and spasmodic eruptions of protests. This weakened political perspective of resistance stands in contrast to the vision of liberation offered by Lefebvre's utopic spaces.

Unlike Foucault's power/knowledges and truth-regimes, Castoriadis's concept of social imaginary significations can explain the form within which Lefebvre's representations of space are constructed, the meaning of representational spaces, and indeed the way spatial practices are disrupted or smoothed out by the workings of dominant social imaginaries. This makes the integration of Lefebvre's and Castoriadis's theories of space useful in moving beyond a mere descriptive typology of urban spaces and toward an analytical examination of how social and physical spaces are assembled within our society. A social imaginary predicated upon a white supremacist and patriarchal perspective, for example, can set the boundaries of discourse within which expert technicians, engineers, and policy makers may conceive of race as black and gender as women, just as such imaginaries can alter representational spaces by giving form to the meanings of burning crosses or civil rights marches. Representational space, as shaped by social imaginaries working through writers, artists, philosophers, and activists, can also provide the base for alternative imaginaries, utopic images; alternative representations that can collide with dominant social imaginaries worked out in the spaces of representation. Given these relationships, power and privilege in society will always emerge as a negotiated process between these three forms of space, informed by the struggles between dominant social imaginaries and counter social imaginaries. The social imaginary may be viewed as the bridge between representations of space, representative spaces, and spatial practices.

According to Lefebvre, the active development of private property disrupts the organic lived relations of everyday life, fragmenting the landscape, reducing space to fragmented, homogeneous, and hierarchically organized landscapes, creating an *abstract space* as opposed to developing personal and collectivized spaces (Martins 1982, 178; Lefebvre 1976, 83–84; 1979, 289–90; Gottdiener 1985, 121–32). The imposition of technical urban planning schemas, for example, restricts the multidimensional character of everyday life, fragments life activities, even as such schemas integrate transportation, energy, or housing developments. The inherent diversity of social-physical spaces is dominated by the imposed homogeneity of the "plan."[17] This is quite obvious from a cursory look at urban downtown redevelopment plans. The goal of downtown revitalization is not to increase the race and class diversity of city patrons, but rather to create an attractive consumer climate for those who have the money to spend. Given the socially unequal distribution of wealth, power, and prestige, particular racial/ethnic groups and class segments, will be privileged over others for inhabiting downtown spaces. Those who are poor and homeless will find an unsympathetic downtown climate in the newly redeveloped urban spaces.

The division of spaces, engineered through an intersection of private property interests with technical representations of space, produces distinct hierarchies of urban space organized around limited concepts of social life and cultural difference.[18] And yet, even as city planners and developers seek to construct new abstract spaces within specific affluent markets, poor squatters can "seize" spaces in actions that directly refute the premises imposed by abstract space.

This increasingly chaotic expansion of abstract spaces, what I believe Lash and Urry (1987) incorrectly view as disorganized capitalism, calls forth a differently organized capitalism in which this chaos of production and reproduction is reorganized into containable sites. Abstract space mutates into a form where the very chaos produced by the advanced forms of production are used to create new markets, new consumers, new relations of production, and new spaces, along with expanded forms of surveillance and control. Capitalist flexibility increases to accommodate this new global "chaos," another opportunity for investment, while casting aside whole segments of national populations, generating armies of the unemployed and legions of homeless wanderers. Those who are no longer useful within this new production/consumption system can be effectively isolated through expanded surveillance, and physical and social isolation. These radical spatial exclusions and concentrations, which Lefebvre understood as basic to the creation of industrial capital, are now assisted by advanced technology that accelerates control, surveillance, and consumption. Modern cities mutate into *hypermodern* cities. If hypermodern cities and regions are those in which social and economic tendencies specified in earlier periods are amplified and augmented, then how far can these social spatial polarizations progress before producing a reversal in capitalist fortunes and a crisis in political legitimacy? This can be answered only through the use of an active concept of social practice, a deployment of strategy and tactics, and not an overarching "logic," economic or otherwise.

The imposition of abstract space is not the result of some autonomous logic of capital but derives from strategies employed by groups and individuals acting on behalf of institutional interests within well-defined spatial and temporal boundaries (Lefebvre 1976, 28), strategies shaped by the dominant social imaginary of a given society. As city spatial boundaries change due to financial and or community conflicts, local officials may alter their strategies of controlling and producing space. Established social-physical spaces are organized strategically and historically, and therefore can be disrupted, negotiated, abolished, or assimilated through what de Certeau (1984, 34–38) termed "tactics." Official strategies are strategies that establish a place as "proper" in the eyes of city authorities and the general public. Authoritative control over, and division of, urban space "makes possible a panoptic practice proceeding from a place whence the eye can transform foreign forces into objects that can be observed and measured, and thus control and 'include' them within its scope of vision" (de Certeau 1984, 36). This control is clear in the police practice of sweeping homeless encampments. But, such control is countered in the tactical resistances generated by those living in street encampments.

The rapid expansion of newly created spaces, new spatial distinctions, an "explosion of spaces," "results in a chaos of contradictory spaces that proliferate the boundaries at which sociospatial conflict appears" (Gottdiener 1985, 126). The emergence during the 1970s and

1980s of social movements based on identity politics derived from this "explosion of spaces," from the expansion and creation of new social-physical spatial boundaries.[19] Similarly, as social inequality expands, new movements of the very poor and the homeless begin to appear at the borders of the newly created social and physical spaces. To expand struggles against alienation beyond the factory floor to the community is to extend the terrain of conflict from the factory to everyday life, to the social and physical spaces of the city. However, these expanding struggles can often work at cross-purposes. For example, unemployed workers who find themselves on the streets without a home often come into conflict with community organizations and homeowners' associations who want to keep shelters and mental health community clinics out of their neighborhoods. Fearing a decline in property values and crime, many otherwise progressive community groups often work to exclude shelters and group homes. The definition of who is and who is not acceptable to a given community, therefore, hinges upon the type of social imaginary operating within a given community, and this will be determined by the nature of social struggles occurring within the city. Conflicting social imaginaries can also generate conflicting definitions of acceptability, leading to clashing perceptions on a given social issue.

The inability of communities to assimilate rapidly proliferating social-physical spatial boundaries generates antagonisms that work to isolate individuals and groups on the basis of race, ethnicity, class, and gender. However, growing community antagonisms can also provide new opportunities to integrate the newly developed spaces within broader oppositional spatial forms, a manifestation of the utopian gesture. Imagining what might be, the realm of the possible, the dreams of hope (Bloch 1986; Geoghegan 1987), also provides the visions necessary for social change. Struggles move directly into the community (tenants' rights), into the university (multiculturalism), into media organs, into the administrative apparatus, into the home, into the bedroom, into all crevices of everyday life. Integrating these struggles to prevent working at cross-purposes is the task of a developing vision, of the utopic gesture. In modern society, abstract space assumes a form acceptable to multinational capital—everywhere revealed and simultaneously concealed beneath a marketing culture specializing in flashier graphics, speedier messages, and louder sounds. For Lefebvre the crushing of lived everyday spaces by the imposition of abstract space results in the ghettoization of all sectors of society:

> Social space became a collection of ghettos. Those of the elite, of the bourgeoisie, of the intellectuals, of the immigrant workers, etc.

These ghettos are not juxtaposed, they are hierarchial, spatially representing the economic and social hierarchy, dominant and subordinated sectors. (quoted in Martin, 1982, 179)

These fragmented spatial forms, the ghettos, fragmented racially, ethnically, and by class, lead to the creation of new borders and hence new conflicts. From the margins come new contestations of established urban spaces—even when those margins now occupy center stage.

The "Fixing" of Partial Truths, Differences, Identities, and Bodies in Space

It is an illusion that society has comprehensive and relatively complete social divisions and social coordinations, because all coordinations, all divisions, are partial, ongoing, and strategic. Making final judgments about societal directions, ideology, or functions, is necessarily partial. This absence of final, total knowledge, of any final understandings of the social as a completed project, also means that all subject knowledge is partial (McLaren 1991, 1989, 1993; Collins 1990; Giroux 1988; Haraway 1988), whether it is the knowledge of city officials or of homeless street persons. However, even though all knowledge is partial, knowledge still requires coordination for city and state power to effectively produce and maintain specific configurations of urban space. Social power, expressed in the control over space and the power to define others, is neither manifested on a completely contingent, arbitrary basis nor managed in a totalizing fashion. Rather, the correspondence between social institutions of society (whether it is work, family, school, or the state) and some professed unity can be understood only in reference to a social imaginary that works through authoritative agents, as they perform their jobs.[20] And it is the social imaginary that acts to shape the direction, flow, and target of power and privilege, to shape the direction of interpretive understandings of specific arrangements of institutional coordinations. The partial nature of subject knowledge does not stop us from "fixing" truth to partial knowledges, a fixing accomplished in order to live and work in the world no matter how unequal that world may be. We entertain the illusion of social stability and comprehensibility in order to act in the world.

The coordination of partial knowledges and the "fixing" of that knowledge into an understanding takes place through the body's operating within various urban spaces. The coordinated partial systems of discourses and practices make themselves felt on the body, inscribed on the body through social practices that McLaren (1989; 1991, 154) terms "enfleshment." The body/subject, "a terrain of the flesh in which meaning is inscribed, constructed, and reconstituted" (McLaren, 1991, 150), is the "interface of the individual and society." For example, people living on the street, homeless persons, are not just neutral bodies, but subjugated bodies and resisting bodies moving through, sitting, lying down, and sleeping in, the social-physical spaces of the city, a negative trope for surrounding housed society. As we shall see in chapter 4, homeless persons and city officials play out their power differences in struggles over where homeless people should be: How should homeless bodies look, and where should they sleep?

How this "fixing" of partial truths occurs, the creation of *habitus* (Bourdieu 1984), may be examined by looking at the social practices people engage in, often ritually, that reconfirm their initial understandings of the world. Often these practices are repetitive and work to maintain borders between types of knowledge by routinizing action (Giddens 1979, 128; 1984, 60–63). These repetitive border-maintenance actions are social practices that suffer from the body's own vulnerabilities and irregularities. People get sick, or they are hurt, challenging these everyday repetitive patterns. Homeless street people constantly challenge the routinized assumption of the "healthy," "active," and "housed" body, disciplined, focused, and hardworking, simply by sleeping on a city sidewalk.

Social institutions, social definitions, and the configurations of urban spaces shift and change, assuming new relationships through dynamic human activity expressed in the "fixing" of partial knowledges. These changes are often registered in both direct and indirect social struggles around issues of power, prestige, and privilege. In these struggles and routinizations, different societies will organize their social institutions differently, positing different categorical arrangements, different ways of judging the validity of particular forms of knowledge, different ways of judging the worth of bodies, homeless or otherwise. The hierarchies of social knowledge, structured by dominant social imaginaries, common in one society might be absent in another. For example, the preoccupation with distinguishing between deserving and undeserving poor, between who is and who is not to be labeled "homeless," common to Western European culture, is not necessarily going to exist in a different society, with a different social imaginary.

The fixing of particular ensembles of institutional meanings, of symbols and partial knowledges, of arrangements of urban space, through the social practices of individuals, reveals the workings of the social imaginary (Castoriadis 1987, 355). It is not simply an issue of ideology, of text, or of spoken language; it encompasses all forms of human creative expression in the material world, from the particular designs of fashion jeans to the construction of shelter facilities and the partitioning of city spaces. Therefore it is through the practices of individuals and groups of individuals, and the mutability of objects, their specific configurations, that society makes material, makes "real," the social imaginary significations. In their social practices, individuals in groups and institutions, embedded in varying relationships of power and privilege, produce the society they live in, and reproduce the existing power relationships—that which holds the network of significations together in a particular form.

The practices of the city planner, the architect and developer, the banker and real estate agent, the police officer, the politician, and the social worker create not only the city they live in but themselves as well, through the active re-creation of the dominant social imaginary significations of that society. However, the ocean of significations[21] from which such practices spring is constantly and intensely fluid, always subject to change, to dissociations, new juxtapositions, eruptions, negotiations, and reformulations. The social world is never stable, but only contingent upon practices of the moment, practices that create the illusion of stability, of cemented sets of social imaginary significations.

Privileged individuals must act, either consciously or unconsciously, to reproduce an illusion of social order and stability that will reinforce the social imaginary that constructs their very selves as "privileged" or "housed" persons, if they wish to maintain their power and privileges. What holds a social order together, what creates its apparent stability, is the coalescing of its particular realms of significations through material actions that work to police significant boundaries (Castoriadis 1987, 359). Social imaginaries work their presence upon our flesh, and that flesh walks, runs, crawls, and jumps through social and physical spaces; so it becomes quite obvious that the ongoing dynamic configurations of the body and of the city are contested terrain for fashioning and refashioning the social, for embodying both the dominant social imaginary and counter-imaginaries.

At the level of discursive formation, clear choices and human agency appear most confusing and conflicting. However, when we understand that the discursive works through the somatic, and that we identify with both our discourse and our bodies, then subjective agency and choice take on the appearance of solidness, of clarity. No matter how confused our decisions, they become anchored to our bodies. And these bodies are socially coded, a welter of signs and symbols. The body exists as a semiotic system, communicating codes of meaning derived from the outcomes of historical race, class, and gender struggles.[22] And because social struggles are often conflicting and contradictory, the body's meanings are often coded ambivalently. Language mediates the world for us, but it is the lived body in social-physical space, in material reality, that socially grounds discursive formations. We might loose our ability to understand our bodies cognitively or discursively, but with the death of the body comes the death of language (our own). Our bodies might rebel against our perceived subjectivity. We are both attached and not attached to our bodies. Insofar as our bodies combined with discourse constitute a world of "common sense," we need to ask how it is that "sense" is produced, or "fixed," through social-physical space. The process of "fixing" particular discursive forms historically is what we often term "ideology."

Here I refer to ideology not as an aspect of "false consciousness," or as an idealized concept of truth, but rather, following Michel Foucault (1991b, 75; 1979; 1980), as the outcome of the production and legitimation of a particular truth regime, of a particular discursive formation that takes on the mantle of "truth" historically and socially, a result of "regimes of practices," of material practices shaped by race, class, and gender social relationships, which both proscribe and codify what is to be done and by whom. As power knowledges, these formations operate on the body in ways that may often be contradictory and can thus be exploited as openings for micro-level resistances. According to McLaren (1989), "Power-knowledge regimes of truth govern social relations not by producing coherent subjects with fixed identities but through discursive practices that produce subject positions, which are always potentially contradictory" (177). Hence, identities are constantly negotiated and renegotiated to mediate such contradictions. Institutions, groups, organizations, and associations are constantly disintegrating, reforming, reshaping, in an attempt to produce a sense of fixed identity for their members. Those with greater access to material and social resources are better able to secure this continuous reformation of identity than are those with few resources.[23]

Ideology and identity are not based simply on discursive formations, embodied within texts, but emerge out of an individual's actions in the world, producing both pleasure and pain, a real physical engagement within the world (McLaren 1989, 191). This can happen only within the realms of social-physical space. Ideology is not merely produced in written texts but inscribed in and on the flesh, in the ritual moving of the body in social settings,[24] and the social imaginary significations crystallized in particular body movements, from the authoritarian pose of the soldier at attention to the downcast look of those forced to live in the streets. The occupation of a city council chamber during a demonstration by homeless persons contrasts with the infusion of police agents arresting those who are willing to put their "bodies on the line," to collapse the artificially created distance between the privileged and the poor. Bodies are not about power, bodies are power.

The body cannot be left behind, no matter how many times one engages in flights of textual fantasy (Megill 1985; McLaren 1991; De Lauretis 1987; Levin 1987; Yudice 1988) or in the fantasies of technical, instrumental reasoning. Nonetheless, Western Cartesian thinking, a mode of thinking easily traced back to Descartes and Kant, as the manifestation of a particular social imaginary, is deeply implicated in dissociating reason, intellect, and belief, from affect and the body.[25] This dissociation is expressed in socially created dualities such as rational/irrational, feeling/thinking, good/evil, body/mind, male/female, and black/white. These dualisms serve as vehicles to maintain authoritative control over bodily behavior and regulate the interpretation of difference, including perceptions of homeless bodies.

The generation of social identities based upon these constructed binaries can be attributed to the social imaginary that privileges a *logic of identity*, a logic that denies, deflects, or represses differences (Young 1990, 98; Adorno 1973) at the service of those who have the power to enforce such distinctions. You are female, not male; you are homeless, not housed; you are black, not white; you are reasonable, not unreasonable; etc. Since the imposition of Reason is an attempt to order partial knowledges, to assemble fragmented bits and pieces of experience, it is also clear that a particular type of authoritarian reason, a reason based upon a *rigid* logic of identity, seeks to solidify clear, stable, unambiguous categories while avoiding the sensuous, the unstable, the contradictory, the messiness of the material world (Young 1990, 98).

Gendered and Racialized Bodies: the "Other" and Social-Physical Space

A rigid logic of identity works to "normalize" differences among racial/ethnic, class, and gender groups. Racial, ethnic, and gender differences expressed in the many different experiences social groups bring to our society are understood under this rigid logic as a simple "plurality" of difference. Multiculturalism as fashion show. One has merely to think of the attempt to communicate a multicultural society by the Benneton ads in which typified images of racial and ethnic groups are presented for public consumption wearing the latest in fashionable attire. The concrete historical and political differences within which each ethnic/racial group must exist are reduced to merely an outside context that unites all in the "American experience." Any experiences or differences of groups outside this created set of "normal" differences is projected, pushed out as an absolute "Other," as that which does not fit into the socially produced identities, the identities recognized in the dominant social imaginary.

This occurs not just at the level of consciousness, but also materially in the physical ghettoization of those deemed unfit, or "Other." It is not difficult to see that with specific sociohistorical circumstances of deprivation and social inequality, of struggles over race, class, and gender, fear and desire can lead to an identification with those who depend upon a rigid insistence on difference, supplemented by a rigid logic of identity, in order to realize their ambitions. In this instance the potential civility of Reason is transformed easily into a rationalized hatred of difference, supported by the social imaginary of "purity," the consequences of which have been quite obvious in the concentration camps of World War II, the "ethnic cleansing" in former Yugoslavia, and the persistent deep-seated racism in the contemporary United States. In this instance the body, the social body, calls for discipline, the imposition of a moral regime, a purification of sin, and the private body is viewed only as an instrument of Reason, a foreign "Object" to one's self, an object to be subjected to rigid controls. It is no accident that the disabled and the deformed, those thought to have "impure" bodies, were the first to die in the Nazi pogroms of World War II. Disabled and impure reasoning was equated with the visible condition of the disabled body, an object to be purged by a social imaginary that normalizes "purity" as goodness.

Clearly with the merging of the visual and a rigid logic of identity, those who give visible evidence of their status—the abject poor, the disabled, the homeless—would all be considered less than human, where human is equated with the negation of the "impure body" and the elevation of a truncated Reason. According to Iris Young (1990):

> Difference, as the relatedness of things with more or less similarity in a multiplicity of possible respects, here congeals as the binary opposition a/not-a. In every case the unity of the positive category is achieved only at the expense of an expelled, unac-

counted for chaotic realm of the accidental . . . These dichotomies in Western discourse are structured by the dichotomy good/bad, pure/impure. The first side of the dichotomy is elevated over the second because it designates the unified, the self-identifical, whereas the second side lies outside the unified as the chaotic, unformed, transforming, that always threatens to cross the border and break up the unity of the good. (99)

The body is thought of as "Other," as what is estranged or foreign, as a lack of something, the root of desire, in opposition to an all-powerful, fulfilled reason, the controller of desire. Given the social imaginary of a historically white and patriarchal Western culture with its fantasies of technical progress and purity, it is easy to see how women, people of color, the disabled, the homeless, are constructed as outside the "norm," as objects to be controlled, not subjects in their own right. As Judith Butler (1987) points out, "from this belief that the body is Other, it is not a far leap to the conclusion that others are their bodies, while the masculine 'I' is a non-corporeal soul." (133). And to make the equation "Others are their bodies" means resorting to judgments based on physical appearance, on the visual. Women end up experiencing themselves in a fragmented manner through the eyes fashioned for them by male gazes, defining their self-worth through commercial media images of women's and men's bodies. This politics of appearances plays itself out in the rapacious pursuit of beauty, fueled by the fashion industry, in which women have been expected to take responsibility and authority for their appearances, fashioned through the lens of male desires (Chapkis 1986).

Women's bodies become the visual objects for male and female desires manifested in the gaze, in the same way particular homeless street bodies, those that appear as disorderly, dirty, and unclean, are viewed as objects of repulsion, as objects from which to avert one's gaze, but also as objects of fascination. While understood as applying to the reduction of women's bodies as Other, as objects, this observation may easily be applied to the very poor, the homeless, who are looked on as the Other, as objects to be controlled. Butler's model suggests clearly how shelter providers, social service agencies, and police officers, the caregivers and judges of the very poor, can invoke the categories deserving and undeserving, while remaining above, in the clouds of saintly help freed of any implication in the oppression of those they assist.[26]

Indeed, bodies are powerful. The question then becomes, Whose power is expressed and for what purpose? Yes, bodies are written on by discourses of power, by the working of social imaginary significations, but often we separate and forget the physical body in favor of the discursive body. For example, preoccupation with the inscribed homeless body, inscribed by the imposition of limited categories of status, of deserving or nondeserving, of abled versus non-abled body, draws us into endless battles over which category a body belongs to, rather than thinking of "poor" bodies, of all humans as "deserving" bodies. Too often technocratic discourses of service replace the language of social justice.

It is important to understand, following Mclaren's concept of enfleshment, that language is not separated from the body but is the extension and intensification of body power (McLaren 1991; Turner 1984). According to McLaren (1991), "discourses do not sit on the surface of the flesh nor float about in the formless ether of the mind but are enfolded into the very structures of our desire in as much as desire itself is formed by the anonymous historical rules of discourse." (154). Conflicts over these questions mean that conflict is not merely cognitive, a battle over ideas, but fundamentally a battle over bodies, over affect, and over where those bodies are to be placed and what those bodies say. Quite simply the formation of identities works through human bodies, but can be located within social-physical spaces. In the words of the artist Barbara Kruegar, *Your Body is a Battleground.*[27]

The linking of women to body and the elevating of men to abstract conceptual work offers the appearance of "naturalness" while concealing the fact that, as Dorothy Smith (1979), Emily Martin (1992), Nancy Hartsock, (1983) and others point out, such splitting is made possible because women do the work that men ignore or demean. Hence, the social imaginary significations that resolve identity issues into male/female are also those that work to both conceal and repro-duce relationships of oppression between men and women. Rigid gender roles among male homeless members of the Student-Homeless Alliance and "Tranquility City" encampments were pronounced and in some instances bordered upon a "hyper-masculinization" of protector/preda-tor. Homeless males assumed the position of "protector" of other home-less men and women on the street in exchange for increased status. Some homeless encampment members refused what they understood as elements of respectability, but others attempted to conform in their appearance and respect for established institutions. However, such comportment and respect was always contingent and subject to reversal at the first perceived slight or discriminatory remark.

Given the extreme gender distinctions within American culture, living on the streets can be particularly perilous for women. Abuse is common. Rape is experienced by homeless women at a rate about 20 times greater than housed women (Jahiel 1987, 112). In addition, men and women exhibit different paths in becoming homeless and different strategies for survival (Rosenthal 1993; Golden 1992; Merves 1992; Watson and Austerberry 1986). For example, according to one Chicago study of 258 women who entered the shelter system, 46 percent had left their housing because of abuse and 24 percent had left because of harassment by an ex-partner (McCourt and Nyden, 1990). Of these women, 77 percent were African American, 12 percent were white, 10 percent were Hispanic, and 1 percent were Native American. For these women the streets became the only alternative to a violent domestic situation. For men, unemployment and failure to pay rent are often the most common reasons for entering the streets. The multiplicity of paths that people take in becoming homeless should not blind us to the gendered nature of that progression. It is also clear that homeless men and women have quite different coping strategies for living without a home. Homeless women, unlike homeless men, often appear invisible, since they are able to draw upon their support networks for assistance, are taken in by shelters, especially if they have children, and are generally willing to do household work contributing to their ability to stay off the street (Rosenthal 1993, 217). This underscores the fact that while bodies are power, not all bodies are granted equal power.

Social identities are constructed from class, gender, race, ethnicity, and sexual distinctions that are integrated in and through social-physical space. According to Amott and Matthaei (1991), "race-ethnicity, gender, and class are interconnected, interdetermining historical processes, rather than separate systems." (13). Economic oppression of particular groups in a society is not simply about resources or class position, but also about one's racial/ethnic, gender and sexual identity. When we talk about the oppression of the very poor, the homeless, then, it is with particular concrete historical and political processes in mind, processes that are received and interpreted differently according to the complex interrelationships among race, sexuality, ethnicity, class, and gender. In the United States, for example, homeless men are treated quite differently from homeless women, often being perceived as less "deserving" of aid. And single homeless women are perceived as less deserving than women with children. Categories of moral worth, refracted through the lens of race, gender, and class distinctions, may be deployed in ways that "normalize" existing systems of power and privilege. This understanding is crucial within a society that imagines race to be black, gender to be woman, class to be middle or underclass, and sexuality to be heterosexuality. The social visibility of black lower-class women contrasts with the invisibility of white middle-class men. The ongoing rancorous debates over affirmative action, "family" values, and welfare reform illustrate only too well this process of creating "moral" distinctions.

What transforms the invisible workings of race, class, and gender into the visible revelations of power are precisely those political, economic, and cultural struggles, often expressed in social movements, shaped by counter social imaginary significations, in which those who have been oppressed, those who have always had their stories told through the eyes of others, are able to speak with their own voices and, more importantly, be heard. Identities that have been fashioned through a set of rigid logics can collapse under social pressures, leading to new identities of contestation. As Omi and Winant (1994) illustrate, the social construction of race and ethnicity, and I would add gender and class, develops out of struggles formed through a sociohistorical process that itself emerges out of historically situated projects (54) that redefine, organize, and situate the relationship between people and the institutions through which they live and work. Racial projects connect the racial meanings of particular discursive practices to the manner in which social structures and everyday life are organized along racial lines, an organization based on the meanings generated by that project (56). These meanings are organized through the dominant set of social imaginary significations.[28]

The sheer number of racial and ethnic projects guarantees their invisibility. The workings of such diverse projects are granted the status of "normal," a democratic plurality, from which all other decisions, interpretations, and judgments may be generated. For the subjects of such projects, however, the visibility and privileging of some racial projects over others is all too clear, the reminders all too painful. Ignoring the manner in which hierarchies of worth are created through specific racial projects is one of the cornerstones of institutional racism. We should understand that not all racial projects are equal, and that what constitutes racism is the elevation of racial projects that generate forms of domination anchored in "essential" categories and concepts of race (Omi and Winant, 1994, 71), which maintain hierarchies of domination and submission. Different subordinated groups have experienced different histories of oppression, which should not be blended into a generic "oppression." And these differences are experienced concretely within varying social-physical spaces, themselves affected by the dominant social imaginaries of a given society. For example, homeless participants in SHA and Tranquility City gave radically different responses to the question of race and homelessness. The diversified ethnic and racial sample of SHA clearly communicated that race was a central factor in homelessness, while the predominantly African American males of "Tranquility City" stated that "race wasn't a problem," that "we're all homeless" regardless of race.

Given our prior understandings of social imaginary significations, it is not difficult to see that racial projects, indeed gender and class projects, find the representative forms that they occupy, their symbols, through the working of the social imaginary on the large number of possible significations for any given society. The historical struggles that create the ability for groups, or social classes, to attain what they need to survive and prosper will then determine the shape of the social imaginary, the specificity of symbol usage, every bit as much as the social imaginary will shape the initial historical struggles. As human actors go about their everyday lives, they do the necessary work of understanding the world through the social imaginary, an imaginary that organizes signification, "integrating" social conflicts, fractures, and contradictions along socially constructed race, class, and gender lines. In so far as this organizing remains obscured, through either privilege or trauma, for particular groups such as the homeless, then such constructions are made to appear as "invisible" and are perceived as "natural." The constellation of social imaginary significations that surround specific images of African Americans, Latinos, whites, Asians, Native Americans, and others of different racial/ethnic and class backgrounds further complicates the relationships among social classes in modern society. Not all bodies are treated equally, nor do they occupy similar social-physical spaces.

As Fanon (1967) points out in *Black Skin, White Masks*, the repeating sentence, "Look, a Negro!", reveals that the black male body is constructed through a "pointing" that names black bodies as "dangerous." For example, Judith Butler (1993), commenting on the Rodney King trial, discusses how the videotape of the beating of Rodney King was systematically broken into individual stills by defense attorneys, with each still given an interpretation, "decontextualized," in a manner that reconfirmed white paranoia of black bodies. For Butler, the identification of white paranoia with the symbolization of police security was contrasted with the abject fear of, the threat of, the black male body, represented by Rodney King, a body always ready to spring into action, a body needing control and discipline (19).

Within a white supremacist and patriarchal social imaginary, black male bodies are always suspect, always dangerous, always ready for action prior to any video image. In a similar manner, Robert Gooding-Williams (1993, 166), using the Fanon quote as a descriptive motif to examine the Rodney King beating, understands that the King trial depended upon organizing and mobilizing, "a battery of common prejudices," which the jurors could identify with. As Gooding-Williams points out, the defense attorneys in the King trial were adept at pointing out to the white jury, in each frame of the video, "Look, a Negro!," playing upon the constructed social imaginary significations of blackness in a society built upon, as Steven Haymes (1995) mentions, a white supremacist social imaginary.[29] The fact that white supremacist and patriarchal concepts still undergird many white responses to blacks' experiences of themselves is evident in the belief that blacks "are "always whining about racism." This was the response of 46 percent of whites queried in a CNN poll conducted during the weekend of the LA uprising.[30] As Gooding-Williams (1995) points out, "for many whites, then, black speech is not the speech of fellow citizens, but the always-complaining speech of spoiled children" (170). We should also realize that such a demonstrative supremacist social imaginary is opposed by the majority of citizens, who can hold counter-imaginaries. For the patriarch, "whining" is something performed by women and children, both equal in status in his eyes. Black bodies, like women's bodies, like homeless bodies, are understood through the dominant social imaginary that privileges whiteness and maleness, a social imaginary that encourages the interpretation of black bodies as both childlike and threatening, a syntagm of unbridled emotion, sensuality, and terror.

Degeneracy, Moral Worth, and the "Scaling of Bodies"

From the early writings of Kant through the nineteenth- and early-twentieth century preoccupation with eugenics, phrenology, medicine, and natural history, science was influenced by the social imaginary that worked to establish difference based on visual attributes, where "one sees not with the fallible senses, but with the mind's eye, a vision standing outside all, surveying like a proud and watchful lord" (Young 1990, 125). Although the most blatant forms of discrimination have disappeared, hierarchical concepts of privilege related to body type, skin color, and gender remain in the everyday habits and cultural meanings we bring to bear on our daily interactions, from communication styles, to expectations of dress and comportment. This "scaling of bodies," as Young (1990) terms it, is anchored in a logic of identity that works through visual metaphors and that flourished in the nineteenth century, where "the normalizing gaze of science endowed the aesthetic scaling of bodies with the authoritativeness of objective truth. All bodies can be located in a single scale whose apex is the strong and beautiful youth and whose nadir is the degenerate" (128).[31]

The homeless body in the public imagination represents the body of decay, the degenerate body, a body that is constantly rejected by the public as "sick," "scary," "dirty and smelly," and a host of other pejoratives used to create social distance between housed and unhoused persons. This visual logic of identity, a product of a specific social imaginary that bifurcates bodies into "sick" versus "well," in turn affects the production of social-physical spaces by privileging urban spaces of surveillance, both self-surveillance and control over one's "deviant" body, and the surveillance of those external bodies perceived as too fat, too dirty, too dark, or too sexual. One has merely to look at the social organization of beaches, shelters, jails, TV contests, and sports competition to see the radical emergence of body difference.

Historically, degeneracy was judged by the lack of physical or mental health or moral soundness. From the eighteenth into the twentieth century, physical frailness, ranting and raving or expressing undue emotion, and sexual indulgences were just some of the features which were thought to lead to ill health and degeneracy. The homosexual, the prostitute, the thief, the beggar were all considered degenerates in a culture whose social imaginary associated moral worth and power with young athletic white male bodies whose bodily functions were carefully controlled. As Gilman (1985) points out, degeneracy was equated with the surface appearance of the body, measured by the size, color, and complexion of the skin, bones, and musculature. It was once thought that one could easily spot a criminal by their obvious "criminal-like appearance." Women were identified by their sexual difference from men, and other groups—blacks, Jews, homosexuals, working people, or those considered members of the criminal class—were classed as degenerates simply because of their visual difference from whiteness and maleness (Young 1990, 129). The normal/abnormal distinction was converted into the good/bad dualism through the medicalization of difference, creating the rationale behind establishing nineteenth century poorhouses for the destitute, where inmates were expected to work to correct the moral deficiencies that had led them to such poverty in the first place, to reverse their degenerate status.

While such obvious theories of racial and sexual subordination continue in small eruptions here and there, often covertly coded in the debate over IQ and present in such publications as *The Bell Curve*

(Murray and Herrnstein 1994), Young (1990, 131–33) suggests that contemporary forms of group oppression occur at the level Anthony Giddens (1984) would term "practical consciousness," the level concerned with security and survival, a level often unconscious to the actors involved. This manifests itself in tone of voice, body comportment, language usage, and a host of other verbal and nonverbal signifiers. These expressions of practical consciousness were observed in the way public officials, police and the general public responded to homeless encampment members of "Tranquility City" and of the Student-Homeless Alliance. This raises questions: Whose accounts get treated as legitimate? Whose body is taken seriously? Other examples abound of women being touched by men inappropriately in the workplace, of white people crossing to the other side of the street when a black pedestrian approaches, and also in the turning of the gaze away from the panhandler with the outstretched hand. This "scaling of bodies" occurs throughout our culture, with the media acting as a large storehouse for images that reconfirm the dominant social imaginaries. Analyzing media images of the very poor, therefore, is an excellent way of examining how this "scaling of bodies" operates to define what is "natural" or "normal."

To be out of place is also to be without respect, and hence without the ability to summon the power, the resources, to change one's conditions, to contest the "scaling of bodies" effectively. Hence, placemaking is a key element of resistance to the gaze that fragments, breaks up, dissociates the poor and homeless subject. Placemaking, in the form of autonomous collective street encampments, allows for the possibility of breaking the public gaze with attached authoritative judgments. By engaging in placemaking, homeless members of "Tranquility City" were able to force Chicago's public officials to negotiate seriously, securing housing for all of its members. If respectability means following conventional rules that regulate sexuality, bodily functions, and emotional expression, (Young 1990, 136), respectability is connected to a desire for order in which excessive emotions, passions, desires, or exclamations are censored in favor of the calm, mild-mannered, soft-spoken, and above all a clean persona. Keeping order, being respectable, means not crossing boundaries established by privilege and power. It means being in your place. Skillfull transgressing of these boundaries is essential for securing any real power for marginalized groups.

Since cleanliness is linked with respectability as a visual sign of moral worth, those who are living on the streets and who present appearances of soiled clothing are perceived as disrespectable and therefore unworthy of attention, except through charity, which in turn judges whether the street person is deserving and undeserving. To live on the streets is to cross borders simply by not having a place to call one's own. In this instance, to rebel individually is not radical, merely a confirmation of one's status of being disrespectable in the eyes of privileged citizens. As Young (1990) maintains, in the nineteenth century respectability was associated with white, male professional comportment, while blacks, Jews, women, homosexuals, and members of the working class were associated with the messiness of the body, marginal to those who knew respectability (140). While we no longer have such blatant categorizations at the practical level of everyday behavior, associations of respectability have been refracted away from the above specific groups and onto the poor as a class in general—specifically those classed as "criminal," which now include those homeless who do not know their proper "place," young black males, and drug users. In this context, the purpose of homeless shelters, beyond simple warehousing, is "reforming" disrespectable behavior, an attempt to fashion behavior that conforms with the socially imagined dictates of "respectable" comportment. Social control is assured as disrespectable behavior is contained and disciplined. As will be quite obvious from a cursory examination of Hollywood films in chapter 4, homeless street people have served as the symbol for the outer limits of respectability, the margins of proper comportment, a tool to normalize body comportment within the framework of a particular privileged standard of respectability. Homeless persons wearing soiled clothing are a trope for the margins of society, a symbol of abjection, of the combination of revulsion and intense attraction.[32]

The conflicting nature of ideologies of respectability, of differing discursive formations and emergent ritual knowledges operating through the body, mean, as McLaren points out, that any concept of resistance will be multifaceted and negotiable. Sandra Lee Bartky (1988) claims that the body is not simply the subject of power, but also a site of resistance, a site of disrespectability. However, resistance against dominant social imaginaries does not necessarily have to be positive and liberatory, since resistance occurs within the very processes of domination through which the social imaginary operates. Resistance may operate through particular ideological, somatic, and discursive formations that reinforce status quo arrangements of power and wealth, inverting the violence performed on the body of the poor by directing anger and frustration at other homeless persons. Resistance can be regressive as well as progressive. Resistance can be found in actions which bind one closer to authority and conversely actions that distance one from authority. To the degree that homeless persons adopt a position identified with the dominant social imaginary, in which they are perceived as "out of place" and disrespectable, as a locus of abjection, they will perceive members of their own group (other homeless people) as objects of horror. Tactical resistances by homeless encampment members and authoritative strategies of control by city officials can exclude, repress, assimilate, or displace contested populations and urban spaces. This will be explored in detail in chapter 4.

The specific race/ethnicity, class, and gender compositions of groups of homeless persons are socially constructed in the interplay between historical movements of resistance and established practices of privilege, operating in and through social-physical space, on and through the very body of subjects. Therefore we come to know race/ethnicity, class, and gender, and the resistances and oppressions that surround their expressions, only within the realm of social-physical space, and only with specific populations that we have come to judge via the "scaling of bodies." The race/ethnicity, gendered, classed categorical knowledge of who is and who is not deserving of assistance, of who is and is not impoverished, is useful to those who have the authority to impose such distinctions only if such categorical knowledge can be put into practice. This can be accomplished only in and through the organization and production of urban space, and in fact spaces are produced in order to contain and reproduce highly developed categorizations. In this sense, dominant social imaginary significations can be grasped indirectly by examining the types of spatial segmentations and varied practices that are used to categorize populations; the shelter for the mentally ill, the transitional shelter, the detoxification center, city and county jails, the local welfare office, the planning of city redevelopment places. The planning and development of institutional and noninstitutional settings are ways of embodying categorizations in and through social-physical spaces.[33] Bodies and texts exist somewhere, and that somewhere is in both cities and suburbs for most contemporary Americans. In these cities and suburbs, planning is conducted: zoning, regulating, excluding, and including population segments, dependent upon their differentiation through the dominant social imaginary of a given society. Understanding the formation of urban and suburban areas is critical for making the linkages between the diverse forms of everyday life and the social imaginaries that go into the production of the spaces through which everyday life is manifested. In what manner do social-physical space and social imaginary significations intersect to produce the particular morphological characteristics of modern cities through which our bodies move and on which our texts are written?

The ability of city and state officials to enforce particular categorizations of spatial usage and to produce specific spatial forms is captured in the making and legitimation of texts and the police practices of social control. Contracts and tort law, civil law, manuals, professional papers and books, zoning laws, building codes—all acquire the status of legitimate versions of how others are to be categorized and how one is to behave in particular places. These texts, legitimated with official explanations and combined with the practices of courts and police, allow for the setting up of agencies, employment, dispensations, and other features of everyday life; they impact the body through the regulation of social-physical space. Although not all bodies are regulated equally, as we have witnessed, and the effects of such spatial regulation are experienced unevenly, depending upon one's race, class, and gender position. The effect of such spatial regulation is the generation of uneven development expressed in increased disparities among city neighborhoods, between city and suburb, and among regions.

Social-Physical Space, Social Imaginaries, and the City

David Harvey, following Lefebvre, attempts to explain how city spaces are rapidly and unevenly developed by applying a traditional political economic argument to the production of urban space. Harvey's concept of urban space is based on a model in which capital accumulation and class struggle are central to the configuration of cities (Harvey 1973, 1981, 1989b). Borrowing heavily from Lefebvre, Harvey makes the argument that capital (money, labor, commodities) flows through the geographical spaces of the city, determining the objective form of the built environment. Although the built environment is critical to the capital accumulation process, investments transferred into the "second circuit" of capital[34] (fixed assets, consumer goods, land development, museums, and the like) from the primary circuit to increase capital's productive potential (Harvey 1981, 96) suffer eventually from capital devalorization (Gottdiener 1985, 97) with the onset of overaccumulation.

The problems of overaccumulation begin in the primary circuit with an overproduction of commodities, falling rates of profit, idle productive capacity (surplus capital), and rising rates of labor exploitation (surplus labor) (Harvey 1981, 94). These devalorizations are expressed in the periodic boom and bust cycles of capitalist economies, which for Harvey (1981) involve a periodic sweeping away of built forms, a point analogous to Schumpeter's metaphor of "creative de-struction." Since, according to Harvey, individual capitalists cannot easily make the switch from primary to secondary circuits, what must exist is a fluid capital market and a state willing to underwrite large capital building projects. City redevelopment agencies entering into public private partnerships may be viewed as facilitating this transition. Harvey conceives of the production of money and credit as a "relatively au-tonomous processes" in which "financial and state institutions control-ling them" act as a "collective nerve centre governing and mediating the relations between the primary and secondary circuits of capital" (97). This presumed close attachment between the state and the economy, however, conceals the complex manner in which investment decisions are made within cities and regions, neglecting the role of race, ethnic, gender factors and the role played by the constant negotiations of spatial meanings acted out by oppositional community groups, includ-ing well-organized homeless organizations and countervailing capital interests. Relying upon a model that privileges the logic of capital accumulation, can act to conceal the manner in which city investment decisions are actually made in reality, by collapsing the often conflict-ing demands made by differing fractions of owners/capitalists into a single ruling elite. This is one of the problems with using Logan and Molotch's (1987) concept of the "growth-machine"—the unitary nature of a ruling coalition remains unquestioned.

By stating the loss of value of built environments, simply through the devaluation (Harvey 1981, 101) of exchange value tied to buildings, parks, warehouses, and the like, Harvey, according to Gottdiener (1985, 97) substitutes a "functionalist theory of devalorization" for one of complex uneven development.[35] Why secondary-circuit investments reach a limit is never explained but simply assumed under the logic of capital accumulation. Harvey states that there is a limit to overaccumulation in the secondary circuit, a point at which such investments become un-productive, but that point is neither explained, except in the language of crisis theory, nor are any actors pointed to who might determine such a decision. All is absorbed by the logic of capital accumulation.

Although the use of a logic of capital accumulation is helpful in understanding broad social trends, it might actually work to conceal the concrete nature of city spatial production and the impact of gendered and racialized imaginaries. In addition, an overreliance on this model might obscure the manifold ways in which resistances are generated against city development decisions, and the differences that may exist in such issues as redevelopment strategies. The logic of accumulation subsumes the complexity of both elite strategizing and community resistance. An example that illustrates this point is the struggle over how to spend the City of Chicago's newly acquired $100 million in federal funds, dedicated for city-designated "empowerment zones." Since $100 million over a ten-year period is next to nothing for developing poor areas of the city, plans have been floated to leverage the $100 million into a sizable sum of $2.5 billion. To accomplish this, concessions have to be made, creating new conflicts between those federal agencies giving the funds and city agencies responsible for dispersing the funds. In addition, community agencies, small businesses, activist groups and others are all maneuvering for an advantageous political position that will determine how and where this money is spent. What is the price the community, the businesses, the state, will have to pay in order to leverage this capital, and why is this process happening the way that it is? To ask these questions is to move beyond an oversimplistic theory of capital accumulation to examine the complexities of social-political change. The difficulty of answering these question from Harvey's model is, according to Gottdiener (1985), the problem of ascribing "far too much rationality to the capital accumulation process as well as, more significantly, to the state-capital articulation" (92). Harvey's embrace of the state as an agent of the ruling class conceals the manifold differences within the state and the divisions within ruling elites. Development is quite a bit more chaotic than the logic of capital accumulation allows.

Harvey (1973) discuses the issue of class and class struggle directly, but race, ethnicity, and gender are absent, raising questions about the relationship between the logic of accumulation and cultural issues of identity and body. Even where class is discussed, as in Harvey's mention of "poverty populations" (272), poor people are subsumed under the classical Marxist category of the "industrial reserve army" as a stagnant group, often debased as the lumpen. The very poor are considered to be out of the labor market with few usable skills; they are erased as agents, reduced to mere "stabilizing devices within capitalist economics—stabilizing devices which rest upon suffering and degradation" (272).

On the other hand, Harvey does point to concrete economic processes involved in the creation of redeveloped leisure areas and the rapidly spreading crises that many cities are experiencing. But his insights must be balanced by moving away from a strict logic of capital accumulation thesis to a process that is more open-ended and integrates the insights of cultural theory foreshadowed in the work of

Lefebvre and Castoriadis. By consciously developing a dialectical perspective, Lefebvre offers, I believe, a broader vision of ways to incor-
porate race, class, and gender into the consideration of spatial production, through his concept of the "explosion of spaces" mentioned earlier, and the tripartite division into spatial practices, spaces of representation, and representational spaces. In addition, Lefebvre's theory integrates quite nicely with that of Castoriadis, as we discussed earlier.
Lefebvre's recognition of the proliferation of social-physical spaces under
contemporary capital creates an opening from which race, class, and
gender identities may be considered. We can, therefore, using those
concepts discussed from Lefebvre and Castoriadis, expand on Harvey's
class-based analysis by incorporating race/ethnicity and gender into the
creation and re-creation of urban social-physical spaces.

The dominant social imaginaries that inform the production of
city spaces point to the "racialization of space" (Keith and Cross 1993)
in the continuing persistence of racial segregation in residence and
labor patterns, and in the almost complete absence of nonwhites from
imagined city spaces, such as the spaces of representations discussed
in Jane Jacobs's, *Death and Life of Great American Cities* (1963), or
Ed Soja's (1989) mapping of Los Angeles, in which race formation is
perceived simply as reactionary politics (Keith and Cross 1993, 8). As
we discussed earlier, race is distinguished by its absence. In the vast
discourses about the "postmodern" city and consumption, in an attempt to understand the intersection of contemporary culture and city
economies, cultural theorists have neglected the role of immigrant
labor and racialized minorities as central to the operating of these
increasingly polarized topographies.[36] Rarely do we get a glimpse of
the voices of nonwhites in the shaping of urban space, much less of
their direct participation in the planning of key economic areas within
a city.

Accompanying the absence of race is usually the absence of
the very poor, those not registered as members of the "working
class," those often thought of as poor renters or the homeless, who
are members of nonwhite populations for the most part in the larger
cities of America. Planned corporate images of cities are often imagined as if there were no poor, no racial conflict, no gender issues
to be dealt with, merely the domination of a visual aesthetic oriented toward "family life" and commodity consumption. The lifestyles
promoted by mainstream city developers and planners are ones that
remain detached from the spatial considerations of race, class, and
gender—or, perhaps I should say, that are deeply implicated in

fostering a particular type of city, as understood by Boyer (1990, 1995, 1983).

As we discussed earlier, being black is often contained within the social imaginary of sublime European white versus black savage/exotic "Other" (Hesse 1993, 166). In the context of city social imaginaries, "blackness now commonly serves as the cautionary urban other. A racialized metaphor articulates the new urbanism, even in its apparent absence" (Keith and Cross 1993, 10). With the exploitation of crime as blackness, and to some degree crime as Latino and poor white, present in the image of Willy Horton in the 1988 presidential elections and currently in such television shows as "Cops," and "Real Stories of the Highway Patrol," the dominant social imaginary that equates crime with being black also works to reinforce whiteness and the desire for safety and security. Local tabloids contribute their portion of fear in lurid stories of murder and rape. Within this panic culture, as Krocker terms it, notions of defensible spaces, inherited from Oscar Newman's designs of the early 1970s, take root, mutating into everything from physically designed landscape barriers to walled off communities and armed security guards. As Keith (1993) points out, "race could be used systematically to conjure up the urban crisis" (203). It is taught that safe streets are possible only within an urban fortress (Davis 1990).

Degeneracy, as we discussed earlier, historically has been associated with nonwhites and the very poor, the "mark of the pathological other" (Goldberg 1993a, 55), a sign of disorder that must be contained. In the hypermodern city, stratified by racialized, gendered, and class-oriented social-physical spaces, within growing sets of polarized landscapes, "the paranoia of losing power assumes the image of becoming the other, to be avoided like the plague" (Goldberg, 1996b, 55). As Goldberg (1993b) points out, city social space is a racialized space in which "the racial poor were simultaneously rendered peripheral in terms of urban location and marginalized in terms of power" (188). This does not require the absolute physical isolation of the racial poor, merely their "circumscription in terms of location and their limitation in terms of access to power" (188). African Americans, Puerto Ricans, and Mexican Americans are associated through media representations with inner-city poverty, crime, and drugs while the very physical spaces of their everyday lives are dismantled through racially charged planning policies.

Homeless street people are associated with degeneracy and petty crime, or, conversely, with complete abjection remedied by putting them in their "place." A product of intentional design imposed by local politicians and city planners, structural relationships produced by corporate business practices, concrete activities of real estate agencies, financial lending practices, and flights of particular racial and ethnic groups, a racialized space begins with the created social imaginary of the "Other," combined with real physical limitations on material resources. Such social imaginaries translated into social practices can lead to determined efforts either to contain very poor people of color in public housing projects or shelters, or to disperse them in scattered-site housing to lesson a perceived threat. As Paul Gilroy (1991) points out, black settlement areas in London were defined as "no-go" areas after the 1976 race riots, subject to containment "proven" by reference to comparative statistics of "muggings" (97–98). Containment is predicated upon a racial social imaginary that works through spaces of representation that equate blacks with disorder and create a representative space (national crisis) that takes form as a moral panic (Gilroy 1991, 74; Hall 1978). For those who are homeless these efforts appear more extreme and are more visible in the expansion of street sweeps and punitive arrest procedures.

Gender is a another primary component of the dominant social imaginary produced through spatial practices. From the design of housing to the organization of urban-suburban space (Hayden 1984, 1981; Wright 1981; Weisman 1992; Spain 1992), the dominant design of social-physical space in America has been predicated upon the social imaginary of patriarchy. Spatial arrangements segregating men from women have been used to prevent women from learning particular knowledges, especially in the workplace, where 20 to 25 percent of workers have no contact with the opposite sex (Spain 1992, 210). The gendered space of suburban homes was predicated upon families (Coontz 1992) where "respectable" women were expected to remain at home while their husbands worked, a space that gave short shrift to working women both economically and spatially. This devaluation of women's work, both domestically and in the office or factory, is reflected in the lack of comparable wages for the same work accomplished by men, and in the division of social-physical space into public and private realms.[37] The very spatial patterns produced through capitalist investment reproduces gendered spatial distinctions in a society ruled by a patriarchal social imaginary.[38] The difference between work and home spatially works to the disadvantage of women, who often suffer from a decrease in geographic mobility, and this is reflected in the types of employment women are able to secure.[39]

The planning of gender segregation is quite pronounced in the organization of shelters and group homes. Institutional planning of shelter spaces will divide up buildings into separate facilities for men and women, for married versus nonmarried couples, for single men and for single women. Quite often homeless married couples will have to go to completely different shelters to find beds for the night. This generation of institutional space therefore explicitly practices gender segregation and works indirectly to maintain the dominant social imaginary of gender within the society.

The combination of unequal pay in the workplace and gendered spatial segregation in the community reinforces the split between socially constructed categories of private and public space.[40] Hence, the material reality of gender discrimination reinforces a patriarchal social imaginary by presenting *visible* evidence of differences between artificially created distinctions of public and private spaces. The crude equation of emotional nurturing with private space, and cold reasoning with public space, belies the fact that women's movements have successfully contested these arbitrary divisions through social and political mobilization, taking advantage of the city's contested landscapes. Indeed, the new social movements emerging out of the late 1960s have indirectly and often directly fought the reduction of social-physical space to a simple private/public dualism, a dualism established through the patriarchal aspects of the dominant social imaginary. According to Young (1988), "liberating public expression means not only lifting formerly privatized issues into the open of public and rational discussion which considers the good of ends as well as means, but also affirming in the practice of such discussion the proper place of passion and play in public" (75).

An alternative to a dominant patriarchal social imaginary will involve developing a representational space beyond "the violence and repression of the master subject," a paradoxical space in which "a troubled relation to the hegemonic discourses of masculinism" (Rose 1993, 159) may be nurtured. I would add that this paradoxical space must be free from coercion. For Elizabeth Wilson, paradoxical space must be an urban location. In her work the *Sphinx in the City*, (1991) Wilson defines the city as a place where women can escape the dangers of patriarchal violence, but at the price of reinforcing social imaginaries of women as representing disorder; "women without men in the city symbolize the menace of disorder in all spheres once, rigid patriarchal control weakened" (157). Accompanying the context of urban woman as disorder, woman as "uncontrolled and chaotic sexual license," is the male desire for rigid control of female behavior, to put women in their "place." For Wilson, this becomes much harder to accomplish in the city, where women are freed from the gazes of male authority so prevalent in small towns and suburban confines. The attempt to control the defined "unruly" is, of course, quite evident in the policing of homeless bodies, both male and female, by established institutions of power.

The possibility, then, of resistant heterotopic urban and suburban areas, or utopic spaces (à la Lefebvre) emerges from the liberatory possibilities represented by the contested nature of city social-physical spaces. The social-physical spaces of the city are truly contested land-scapes through which "fixed" identities are rendered ephemeral. Domi-nant social imaginaries may inform authoritative constructions of social-physical space, but they are not the only imaginaries; city and suburban spaces still remain landscapes in flux.

CHAPTER 2

Urban Redevelopment Visions, Social Imaginaries, and Polarized Topographies

You know, we're right beneath you. We're right up under your nose and you go by as if we don't exist, you know. But all of a sudden we exist and you just want to move us out. (Taylor, a homeless resident of Chicago's "Tranquility City")

The development of a city's social-physical spaces is a product of the struggle between competing social imaginaries, working through the spatial practices, representations of spaces, and representative spaces, of land use and redevelopment. Of course, how those spaces are interpreted and utilized on the basis of gender and class, by different racial or ethnic groups, homeless or otherwise, will generate conflict or consensus depending upon the degree to which effected groups understand their stake in the city's resources. Homeless people have few resources, other than their social networks, so it is reasonable to assume that their interpretations of city social-physical spaces will be quite different from those of persons who are wealthier and housed. It is no secret that the redevelopment of a city's central business district often leads to gentrification of the immediate and surrounding area, displacing poor, often minority, populations and local industries. The vast body of literature on redevelopment, gentrification, and displacement,[1] however, will not be reviewed here except to point to the paucity of studies examining redevelopment in relationship to displacement of the homeless and very poor. The majority of studies on land use and redevelopment are concerned with housed populations.

Economic Restructuring, Downsizing, and Homelessness

The roots of homelessness can be found in global and local economic restructuring. Hopper, Susser, and Conover (1985), for example, argue that large cities have shifted from industrial manufacturing to consumer

Sociology

services as a result of deindustrialization (and, I would add the automation and restructuring of large components of the labor process).
This is reflected in the loss of union wage jobs and the growth of
low-wage service-sector employment. In addition, cities have also experienced a declining stock of affordable housing combined with the
release of the mentally ill without adequate community services, a
frequent resort to the streets and shelters as part of a larger subsistence
strategy by the poor, and the integration of shelters as "an important
institutional resource within broader subsistence strategies ... an integral part of life at the periphery" (85). Increasingly, "economies of
makeshift" are replacing steady incomes, as labor markets are polarized
between high-wage professional employment and low-wage contingency work in the midst of massive corporate downsizing.[2] In examining the loss of manufacturing jobs in New York City, in particular the
loss of public-sector jobs, Hopper, Susser, and Conover (1985) noted
the subsequent expansion of low-wage private-sector jobs. Under these
conditions, low-wage sweatshops proliferate, particularly in the gar-
ment industry.

These economic changes are expressed spatially in the increase
in the number of abandoned buildings and in the redevelopment
and gentrification of large swaths of the central city. Competition for
scarce housing stock has expanded with a decline in wage growth.
Housing that once was available to people at the bottom of the
economic ladder now goes to those with greater financial resources,
leaving the streets and shelters for the poorest of the poor. This
decline in low-cost housing units is also accompanied by a massive
loss of inexpensive single-room-occupancy units (SROs).[3] The loss of
low-cost housing is not new; the scale at which it is occurring is.
Urban investment-disinvestment generally results in a net loss of low-
rent housing units in favor of moderate- to high-rent units. City redevelopment strategies are oriented toward attracting stable and market-
paying tenants, so housing for the poor receives a secondary nod at
best. According to Feagin and Parker (1990):

> In the decade 1970-1980 various urban investment-disinvestment
> processes resulted in an average loss of 125,000 low-rent units a
> year in the United States. Approximately half the 2 million units
> in single-row occupancy hotels ... were razed, abandoned, or
> gentrified. And since 1980 the trend toward abandonment and
> conversion has continued. Another million low-rent housing units
> were lost between 1980 and 1988. (132)

For the past fifty years the federal government was actively involved in providing low-income housing for poor tenants, through either the funding of public housing, Section 8 certificates and vouchers, landlord subsidies for low-income tenants, or rehabilitating or constructing new housing units. Since the late 1970s, however, federal commitment to providing safe, decent and affordable housing has gradually eroded to a practice of merely "containing" the poor and homeless on very limited budgets in deteriorated public housing projects and shelters and through very limited numbers of Section 8 vouchers. We should be cautious about assuming, however, that these large-scale economic changes are the primary causes of homelessness.

What is often ignored in the literature on homelessness is the functioning of the dual-housing market (Massey and Denton 1988a, 1993; Taub, Taylor, and Dunham 1984; Galster 1990; Greenbaum 1993, 141–43; Zarembka 1990). Racially based dual-housing markets generate increased competition over limited housing resources in predominantly minority areas. Originating with real estate practices in the 1920s that were designed to create white and black homogeneous communities, ostensibly to protect "property values and neighborhood character" during a period of legal segregation, such discriminatory real estate practices continue to this day, although covertly. The Fair Housing Act of 1968 made such practices illegal, but they continue due to weak enforcement of the law and weak commitment by the states and federal government to invest in the legal resources needed to prosecute violators. In addition, discrimination in the housing market is difficult to detect without using "testers" who can canvass specific known violators. Fair Housing Councils, entrusted with enforcing the Fair Housing Act, are often struggling to survive financially and have difficulty covering more than a fraction of the cases they receive each week. During periods of fiscal belt-tightening, such nonprofit organizations may be shortchanged by cities looking to cut budgets where they can, since many Fair Housing Councils depend on community development block grants granted by local cities to accomplish their mission. When real-estate, banking, and mortgage lending institutions divide housing areas into white and black regions, redlining specific areas known to have large concentrations of minority residents, and starving predominantly minority regions of investment capital, blacks are "locked out" of white areas and commercial and residential housing deterioration is accelerated, contributing to higher rates of housing abandonment and to increased competition for whatever housing resources remain within an area (Jakle and Wilson 1992, 153–80). In this situation, the poorest of the poor may find the streets or shelters their only resort. In essence, the dual-housing market destroys minority neighborhoods.

These economic trends, occurring regionally and internationally, involve a large-scale transformation from an economy that emphasizes increasing wages and benefits, in exchange for union peace, to a brutal corporate downsizing that seeks the abolition of the social wage, the destruction of labor unions, and the replacement of workers through automated production systems. Corporate downsizing is assisted by changing production techniques, such as "flexible manufacturing" and "just-in-time" production, global niche marketing to allow increased profits within smaller markets, expanded communication and computer networks that allow for centralization of control and decentralized production, and the expansion of part-time contract labor. The extensive use of nonunion workers and temporary workers has caused worker wages to stagnate and benefits to decline over a steady twenty-year period.[4] The expansion of global social and economic inequality is refracted through changes in the urban spaces of all of the world's major cities.

Polarized topographies,[5] common in developing countries, are now increasingly evident throughout all of the world's major cities as national governments take up the banner of conservative fiscal belt-tightening. These intensified polarizations are not natural; rather, they are a direct by-product of political decision making that chooses a politics of exclusion over that of inclusion (Kantor 1993). In cities and older suburban areas, budgets are increasingly depleted, services are stripped, and the poor are segregated in pockets of misery (Wilson 1987; Massey and Denton 1993, 1988b, 1988a, 1989; Goldsmith and Blakely 1992, 96–137; Davis 1992), competing for menial low-paying service jobs and light industrial work.

Homelessness, therefore, is a global problem connected directly to the forces of world political, social, and economic restructuring. Cities around the world are experiencing enormous stresses due to the accelerated movement of economic resources from one region or country to another, increasing political fragmentation, an expanded flow of refugees internationally, the migration of manufacturing and light manufacturing businesses from the city to the suburbs and beyond, and a general global economic restructuring with an emphasis on downsizing (Sassen 1991, 1990; Fainstein, Gordon, and Harloe 1992; Mollenkopf and Castells 1991). Investment and land development are no longer local affairs, if they ever were.

Today, as Healey (1990) points out, "this game is increasingly played out in the international sphere of product development, marketing and financial flows" producing effects on local cities, which are subject to the "ebb and flow of the international game" (10). It is a game wrapped up in the burgeoning problems and continuing crisises of world market economies.[6] This has meant that cities have had to scramble to find ways to attract new businesses downtown, to raise revenues to service their remaining populations, and to refashion a new image of the city attractive to those with capital to invest. City redevelopment is crucial in coping with these changes. Redevelopment also directly invokes the specter of poor and homeless populations as it creates "safe" areas for middle-income consumers.

Plotnicov (1991) makes the argument that global economic restructuring has changed the very industrial base of American cities, generating increased levels of poverty and forcing cities to seek funds by building facilities that will attract tourists downtown, a "strategy of diversification." In addition to traditional land use planning, the development of services, and marketing a city's image, have become the principle preoccupations of city planning departments and redevelopment agencies, Most cities have historically engaged in various forms of boosterism, but the regional and global competition for scarce dollars has pushed such boosterism to the front in an attempt to solve the increasing problems presented by periodic fiscal crises, prompted by a decline in federal and state revenues in a stagnant economy (Logan and Swanstron 1990; Beauregard 1991).

Global investors can easily play one region, city, or state off against the other to cut the best deal for their firm. With a large portion of the workforce experiencing stagnation or a steady decline in their wages, combined with an increase in housing costs, cities are faced with an impossible task of providing services in a deficit economy with a citizenry who increasingly cannot afford to pay for them. Reducing deficit spending as an attempt to cope with these changes might, in fact, work to heighten urban social problems by accelerating the creation of polarized topographies, generating long-term social unrest. In the hypermodern city, social fractures often emerge along geographic fault lines, border areas between contested zones of the city, where social problems make their appearances.

City Redevelopment Strategies: Inclusion or Exclusion?

Cities may utilize a set of strategies to cope with these problems, promoting urban development and redevelopment, often with the assistance of the private sector. Solesbury (1990) defines three such strategies involved in land use related to the spatial practices of redevelopment: (1) building flagship properties, used to symbolize regeneration of an area and pursued through private-public relationships (192); (2) using the "big bang" strategy, where major economic changes in an area are spearheaded by large-scale property development, effectively creating demand by offering supply [development of wharfs, abandoned railway yards, warehouse districts, etc.], and (3) developing property in order to diversify an area's mix of households or businesses. The third form of development generally relies upon a specialty developer who can build sites crafted to specific types of businesses or housing, usually "owner-occupied housing in areas of predominantly rental housing; otherwise the diversification might be pursued through developing office premises, tourist attractions or specialist industrial buildings" (193). In Chicago, the development of Central Station and Dearborn Park, as we shall see in the next chapter, fall into the "big bang" strategy.

The ability to practice any of these three forms of strategic development is predicated, according to Logan (1993), on the increasing global integration between real estate developers and financial markets combined with the expansion of corporate organizations who are "more closely tied to non-real-estate organizations than were developers in the recent past and are . . . capable of operating in multiple regions, even countries" (36).[7] The attempt by city officials to handle the expanded organizational abilities of private development firms has meant coordinating private-public schemes in which cities may trade off tax revenues for a given period of time, as we shall see in Chicago's tax increment financing arrangements in the next chapter, or offer new locations of affordable housing, land writedowns, and a host of other financial and social plans to make the city more palatable to developers.[8] For example, more than a thousand business improvement districts (BIDs) have expanded across the United States, creating special districts where taxes are raised or lowered independent of the majority of the population within a given city (Gallagher 1995). This raises a key issue in the preservation of public democratic city spaces. The privatization of public space promoted by such schemes means that political and economic decisions will be made by those who own the most property. Democratic input into city development can be forstalled through implementing such special districts.

In exchange for tax district privileges, developers might promise to build infrastructure and provide needed employment to sectors of the population. In the face of extensive federal and state cutbacks, these public-private partnerships have become one more tool for many development professionals, planners, and local politicians to redevelop and revitalize modern cities, often with mixed success (Davis 1986; Squires 1991, 1989). As Squires (1991) points out, the granting of financial incentives to private investors has not substantially increased redevelopment benefits for local cities; "the array of subsidies and related supply-side incentives has not created the anticipated number of jobs or jobs for the intended recipients, tax revenues have not been stabilized as initially expected" (201).

Financed with public subsidies, private development companies are rapidly transforming downtown areas into middle-class consumer landscapes with expensive shopping districts, luxury townhouses, franchise shops, and entertainment complexes, often at the expense of the city's poorer clients (Feagin and Parker 1990). In Chicago, for example, between 1979 and 1987 over $6 billion was invested downtown in new office towers, expensive restaurants, and luxury housing, replacing many single-room-occupancy hotels, small shops, and local services (Squires 1991, 209). Neighborhood investments did not come anywhere near such levels of investment. Not surprisingly these trends have had a significant racial component as larger and larger numbers of upper-income whites have either moved into city or moved from other parts of the city to more expensive housing downtown, displacing a largely poor black and Latino population. We will look at a brief example of this in the next chapter.

The attempt to politically coordinate these public-private partnerships has been variously ascribed to city growth networks (Gottdiener 1985), growth machines (Logan and Molotch 1987) and/or urban regimes (Stone, Orr, and Imbroscio 1991). While each of these conceptions have their differences, depending on the strength of governing coalitions that are established, they all share the understanding that business elites, often with community leader support, attempt to steer development to the advantage of business. Unlike Logan and Molotch's assumption of community solidarity,[9] however, Gottdiener's concept of *growth networks* understands that actors within the city elite and those in the community often have conflicting interests, and contrary to a rational assumption of interest, might work at cross-purposes. In fact, communities are often as fractured as growth networks or coalitions. These competing growth networks have attempted to fashion a unity of sorts through the politics of redevelopment (Mollenkopf 1983), and via city council decisions related to building and zoning changes that directly alter the spatial landscape of cities. Such decisions are often exacted at a price. Similarly, community organizations and activist groups often have to struggle with each other, in addition to city policy makers, before a coherent position can be taken to oppose or approve redevelopment projects.

The reader should be aware that I am not blaming redevelopment directly for the problems of city displacement and gentrification. However, redevelopment does amplify the larger trends of social inequality, thereby calling into question whether it is possible to have "responsible" redevelopment that takes into account all citizens of the city, not just those who can afford its services. The choice is between "inclusive" and "exclusive" redevelopment. Whether "inclusive" redevelopment is possible under a capitalist market economy in which the main actors are global multinational corporations is still open to question. To date redevelopment has been almost entirely oriented toward exclusion and displacement.

In their study of Philadelphia, Adams et al. (1991) argue that redevelopment itself does not produce an economic polarization of high-waged professionals and low-waged service workers. However, redevelopment does serve to strengthen spatial displacement produced by larger regional economic changes. Indeed, "The point is not that these trends have been caused by redevelopment, but rather that redevelopment has not—and we argue cannot—help redistribute job opportunities downward. Rather, redevelopment has reinforced these economic trends, playing 'midwife' to the emerging corporate economy that now characterizes the major cities" (119). One often hears that by supporting this or that redevelopment project, new jobs will be created and new services provided. Clearly, the data show only a limited effect on downward job dispersion. It is more likely that displacement will act to counter any benefits of expensive redevelopment projects. In addition, as Savage and Warde (1993) point out, the attempt by cities to attract suburban dwellers through redevelopment and gentrification may be misguided since, "gentrification [is] not a return of the professional and managerial classes from the suburbs, rather it merely represented movement with the city boundaries of such people" (81). Gentrification, then, works by increasing the concentration of city-based professionals and managers in specialized locales that cater to their needs and desires, further accentuating the development of polarized topographies.

Redevelopment is not a secondary cause to economic restructuring, but rather a mutually reinforcing process. Redevelopment works to amplify existing social and economic inequality produced by economic restructuring, forcing the dispersion of poor populations and the concentration of wealthier clients in marketable residential enclaves. There-fore, two points of attack on social inequality and homelessness would be (1) to address the issues of city redevelopment as either "inclusive" or "exclusive," and (2) to address the larger global trends of economic mismanagement and their ramifications at the local and regional levels. While Adams et al. (1991) may be correct that redevelopment exists within a mutually reinforcing position with larger economic forces, in particular the impact of labor market changes, they underestimate the effects of cultural representations on spatial practices, representations reproduced through city redevelopment schemes. Redevelopment am-plifies social and economic inequality through the employment of culturally based social imaginaries, and it does so through the direct production of exclusive forms of social-physical space via the genera-tion of polarized topographies.

The consequence of city redevelopment for the very poor and homeless is dispersion to the city periphery or to the interstices be-tween developed city locations. Lest we understand this dispersion as simply a "natural" by-product of redevelopment, Mair (1986) reminds us, in his examination of the conflict over the location of homeless shelters in Columbus, Ohio, that such redevelopments *necessarily* de-mand the removal of very poor and homeless populations. Drawing upon the central-city rent gap thesis of Neil Smith and David Harvey, according to which investors seek out land areas with low rents in order to secure profits in a crisis economy, and the aggregation argu-ments of Dear and Wolch (1987) that homeless people cluster down-town to take advantage of social service facilities, Mair argues that the very nature of what he terms the "post-industrial city" calls for the exclusion of the homeless. Following Kantor (1993) I would define these trends less as some mystical result of postindustrialism, and more the result of conscious political choices made by Columbus business elites. Of course, one could argue that the orientation of the city toward consumption and services, and not industrial production, leads to changes in the sensibilities of consumers who would rather not be offended by the sight of poverty while shopping.

The expansion of downtown cultural facilities in Columbus, Ohio—in particular, the growth of the Columbus Symphony Orchestra, street fairs, a new arts complex, and luxury condominiums—is counterbal-anced by the status-seeking anxiety of their patrons (Mair 1986, 359). This has had the effect of reinforcing negative stereotypes of homeless individuals and reinforcing value sanctions on behavior considered "deviant" or outside the "mainstream." The homeless are reconstructed by those consuming the facilities downtown as the "degenerate other," better to avoid and expel than to assist. Given the nature of city redevelopment, as marketing a particular *visual* image and competing with other cities for consuming patrons, such sights as persons wandering the streets without a place to sleep are most disturbing. The very visibility of homeless street persons in public places transforms them into "symbols of incivility" (Hunter 1985), symbols which counter the development myth of a carefully marketed consumer aesthetic. According to Mair (1986), "the post-industrial city is a space reserved for post-industrial activities; a space from which all intruders must be banished, in order that its realization as a commodity not be jeopardized by the tarnishes of industry or poverty" (363).[10] Mair concludes by stating that businesspersons protested the location of shelters in their neighborhood because they feared that they would not be able to sell their properties in a city where land values are fragmented and the city image is marketed for the city as a whole.

The very poor are being forcibly excluded from downtown areas in city after city across America, often through the passage of restrictive ordinances (Ades 1989; Collin and Barry 1987; Stoner 1995) covering shelters, group homes, soup kitchens, and low-income housing locations. Peter Marcuse (1989) invokes a slight variant of Mair's argument by claiming that "the former housing of the homeless and their current non-housing quarters, whether in a bus station, [or a] railroad terminal . . . are incompatible with the content of work being done downtown" (216). That is, the labor being accomplished in the central business district produces neither products, nor goods, but rather financial accumulation, information circulation, and consumption—all forms of labor that come into direct conflict with those who are perceived as "lazy," as rejecting the values of capital and commodity accumulation. One reservation with Mair's and Marcuse's arguments that I share with Ruddick (1990, 192) is the neglect of how the homeless understand their position. By not addressing how the homeless understand these actions, how they talk back from the street, ignores, as Ruddick comments, "the multiple and singular acts of resistance by the homeless and their advocates to confront and transform both these images of themselves as deviant, and the spaces they occupy" (192). Mobilization of resistance against gentrification and displacement by and for homeless persons is often ignored in favor of housed working-class resistance, from either renters or homeowners.[11] Homeless persons are treated principally as charitable victims, and the significance of homeless encampments, as a de facto resistance to displacement is ignored.

To confine the debate over redevelopment and homelessness to forms of political economy, however, ignores the significance of cultural factors in the generation of particular forms of social-physical space. Fainstein (1994), in comparing redevelopment in London and in New York, broadens the debate by examining the role of private decision making among real estate developers, politicians, and community groups, moving the debate beyond the general examination of political or economic forces inherent in Harvey's capital accumulation model.[12] Fainstein (1994) broadens the debate over the impact of redevelopment by focusing on the "beliefs and actions of its leaders operating under conditions of uncertainty" (18). In contemporary cities, planners, as one of the actors in the development process, "perform a mediating function, bringing together private investors and public sponsors . . . dealing with outraged members of the public, and cajoling developers for exactions" (101).

Planners assume the position of negotiator between various interests, as opposed to a total planning function. As a result, the planning of land use and real-estate investment remains a chaotic process, except for those rare opportunities when developers and local governments are presented with large tracts of unused land, often adjacent to a low-income areas, such as deteriorated wharfs, warehouses, railway yards, and areas with large tracts of abandoned housing or commercial properties. Hence, planners and developers alike target areas of opportunity that they think would be the most profitable for investment; they avoid grand schemes, except when large projects might be used in a "big bang" strategy, such as the development of Harbor Place in Baltimore (Harvey 1989a, 256–78), South Street Seaport in New York (Boyer 1992), Faneuil Hall Marketplace in Boston, or Canary Wharf in London. However, whether local politicians or city council members listen to their planning departments is another matter. In many cases, planning departments operate only in an advisory capacity. According to Fainstein, this style of chaotic planning further fragments land use, making coordination difficult, and while citizens might have input into which projects are built, the question of which citizens have the most input to effect development decisions remains an open one. In her analysis of Battery Park City, in New York, Fainstein (1994, 184) demonstrated how the developers of Battery Park justified the exclusion of the poor and working classes from the project by supporting the construction of affordable housing elsewhere in New York City.[13] A similar negotiation was concluded with Presidential Towers in Chicago, as we shall soon see.

While Fainstein (1994) correctly points out the limitations of David Harvey's capital accumulation model, her reliance upon the assumption that "a large proportion of the population chooses to exclude others, based on rational calculation and genuine preference" (235) ignores how such calculations and preferences are often neither rational nor genuine. That is, Fainstein's own analysis excludes a cultural analysis that might help us understand how such calculations or preferences are developed in the first place.

Culture and Images of Redevelopment

Because redevelopment works through gentrification,[14] the vision of the type of community gentrifiers want is crucial to the success of any project. Gentrification might benefit middle-class and some working class homeowners and tenants; for the very poor such benefits may indeed be mixed. Often the influx of new persons into a neighborhood with wealth will create a rupture in that community's sense of "place," generating class-based rifts, which, when and if one is forced to leave, can produce severe emotional distress, as Cybriwsky (1978) discovered when tenants and homeowners were forced out of a gentrifying Philadelphia neighborhood. Often the gentrifiers remain oblivious to such a sense of community "place," except their own version of what "place" should be. According to Plotnicov (1991), "gentrifiers view themselves not as displacing old neighborhood residents but as replacing outmoded institutions and customs that have shackled progress toward creating a better city" (107). In this instance, redevelopment and gentrification are not simply about the workings of political economy, the workings of capital accumulation in the second circuit of capital. They are about transforming the culture of the city.

Gentrification is the vehicle through which displacement and concentration are accomplished. It is more than a consequence of the workings of the market, a product of redevelopment; it is about who is allowed "in," who is to be accepted and who is to be excluded. According to Haymes (1995), "gentrification of the city cannot be explained solely with reference to the redevelopment of space; it also involves the image of redevelopment" (106).

The necessary mechanisms for the construction of spaces and places are political and economic forces, from financing (Budd and Whimster 1992) and taxation strategies to political negotiations among developers and city officials (Fainstein 1994). But privileging political economy, or a logic of capital accumulation, as the sole explanation for developed and redeveloped city spaces is insufficient; it cannot answer the question of why social-physical space assumes the form that it does, rather than some other form, especially aesthetic form. Integrating a cultural analysis with a political economy of redevelopment will assist in understanding the specificity of particular forms of city social-physical spaces.

What is the role of culture in assisting in the configuration of redeveloped spaces? How does the social imaginary shape social-physical space, or, how does the struggle between dominant and oppositional social imaginaries shape social-physical space—in particular, those spaces created through redevelopment? What do the city visions of those responsible for shaping redeveloped city spaces look like? Those responsible for constructing representations of spaces—planners, engineers, architects, social scientists and politicians—often have specific ways of understanding cities, which in turn shape the designs, plans, and concepts of how social-physical spaces should be designed and utilized. For our purposes we can ask, how do these actors conceive of the role of the very poor within their designed spaces? Where do the very poor or homeless belong, what is their place?

In Dreaming the Rational City (1983), Boyer outlines how the dreams of early city planners and the designers of urban aesthetics were heavily influenced by middle-class concerns over social order and sanitation. The city, perceived as a site of danger and opportunity by the privileged classes, was a natural target for social reformers at the turn of the nineteenth century. The early City Beautiful movement inspired planners and city politicians to add park landscapes, promenades, playgrounds, and gymnasiums, with linking streets and boulevards which would open the city to light and air, that somehow civilized values could be brought to bear on a perceived urban disorder. According to Boyer (1983), "The realities of urban life, the devastations and degradations of congested city environments were displaced through images of a rural order infused across the fabric of the city, the fears of social unrest dispelled by the calming presence of open vistas and pastoral promenades, by the pedagogical order imposed through supervised playgrounds and rigorous games" (37). During this early period of the late 1800s, public health dangers were invoked and social reformers warned of the dangers of poverty-stricken mass spreading disease and disorder. Therefore, the recreation of "second nature" was to "recover the harmonies of nature that had been destroyed by the accumulation of such a mass of humans in cities" (37) While some city reformers thought of improving the city, others believed that only dispersion of the city's population to the newly developing suburbs would cure society's ills, a sentiment fueled by the historical anti-city bias of American ideology, the equation of small-town America with moral values and community.

Likewise it was assumed that by making the city beautiful, by refashioning urban aesthetics, the new environments "would help to influence the moral and intellectual improvement of the whole social order" (45). This led to focusing on municipal improvements, monuments, museums, street vistas, classical and neoclassical fronts for businesses, allegorical murals, parks, promenades, color in buildings, clean streets, and such. These ideals were well expressed in the design of the "Great White City" at the 1893 World's Columbian Exposition in Chicago. The city was to be a personification of purity and light, of whiteness and order. The birth of American city planning, according to Boyer, emerging from the 1893 exposition, can be viewed, then, as embodying the contradictions between the desire for purity and lightness and the desire to contain the rabble, the dark, the unruly, which were represented at the Columbian Exposition by the tawdry booths, circus hawkers, sideshows, and "exotic" exhibitions on the margins of the Exposition. From shows featuring exotic animals to representatives of "ethnic" groups from afar, the very distance of these sideshows from the center of the Expo was proof of both their danger and their spectacle nature. This dual quest for monumentality and containment came to Chicago in the plans of Daniel Burnham, the principal designer of Chicago's lakefront and, as we shall see in the next chapter, still a major influence on how the city should "look." Symmetry and the balance of shapes and volumes were considered necessary in design to emphasis the importance of civic duty and the role of civic society. Models of aesthetics dating back to classical Greece were embraced with the assumptions that such models were representative of a rational, well-ordered mind, a mind founded upon order, proportion, rhythm, equilibrium, and harmony. The impurities and baseness of the American city were to be purified by the imposition of a neoclassical disciplinary order. Architecture and city space were to be designed to uplift the individual, to embrace a civic totality based on the conquering of disorder. In Burnham's 1909 plan for the city of Chicago, civic monuments alternated with grand vistas and diagonal streets. Parks alternated with well-ordered highways.

The city envisioned as a disciplined spatial order stood in contrast to the corruption, disease, filth, and squalor that occupied early American cities, results of the chaotic market development of lot sizes, insufficient drainage, industrial waste combined with mud streets, drainage ditches in place of sewer systems, and a fragmented local political structure. With the arrival of comprehensive city planning, dating to around 1907, came the attempt to impose disciplinary order and supervisory direction upon the city. Attempts were made to organize transportation and water systems, commercial and manufacturing districts, and to regulate housing to improve conditions for all city dwellers, usually through the development of zoning laws. Private ownership of property proved to be an impediment to these schemes. This created pressures to reform some areas over others, affecting some plans more than others. Landowners argued with each other over access to limited resources. Housing reformers fought land speculators and corrupt politicians. The art of city planning attempted to negotiate these conflicts. According to Boyer (1983), "the diverse and opposing strategies of industrial and financial capital, small businesses and trade groups, professional concerns and middle-class outrages formed a network across which the power of capital was intricately webbed" (67). Planning documents and backroom deals became the battleground for these struggles. Conflicts over land use were presented in a new, "neutral" language of aesthetic engineering which carefully avoided the appearance of political or social conflict.[15] To smooth out the problems of capital accumulation, to impose a normative order bound by visual interest, and to make for attractive investments in order to hold business confidence in the city—these were the purposes of planning.

Visual ideologies were, and still are, deeply implicated in the spatial practices of urban design (Rubin 1979). I am by no means making the argument that planning is all-powerful. Clearly, planners' schemes may be ignored, replaced by arbitrary forces of development based on political patronage, arbitrary whims, or multinational corporate development. However, an examination of planners' schemes and architects' plans does provide insight into the representation of spaces often shared by politicians, developers, real estate agents, bankers, and a middle-class public, representations that both exclude and include particular populations. In an attempt to manage the inequalities produced by market capital, planning worked by allocating a place to individual, class, group, or association. "Disciplinary control proceeded by distributing bodies in space, allocating each individual to a cellular partition, creating a functional space out of this analytic spatial arrangement. In the end this spatial matrix became both real and ideal: a hierarchical organization of cellular space and a purely ideal order that was imposed upon its form" (Boyer 1983, 70–71). Architectural models were developed to house the disciplinary system formed out of these operations, an architecture that would maximize surveillance, operating on the body, and communicate the appropriate space each was to occupy. We have seen how some bodies are treated as more equal than others; such surveillance would be extended to the poor and homeless with greater energy than to those who were propertied and wealthy, in order to contain "unruly" behavior.

An analogous process of cataloging the very poor, described in the introduction, also operates through land-use planning. Disciplinary control over land use is created by classifying social-physical spaces into particular functional entities and locations. "Proper" places are established for specific functions and specific populations.[16] The cellular nature of disciplinary space makes it possible to organize and increase communication between diverse land areas, to increase the organizational ability of production and reproduction of capital. Requiring the surveying of housing stock, businesses, people, and other features of the city landscape, planning works to unite the diverse aspects of the city into a rational whole. For example, in 1907 the Russell Sage Foundation sponsored the first citywide survey (the Pittsburgh Survey) in an attempt to assess the various social and environmental factors effecting the city. The development of these city surveys, now codified in each city's general plan, and, for our purposes in dealing with housing and homeless, in their Comprehensive Housing Affordability Strategy (CHAS) reports, was subjected to increasingly finer quantitative and qualitative methodologies, always with an eye toward a rational integration of city functions. Aside from tabulating the various features of the city and its population, disciplinary space also assigned functional locations to all land use, the purpose being, to separate conflicting land uses and improve the efficiency with which land was utilized. Conflicts occurred between residential and industrial uses, as well as commercial and industrial, necessitating the development of functional topologies. Industrial, commercial, and residential land uses often were mixed together randomly, so city plans began to emphasize the division of specific land areas into separate functions—what we now have come to know as "zoning."

Limited control over zoning processes and building codes by local growth networks is connected closely to real estate and financial interests (Faegin and Parker 1989; Logan and Molotch 1987) through the demarcation, marketing, and advertising of social-physical spaces. City boosterism, which is part of this process, attempts to create social-physical spaces of artificial "marketed" identities—distinctive spaces for the urban consumer, pleasure spaces for leisure-time tourists and local residents (shopping malls, shopping districts, redeveloped wharf or industrial areas, museums, entertainment complexes, sporting complexes including stadiums), and functional areas of production, commercial services, transportation, and residential development for work-time residents (office construction, transportation improvements, convention halls, residential housing). Control is not completely assured or uniform but subject to serious contestation between social groups, environmentalists, social activists, churches, and neighborhood associations (Perin 1977). The use of zoning as a strategy for disciplining social-physical space imposes abstract space upon everyday life, which I would claim leads to the production of spatially segregated landscapes, polarized topographies that enlist representations of pleasure (Zukin 1988, 438) and refuse (Winchester and White 1988; Mair 1986; Jakle and Wilson 1992), often mixing with engineered functional spaces involved in transportation and communication.

Polarized Topographies, Spatial Hierarchies

The intensity of contemporary social and spatial polarizations is captured well by Mike Davis (1990, 223–322; 1992) in his analysis of the increased militarization of south central Los Angeles in contrast to the pleasurable proliferation of consumer goods on Hollywood's Rodeo Drive. Private wealthy enclaves are increasingly isolated from deteriorating public spaces with locked gates, private security systems, and spatial segregation patterns dependent upon the production of "second nature" landscapes, manicured parks, and controlled "natural" environments. The dysutopic images from *Blade Runner, Brazil, Escape from New York,* and the *Mad Max* films constitute the socially imagined "other half," the homeless and the poor, segregated from glittering shopping/entertainment malls and theme parks.

Introduced in 1980, the "dual city" concept (Sternlieb and Hughes 1980) was intended to illustrate how the capitalist market operating within the city would lead inexorably to binary divisions of city spaces (e.g., rich/poor, safe/unsafe) as a result of conflict between workers and capitalists or between differentiated geographic areas, or both. Clearly, since that time the "dual city" concept has fallen out of favor because of its inability to explain the contradictions of post-Fordist societies and hypermodern cities. The terrain of social inequality, both geographically and socially, has grown more complex over time. The ever-changing binary divisions of city spaces are not fixed, static, or immutable. What I have chosen to call "pleasure spaces" and "refuse spaces" should not be thought of as "fixed" entities, but rather as ways of conceptualizing social-physical spaces that emerge out of the production of polarized topographies, which is subject to radical shifts given changes in cultural and economic productions.

Practically speaking, there is a multiplicity of cities, not just "dual cities." On the other hand, one could say that in a panic society (Goode and Ben-Yehuda 1994; Hall et al. 1978), where daily crises are fed through news broadcasts supplemented by increased tensions from dwindling economic resources for greater and greater numbers of families and complete destitution for those without homes, in fact a "dual city" is not far from the truth of individual experiences. Perhaps those with sufficient means experience far broader and more subtle distinctions within city spaces; for those having to figure out where their next paycheck, or next meal, is coming from, or worry about where to sleep the next night, the city does indeed take on a dual character, indeed a desperate one.

The division of social-physical space into pleasure and refuse spaces may be understood as the outgrowth of the production of polarized topographies, themselves a result of the interactions between social, economic, and cultural inequality expressed materially, and in turn affecting the relationships constituting both dominant social imaginaries and oppositional social imaginaries. Conceivably, in a society of social, political, and economic equality such distinctions would evaporate under the heat of justice, and the passions of pleasurable creative expansion would suffuse everyday life for all people, not just a select few. The risk in using the terms *pleasure spaces* and *refuse spaces* is the possibility that this will serve only to reify social, cultural, and economic inequalities by drawing spurious distinctions and reinforcing a spatial hierarchy that considers some spaces more worthy than others. This is a typical problem with using dualistic notions of the city, as Beauregard (1993) warns us about.[17] Therefore distinctions between pleasure spaces and refuse spaces must be followed by Beauregard's five recommendations for resolving this dilemma. He explains that dual representations, if they are not to be reified into some "natural" phenomenon must (1) be viewed in a dialectical fashion, (2) be understood as socially mediated, (3) be subject to reflection, (4) recognize the historical and cultural specificity of such dualism, and (5) recognize the political ramifications inherent in all dualism (227).

I hope that the reader will have by now concluded that I have attempted to keep these five points in mind in my guarded use of the terms *pleasure spaces* and *refuse spaces*. I am not attempting to carve up the social-physical spaces of the city into "dual," "tertiary," or "quartered" sections, each with its distinctive flavor, like so many select cuts of meat.[18] These distinctions are often based on degrees of inequality—rich versus poor, hovels versus palaces. Clearly, these types of inequality have persisted for a very long time. But, rather than abolish the use of the term *inequality*, it may be more helpful to invoke Marcuse's notion of "invidious differentiation." According to Marcuse (1993), the problem is "not inequality per se, but inequality that reflects a hierarchical relationship, one of domination and subordination, inclusion and exclusion, privilege and deprivation" (357). This definition best underscores my own use of the distinctions between pleasure and refuse spaces.

Clearly, the understanding of relationships of race, ethnicity, class, and gender in the production of social-physical spaces will have elaborate manifestations far beyond any simple dualism. On the other hand, these dualisms are deeply embedded in the popular and dominant social imaginary of any society predicated upon a high degree of social, economic, and cultural inequality, and they function as ideological tools in the creation of moral panics or in city redevelopment campaigns with their subsequent expulsion of the poor. Hence, dualistic notions might help us understand, less the "objective" reality of cities, and more the ideological baggage demanded by the planning of cities under conditions of social inequality.

How do we understand the spatial hierarchies, homogenizations, and increasingly polarized landscapes we drive, run, or walk through on our way to work? And how does the scheme we come up with affect our perception of the very poor, the homeless? In fact, as we have seen, developers and city planners clearly make distinctions of land value through the planning and investment process, which generate new boundaries between areas of differing values. It is often at and in these border areas between zones, between urban spaces of heterogeneous class, race/ethnic, and gender sites, that conflict occurs. Urban spaces are broken into polarized and fragmented topographies of varying levels of pleasure and refuse spaces through the demarcations of zoning ordinances, investment profiles of geographic areas, relative policing of city spaces, and so on. As Marcuse argues, it is not the abstraction of social inequality per se, but rather the spatial practices of redevelopment, informed by dominant social imaginaries and enforced by city officials and police, that generate the polarized topographies of pleasure and refuse spaces. Hence, a polarized topography might become evident, not when one is in the center of a particular site, but rather as one crosses the border from one site into another. These subjective and often physical borders are often those areas subject to the greatest community struggles—who will define their uses, where are they to be placed, and who will benefit and suffer from their location.

Snow and Anderson (1993), following Duncan (1979),[19] attempt to apply the "dualistic" notions of marginal space and prime space to distinguish how homeless persons in Austin, Texas, interact with the symbolized value of land, both public or private. According to Snow and Anderson the key point is not land ownership, whether public or private, but whether or not the land "is of importance for domiciled citizens" (102). Integrating the social constructionist approach (Duncan 1979) with the political economy perspective from Castells (1983), Logan and Molotch (1987), and Feagin (1986), Snow and Anderson understand that the value of space is "subject to change as its use and meaning change" (333) and that because different degrees of significance will be attached to the same space, community conflict and struggles over spatial meaning are "ultimately a political issue."

Prime space is defined by Snow and Anderson "as space that is either being used routinely by domiciled citizens for residential, commercial, recreational, or navigational purposes or has symbolic significance" (103). Marginal space, as the inverse of prime space, has "little value to regular citizens" and is "ceded both intentionally and unwittingly to the powerless and propertyless" (103). Whether or not this is conscious, as in the containments offered by skid rows or shelters, or unintentional, the result is that space can be redefined quickly by those who have the power to do so. Marginal space can be redefined as prime space. In Austin, neighborhood organizations redefined marginal space as prime space in order to prevent the Salvation Army from relocating to their neighborhood. Similarly, the gentrification of downtown areas through redevelopment has redefined many so-called marginal spaces, as prime spaces forcing out the very poor and homeless from previously defined marginal areas into prime space locations where they are more visible. The end result of the appropriation of marginal space and its conversion into prime space by developers is the further dispersion of social services and commercial facilities catering to the homeless, which means long walks every day between distant sources of food, shelter, medical care, and money-making shadow work. I believe it is important to move beyond the simple notion of "prime" space that Snow and Anderson invoke to escape the trap of static dualism. One way to accomplish this, borrowing from Henri Lefebvre, is by introducing third terms. In addition to pleasure and refuse spaces, I would like to add functional spaces—as those spaces that are neither ones of pleasure, entertainment, relaxation, or stimulation, nor spaces of abandonment, neglect, or violence. I shall discuss this later in this chapter.

Producing/Consuming Pleasure Spaces

Pleasure spaces can assume a wide variety of guises—from commercial tourist, club, and dining complexes that satisfy food, drink, touch, visual, or acoustic cravings, to private residencies with "historical" themes, to theme parks, museums (cultural capital), beaches and parks, and shopping malls. The list may go on endlessly, like pleasure itself. Not well defined, pleasure spaces may have the fixity of a historical monument like Mount Rushmore or the fleeting appearance of Chicago's Printer's Row Book Fair. The question that arises within pleasure spaces, and that is always suppressed, is who cleans the buildings, the sites, the bathrooms? And where do the workers who service these buildings and sites live? And who benefits from this landscape production and how much? According to Mitchell, "squatter camps, tenement buildings and suburbs . . . are often produced as 'answers' to the questions raised by the skyscrapers" (Mitchell, 1994, 11; see Deutsche and Ryan 1984).

Pleasure spaces are not simply created sui generis but are invested with symbolic capital by both producers and consumers, a meaning that is explicitly class, race, and gender based (Bourdieu 1984; Goldberg 1993a, 185–204) and subject to contestation, a product of ongoing cultural struggles over representation and identity. Landscapes are endowed with symbolic significance and grandeur according to the history of their users, even as remaining landscapes are maginalized, pushed to the periphery of desire, often into ascribed refuse spaces. When local and regional histories are reproduced within a corporate marketing culture, it is not surprising that regional historical differences will be resurrected as corporate-sponsored design themes, or conversely that historical sites will be redesigned and repackaged as tourist places that work to create a simulated history, a nostalgic recreation of mythical past imaginaries.

One brief illustration of this point is the Walt Disney Company's proposal to build a Disney American history theme park on a site adjacent to one of suburban Virginia's "real" historical locations. The proposed theme park, finally defeated by local residents, was to have included a simulated Civil War fort with reenactments of land battles, an Ellis Island Replica, the Enterprise, a model factory town with a ride through a steel mill, Native America complete with an Indian village, a President's Square, and much more (Wines 1994). The boundaries of what constitutes pleasure spaces are constantly changing and subject to negotiation.

Fluid boundaries mean that such pleasure spaces may be produced by planners and designers only to change with new uses by the public in ways planners have never thought of, the public appropriation of private pleasure spaces is one such possibility; what is more common with people living on the street is the appropriation of a public pleasure space for private uses. The latter, however, usually leads to severe conflict, which may turn dangerous for street persons who attempt such a strategy. Hence, the policing of boundaries, the regulation of social-physical spaces, is another mechanism for producing pleasure spaces that designated persons can then consume.

The spatial practices of redevelopment integrate planning with marketing and advertising to ensure the proper tenant mix in a residential pleasure space, linking and unifying the fragmented nature of city social-physical space with a "theme," historic or otherwise. This decontextualizes a historically developed sense of place through recreating a "nostalgic" link to past events designed for specific niche markets. For example, Boston's Faneuil Hall Marketplace, a specialty center, made maximum use of the historical associations affiliated with Boston's waterfront to generate a "nostalgic" sense of history. Built in the late 1970s, Quincy Hall, one of the main buildings in the Faneuil Hall Marketplace, produced sales of $233 per square foot within the first year of its operation (Frieden and Sagalyn 1989). Existing as a declining refuse space, a neglected area of Boston for many years, the waterfront became a prime site for redevelopment at a time when cities were casting around for schemes to improve their financial status. To accomplish this the city of Boston paid $12 million in public funds, almost 30 percent of the total costs to redevelop three adjacent buildings next to Faneuil Hall (Frieden and Sagalyn 1989, 4). The Rouse Company, Faneuil Hall's developer, received a ninety-nine year lease in exchange for a small annual payment and a portion of the projected income from the retail rents to be returned to the city of Boston. The materials used in the renovations to the old marketplace—worn bricks, rough wooden beams, antique business signs, and other symbols of "tradition"—were deliberately chosen for their ability to communicate a "nostalgic" sense of history, to connect the consumer with an imagined past.

Pike Place Market in Seattle, another specialty center, is unlike any other with its emphasis on a plethora of exotic shops and food stalls and its commitment to bring in poor people by sponsoring three hundred subsidized apartments on site. Its renovation was conducted by Seattle's Historical Commission in conjunction with the city of Seattle, assisted by federal dollars. Pike Place Market proved to be a huge success, attracting all classes and races of people. Unlike most other commercial complexe, Pike Place garnished a reputation for tolerance of "deviant" behavior and for street clientele. A 22-acre complex with 235 businesses, 40 percent of them food services and another 40 percent selling handicrafts, gifts, and household goods, Pike Place Market attracts a wider cross-section of people than most traditional shopping malls. Unlike most redevelopment projects, Pike Place Market rents only to independent business persons, who must be present in the market. In addition, lower rental rates allow businesses that would normally be forced out of a redeveloping downtown, such as pawnshops and kitchenware stores, to remain in the area. In commenting upon Pike Place Market's image, John Turnball, a former staff director for the Historical Commission commented, "Vagrants and street people are part of the scene; they have a right to be here" (quoted in Frieden and Sagalyn 1989, 181). Turnball commented that it is the "un-touristy" character of the place that attracts tourists. However, according to Tim Harris, editor of *Real Change*, Seattle's homeless newspaper, panhandlers are escorted out of the market on a regular basis even though a decision by the district court upheld panhandling as a protected form of free speech (Harris, personal communication, 26 June, 1995). *Real Change* vendors were also being run out of the Market by Market Security until an agreement was reached between *Real Change* and Pike Place Market. Graffiti is encouraged, but only in certain locations, all carefully monitored by a committee of local artists. Compared with most shopping malls and commercial redevelopment projects, Pike Place Market relies more on a policy of "containment" than on simple "exclusion" of those stigmatized by homelessness.

Rather than attempting to house all classes or races, development projects now seek to exclude the street, to contain and develop services within large development complexes so tenants will not have to wander out into the street, while wanderers from adjacent run-down developments are kept at bay by guards at the gate. This is true for both residential and commercial pleasure spaces. Hence, the social-physical spaces of pleasurable consumption (either housing or shopping) may coexist with neglected areas of the city, with refuse spaces, sometimes within the same block—the boundaries between these two radically different areas a very faded version of the historic public spaces of old. The concentration of wealthier tenants in integrated, security controlled luxury residences has its counterpart in the expanding production of commercial/entertainment complexes.

In both downtown and suburban areas, regional malls, as pleasure spaces, are integrating entertainment complexes into their designs, further concentrating consumption in a carefully controlled pleasure space from which homeless persons can be easily excluded. One has only to think of the West Edmonton Mall in Canada (Crawford 1992), the Mall of America in Minnesota, or the newly developing 21-screen theater entertainment complex—complete with Egyptian, Chinese, and Art Deco aesthetics, four restaurants, a food court, a large chain bookstore and a music shop—developing in Irvine, California (Adelson 1995), to envision the increasing integration between entertainment and shopping. This hyper-intensification of consumption, the integration of entertainment, consumption, and aesthetics, increases the distance between redeveloped pleasure spaces and excluded refuse spaces, reducing public spaces to mere accessories to privately owned theme parks and malls. With the expansion of larger numbers of the very poor and homeless, and the spread of commercially integrated shopping complexes that function as de facto public spaces, the question "When is a private space a public place?" (Benard 1988) is asked more and more frequently.

In today's budget-strapped cities, investment in public places is overshadowed by the public-private partnerships designed to cater to those who can afford private services and live in luxury housing. As the designs of pleasure spaces collide with the realities of street life, border conflicts arise as to what is permissible in privately owned pleasure spaces. To keep their customers, businesses have pressured cities to develope and enforce tougher antivagrancy ordinances that can be utilized to exclude the very poor, the homeless, and any who decide to use the de facto public space as a political forum. The effort to exclude any form of political expression from shopping malls, for example, was supported by 73 percent of the American population in a 1990 Gallup poll (Rybczynski 1993, 101). The gradual introduction of civic facilities, such as police stations, libraries, and post offices, into suburban shopping malls may work to counter this trend. However, it is unlikely that in major cities one will see this crossover between public and private facilities anytime soon.

Although it is true that malls, as pleasure spaces, are a "functional machine for the transformation of production into consumption"

(Gottdiener 1995, 94), they are also "dream-like fantasies . . . places of unabashed contradictions of time, place and subjectivity that exist as much in imagination as reality" (Langman 1992). The social imaginaries from which pleasure spaces emerge, then, invoke the dualisms safety/danger, purity/order, degenerate/moral. Therefore, the attachment to a visual aesthetic that defines body comportment or shabby dress as a "sign" of one's moral worth, while other visual aesthetic "signs"—the graphics, wrapping, architecture of the new shopping complexes—are eagerly embraced and consumed as pleasurable purities, allows for the forcible exclusion of those who correspond to the "sign" of low moral worth, and subsequently the embrace of those aesthetic "signs" associated with pleasure. Binge and purge then becomes synonymous with a consumer culture that bifurcates the city into pleasure and refuse spaces. The avid consumption of products, experiences, and spaces in pleasure spaces is offset by the repulsion and exclusion of products, experiences, spaces, and people associated with a mythical refuse space.

The integration of entertainment and shopping was foreshadowed by the development of the Disney theme parks, which played off the distinctions between the world outside the magic kingdom and the world inside the gates of the parks. Now such distinctions have broken down, as the "Magic Kingdom" has pervaded all sectors of everyday life, from the ever present Disney stores in nearby malls to Disney's acquisition of major film studios and television stations. Indeed, one could say the world is becoming Disneyfied as consumption is increasingly organized within well-controlled pleasure spaces that are selective about who is admitted and what kind of behavior can occur in them. Suburban areas have been the main recipients of large regional malls and entertainment complexes, but city downtown redevelopers have looked to the reproduction of such complexes as a way to lure in city and suburban dollars. Often termed "entertainment destination centers" (Allen 1995), the shopping mall/theme park is now envisioned as a method of concentrating paying consumers in one location, a money machine to rescue failing city economies.

The recent acquisition of major sites in the Times Square/42nd Street area of New York City by Disney and the nationwide spreading of the Dave & Buster's complexes nationwide, (offering dining, drinking, virtual reality games, and sports within a building the size of a supermarket) appears to be the trend of the future for downtowns. Developers and city officials alike assume that a properly crafted entertainment complex can project a particular city's identity and, according to Michael Rubin, a leisure development consultant based in Philadelphia, "recreate a lost sense of urbanity" (quoted in Allen 1995, 1).

In this context of expanding consumption, investment shifts from office construction to entertainment complexes and shopping areas, to pleasure spaces.

Producing/Consuming Refuse Spaces

Refuse space, derelict landscapes (Jackle and Wilson 1992), empty spaces (McDonogh 1993), or "lost spaces" (Trancik 1986; Greenberg, Popper, and West 1990), can be defined as space that is excluded from development, held in reserve for future development, or residual space from a particular development, such as spaces under freeway overpasses. Social-physical spaces already established for other uses, such as functional spaces, may assume the status of refuse spaces, especially when associated with crime, violence, and overt deterioration. In the period of urban renewal during the 1960s, blight was defined as anything that visually communicated a sense of deterioration—such as abandoned buildings, graffiti, broken windows—and was subject to immediate leveling by city bulldozers. Blight would match my description of refuse spaces. However, my definition goes beyond the simple visual appearance of a social-physical space, which, in any case, is often judged by those with middle- or upper-income status at the expense of the poor. Refuse spaces are spaces in which one is refused—refused services, refused dignity, refused human rights, refused the basics of food, clothing, and shelter, and refused medical care. This is what makes refuse spaces different from a simple notion of marginal space, which communicates a distance from a mythical "center." Refuse spaces can exist within the center, infused throughout, and can remain invisible to those not affected by it, just as race is often invisible to whites but never to blacks. "Proper" behavior is considered problematic within a refuse space, open to contestation.

Winchester and White (1988) say that, what they term "marginal spaces," are characterized not merely by physical marginality but also by social, economic, and legal marginality. Homeless populations occupy the most extreme form of marginal residential space (Winchester and White 1988, 44), the space of shelters, alleyways, bushes, and abandoned buildings. Refuse spaces are social-physical spaces, both invisible and visible, that carry low social status, often stigmatizing its inhabitants even more than the label *poor*. The city is a patchwork quilt of such pleasure and refuse spaces, shaped by the developing polarized topographies of investment and social exclusions that prevail. For example, in San Jose, California, the Guadalupe river running through the center of the downtown was home to many homeless persons, as we shall see in the next several chapters. Undeveloped, the river remained a refuse space in the eyes of city planners, developers, real estate agents, and many homeowners. Viewed by them as a site of filth, of untamed "nature," of threat, and of crime, reflected in media reports about drug sales in the riverbed, the Guadalupe River was produced as a refuse space, an eyesore that had to be "cleaned up" to fulfill the planners' image of a pleasurable downtown area. Those who live in such places, such as the homeless, are then treated by association as equivalent to human "refuse." However, refuse spaces do not all have equal value, just as not all pleasure or functional spaces have the same value. Social-physical spatial hierarchies operate by grading the various degrees of refuse, pleasure, and functional spaces. Shelters may be considered a refuse space in relationship to the luxury Fairmont Hotel, but they are definitely of higher value than the Guadalupe River, at least for homeowners and middle-class constituencies. The homeless themselves might prefer the Guadalupe River over shelters because of their belief that the Guadalupe offers freedom from daily forms of intimate institutional surveillance, something middle-class homeowners are removed from on a daily basis.

Another brief example of the production of refuse space was the completion of the Dan Ryan Expressway, which cuts south from Chicago's downtown Loop through the heart of the Southside black community. Built during the 1960s as part of the urban renewal trend throughout the United States, the effect of the Dan Ryan was to destroy large parts of the black community, to produce and treat the black community as a refuse space, by the imposition of the functional space of freeway transportation, of abstract space, to use Lefebvre's term. Driven by fears of "invading" blacks, prompted by the developments of the civil rights movements, white homeowners and renters to the west of the largely black Southside area lobbied extensively for the construction of the Dan Ryan to provide a barrier between themselves and "those" people. To this day the area underneath and adjacent to the Dan Ryan remains a refuse space, a "no man's-land" of competing turf battles and neighborhood struggles. The assumption that a poor black community contains nothing but drug deals, crime, and violence rhetorically works to direct public attention away from placemaking and community involvement in the black community. In the dominant social-imaginary where whiteness is equated with goodness, examining the strengths of the black community is given low priority. Hence, it is all to easy to produce refuse spaces in those areas, which are given little value to begin with.

direct contradiction b/t social imaginaries.

Changing and building upon the concept of "openness" developed by Kevin Lynch and Gary Hack,[20] McDonogh (1993) coins the term *emptiness* to talk about the form of space, both subjective and objective, that is empty, devoid, vacant, that is 'underused,' 'unfashionable,' 'forbidden,' 'voided,' or it may have been planned to preclude social activities" (3). While for Lynch and Hack emptiness connotes freedom, for McDonogh it connotes social conflict. For McDonogh, empty space is a form of spatial consciousness, perhaps closer to the spatial practices and representation of spaces evoked by Lefebvre, and yet empty spaces are embodied physically in such things as the social-physical makeup of a small park. Tracking the use of a small park in Barcelona's Raval, a predominantly poor immigrant neighborhood, specifically the area known as the Jardins d'Emili Vendrell, between 1980 and 1990, McDonogh observed that the park had been abandoned, treated as an "empty" space, a location where residents "complained about both pollution and safety" (6). Local residents' concerns and fears about Barcelona were distilled within the representational space of the city square. The empty spaces of the Jardins came to stand for all of Barcelona.

As McDonogh understands, and as we have discussed, speculative investments often leave large tracts of abandoned buildings, vacant lots, and unused parks in their wake. Similarly, empty spaces are created through the struggles between different groups with contrasting visions of the city (7). One can think of examples where redevelopment projects have been started only to fail at the last minute because of insufficient funds, leaving an "empty" space to fill in the future. Likewise urban redevelopment may focus on developing downtown public spaces, without the "public," through the design of homeless-proof benches or uninviting wall alcoves, as William Whyte documents (Whyte 1988). This desire to plan for only certain kinds of citizens has the effect of creating barren, empty, windswept plazas, empty spaces downtown, especially after hours. This restriction of public space has been followed by increasing control over the remaining public spaces by the ever expanding role of private interests, such as the shopping malls and theme parks mentioned above. This de facto exclusion of the very poor from public spaces creates refuse spaces. The refusal does not have to be direct to be effective.

In defiance of the planned or unplanned production of empty or refuse spaces, people might organize, gather, or petition, developing a mini-movement through engagement with authority in empty or refuse spaces. According to McDonogh (1993), "When an empty space fills, its actors controvert its social construction or planned meaning" (15). Empty space—refuse space—can become the birthing area for revolutions, revolts, and protests far beyond the immediate claims of those using that space. The conversion of that empty or refuse space into what Sara Evans and Harry Boyte (1992) term "free spaces" can form the beginning of a large grassroots movement motivated by counter social imaginaries. The large-scale production of refuse spaces can set the stage for a revolt of the marginalized.

Examples of this type of revolt are the increasingly larger movements for homeless squatting (Yeich 1994; Ruddick 1990, 1995; Wagner 1993; Wright and Vermund forthcoming), the most notable being the occupation of Thompkins Square Park in New York City. Occupied by persons who were homeless, anarchists, local community activists, and some local residents, Thompkins Square was a magnet, a refuse space to middle-class residents, a space of opposition for the squatters. The refuse space of the park permitted the growth of a brief social movement that highlighted New York City's failed housing and shelter policies for the homeless (Abu-lughod 1994; Smith, Duncan, and Reid 1994). The pitched battles with New York police resulted in the eventual exclusion of squatters and the construction of a large chain link fence around the circumference of the park. It appears that, from the city's point of view, if the park was not going to exist as a pleasure space, then it was not going to exist as a refuse space either, although through its actions the city did, in fact, guarantee that the park would remain as a refuse space, empty and secure.

Producing/Consuming Functional Spaces

Functional spaces may be understood as places through which one moves to get to a particular destination, or a space planned for moving through to get to a particular destination. It is easy enough to understand bus stations, airports, railroad stations as way stations functionally created for travelers on their way between two or more points. Not in essence, designed for consumption, although those features might be included to market the space, such places are engineered for ease of transport and to relieve the burden of waiting.

The Weberian concepts of rationalization and calculability inform the design of functional spaces, social-physical spaces reduced to single purposes of performance and efficiency. For those who are homeless, however, such functional spaces may become surrogate homes. Airports have been frequent ad hoc homes for many people on the street

(Hopper 1991).[21] O'Hare airport in Chicago was home to about 150 homeless people for quite some time until police sweeps forced them back under Lower Wacker Drive in the downtown Loop area of Chicago or into local shelters. These homeless used restrooms on a regular basis for bathing and general cleanup, and many comported themselves in ways that made them invisible to the casual traveler. Looking like many who are traveling, waiting, or rushing to catch the next plane, those living in the airport had already arrived at their destination, waiting, and waiting some more. Other functional spaces of waiting may serve a similar purpose. Border maintenance between these spaces is conducted by local security guards who are often ambivalent about enforcing local loitering laws.

Functional spaces are particularly important for those living on the streets—not just for the amenities they offer, but also for the cultural power that resides in occupying such a transitory space. Living and sleeping in functional spaces means that one may be constantly on view by the public. That can be both a blessing and a curse. On the one hand, you are better protected against thieves and muggers, but on the other hand, you are subject to daily degradation ceremonies in dealing with other people's expressions and statements about your condition. Many other functional areas immediately come to mind, such as lobbies, doorways, service rooms, subway tunnels and trains, buses, cars and trucks, service tunnels, waiting areas of offices and residential buildings, parking garages, and restrooms. The point is, each of these social-physical spaces serves a specific engineered and designed function, usually a function separated from other functions by the physical boundaries of the building, rooms, or openings.

For those living on the street, these separations between functions, between functional spaces, can also provide a wedge within which to insert themselves, to find a space "in between" where they can sleep or do their business and survive without having a permanent residence. Often, refuse spaces and functional spaces overlap, such as railway lines cutting through an abandoned industrial area. In Chicago's "Tranquility City" hut encampments, the space occupied was both functional, insofar as it provided the corridor through which Chicago's western commuter trains passed, and refuse, due to the abandoned buildings and debris in the area, a place middle-class residents would avoid. On the other hand, for those living in the huts, the area constituted a pleasure space where they could relax after doing day labor or scavenging all day, as we shall see in chapters 4 and 5. The key point is that functional spaces are spaces through which one moves and waits to move. They are transitional areas, which for many homeless are converted, reappropriated, into residential places, places where one stays. The point for those living on the streets is not to travel through functional spaces to go somewhere; the point is you are already "there."

Zoned and Redeveloped Exclusions and Dispersions

Traditionally the spatial hierarchies reproduced through zoning functions were tainted by white supremacist and patriarchal imaginaries that maintained economic, political, and social segregation. Pleasure, refuse, and functional spaces shifted in form and content with the implementation of racist and sexist imaginaries. Boyer (1983) cites the example of one of the earliest zoning ordinances developed in California, between the 1870s and 1890s, which restricted the location of Chinese laundries to areas away from dominant white interests; "since zoning was supported by financial and banking interests as a guarantor of property values, it necessarily meant economic and racial segregation" (167).

In the 1920s Robert Whitten praised the zoning plan for Atlanta, Georgia, for its segregation of city social-physical space into all-white, all-black, and undetermined areas. Blacks were excluded from living in white areas and vice versa. Although the most visible features of this overt discrimination have disappeared in the 1990s with the abolishment of legal segregation, de facto segregation still remains the norm in many American cities.[22] The city of Memphis, for example, during the 1970s, constructed a wall between white and black sections of the city, ostensibly to protect property and preserve order (Young 1990, 135).

For the very poor and homeless, those without places to live, such segregation is a moot point because the segregation they experience is differing degrees of exclusion from all areas of the city, and containment within allocated shelters or other institutional settings. The racial and gender nature of homelessness continues this legacy of segregation, this time over the meaning of city streets for the very poor versus which neighborhood one is allowed to live in. As Haymes (1995) well understands, the production of the built environment, the actual form of capital investments, is "bound up with images and fantasies about racial difference, thereby linking the politics of race and ethnicity to the process of place making" (100). These images and fantasies are also about gender and about class, about where and how the poor should be treated.

Drawing upon the work of Rosalyn Deutsche (1991), Haymes explains that the act of looking, structured by highly mediated fantasies involving racial difference, is implicated in the very production of the built environment. This is most obvious when examining the aesthetics of redevelopment projects and historical renovations. Spaces are not merely produced, but also consumed as nostalgic signifiers, or as visual symbols of security, progress, and a host of other meanings generated through the dominant set of social imaginaries. And again, as we discussed before, the consumption of these visual attributes is closely connected to class.

Redevelopment and gentrification of city areas, is predicated not merely on the operation of land speculation and real estate practices, but also on cultural practices that connect the visual imagery of a project, building, or plaza to the visual fantasies entertained by the target consumer, fantasies highly dependent upon the class, race, and gender composition of the buyers.[23] According to Haymes (1995), "contemporary efforts by city planners to gentrify and redevelop downtown" are a conscious "attempt to regulate and control racial differences in terms of the city's visual space" (102). This control operates through the production of projects that evoke "the nostalgic image of the harmonious city" (103), often referring to a past historical referent, which is then counterpointed to a contemporary problem, usually defined by class and or race, necessitating the rationalization or "need" to disperse "those people" in order to make the neighborhood "economically viable," "safe," or any host of other signifiers that communicate who is to be excluded from a given area and who is to be included. The production of nostalgic images of tradition, of a mythical time when cities worked, demands labor that will preserve this illusion in the form of gated communities, security guards, elaborate aesthetic designs, and specialized stores. The preserving of this type of nostalgic illusion, according to Deutsche (1990), demands "a cost in representational violence: the city can only be constructed as a cohesive entity by expelling the differences and conflicts within it" (160).

The fact that homeless persons can not "go home," for lack of a stable residence, means that their explusion from a given area cannot occur except by employing various forms of repression. Antipanhandling laws or anticamping ordinances will be passed, and increased harassment from local police implemented to remove unwanted persons from a specific area of the city.[24] However, by demolishing or dispersing the facilities, shelters, single-room-occupancy hotels, flophouses, soup kitchens, and out-patient treatment centers that serve the homeless, the same result may be achieved—the exclusion of the very poor from neighborhoods redeveloped for more marketable classes. For example,

Kasinitz (1986, 250) reported that New York City built a new men's shelter on Ward's Island away from populated areas. Churches attempting to operate soup kitchens have encountered similar obstacles.

The Western Presbyterian Church in Washington, D.C., entered into an agreement with the International Monetary Fund (IMF) to exchange properties; the IMF agreed to build a new church with a feeding center in a mixed residential and special purpose zone. The zoning allowed churches to develop "customarily incidental uses" (Gammon and Grange 1994, 23). A permit was granted and construction proceeded in June 1992. After receiving complaints from two neighborhood associations in the area, the local zoning administrator ruled that the church's feeding program was not an accessory use. Appealing the ruling first to the Board of Zoning Adjustments and then in federal district court, the church, claiming that feeding the poor was a central practice of its faith, received an injunction to stop the ruling. In a final verdict by the courts the church was granted a permanent injunction against the city's ruling and continued their feeding program for the very poor and homeless.

Similar battles over shelter or food service relocations were fought in Yakima in Washington state, and in Daytona Beach, Florida (Gammon and Grange 1994). Goetz (1992), in his analysis of city redevelopment, land use, and homeless policy in Los Angeles from 1984 through 1989, demonstrated the conscious attempt by the Community Redevelopment Agency (CRA) to "contain" the homeless within the Skid Row area of the city while expelling them from the central business district. Downtown Los Angeles, whose Skid Row area was spared in the urban renewal programs of the 1960s, prompted the removal of the United Rescue Mission from an area near the central business district to Skid Row at a cost of $6.5 million (Goetz 1992, 545). Community advocacy, however, helped blunt the arbitrary street sweeps of homeless shanties during the summer of 1987 and brought a commitment on the part of the CRA to build more very low-income housing. Undoubtedly, countless instances of other shelter relocations and soup kitchen expulsions from profitable downtown land can be found in the United States and indeed in cities around the world.

Haymes (1995, 105), Smith (1992), Smith and Williams (1986), and Smith, Duncan, and Reid (1994) remind us that the "frontier" myth is used extensively by redevelopers to attract youthful upper-middle-class professionals into the city and to simultaneously warn them of city "dangers," of hostile forces on their doorstep. This play with the dualism civilized/savage, as we have seen, matches the images the dominant social imaginary constructs around racial and gender imagery (pleasure-white, male; refuse-black, female). As we stated before, the construction of such dualistic representations serve the purpose of maintaining control over the dominant social imaginaries through policing the boundaries of discourse and comportment within a given social-physical space. Such representations are not given but are constructed, albeit often unconsciously, for the purpose of reproducing privilege. Areas containing high percentages of poor blacks are considered less worthy than areas containing high percentages of upper-income whites. According to Haymes (1995), "this suggests that the gentrification (architectural redevelopment) of the city is mediated by white supremacist ideology" (106).

The spatial dispersement policies practiced upon low-income tenants presuppose the repression of black and Latino culture in central city areas in favor of the dominant social imaginary fantasies about the mythical "other." The treatment of racial minorities as the dangerous other, is bound up, then, with city planning policies that affect the visual appearance of downtown spaces. Since physical space is the domain within which cultural identities are established, structuring physical space also affects cultural identities as well. A racial binary is constructed that divides the city spatially into "black," and I would add "latino," "poor white," "the homeless," and other excluded groups as disordered, and middle-income "white spaces" as ordered. This imposed cultural code provides the rationale for spatial dispersement policies that homogenize the downtown area and uproot low-income populations, reducing cultural differences to safe theme-park variations developed from a dominant white mainstream cultural perspective.[25] As we shall see in chapter 4, media representations of homeless populations are constructed as the antithesis of orderly middle-class culture, the homeless person as either pathetic victim or dangerous presence. Similar to blacks, homeless persons are treated as a racial minority in a predominantly white culture, regardless of their race, subject to dispersement from downtown areas and containment in city institutional facilities.

Deutsche (1990) summarizes the effects of redevelopment quite nicely, stating, following Lefebvre, that redevelopment depends upon establishing both a spatial hierarchy and a homogenization of social-physical spaces. The production and reenforcement of spatial hierarchies works by establishing aesthetic and physical boundaries between areas of differing class and racial backgrounds, from physical barriers and aesthetic styles to security patrols; the homogenization of social-physical space works by physically excluding undesirable groups from the city and "discursively by inscribing the absence of groups in representations of the city" (173).

Exclusive redevelopment works to both homogenize space and deterritorialize its existing population. The latter exclusion is quite apparent in a cursory examination of real estate promotional literature and redevelopment brochures, which highlight city projects but conceal their effects from inquiring eyes. City planners, who often resort to sketches to communicate their ideas of social-physical space, also engage in excluding typical city residents even within their reports.

In a study examining who appears in published planning reports between 1958 and 1964, Wood, Brower, and Latimer (1966) concluded that those who were presented in the drawings were "young, well dressed, and white—at a time when cities were becoming noticeably older, poorer, and blacker" (Frieden and Sagalyn 1989, 58). It is probably safe to say that these representational exclusions continue into the present.

To complete the illusion, Deutsche (1990, 173) claims that ideology then neutralizes "antagonisms among competing visions of the city by substituting . . . simple dualism for genuine conflicts." Problems of displacement may be reinterpreted as the consequences of "progress" or a need for a "higher and better use of the land." Persons who are made homeless through displacement can then be reinterpreted not as "homeless through displacement," but rather as "deserving/undeserving victims of charity now requiring shelters." Private and public responsibility for excluding the poor is effectively neutralized. The conflicts and struggles over redevelopment are then conveniently hidden from public view through rhetoric maneuvers that play off of the already established social and spatial hierarchies. Dominant social imaginaries may then emerge in the representation of spaces and through spatial practices to allow and shape the particular type of ideology to be employed given the particular nature of city conflicts and contradictions which are encountered. Therefore, city redevelopment is not a given, but rather a highly strategic process subject to conflicting claims from a multitude of parties exercising differing degrees of power within a highly contested landscape, both culturally and economically. It is this struggle that cities actively work to conceal in their promotional literature, advertising, marketing, and boosterism designed to "sell the city."

CHAPTER 3

Making Pleasure and Refuse:
Chicago and San Jose

In the prior chapter I noted the trends in social-physical spatial formations on a national level. A closer examination of several local city case studies, case studies that provided the everyday context for the struggles of SHA and the "Tranquility City" inhabitants, can provide a way to ground the theoretical concepts noted earlier. Chicago and San Jose are two hypermodern "service" cities that offer interesting examples of downtown redeveloped pleasure spaces and refuse spaces, and ongoing battles with housing and homeless activist groups. These cities, like many others, are working to attract tourists and finance capital in the midst of a declining manufacturing base and suburban flight. Increasingly, each city's development of its cultural capital is an attempt to reverse the slow degradation of social-physical space prompted by years of neglect.

In many major cities, Chicago and San Jose included, the financial, insurance, real estate, and business services (FIRE) are the most rapidly expanding areas of the downtown economy, a common phenomenon of the "new," hypermodern city. Architecture affiliated with the growth of cultural capital is also expanding, in the form of new museums, festivals, sports stadiums, entertainment complexes, and redeveloped shopping districts to service this "new" class of office, information workers. Insofar as these hypermodern cities move to embrace consumption and pleasure for those with the ability to pay, it is easy to see how the very poor, the homeless, will be excluded in a de facto manner from this newly fashioned topography. Services and entertainment are refashioned for the privileged, while services for the very poor are either increasingly concentrated in select areas, removed from, or, conversely, widely dispersed to, the edges of the city and or isolated suburban tracts.

In the past, Skid Row was the area close to, if not in, downtown that serviced the needs of the very poor. As Skid Rows have declined across America, spaces where the very poor could survive, where one could be "down and out," have drifted into what I have termed "refuse" places. The small shops and services that catered to the very poor are disappearing as everyday life functions are organized into institutional settings, removed from the sight of downtown patrons. For those not living in shelters, a bed for the night might be under bushes, next to garbage dumpsters, along fast-moving highways, or in abandoned buildings and warehouses.

Chicago, with a population of a little over 2.7 million, represents the prototypical, aging industrial city. It has had a 7.3 percent population decline since 1980 and a loss of 79,744 jobs between 1980 and 1990. Losses to larger Cook County amounted to 106,200 jobs, $3.2 billion in personal income, and $5.4 billion in gross regional product (Ranney 1992) as a result of declining investment. Manufacturing jobs in the metropolitan area declined 19 percent between 1979 and 1989. According to Ranney (1992, 3), this decline in investment, or deindustrialization, was a direct result of a transnational production strategy that closed domestic plants and shifted production to outlying regions.[1]

During the 1980s, what job growth occurred in Chicago did so in the FIRE sectors and the retail industries. As these sectors expanded, so did downtown employment, attracting both suburban commuters and workers who decided to move back into the city. The latter group, primarily white singles and young couples, settled in community areas like Lincoln Park (Bennett 1990, 74–76), and now the South Loop area, choosing to live close to their places of employment. Meanwhile, the very poor, predominantly African Americans and Latinos, either were concentrated in separate areas of the South and West Sides of the city, or have started to move out into segregated suburban areas (Wilson 1987; Massey and Denton 1993; London and Puntenney 1993).

In Chicago, a race- and class-segregated city,[2] declining wages and employment have contributed to a 33.2 percent poverty rate among African Americans and 24.2 percent poverty rate among Hispanics. While the city of Chicago's 1990 median family income of $30,707 was a slight increase from 1980, the larger Primary Metropolitan Statistical Area (PMSA) median family income increased dramatically to $41,745, a reflection of growth in the surrounding suburbs of Cook County but stagnation within the city itself. Thirty-five percent of Chicagoans earn less than 50 percent of the PMSA median family income. Rising rental rates combined with neighborhood disinvestment, housing stock deterioration (Theodore 1991), and redevelopment policies favoring the privileged set the stage for increased homelessness. In 1993, over 18,781 City of Chicago residents took advantage of various shelter programs; the state's homeless population is estimated by local advocates to be 20,000 to 60,000.[3]

San Jose, California, with a population of over 700,000, is the third largest city in California. Located one hour south of San Francisco, San Jose serves as a bedroom community for the nearby "Silicon Valley" electronics industry, which spreads throughout the cities of Santa Clara, Mountain View, Sunnyvale, Campbell, Cupertino, and Palo Alto (Saxenian 1981, 1983, 1995). Since 1992, 46,000 jobs have been added to the Silicon Valley region, a result of large influxes of venture capital (Markoff 1996, C2). With the goal of attracting financial capital and upper-income professionals, San Jose is undertaking a massive 450-acre redevelopment project in the downtown area and in seven neighborhood business districts. San Jose is a good example of a rapidly developing, hypermodern service city. All of the ingredients are present: an emphasis on finance, insurance, real estate, and other service-sector employment; increasing economic polarization; the development of cultural spectacles, entertainment, hotel and retail complexes; an emphasis on "strolling" walkways and plazas; a ubiquitous multiracial environment; rapidly developing systems of surveillance and control; and accelerated spatial exclusions of the poor from the central business district. During the mid to late 1980s intensive redevelopment of the downtown area occurred simultaneously with a 300 percent increase in homeless aid requests (City of San Jose 1988) within the larger Santa Clara County. The bulk of these requests came from San Jose. San Jose is the largest city in Santa Clara County and contains 85 percent of the county's permanent homeless shelter beds and 50 percent of seasonal beds (City of San Jose, 1991a, 32), and contains the largest concentration of homeless persons.

The cities of San Jose and Chicago exhibit quite different racial and ethnic patterns among homeless and nonhomeless populations. San Jose's population is predominately white, with rapidly increasing population sizes for Hispanics and Asians. African Americans represent only a very small fraction of the total population. Comparing the racial and ethnic composition of Santa Clara County's estimated 16,000 to 30,000[4] homeless with the racial and ethnic composition of nonhomeless populations in San Jose, however, reveals disproportionate numbers of African Americans and Hispanics (table 3.1). Approximately 60 percent of Santa Clara County's homeless (about 18,000 persons) reside in San Jose (Homeless Overview Study Task Force 1989; City of San Jose 1993, 22). Chicago's 1990 multiracial population, by contrast, is more evenly balanced between African Americans and whites, even though spatial segregation has clearly created geographic areas of conflict. The majority of Chicago's homeless individuals and

families are African Americans. Eighty-one percent of Chicago's homeless families and individuals who used the Department of Human
Services shelter programs were African American (City of Chicago
1994, 33).

In both cities, Hispanics and Asians have led the way in population growth; Chicago reveals the patterns for the twenty-first-century
city, in which no race or ethnicity has a distinct majority role. In
Chicago, the number of whites declined 19 percent between 1980 and
1990, many moving to surrounding suburbs. The numbers of African
Americans declined by 9 percent over the same time period. Hispanic
and Asian populations grew in Chicago during the 1980s and early
1990s, by 29 and 39 percent, respectively. San Jose, in contrast, had
only a slight decrease in population among whites (–3.51 percent), but
large increases of Hispanic (+48.29 percent) and Asian (+182.0 percent)
populations. African Americans constitute a small percentage of the
overall population of San Jose. By the twenty-first century, San Jose
will, like Chicago, become a true multicultural city if present trends
continue. Table 3.1 illustrates the large differences in racial/ethnic groups
for both homeless and nonhomeless for Chicago and for Santa Clara
County using available data sources.

The disproportionate number of African Americans in both homeless populations reflects the high rates of poverty in the African American communities in those cities. In San Jose, African Americans, Hispanics,
and Native Americans are the poorest populations, although African
Americans make up only 4.7 percent of San Jose's general population.
However, African Americans make up almost one-third of the local
Santa Clara County homeless population (table 3.1). Unlike Chicago's
homeless population, Santa Clara County's homeless population does
reflect a more equitable multiculturalism of poverty.

In examining the ethnic composition of the homeless samples in
24 local area case studies, in 18 U.S. cities, Baker (1994) concluded that
Latinos and African Americans "account for between 20 percent and 88
percent of the local totals" (482). What is clear from this data is that
homelessness is not neutral with respect to race or ethnicity, but directly related to the social position of poor African Americans and
Latinos in the United States. Policies designed to assist the homeless
must take into account the racial composition of the homeless and the
correlation between homelessness and racism. The prevalence of widespread discrimination in mortgage lending practices leading to housing
segregation patterns, in redlining of commercial businesses and subtle
employment discrimination practices, all work to marginalize African

Table 3.1
Racial/Ethnic Composition of Sheltered Homeless and Nonhomeless Populations

	CHICAGO		SANTA CLARA COUNTY	
	SHELTERED HOMELESS (%)[5]	NONHOMELESS (%)	SHELTERED HOMELESS (%)	NONHOMELESS (%)
African American	81.6	38.6	35.0	3.0
White	10.0	37.9	40.0	64.0
Hispanic	7.8	19.1	21.0	20.0
Asian	n/a	3.5	1.0	13.0*
Native American	n/a	0.2	2.0	n/a
Other	0.6	0.1	1.0	n/a

Sources: Homeless Overview Study Task Force 1989; U.S. Bureau of the Census 1990; U.S. Conference of Mayors 1994, 68.

*Includes Asian and other

**Other estimates taken from homeless studies performed in Chicago arrive at slightly different levels of race and ethnic differences. Sosin, Colson, and Grossman's (1988, 30) study of 527 homeless persons revealed a composition of 69 percent African American, 19.4 percent white, 9.2 Hispanics, and 2.1 percent other. In Rossi's (1989, 123) weighted total, combining street and shelter samples (*N*=722), Chicago's homeless were, 5.5 percent Hispanic white, 1.4 percent Hispanic black, 53.0 percent black, 5.1 percent American Indian, 0.7 percent Asian or Pacific Islander, 30.7 percent white, and 3.3 percent other. In Rossi's sample, including his examination of numerous homeless samples around the country, American Indians constituted the largest overrepresented segment of the population compared to the Chicago Indian census population (0.1 percent).

Americans. As pointed out in chapter 2, cities are not neutral spaces for redevelopment with "all citizens" in mind, but instead are ethnically and racially charged, within a class and gendered context. A downtown is not simply a "downtown," but a social space in which some particular segments of the population are catered to, given privilege, over other segments, according to the prevailing social imaginaries of city leaders in conjunction with the structural attributes of social-physical space.

Negotiations between the social-physical spaces of the homeless and those of the housed occur daily on street corners, in front of stores, across parking lots, and in passing on city sidewalks. These negotiations occur within a racialized, class, and gendered social-physical space, quite often of white male and female inclusion and "minority" male and female exclusion. At one level, to be a black or white homeless person is to be the "Other" in the eyes of those who are housed. The housed accord similar degrees of marginality to people living on the street, regardless of their skin color. However, at a second level, race, ethnic, and gender differences do constitute a factor in discrimination. Homeless women and children are accorded different treatment than are homeless men. Homeless families are preserved and acted upon differently than are single homeless persons.

In Chicago, city redevelopment has focused primarily on the downtown Loop, the North Side, the Near South Side, and the Near West Side. These projects include the upper-income Presidential Towers residential project, a proposed casino complex, Navy Pier renovations, the United Center sports arena, the McCormick Place convention center expansion, and the Central Station–Dearborn Park luxury residences. Due to increased land speculation in the southern part of the downtown Loop, single-room-occupancy (SRO) units, the last housing options before shelters—such as the St. James Hotel, the New Ritz Hotel, the Carter Hotel (now the New 7th Street Hotel), the Roosevelt Hotel, and the Ewing Annex—are threatened with extinction. The St. James Hotel, containing 186 units, is at the center of a rapidly gentrifying area. Other SROs south of the Loop, such as Hotel 830 and the Rialto Hotel, remain unaffordable or are not operating.

The most unsavory kinds of SROs, including "cage" hotels and flophouses, historically have provided housing for the marginally employed and unemployed. Many SROs once located on the Near North Side, the Near West Side, and on the Near South Side, just south of the Loop have vanished under urban renewal bulldozers. The decline, by the 1970s, of earlier transient-worker populations, many of whom had been the main occupants of SROs, combined with gentrification and redevelopment, accelerated the decline of Chicago's SROs; most units were decimated by the 1980s (Marcuse 1989; Thomas and Wright 1990; Kasinitz 1986). New SRO units have been established on the North Side in the community areas of Uptown and Edgewater, but not nearly enough to make up for the current need.[5] Since 1975, about 20,000 SRO units have been lost in the city of Chicago (Wright 1992; Hoch and Slayton 1989). There are now only 13,500 SRO units (U.S. Conference of Mayors 1994, 69); one-fourth of these are located downtown. Of those households in Chicago's downtown Loop, 45 percent are considered single households, and of these 16.7 percent are living in SROs.

Downtown redevelopment plans in San Jose have included the development of 4 million gross square feet of new office space, 850 additional hotel rooms, 3,600 new dwelling units, 400,000 gross square feet of retail space, a proposed, publicly funded, baseball stadium to house the San Francisco Giants, the San Jose Sharks hockey arena, and a downtown convention center. Many of the area's homeless, who had made their homes along the banks of the Guadalupe River and in downtown shelters, have been forced to the margins of the city by this redevelopment. Many working poor renters who reside in the downtown area are also being pushed east and south of the downtown area as land values and rents increase. The destruction of the Terry Hotel in 1989, to make way for the adjacent San Jose Opera House, eliminated one of the last major SRO hotels for the downtown poor.

In Chicago and San Jose, as in other American cities, housing and homeless advocates have resisted SRO destruction, gentrification, and displacement. The Chicago Coalition for the Homeless successfully struggled to secure 165 low-cost housing units in the upper-income Presidential Towers, won 1,014 project-based Section 8 certificates, forced the resumption of donations to the City of Chicago's Low-Income Trust Housing, fought police sweeps of Lower Wacker Drive and O'Hare Airport, campaigned for the 21,000-plus Illinois homeless youth, and contested the exclusion of the very poor from the new South Loop development projects, such as Central Station and Dearborn Park.[6] Resistance in San Jose has been led by many housing and activist groups. The San Jose Student-Homeless Alliance (SHA) has been one of the most vocal in defending the rights of the homeless. Integrating homeless individuals, students, and community activists, the SHA protested police sweeps of downtown encampments in 1989 and city council redevelopment plans in 1990. The SHA also engaged in large housing takeovers involving over fifty people from 1991 to the present in an attempt to move the city to alter its redevelopment policies.

Chicago

Like many older industrial cities, Chicago has experienced a net outflow of manufacturing positions and an increase in positions associated with finance, insurance, real estate, business services, and retail trade. Though much of the region's job growth is occurring in the collar suburbs, commuters daily clog the Eisenhower, Dan Ryan, and Kennedy Expressways commuting into Chicago's city center. During the 1970s and 1980s, many middle- and working-class whites moved to the suburbs to take advantage of better schools, lower taxes, and increased job opportunities. For the poor who stayed behind, life has taken on an increasingly desperate tone.

Chicago has a high rate of uneven development; many poor neighborhoods are segregated from wealthy North Side and downtown neighborhoods. City investments are primarily directed toward the privileged central business district as opposed to the surrounding neighborhoods. Examining the areas of the Near South Side and the Near West Side provides an opportunity to demonstrate how this inequality expands and reproduces, accenting widespread economic, racial, and spatial polarization, often extremely localized, contributing to increased rates of homelessness. Overall, Chicago's median household income, including singles and families, increased only slightly between 1979 and 1990. However, Chicago's median family income declined from $31,469 in 1979, to $30,707 in 1989, indicating increased impoverishment among families. Uneven development, the privileging of certain areas of the city, namely the central business district, for increased redevelopment funds and the past politics of racial segregation have produced a very high degree of economic and racial polarization by geographic area.

Chicago's investment strategies in pleasure spaces—the "Magnificent Mile" of North Michigan Avenue,[7] the fashionable townhouses of Lincoln Park and condos of Streeterville, and the newly refurbished Navy Pier[8]—have focused on retaining wealthier, urban taxpayers and attracting young suburbanites into the city through the development of cultural capital, "pleasure spaces," in the form of festivals, entertainment centers, upgraded cultural facilities, redesigned city landscapes, and new luxury housing. From 1979 to 1990 the primary areas for such public and private investments were in the Loop ($3,715.8 million), Streeterville and along North Michigan Avenue ($1,844.3 Million), the West Loop/River West ($987.4 million), and the East Loop ($820.8 million) areas (Ludgin 1989, 39). The South Loop area received $708.7 million in public investment during this time period.[9] Though most private investment has occurred in the northern part of Chicago, over $5 million from banks, savings and loans, and mortgage banks were invested in southern areas of the Loop (census tracts 3205, 3201) and the northern census tracts of the Near South Side (census tracts 3302, 3301) (Woodstock Institute 1993) in 1991. How both public and private investment in redevelopment operate in specific locales of Chicago is important for understanding how social-physical space assumes particular shapes with particular consequences for populations who live within their borders. After discussing labor market data and the general vision for the city of Chicago embraced by the "growth network," I will focus on changes occurring in the communities of the Near South Side, the Loop, and the Near West Side relevant to the production of homelessness.

Changing Chicago Visions

Almost a century ago, Daniel H. Burnham (1846–1912) envisioned Chicago as a workable city, a "city of big shoulders," developed during a period of rapid industrialization, slaughterhouses, factories and belching smokestack industries, of labor organizing, and robber baron violence. The social imaginary of technical progress, rational organization, and capital accumulation mixed with enforced disciplinary work hierarchies. Enduring the Great Fires of 1871 and 1874, Chicago provided a proving ground for new innovations in planning and design. Supported by members of the Progressive movement, Burnham's plans, carried out in the designs of the World Columbian Exposition of 1893 and later expressed in the Chicago Plan of 1909, represented a vision in which "the chaotic city, that had arisen through too-rapid growth and too-rich mixture of nationalities, would be given order by cutting through new thoroughfares, removing slums, and extending parks" (Hall 1988, 179). Lake Michigan and Grant Park would become Chicago's front yard, a waterfront playground for city residents. This imposition of aesthetic order, inspired by Baron von Haussman's class reconfiguration of Paris in the 1800s, blended nicely with upper- and middle-class fears of urban disorder; design became a way to safely contain ethnic working class struggles. Such containments, when applied to Chicago, while directed at urban class-based movements, were also a product of ethnic fear and nativist reactions against "foreign" outsiders—mostly particularly ethnic whites, such as Poles, Italians, depending upon the years of immigration. This fear was later extended to urban blacks after their migration north en masse during the early twentieth century and during the 1940s.

Unlike many other cities, including Washington, D.C., and San Francisco, where such grand visions were often defeated by commercial lobbying, Chicago grew and developed in a manner not unlike that desired by Burnham. Burnham's notions of Europeanized American cities arose, however, within a political economy that depended on the growth and expansion of industrial manufacturing. Today that growth has shifted from manufacturing to services, with the consequence that both city visions and city realities are also shifting. Yet the underlying assumptions about what a locale should "look like" still remain very close to Burnham's planned preoccupation with aesthetics. If anything, the focus on aesthetics has grown stronger as the labor composition of the downtown area and immediate surrounding communities have shifted to emphasizing cultural capital, consumption, and finance activities.

Chicago's transition to a service economy has been slow but steady (Squires, Bennett, McCourt, and Nyden 1987, 23–61; Wintermute and Hicklin 1991; Lawrence 1990) (table 3.2).

Table 3.2

Percentage Employment by Industry, City of Chicago, 1990

	N	1990 (%)	1980–90 (%)
Construction	45,405	3.8	+0.8
Manufacturing	225,307	18.7	−7.5
Transportation	75,234	6.2	−0.2
Communications, public utilities	28,066	2.3	−0.2
Wholesale trade	54,162	4.5	+0.2
Retail trade	181,353	15.0	+0.7
Finance, insurance, and real estate	110,841	9.2	+1.2
Business and repair services	74,203	6.1	+1.3
Personal, entertainment, and recreation services	57,898	4.8	+1.2
Professional and related services	287,992	23.9	+4.2
Public administration	60,564	5.0	−0.3

Sources: U.S. Bureau of the Census, *Census of Population and Housing,* 1980; U.S. Bureau of the Census, *Census of Population and Housing,* Summary Tape File 3A, 1990.

During the 1980s Chicago's economy lost 93,647 residents who worked in manufacturing and 11,433 residents who worked in public administration. However, 44,405 residents were added who worked in professional and related services, boosting Chicago's economy, accompanied by 10,789 in finance, insurance, and real estate, 14,494 in business and repair services, and 13,872 working in personal, entertainment, and recreation services. Much of the growth in professional and related services was in the educational and health fields. Clearly, the Chicago of the 1990s would not be the Chicago of the 1970s.

The movement from Chicago's aging industrial past to the hypermodern service city had begun. While the service sector has boosted job growth, it has not been sufficient to compensate for the decline of the manufacturing sector. In addition, unlike the union-level wages paid in the manufacturing sector, the newly developing service sector pays lower wages overall, demands higher levels of education, and is increasingly operating with greater numbers of part-time, contingent workers. While higher levels of education are demanded, actual wages, relative to the median, will most probably decline as more contingent work is promoted. For those with lower levels of education, few skills, and little mobility, future job prospects are very bleak. High-paying, entry-level union wages are declining, leaving those without college educations competing for scarce positions. Even for those with a college degree, entry-level jobs will not pay at the level they would have paid 20 years ago. Without good-paying entry-level positions for those with little education, economic and social polarization will increase, and in Chicago that polarization most often happens along race and gender lines. Chicago's homeless population remains at the bottom of a pyramid of declining job opportunities. Many with disabilities and reduced skills therefore constitute a population that is no longer needed or wanted in the city economy—an "expendable" population that is dispersed over the city landscape as so much chafe in the wind.

In Chicago between 1980 and 1990, blue-collar occupations, such as operators, fabricators, and laborers, have gone into drastic decline, while white-collar jobs, such as managerial and professional occupations, have greatly increased (table 3.3).

Table 3.3

Percentage Employment by Occupations, City of Chicago, 1980–1990[10]

	N (1980)	N (1990)	1990 (%)	1980–90 (%)
Managerial and professional specialty	245,887	300,246	25.0	+5.2
Technical, sales and administrative support	405,605	398,444	32.7	−0.1
Service occupations	177,727	182,737	15.2	+0.9
Precision production, craft, and repair	122,487	107,131	8.9	−1.0
Operators, fabricators, and laborers	280,441	212,643	17.6	−5.0

Sources: U.S. Bureau of Census, Population and Housing Characteristics, 1980. U.S. Bureau of Census, Population and Housing Characteristics, Summary Tape File 3A, 1990.

While the number of service jobs has only increased by 0.9 percent between 1980 and 1990, the number of positions in managerial and professional specializations has increased by 5.2 percent. This major shift in city occupations has radical implications for the type of city Chicago will become, the type of vision that is now altering Chicago's topography. Indeed, 40 percent of downtown jobs are in finance, insurance, professional services, and public administration, 20 percent are in retailing (Reardon 1995, 13). What are even more disturbing are the internal changes in technical, sales, and administrative support positions. Between 1980 and 1990, only 5,400 positions in technical and support services were added while sales positions increased by 23,265. Those positions available in administrative support, including clerical, however, decreased by 35,826. Clearly the moving of many companies to outlying suburban areas has also meant a draining away of those who work in support capacities and clerical positions. Office automation has also contributed to clerical downsizing. These developments are occurring in middle-class, white-collar occupations following the downsizing of manufacturing positions in Chicago during the 1970s.

One consequence of the loss of many clerical and administrative support personnel is the drop in requirements for office space in the central business district. The speculative overbuilding of offices during the 1980s is now accompanied by high office vacancy rates, although there is some evidence that vacancy rates may be decreasing in the mid 1990s. From 1989 to the present, vacancy rates in the downtown Loop area rose from 14.6 percent to 19.9 percent (Smith, 1994, 43). National office vacancy rates stand at 15 percent, although cities like Dallas and Los Angeles have rates of 35.3 percent and 23.2 percent, respectively (Laing 1996, 34). As corporate downsizing continues, requirements for office space will also shrink in size and quantity as office development moves to the suburbs.[11]

Exotically designed office buildings, developed by "star" architects and real estate firms, compete for corporate attention in a glutted market. Like other products, offices are increasingly marked by their commodity status in a downtown market where product differentiation replaces funtionality. Downtown offices are developed as "hot" addresses or as "fashionable" locations, while suburban offices stress the functional requirements of labor and management. This spatial development of downtown architecture as "symbolic" architecture is consistent with a central business district that is changing into a pleasure space for consumption.

Some Chicago office buildings have been vacant for months. The One North Franklin building, owned by Equity Office Properties, was 85 percent vacant in 1992, although it has since achieved a 91 percent occupancy rate. The Chicago Title & Trust Building, completed in 1992, one of the last Chicago skyscrapers to be completed in the Loop, suffered a 45 percent vacancy rate until its acquisition by Equity Office Properties, the owners of One North Franklin, in 1995. It remains to be seen if the low vacancy rate can be turned around in a glutted market. In an effort to increase occupancy rates for Chicago Title & Trust, Chris Wood, vice president of regional leasing for Equity Office Properties, exclaimed, "We're going to market the building to image-conscious and top-of-the-line tenants such as foreign banks, law firms, and consulting firms" (Briggs 1995, 1). Vacancy rates will probably decrease over time as the service sector continues to expand and marketing campaigns increase, but the high rates are indicative of overinvestment in office space during the 1980s. The Loop alone, accounting for 66.4 percent of all central area office space, expanded from 38.6 million square feet to 77.4 million square feet, a 49 percent increase from 1970 to 1990 (Ludgin 1989, 41). Conversely, the South Loop area witnessed a dramatic drop in office space from 2.7 million square feet to 0.9 million square feet, due to company flight and area deterioration.

Clerical positions and manufacturing positions associated with operators, fabricators, and laborers are common routes of entry into the workforce, but those entry-level positions for low-skill workers are now rapidly disappearing. The losses of manufacturing jobs is most dramatic. The number of Chicago residents working as machine operators, assemblers, and inspectors decreased by 43,165 during the 1980s; the number working as handlers, equipment cleaners, helpers, and laborers decreased by 13,386. Not only are fewer residents working in lower-level clerical positions, but there are also fewer working in entry-level manufacturing positions. Clearly, given these bleak job prospects and the difficulty inner-city residents have in traveling to suburban jobs, the economies that are flourishing in economically depressed areas are criminal and shadow economies. With a net loss of population to the collar suburbs, Chicago attracts large numbers of suburbanites who return to the city every day to work in the downtown areas. Therefore the figures indicating the occupational changes for those who are living in the city might underestimate the actual job growth in the FIRE sectors in the city. But it is clear that the bulk of economic growth is happening outside of the city in the surrounding suburbs.

What are the implications of these changes in Chicago's economy for worker wages and the ability to afford housing and services? Will these lead to higher rates of homelessness among the working and nonworking poor? How does the process of redevelopment facilitate these changes? Wage rates by economic sector will have a direct impact on the very poor, both in their ability to find decent housing and in their ability to find employment that pays a livable wage. With a decline in manufacturing and a subsequent loss in high-paying union jobs, and with the increase of lower-paying service-sector jobs, the ability to pay steadily increasing rents becomes more and more difficult. The sample of Chicago-area wages listed in table 3.4 illustrates the extremely wide range of incomes in the Chicago area. Clearly, those with upper-level wages in the professional, managerial, and technical fields are on the ascent; persons working at low-skilled labor are at a clear disadvantage in the new, hypermodern Chicago.

Table 3.4

Pay for Selected Occupations in Chicago, Illinois, Metropolitan Area, 1991

	MEDIAN WEEKLY PAY	MIDDLE-RANGE PAY
Accountant	$672	$568– 830
Attorney	$1,357	$1,089–1,702
Engineer	$908	$751–1,107
Registered nurse	$591	$539– 636
Computer programmer	$672	$587– 783
Nursing assistant	$232	$196– 268
Computer operator	$464	$399– 528
General clerk	$330	$288– 390
Key entry operator	$316	$273– 359
Secretary	$470	$408– 544
Accounting clerk	$372	$329– 432
	MEDIAN HOURLY PAY	**MIDDLE-RANGE PAY**
General maintenance worker	$10.90	$9.77–11.96
Tool and die maker	$18.10	$16.70–19.39
Guard	$5.75	$5.00– 7.25
Janitor	$7.65	$5.40–10.10

Source: U.S. Department of Labor, Bureau of Labor Statistics, *Occupational Compensation Survey: Pay and Benefits: Chicago, Illinois, Metropolitan Area, May 1991.*

Given the wide disparities in incomes by sector and the decline of union manufacturing jobs paying high wages, the demand for lower-paid service workers conflicts with a housing market that is rapidly pricing many out of both owners' and renters' markets. The changing labor market reflects the trend toward a larger service sector, unlike manufacturing, where one could acquire skills on the job and move up the career ladder to a secure position paying high union wages, the service sector is noted for not providing on the job training for higher level positions and therefore holds little promise for career advancement (Wintermute and Hickline 1991; Spilerman 1977). Between 1988 and the year 2000, service occupations are expected to add 173,200 workers to the state of Illinois, most of them (63,200) in food and beverage preparation services (State of Illinois 1992), traditionally a low-paying industry. In addition, the trend toward contingent part-time work makes it difficult for marginal workers to maintain a steady income even if some service positions may pay higher wages. Advanced education is required for upward mobility, but the tremendous problems in the Chicago school system make it difficult for the poor to get adequate education.

Race and gender disparities are widespread within Chicago's labor market. According to Wintermute and Hicklin (1991) "Nine of the ten industries with the highest percentage of women are service industries" (152). In contrast, men dominate manufacturing and five service industries. The expansion of Chicago's service economy can offer increased opportunities for women, but the low wages and contingent nature of service work prevents women from acquiring the same benefits as men. Hispanics dominate manufacturing and sales; African Americans dominate eight out of ten service sector industries: U.S. postal service, private households, railroads, other transportation, communications, public administration, hospitals, and other personal services (152). Whites are the majority in the advanced corporate services, public education, entertainment, and transportation industries. African Americans make up the largest segment of workers in middle-level service occupations. Hispanics employed in services make up the majority of food service industry workers, clerks, mechanics and repair work, and cleaning and building maintenance. These positions all suffer from low pay, unlike the blue-collar jobs of yesteryear (Wiewel 1990, 41). Women and African Americans "are concentrated primarily in occupations at the middle and lower ends of service sector employment" (Wintermute and Hicklin 1991, 154). These sectors of service employment are the most susceptible to reorganization and elimination (corporate downsizing).

With the majority of minority workers and women employed in the service sector, local changes in the economy, often boosted by global economic changes, can have drastic effects on incomes and therefore the worker's ability to remain housed. Multinational development companies and service-sector industries such as major hotel chains can dictate local city development policies by offering or withdrawing development capital and promising employment and construction contracts in a given local area. If turned down, they have many other places to invest.

With job expansion in the suburban collar counties, minorities and women must be able to commute to outlying jobs and attain higher levels of education if they are able to escape "dead end" service-sector employment. Conversely, concerted efforts must be made to bring good entry-level jobs back to Chicago to provide the necessary stepping stones to success for the city's poor. Attracting professionals, administrators, and management will not subsequently attract entry-level positions, since many companies now "farm out" their lower-level administrative operations to distant suburban or out-of-state locations connected with the main office through extensive communication and computer networks. Failure to bring entry-level positions with a clear career ladder into Chicago will simply increase the already high levels of poverty in the city, contributing to increased crime and health problems and an expanded set of polarized topographies.

The inability of African American men to find unskilled and skilled work at good pay can be traced to one of the factors in the production of homelessness. With only several exceptions, all of the homeless men interviewed in Chicago's Tranquility City had parents who had worked in blue-collar occupations. The decline in manufacturing jobs, jobs that paid well but required only minimal skills, has left those with few skills in the new economy at a distinct disadvantage. Sons and daughters of blue-collar workers can no longer expect to follow their fathers and mothers into union industrial jobs. With only low-level, low-skilled, low-pay service work to look forward to, combined with a weak public educational system and a contracting housing market, many African American and Hispanic males are at extreme risk of homelessness and job loss.

While some can and choose to pay excessive amounts for rent, others, earning lower wages have very little choice in the matter. Those working in professional, administrative, and technical occupations are easily able to afford the median rents for Chicago. The same cannot be said for those who form the backbone of the service industry. Paying more than 30 percent of one's monthly income for rent is considered by the Department of Housing and Urban Development to be paying an excessive amount. According to the Department of Housing and Urban Development (1993) the median gross rents for household renters in metropolitan Chicago was $506 a month in 1991. Using the $506 a month as a guide, and referring to the middle-range incomes listed in table 3.4, the 10,251 accounting clerks will pay between 27 and 36 percent of their income each month on rents.[12] 8,981 general clerks would pay between 30 and 41 percent. Secretaries as a whole are paying a maximum of 29 percent of their income for rent; however, beginning secretaries at Level I may pay as much as 35 percent.

Workers in manufacturing-related industries, such as tool and die makers, are generally unionized and have fewer problems paying rent.

However, workers at the low end of occupations related to materials movement and custodial work, such as janitors and guards, are at a clear disadvantage. The 16,166 Chicago janitors, porters, and cleaners pay between 29 and 55 percent of their incomes for rent, and the 19,010 security guards spend between 41 and 60 percent. Single parents who are poor are at an even greater disadvantage, since they require larger rental units to house their children and therefore must pay higher rent. In 1990, when Chicago's median gross rent was $445, only 15.4 percent of rental units were affordable to the Chicago households earning less than 30 percent of the median family income of $30,707. Not only are wages for unskilled labor insufficient to keep up with housing costs, but good low-cost housing is also in serious short supply.

The total number of rental units in the city declined 10.1 percent between 1980 and 1990 (City of Chicago 1994, 7). Of Chicago's total of 1,025,174 occupied units, 58.5 percent are rental units. The number of studios and one-bedroom units declined by 12.4 percent between 1980 and 1990. The number of four-bedroom rental units declined even more, at 16.9 percent for the same time period. The decline in numbers of large rental units has placed an unfair burden on low-income family renters, while the decline in numbers of studio and one-bedroom units has forced competition over a limited supply of low cost units for singles. The effects of this contracting housing market are increased overcrowding, family stress, and ultimately homelessness, as those least able to pay are shunted to the streets.

It is tempting to assume that Chicago's past high vacancy rates mark a vibrant and rich housing market and that overcrowding was simply a transitory phenomenon. City housing vacancy rates increased 33.8 percent between 1980 and 1990. However, according to a rental survey conducted by Grubb & Ellis, average vacancy rates dropped from 4.3 percent in 1994 to 2.7 percent in 1996 (Allen 1996, 1), accompanied by 6.6 percent increase in rents in 1996. Previous causes of high vacancy rates in Chicago may be traced to aging housing stock, since most housing is over 40 years old, not simply more affordable housing or outmigration from the city. Much of Chicago's housing for the poor is in extreme disrepair. In addition, new rental housing is designed not for very-low-income families but for low- and middle-income families and single persons. Judgments of very-low (0–50 percent of median family income [MFI]), low (51–80 percent of MFI), and moderate (81–95 percent MFI) incomes for the City of Chicago[13] are established based upon the Chicago Primary Metropolitan Statistical Area (PMSA) median family income of $41,745, which includes the larger metropolitan area surrounding Chicago. The median family income of $30,707 for the city center is a more accurate measure of Chicago incomes. The difference is the difference between constructing units for very-low-income families affordable to families making up to $20,872 a year (using PMSA Median Family Incomes), versus constructing units for families making up to $15,353 a year (using MFI figure for the city of Chicago). Even so, fully 76 percent of those renters making 0–30 percent of the (PMSA) median family income pay excessive amounts of rent. The city chooses to use the PMSA figure.

Clearly, for many Chicago families and individuals, even very-low income units are not affordable. According to city officials, there are insufficient units that are affordable and of the right size for Chicago's population. They admit that "excessive cost burdens and overcrowded conditions" have led to this condition: "The combination of declining incomes and increasing housing costs have created substantial market inefficiencies. Vacant units at all levels of affordability are not sufficient to meet the demand for affordable, decent and uncrowded units" (City of Chicago 1994, iv).[14]

The housing of last resort for Chicago's poor, before shelters and SRO units, is public housing. The high vacancy rate of 15.5 percent for Chicago's public housing reflects the very poor physical condition and location of units. The Chicago Public Housing Authority (CHA) has a total of 40,000 units and 26,967 households on its waiting list. Homeless persons are given priority on the waiting lists. All "Tranquility City" residents were able to secure housing in CHA buildings after they were forced from their encampments by the city of Chicago.

Given the conditions of social and economic polarization within a restricted housing market, how does Chicago's vision of a "workable" city fit into these dynamic societal changes? For whom is Chicago building? Are considerations of affordable low-cost housing built into developer plans for all areas of the city, not just selected communities? While plans clearly change with political winds and pragmatic considerations, examining the vision of "growth networks," of what Chicago movers and shakers imagine Chicago should look like, what type of city Chicago should be, is helpful in understanding the relationship between redevelopment and homelessness. To understand Chicago's changing topography, we must examine the heir to Burnham's general plan, the Chicago 21: A Plan for Central Area Communities.

The Chicago 21 Plan, a corporate vision of downtown Chicago promoted by the Chicago Central Area Committee (CCAC) in 1973, was framed within the context of an anticipated increase in leisure and consumption activities, corresponding to a predicted shift from manufacturing to services. The CCAC, heavily dominated by business elites, with some community representation, has a fairly typical class composition for business-oriented urban regimes. The Chicago 21 Plan, which has been the cornerstone for all city development since 1973, states, "The vision of the future is of tightly knit communities in the heart of the City with widely diverse options for the use of leisure time and with plentiful close-in open space" (City of Chicago 1973, 10).

As a plan designed to increase the degree of visible, aesthetically designed spaces, the Chicago 21 Plan was surprisingly quiet on issues of race and class. Language is couched in aesthetic terms, with concern for the visual and traffic attributes of the landscape considered paramount. Two areas the plan examined were the former railroad yards at the south end of Grant Park and the abandoned yards further west, next to the Chicago River. The six-hundred acres of vacant land, formerly property of the Rock Island, the Illinois Central, and the Illinois Central-Gulf Railroads, between Michigan Avenue and the waterfront, were destined for a "new family living environment." The south end of Grant Park is also a prime summer sleeping location for many of Chicago's downtown homeless. It has now become the location for the market-rate housing units of Central Station–Burnham Place.

The Chicago 21 Plan also argued for the development of a South Loop New Town, which was expected to contain 15,000 new housing units by 1985 (City of Chicago 1973, 3). While not quite on schedule, South Loop New Town is beginning to take shape in the redevelopment plans for the South Loop area. However, the plan increasingly appears to be aimed at excluding persons of undesirable appearance or income. The city of Chicago, according to Betancur, Bennett, and Wright (1991, 204), is now designed as a fortress city, "aimed to redevelop the land that circled a booming service sector downtown for middle- and upper-class residents." The creation of a "buffer zone" between middle- and upper-class residents and the poor was predicated on forcing the poor out of the areas they already occupied on the Near North Side, the Near South Side, and the Near West Side. This proposal did not go uncontested by community organizations. However, initial protests against the plan were diffused as community groups became absorbed in their own local issues. The catalyst that revived their interest in city planning was the attempt by the city of Chicago to host the 1992 World's Fair, a plan that was ultimately defeated.

With the decimation of Chicago's union-wage manufacturing economy during the late 1970s and early 1980s, community opposition

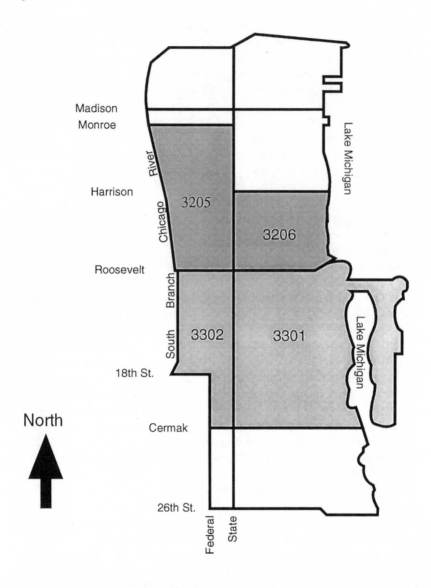

Map 3.1 *City of Chicago, Downtown Loop and Near South Side*

shifted to focus more closely on the relationship between neighborhood and downtown investments. While pressuring the city for increased funding in their neighborhoods, emerging community coalitions
pressed for more economic development allocations. Urban Develop-

ment Action Grants (UDAG), initiated by the Carter administration and funneled through the cities, were utilized by Chicago to further the aims of the Chicago 21 plan during the 1980s (Betancur, Bennett, and Wright 1991, 205).

According to Giloth and Betancur (1988, 237–38), between 1979 and 1986 Chicago spent 42 percent of its UDAG funds on downtown projects and only 17 percent on manufacturing. UDAGs were used for loft conversions in the South Loop area and commercial/office lofts in the West Loop area. During the Reagan years, federal funding for community development projects and affordable housing were reduced, even as city corporate developers continued to push ahead with the Chicago 21 Plan. Mayor Harold Washington, during his brief reign, attempted to reverse many of the investment priorities of Chicago, but the need remained overwhelming and the resources meager. Even though the 1986 defeat of the 1992 World's Fair proposal brought together many diverse community organizations, the lack of real federal dollars insured that, in relation to corporate spending, such groups would lack overall clout with city redevelopers. Even though small victories were won—such as the promotion of linked development in which private developers assisted Chicago with limited public development in exchange for privileged private development, the establishment of the low-income housing trust fund and various legislative changes, such as the changes to the housing tax delinquency regulations—the overall impact of organized community opposition on the direction of corporate plans for Chicago remained weak. With the granting of new federal dollars for economic empowerment zones under the Clinton administration, new possibilities have opened for Chicago to apportion the funds to the community. Whether or not city elites will be persuaded to do this remains an open question and a source of struggle between communities and city officials.

Polarized Topographies I: The Near South Side/South Loop

There are many local polarized topographies throughout Chicago; the accelerated redevelopment of the Near South Side/South Loop area is especially noteworthy for its scale and speed of changes. The Near South Side, and specifically the South Loop area extending south of Jackson Street to Roosevelt Road, is currently the site of intense redevelopment. Understanding the changing demographics of this area and the transformed social-physical space prompted by redevelopment investments allows us to witness the dynamics of displacement, and therefore of the preconditions for homelessness.

Because much of current redevelopment is occurring close to the downtown Loop, I have chosen four census tracts (3206, 3205, 3301, 3302) (map 3.1), encompassing parts of the Loop and the Near South Side (the major sections of what is known as the "South Loop"), for an in-depth examination. This area is the former home of Printer's Row, abandoned railroad yards, light industry, the Dearborn railway station, the south end of Grant Park, the Chicago Mercantile Exchange, luxury residential complexes of River City, single-room-occupancy hotels, the Pacific Garden Mission, and flophouses. Often thought of as a "zone in transition," following the classical model of urban ecology, the South Loop comprises a curious mixture of developing residential pleasure spaces and what city officials define as "blighted" areas or created refuse places, a borderland from which one can detect future city visions. Facilities that serve the South Loop's poor are now sandwiched between the redevelopment "pleasure" residential projects of Dearborn Place to the west, Roosevelt Road improvements in the middle, and Central Station "pleasure" residential developments to the east.

The increased numbers of people who have moved into these four census tract areas mask trends of racial and class displacement. Since 1980, the majority population in this area, African Americans, have been increasingly supplanted by whites. While the number of African Americans (N=5,763 in 1990) increased by 22 percent from 1980, the number of whites (N=5,054) grew by 52.8 percent. The number of Asians (N=544 in 1990) has grown 87.7 percent since 1980, the fastest growth rate of all racial/ethnic groups in the area.

Clearly, at the current rate of growth, and given the fact that redevelopment is proceeding without adequate provisions for the very poor, whites will quickly overtake African Americans as the majority population in this area. Greater numbers of professionals, sales, technicians, and service persons (table 3.5) are moving into the area, increasing the area's median income, while others associated with manufacturing are moving out. For the remaining working poor, who are a paycheck away from homelessness, and those living in SRO's, the rapid increase in rents and a decline in income can have disastrous effects.

The outflow of occupations associated with manufacturing has been occurring since the 1970s; those workers remaining in low-income occupations will find it extremely difficult to secure decent low-cost housing in the South Loop area to match their income. For those living in the SROs along State Street, Clark Street, and Wabash Avenue, the situation looks even more desperate, because little replacement housing is being planned in the area to accommodate their needs. High-salaried

Table 3.5

Occupational Employment for Combined Census Tracts, South Loop, 1990*

	N	1980–90 (%)
Executive, administrative, managerial	1,438	+83.6
Professional speciality	1,416	+67.6
Technicians and support	255	+71.8
Sales	785	+81.0
Administrative support, clerical	1,000	+47.2
Private household	17	+100.0
Protective services	132	+71.2
Services, except protective and household	330	−21.1
Precision production, craft, and repair	145	−1.4
Machine operators, assemblers, inspectors	65	−70.8
Transportation, material movers	45	−55.4
Handlers, cleaners, helpers, and laborers	84	−4.5

Source: U.S. Bureau of Census, Centers of Population and Housing, Summary Tape File 3A, Illinois, Adams County-Cook County. 1990.

* This includes census tract data from tracts 3301, 3302, 3205, and 3206. I have excluded the occupational category for farming, forestry, and fishing because the numbers were very low and there was very little change between 1980 and 1990.

executives, sales, and administrative support people are moving in. It is the upper-income tier of these occupations to which the new development plans for the South Loop are now directed.

However, the aggregate features of these four census tracts, while clearly showing patterns of gentrification and displacement, cannot capture the internal dynamics happening at the micro level in the South Loop. By examining briefly each of the quadrants, divided north and south by State Street and east and west by Roosevelt Road, we can better understand the potential for displacement as a product of Chicago's redevelopment plans. For example, of all the quadrants, the northwest quadrant (tract 3205) has witnessed the most changes since 1980. Home to the luxury housing of River City, built in 1986, renovated Dearborn Station, and the Pacific Garden Mission, the northwest quadrant experienced an 88.6 percent increase in median family income since 1980 and an 86 percent increase in median rents. By 1990 median family income for the area had increased to $68,594. Median rents had increased to $843 a month. Of the 5,233 people who currently live in this area, 246 are in emergency shelters (Pacific Garden Mission) and 714 are in correctional institutions. Of all the quadrants, the northwest quadrant has the lowest overall poverty rate (9.2 percent), a decrease from 1980 of 34.3 percent and the lowest percentage of female heads of households (16.7 percent). It also has the lowest rate for those paying more than 30 percent of their income for rent (6.6 percent).

Occupying an area bounded by Monroe Street, Roosevelt Road, the south fork of the Chicago River, and State Street, the northwest quadrant is prime development land for future "pleasure" spaces emerging along the banks of the Chicago River. Suggestions have been made that these new "pleasure" spaces include riverfront gambling casinos. Of all the four quadrants, the northwest tract experienced the largest increase in numbers of residents employed in executive, administrative, and managerial occupations, in professional occupations, in sales, and in clerical and administrative support occupations. Interestingly, the numbers of those employed in all service occupations, with the exception of protective services, decreased, as they did in all of the other tracts studied. Rapid declines were also noted in the numbers of residents employed in the manufacturing occupations, with the exception of about 42 handlers, equipment cleaners, helpers, and laborers who moved into the tract during the 1980s. All other tracts experienced a net decline in this group.

Racially, Asians and Pacific Islanders increased the fastest in tract 3205 (+83.4 percent) between 1980 and 1990, although they totaled only 247 individuals in 1990. From 1980 to 1990 whites grew at a rate of 67 percent numbering 3,754 individuals in 1990. While the number of blacks stood at 1,154 in 1990, a 54 percent increase from 1980, this was only about half the size of the white population. The other tract with a high rate of increase for whites, track 3302, is immediately south of the northwest quadrant. However, the rapid increase of whites in this area is offset by their small numbers (N=86 in 1990). While the 1,483 blacks in tract 3302 constituted the majority in 1990 they witnessed a 14.2 percent decline in their numbers from 1980.

Clearly, the development of housing in Dearborn Park and River City and the conversion of old manufacturing facilities into lofts and condos have had a decided change on the racial and class composition of the northwest quadrant. The redevelopment of abandoned railroad property south of Dearborn Station provided the opportunity to change the dynamics of the area. The decline of railroad activity in the area during the 1960s prompted calls for developing the South Loop area. Following the Chicago 21 Plan, the document *South Loop New Town: Guideline for Development* (City of Chicago 1975) outlined how the city intended to use such newly vacant land. Such large tracts of vacant land contrasted with poor housing in the area at the time. While the

South Loop plan called for adopting the Chicago 21 guidelines, to create an "in-town residential environment," the sole thrust for development was to be for "family living and available and primarily attractive to moderate- and middle-income families" (City of Chicago 1975, 11). Anticipating the construction of 13,000 dwelling units and an influx of 30,000 people the South Loop New Town, the plan also wished to "insure that there is equal opportunity for all to reside in and participate in the development of the South Loop area" (City of Chicago 1975, 11). Initiating this development, a segment of the local growth network put together $14 million in investment capital, negotiated with the railroads to purchase their abandoned property at $3.25 a square foot, and worked with architects Skidmore, Ownings & Merrill to draw up the initial plans for what would become a set of enclosed 6- to 11-story midrises, townhouses, and freestanding homes, complete with an enclosed park area.

With the exception of senior apartment units, almost the entire Dearborn Park development is made up of homeowner townhouses costing approximately $200,000 to $300,000. The political rhetoric of "equal opportunity for all to reside" seems to be contradicted by the realities of these housing development projects. The perception that the construction of Dearborn Park would become an island of white upper-income residents within an area housing predominantly poor African Americans was reflected in criticism the Dearborn Park Corporation received during the 1970s in response to the construction of its residential units. The security plan (Dearborn Park Corporation 1977) initially proposed for the residential units, between Harrison and Roosevelt, was criticized as creating a "white fortress," isolated from the outside community. The Pacific Garden Mission (fig. 3.1), housing primarily single African American homeless men, is located on State Street near Harrison, about two city blocks away from Dearborn Station. This was clearly reflected in the stated criteria for security: "Direct uncontrolled movement between communities, neighborhoods and clusters should be discouraged and if necessary not allowed" (Dearborn Park Corporation 1977, 9). The developers rebutted criticism from the city of Chicago with the assertion that while vehicular access will be restricted, pedestrian and bicycle access will be allowed.[15] Instead surveillance would be promoted through "natural surveillance" using informal monitoring and "sophisticated landscaping" to create defensible spaces.

From State Street one easily notices that almost every window facing the street of Dearborn Park is set high above the sidewalk, leaving blank walls facing the pedestrian. The distance between Dearborn

Figure 3.1 *The Pacific Garden Mission looking south on State Street. Dearborn Park is visible on the right, beyond the mission.*

Park residents and surrounding low-income families is clearly illustrated in the struggles over the opening of a nearby public elementary school in 1987. According to Bennett (1990), many Dearborn Park residents resented having to share the school with children from the nearby public housing projects; this was reflected in conflicts over the local school's "standards" (47). The city of Chicago spent $50 million between 1979 and 1990 for the entire South Loop area; private corporations spent $700 million. These public/private partnerships enabled the production of 36 residential units at Ninth and Wabash (Fairbanks Lofts, built in 1988), 84 rental units at Wells and Harrison across from River City (the Regal), and 225 new residential townhouses south of Roosevelt Road at Dearborn Park II. Rents range from a low of $700 a month at Fairbanks Lofts to $2,900 at River City. One of the reasons for the rapid demographic change in the northwest quadrant is because South Loop residential development began with the transformation of Printer's Row in the 1970s. Other conversions, such as the transformation of the South Loop YMCA into 281 rental units and the construction of the Dearborn Park Plaza, helped link Michigan Avenue to the east with Printer's Row (Ludgin 1989). A result of overall South Loop redevelopment is the displacement of 96 firms and the loss of 1,700 jobs since 1970 (Giloth and Betancur 1988, 281).

The transformation of the northwest quadrant foreshadows the future for tract 3302 immediately south of Roosevelt Road. The 1990 census does not capture the changes to this area in the past few years. With the construction of Dearborn Park II (fig. 3.2), 34 single family homes, 89 townhouses, and 92 condos will now occupy the area bordered by Roosevelt Road, State Street, Clark, and Fifteenth Street. With houses selling for between $425,000 and $495,000, it is clear that this neighborhood will experience a rapid rise in median income in the future. In the ten years prior to the construction of Dearborn Park II, the median family income had increased only 10.1 percent to $5,777 a year for the 1,569 people who lived here. However, median rents in the area jumped 63.7 percent to $135/month. Racially, the division falls between renters and owners—40 white households own their own homes, and 619 black households rent. A little under half the population (N=725) who live here and are between 16 and 64 years of age are disabled and not institutionalized. Unemployment in the area prior to 1990 was 50.9 percent. A small number of executives, administrators, and managers have moved into the area along with professionals; the

Figure 3.2 *Dearborn Park II townhouses, looking south on State Street.*

number of residents employed in sales, administrative support work, including clerical, service occupations, and manufacturing, has declined as in the other quadrants. Between 1980 and 1989 the percentage of residents at or below the poverty level increased 22.6 percent to 71.2 percent. Of the residents, 81.9 percent were female heads of households and 42.5 percent paid more than 30 percent of their income for rent. The majority of residents in this area were African American women, who will be forced out of the area as rents rise and as more moderate- and high-income housing is built. So one can ask, of what good is redevelopment for these citizens?

Between Harrison and Roosevelt, with State Street to the west and Lake Michigan to the east, the northeast quadrant (census tract 3206) is home for many who live in the last SROs in the South Loop, including the Roosevelt and the New Ritz (fig. 3.3). The area south of Harrison, along Wabash and State Street, has historically served as the city's red-light district, the location for honky-tonks, porn shops, and bars. Some of the last SROs in the area are increasing their rents or changing their policies on boarders. The former Carter Hotel, now the New 7th Hotel, adjacent to the Pacific Garden Mission, charges $70/week for rent, the New Ritz charges $12/night, and the Roosevelt Hotel, at the corner of Roosevelt and Wabash, charges $19/day. For those very-low-income persons who can scrape up the necessary funds, such hotels can provide the necessary housing often missing in more expensive units.

Declining for the past forty years, the northeast quadrant has begun to change with the infusion of redevelopment funds and the planning of new developments in the area. With a 1990 population of 1,878, the northeast quadrant is roughly equal in numbers of blacks and whites, although Blacks have increased 50 percent since 1980 while Whites have declined in the area by 2.6 percent. The count of people living in emergency shelters is 465. Since 1980, median family income has risen 51.2 percent in the area to $41,667, while median rent has increased 62.2 percent to $749/month. This can be explained by the changes in the labor market. Since 1980 the numbers of residents associated with managerial, professional, technical, sales, and administrative support occupations have increased while the numbers associated with manufacturing and service have declined quite dramatically. For example, the number of residents in executive, administrative, and managerial occupations jumped from 78 residents to 211, while the number of those working as machine operators, assemblers, or inspectors declined from 71 to 27. Residents left behind are either very poor or upper middle income. With a 12.3 percent unemployment rate in

Figure 3.3 *The New Ritz single-room-occupancy hotel on State Street, across from the Dearborn Park developments.*

1989, this area's poverty rate increased 48.8 percent, to 24.6 percent of the population. Of the residents, 35.4 percent are female heads of households. This area also has the highest rate (49.3 percent) of people paying more than 30 percent of their income for rent.

The major centers of redevelopment activity for this sector are along State and Wabash, from Harrison to Roosevelt Road, with many new projects initiated close to Harrison. With the redevelopment of buildings close to Buddy Guy's Legends Club and the promotion of cultural and artistic activities in the area, including the development of local art galleries, the northeast quadrant is preparing the ground for expanded commercial activity and for linking activities along the lakefront with the northwest quadrant (fig. 3.4).

The other major site for current redevelopment activity is south of Roosevelt Road in the southeast quadrant (census tract 3301). This area and the areas to the west of State street are sites of massive residential construction and rapid demographic changes. The southeast quadrant, home to the St. James Hotel, one of the last SROs, and the site of struggles between homeless activist groups and the city of Chicago, is undergoing profound change (fig. 3.5).

Extending from Roosevelt down to Cermack, the southeast quadrant is home to the new upper-income residential projects of Central

Figure 3.4 *Luxury lofts along Wabash Avenue, north of Roosevelt Road.*

Figure 3.5 *Roosevelt and Saint James single-room-occupancy hotels, looking south on Wabash Avenue.*

Station and numerous loft and condo conversions. Along Wabash Avenue are the offices of CCH, and just around the corner, to the north, are the offices of *Streetwise*, Chicago's homeless newspaper. Racially, the southeast quadrant contained 2,241 blacks and 259 whites in 1990. The number of black residents grew 22 percent between 1980 and 1990, matched by a 31 percent growth rate for whites during the same time period. Principally an area of African American residents, the southeast quadrant has experienced a 27.7 percent increase in median income (to $21,014) since 1980 and a 47 percent increase in median rent (to $459/month.). The unemployment rate is the second lowest in the area (8 percent), but the poverty rate has climbed 69.1 percent since 1980, to 31.2 percent of the population.

Repeating patterns consistent in the other quadrants, resident occupations moved heavily toward an increase in managerial, professional, technical, sales, and administrative support occupations while declining in manufacturing. The southeast quadrant also has the second-lowest rate of female heads of households (19.7 percent). Given the rapid changes in median income and rents, it is not surprising that 21 percent of the residents paid more than 30 percent of their income for rent. Blacks constituted the majority of renters, along with whites;

Figure 3.6 *Central Station sign—"A Magnificent New World."*

Asian and Pacific Islanders were the only residential owners in the quadrant according to the 1990 census data.

Across from Dearborn Park to the east, Central Station (fig. 3.6) is one of the largest redevelopment projects in Chicago, costing a projected $1 billion, with planned 9,500 residential units, 7.5 million square feet of office space, 3 million square feet of exhibition space, and 1 million square feet of retail space. Currently under development by MCL and Central Station Corp., completed sections of Central Station include "The Residences," composed of "Harbor Square," which has residential unit complexes facing inward, with a fortresslike exterior, and to the north "Park Row," consisting of luxury 3-bedroom, two-and-a-half bath townhouses (fig. 3.7). Across Indiana Street, to the west, the abandoned St. Luke's Hospital will be replaced with "Burnham Commons," consisting of one- and two-bedroom single- and two-level condos, advertised as a "gated community, surrounding a private park." Such a massive infusion of upper-income housing into this area without adequate provisions for low-income tenants will force most low-income persons living in the area out of the South Loop area.

For the remainder of this section, I will focus on Central Station, because this development in particular is the key element in a strategy

Figure 3.7 *Central Station—"Harbor Square" with fortress exterior, looking north toward the Loop.*

that is serving to sandwich the remaining poor in the South Loop between two wealthy developments, increasing land pressures for owners to sell and forcing low-income people out of the South Loop area entirely. Approved for development by the Chicago City Council in 1990, Central Station contained no provision in its master plan for any low-income units. The approval of such a large project in an area, formerly home to many low-income SRO hotels, is likely to produce inflated land costs and a rising tax base for the city as upper-income residents move into the area, lured by its proximity to downtown.

Although most of the South Loop SROs have been destroyed, the remaining SROs that provide homes for the city's poor, such as the St. James Hotel and the Roosevelt Hotel, are directly in the path of city redevelopment.[16] According to Hoch and Slayton (1989), "the loss of SRO units in the Loop and North Side area resulted from pressures for conversion and redevelopment, rather than decline and abandonment" (182). This process is now being extended to the Near South Side, with a specific focus on the South Loop area.

To facilitate redevelopment in the South Loop area, the city of Chicago has used a mechanism called "tax increment financing" (TIF)[17] in which the city sells bonds and uses the revenue to make improvements to the infrastructure, effectively subsidizing commercial and upper-income residential developments within a given area. In August 1994, Chicago's finance committee approved a plan to amend the TIF for the South Loop area, originally set at 156 acres and $11.5 Million, expanding the area to 248 acres at a cost of $104 million in city funds (map 3.2). In the amendment the SROs—the St. James Hotel, the Roosevelt Hotel, and others—were included in the TIF boundaries, making the property eligible for redevelopment. On the other hand, the Hillard and Ickle public housing projects, just to the south, were placed just outside the TIF, making them ineligible for redevelopment money. No specific proposals for either new SROs or affordable housing were made, although general targets were agreed upon for the future. City planning officials claimed that those units would be built when the rental portions of the property are developed (Reardon 1994).

In an ordinance adopting and approving the Near South Redevelopment Area Project and Plan, which includes the Central Station area, Chicago's city council expressed city commitment to "provide affordable housing units which may be lost due to redevelopment in the Expanded Redevelopment Project Area," and in Exhibit E of the city council decision expressly stated a commitment to "one for one replacement or a minimum of 300 affordable housing units . . . for 'low

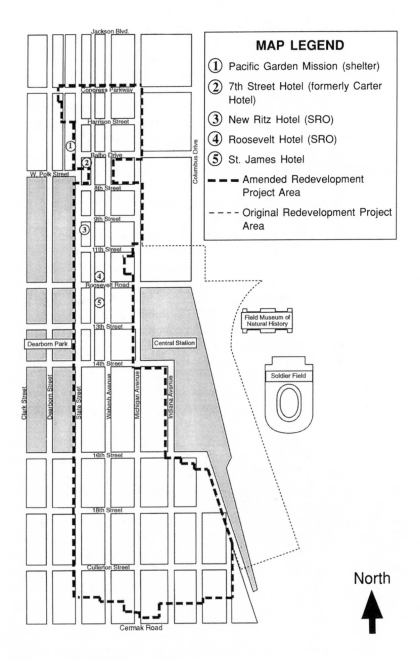

Map 3.2 *City of Chicago, TIF Area*

and moderate income' individuals." However, the construction of these replacement units does not have to be considered until "the estimated date for final completion of the redevelopment project," which for the Central Station project could be as long as eighteen years in the future. In addition, such units do not have to be constructed in the same area, nor is there a call for very-low-income units to provide replacement housing to current SRO tenants.

Chicago city officials claim that calls for affordable housing are "premature" and will be treated on a case-by-case basis, and that the TIF stipulates only the designation for financing a specific area. According to Greg Longhini, spokesperson for the City of Chicago Department of Planning and Development, "We can't tie ourselves down to making a future commitment for a specific program in a specific part of the city" (McRoberts 1994, 1). What this means is that land values will determine where low-income housing will be built—the cheaper areas of the city will receive the most low-income units, continuing the class segregation, and indirectly the racial segregation, of Chicago. Again, Mr. Longhini states, "I don't think we're going to set specific goals to build low-income housing when it might be cheaper somewhere else" (Michaeli 1994, 1). It is that "somewhere else" that is the problem. Given that extensive redevelopment is changing the face of the South Loop area, we can expect property values there to rise over time. This will make the construction of low-income housing in the South Loop area economically unfeasible without massive state or city subsidies, eliminating any professed goal of "mixed-income" housing.

Acting as the "anchor" for South Loop development and connecting the newly renovated McCormick Place with the downtown Loop, Central Station markets itself by reference to the Illinois Central Railroad's Central Station, which was established in 1892 to bring the public to the Columbian Exposition. Conceptualized as a development project that could "integrate" various urban functions as well as commercial, residential, hotel, trade, and retail facilities, Central Station harkens back to the dreams of Daniel H. Burnham. Indeed, according to a promotional brochure for Burnham Place, a subsection of Central Station, "Central Station is the cornerstone in Chicago's ultimate master plan, bringing Daniel H. Burnham's concept to a brilliant conclusion . . . linking the lake and Lake Shore Drive with Michigan Avenue and the city's other major thoroughfares."

Advertised as "private and secure gated communities . . . an easy walk to the city, the lake and museum campus," Burnham Place, consisting of 160 upper-income condominiums and townhouses, will cater specifically to a professional and upper-income population. Rely-ing upon a combination of nostalgic attachment with the original Burnham vision of Chicago and the ease of access to downtown facili-ties, the postmodern aesthetics of Central Station architecture lends itself well to the fabrication of a Chicago modern history, a history in search of its past, while communicating a distinctive upper-income status through the use of fine crafted materials and simulated nineteenth-century aesthetic forms.

The granting of the extended TIF area, and indeed the Central Station concept, has met with protests from CCH, the South Loop Coalition, and other housing groups who claim that such developments will displace those currently living in the South Loop area. When a property owner across the street from the Coalition's offices was granted a $2 million grant under the TIF guidelines, CCH staged a protest, occupying the building and demanding that the developer "either re-turn the $2 million in public financing or commit 20% of the units" for affordable housing (Chicago Coalition for the Homeless 1994–95, 7). The effects of such a massive redevelopment project on surrounding land values is clear. Dearborn Park is a model of what will happen with Central Station. Large-scale redevelopment projects such as residential Central Station and Dearborn Park in the South Loop, and the United Center sports stadium located on the Near West Side, can serve as a "big bang" in the area—a massive investment of capital in a central project that then disrupts surrounding neighborhoods through its im-pact on land values. Large projects for upper-income residents often serve to "colonize" a given area, driving out the local inhabitants in favor of those who use the services of the project.

Polarized Topographies II: The Near West Side

In strips of land between the community areas of the Near West Side and West Town, tussles of prairie grass have reemerged, along with rabbits and waterfowl. Weeds and broken buildings mingle with rusted machinery, aged railway tracks, and dirt mounds (refuse space). In this median strip, the transportation corridor for western suburban com-muter trains (functional space), neither in nor out of a community area, in this borderland, Chicago's homeless encampments called "Tranquility City" were born (fig. 3.8).

For the homeless living in the camps, the Near West Side and the Loop were primary reference points, because both offered possibilities of work, food, and occasional shelter. The Near West Side is the site

Figure 3.8 *Metra railway lines, the site of Tranquility City. A functional/refuse space. Looking southeast toward the Loop with the Sears Tower in the background.*

of many homeless shelters and SROs, Chicago's early skid row, the original Jane Addams Hull House, the University of Illinois campus, Greektown, the former Maxwell Street market, the United Center sports stadium, and numerous public housing projects such as the Henry Horner Homes.

Between 1979 and 1990, median household incomes dropped on the Near West Side from $10,188 to $9,336, accompanied by an 80 percent decline in population. The SROs have closed, some shelters have moved, manufacturing plants left for suburban areas, and housing stock has eroded with age. Rents increased 62.4 percent between 1980 and 1990, making it very difficult for the very poor to survive in the area, except within the local public housing projects. There is about a three-year waiting list to enter the projects. The poverty rate for the area was 54.5 percent in 1990 (London and Puntenney, 1993, vi).

Given the median decline in household income, new tenants, although few in number, have moved into parts of the Near West Side closer to the Loop, occupying newly built lofts and taking advantage of the low median rents compared to the rest of the city. In addition, the construction of Presidential Towers, which houses more than 2,000 people, has tended to attract upper-income professional singles who work downtown. The new tenants are of a different social-economic class and racial grouping than those who previously lived in the area; according to the 1990 census, the largest growth was in skilled, middle-class occupations requiring advanced educations. Workers in management, sales, and finance increased 25 percent, 32 percent, and 55 percent, respectively, from 1980 to 1990. Workers associated with working-class occupations—machine operators, assemblers, inspectors, durable goods manufacturing, and health services—declined dramatically. In addition, those working in low-skill occupations, such as handlers, equipment cleaners, helpers, and handlers, declined 57 percent. African Americans (N=46,197) decreased 27.7 percent and Latinos (N=4,416) 21.8 percent between 1980 and 1990, while whites (N=8,672) and Asians (N=2,283) increased 15.5 and 35.5 percent, respectively, during the same period.

Even though there are fewer whites and Asians than African Americans, the direction of population flow is clear: African Americans are leaving the area. Within this community area one can easily find squatters and homeless individuals mixed in with the new collection of artists and young urban professionals, as the "old" working class has begun to dissipate. Increasingly, facilities for the poor are also beginning to be displaced by the pressures of gentrification as city redevelopment projects progress.

The Near West Side is being transformed into a renewed industrial and commercial base; there are plans for a new industrial park, and the just-completed United Center has already housed the 1996 Democratic National Convention. The closing of the Maxwell Street Market and its relocation to a smaller area further east and south of its original location served to reduce the numbers of peddlers and homeless close to the University of Illinois's Chicago campus. The eastward expansion of the University of Illinois into the formerly occupied area by the Maxwell Street Market promises to further increase the pressure of gentrification and the risk of displacement.

Shelters are closing in the area and being dispersed to other locations. Sousa House, a homeless shelter housing 145 people, is relocating to the Englewood community area, ostensibly to be closer to the community it serves. Part of the Olive Branch Mission, on Madison Street, is moving to West Garfield Park, and the Mission has been pressured by the Department of Human Services (DHS) to relocate the its soup kitchen facilities. According to Jackie Edens, director of homeless services for DHS, soup kitchens were widespread on the Near West Side (Stein 1992, 4).

While Chicago officials state clearly that they have no intentions of moving shelters from the Near West Side, shelters are feeling pressures from rising land costs and the gentrification of the surrounding community. Alderman Ted Mazola, equating homelessness with criminality, has advocated moving shelters out of the area entirely, stating, "When adults with nothing to do, and no hope, are released into a community in a mass, crimes of opportunity go up . . . In the old days, this was an area that didn't have anything going for it. Hobos jumped off the train and stayed here. But now, we're trying to attract business" (Stein 1992, 4). In the shadow of shelters, upscale restaurants, facilities like Oprah Winfrey's Harpo Studios (WCFC-TV), the United Center, and Walsh Construction of Illinois have opened on the Near West Side, raising property values throughout the area. Some shelters, such as the Chicago Christian Industrial League, are vowing to stay on the Near West Side.

The United Center sports facility (fig. 3.9), constructed in the heart of the West Side, typifies the pleasure spaces constructed within the refuse spaces of abandoned buildings and high poverty areas. Built with internal restaurants focused on its interior space, the United Center

Figure 3.9 *United Center sports facility. The Chicago Housing Authority's Henry Horner Homes are in the background.*

is not oriented toward the outer street, as are other facilities. This fortress architecture further insulates the Center from the surrounding community, acting as a pleasure space for those coming in from the suburbs and other parts of Chicago to see Bulls basketball and Blackhawks ice hockey games. Sports stadiums are perceived by city governments as symbols that can economically jump-start an area, but they create their own problems.

While cities scramble to construct stadiums to attract major league players, the owners of those players engage in playing cities off against each other to secure the best possible deal for themselves (Euchner 1993; Goodman 1979). Many other cities use their stadium space to attract local patrons to newly constructed restaurants and shops, but United Center is unique in being located in one of the most devastated areas remaining from the riots of 1968.[18] At the Henry Horner Homes, adjacent public housing projects just one block away, several fourteen-story, 148-unit high-rise structures were leveled before the 1996 Democratic National Convention as part of the Chicago Housing Authority's master plan to develop mixed-income neighborhoods. These high-rises will be replaced with 466 units of scattered-site housing, rent vouchers, two-flats, and townhouse units built nearby. This proposal was initially greeted with a great deal of opposition from Henry Horner Homes residents who feel that they are being asked to leave an area in which they have lived for years in order to accommodate the patrons of the United Center, and who have tired of the promises made and broken over the years by the Chicago Housing Authority. However, in August 1995, after negotiations, two tenant committees voted to approve the $75 million redevelopment plan for the Henry Horner Homes. This is the first time the Chicago Housing Authority has demolished any of its high-rise projects, built between 1956 and 1968. How this plan will work in reality and where Horner residents will eventually end up is open to question.

Presidential Towers (fig. 3.10), a four-tower, forty-nine-story luxury housing complex, is another large development project on the West Side, two blocks from the downtown Loop, in the heart of the former Skid Row area of Chicago. Containing 2,460 market-rate one- and two-bedroom apartment units, Presidential Towers has been the focus of much of Chicago's homeless activism since the late 1980s. Hoch and Slayton (1989, 183–185) extensively discuss the development of Presidential Towers, so I will merely summarize their arguments as an illustration of how redevelopment, in the guise of "higher and better use," can work in contradictory ways.[19] As self-contained towers, providing shopping,

Figure 3.10 *Presidential Towers luxury housing with CCH homeless demonstrators at the front entrance.*

restaurant, and athletic facilities for the residents, Presidential Towers remains well insulated from the surrounding area, a colonizing presence within a refused landscape that historically had been home to numerous SRO that were destroyed in the urban "removal" programs of the 1960s.

One enters at ground floor into a medium-size lobby containing a bar, cafe, newsstand, and restaurant, then moves up the escalator to a security area where residents use their entry cards to gain entrance and visitors can use the phone-in security system. Security guards with two-way radios wander the floor. The fourth floor holds a jogging track, a full-size basketball court, and a health club with a full range of exercise machines. Most of the tenants are single, young, urban professionals who work in the nearby Loop and can afford the moderate to expensive rents. Except for the destruction of the Starr Hotel, displacing almost three hundred residents, Presidential Towers was developed on land that had previously been cleared to make way for the Madison-Canal urban renewal project.[20]

The urban renewal programs of the 1960s ensured the destruction of low-rent SRO units in the Skid Row area. As Hoch and Slayton (1989) point out, "the number of low-rent SRO hotel units declined 80 percent between 1960 and 1980" (182). Extensive public monies were used to subsidize Presidential Towers, from cheap land, low-interest construction loans, a low-risk fixed-interest mortgage, a release from paying penalties incurred from "delaying insignature of the federal mortgage commitment within the standard two-year limit . . . the use of accelerated rather than straight-line depreciation in calculating their tax loss," and "[ignoring] their original commitment to ensure that 20 percent of the units would be rented to low- and moderate-income households" (184). This last point, initiated as an exemption with the aid of former congressperson Daniel Rostenkowski, also became the rallying point for CCH in their campaign to house homeless persons. According to Hoch and Slayton, "the total amount of public expenses associated with Presidential Towers, including direct expenditures and lost revenues to city, state, and federal governments, has been estimated at over $100 million" (185). Presidential Towers received the largest guarantee in history from the Federal Housing Administration (Giloth and Betancur 1988, 281).

Interestingly, even with public subsidies, after the initial success of filling the first tower less than a year after completion, Presidential Towers began to experience occupancy problems in the late 1980s and went into default in the early 1990s. This provided an opportunity for CCH to increase pressure on the owners to negotiate over allowing low-income residents into Presidential Towers. Street marches and demonstrations by CCH and members of the local homeless community were mixed, with attempts to conduct a dialogue with some of the tenants in Presidential Towers over who should have the right to live in the high-rise units. Some tenants were won over to the position of CCH, putting further pressure on the owners of Presidential Towers to negotiate. In final negotiations with the Department of Housing and Urban Development and CCH, Dan Levin of Habitat, Inc., the current owner, agreed to minimal concessions for introducing low- and moderate-income units into Presidential Towers in return for a financial bailout.

San Jose

The city of San Jose has followed policies of redevelopment designed to attract business investment to a moribund downtown, a downtown that is in competition with two major regional shopping malls less than five miles away. The dream: to attract a major department store to the downtown area. Electing to make retailing and entertainment as its center of downtown consumption, San Jose is attempting to adjust to the historical change in the region's political economy. In the words of former mayor Tom McEnery (1994), "My firm intention was to place San Jose among the leaders in what has been called a 'golden age of downtown retail development' (128). Once a thriving center for a regional canning industry closely connected to nearby farms in the Salinas Valley area, San Jose now is courting businesses that will service those employed in the rapidly expanding banking, real estate, and insurance sectors. In the 1950s through the 1970s, San Jose was perceived as a "bedroom community" for nearby Silicon Valley, but it is now attempting to establish itself as a "new financial center" for the electronics industry. As the third-largest city in California, San Jose is indicative of the growth and direction of future West Coast cities.

Like many cities, San Jose has pumped millions of dollars into downtown hotel construction, a new stadium, a convention center, an opera house, and general investments in "pleasure" spaces, such as the downtown Pavilion shopping mall (fig. 3.11). In the 1980s alone over $1.5 billion were pumped into downtown redevelopment. Redevelopment has both anesthetized the downtown environment and brought the city into conflict with its poor and working-class population, most of whom live in the downtown area and directly to the east of the city. Traditional small businesses that serviced this population are being displaced in favor of franchise operations and boutique shops.

The Pavilion shopping mall was developed as an attempt to create a better retail climate in the downtown area. However, prices

Figure 3.11 *Downtown San Jose. The Pavilion shopping mall is to the far left, and the Fairmont Hotel is in the center.*

remain high for consumer items. The daytime professional office crowd is able to afford these items, but large numbers of the local population, including many San Jose State University students, cannot. In addition, the mall is recessed; one has to walk down a set of stairs to get to the below-ground shops. By separating the mall from the street, this design creates an enclave that further divides city spaces from everyday interactions. As William Whyte (1988) pointed out in his analysis of New York commercial development, this type of design discourages inherent street sociability and an active public life.

The local homeless population is dependent upon local shelters and downtown services, and redevelopment has brought them into direct conflict with city officials and their plans. The strategy of dispersing homeless encampments and relocating downtown shelters to mixed zoning areas on the edges of the city has increased the hardships of the local homeless population. Most downtown shelters are now being relocated into former manufacturing districts containing extensive warehouse space. The new homeless, the new expendable surplus population, are warehoused like the former manufacturing machinery and consumer goods were. These strategies will be examined in the next chapter.

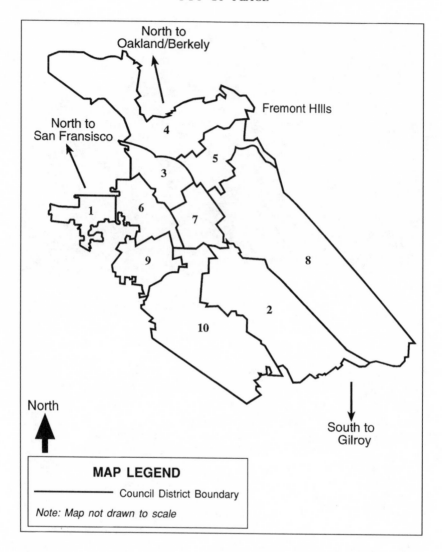

North to
Oakland/Berkely

Fremont HIlls

North to
San Fransisco

4

5

3

1   6

7

9   8

2

10

North

South to
Gilroy

MAP LEGEND

———————— Council District Boundary

Note: Map not drawn to scale

Map 3.3 *City of San Jose: Council District Boundaries*

Most of San Jose's poor are quartered in two areas of the city, downtown (Council District 3) and to the east (Council District 5), against the Fremont Hills (map 3.3). The affluent neighborhoods are to the southwest and northwest of the city. City Council District 3, comprising the downtown center of San Jose, contains the largest service-dependent population in Santa Clara County. Ten percent of Council District 3's population is in institutional or other nontraditional facilities (City of San Jose 1989, 4), and is responsible, in part, for the low median income of the central business district. Dear and Wolch (1987) described this concentration of San Jose's poor as the creation of "service-dependent ghettos." This overt concentration of the poor, in turn, has been used rhetorically by the city council to support an argument for no further construction of service facilities, SRO hotels, or low-income housing units downtown. Rather than channel redevelopment funding into these poor communities, and upgrade housing and health conditions, the city has opted to "disperse low-income housing throughout the City, to avoid concentrations of low-income households and to encourage racial and economic integration" (City of San Jose 1988, 17). The assumptions that concentrations of low-income households have pathological characteristics, that they have a "culture of poverty," heavily tinges San Jose's intent to disperse the poor, as it does in Chicago. A variation on this argument is that new services for the poor should be dispersed into the surrounding area where other cities could take up responsibility for the poor. Nevertheless, the City of San Jose did support the construction of 510 affordable units and 138 shelter/transitional beds in District 3 and in District 5 located on the east side of the city between 1989 and 1995 (personal communication, Department of Housing, City of San Jose, May 31, 1996 and June 3, 1996). 72 percent of these units (368 units) were for very low-incomes, 18 percent (91 units) were built for low-incomes and 10 percent (51 units) were built for moderate income units. While a step in the right direction such levels of construction are simply not enough to meet the demand.

However, most of the "service-dependent population" consists of students living in dorms on the San Jose State University campus. Another third are residents of group homes for the mentally disabled. Inhabitants of halfway houses, shelters, and the county jail make up only about one-third of the service-dependent population. Affordable nondorm housing for students and for group-home inhabitants remains scarce. The downtown area could handle many more low-income people with proper planning, but this would conflict with the goals of the city council to remake downtown San Jose into an area attractive to business investment and middle-class shoppers who may be offended by the presence of the poor.

Problematic Economics

Rapid development from the 1950s through the 1980s, stimulated by commercial semiconductor and software development, federal defense contracts, financial services, and light manufacturing, brought a rapid influx of professionals into the Santa Clara County region. Between 1950 and 1980 San Jose experienced a 500 percent increase in employment, exceeding the growth rate of both California and the nation (City of San Jose 1991b, 39). This raised the median income level and inflated housing costs and services. According to the U.S. Bureau of Census, San Jose had a yearly median income of $46,206 in 1990, an increase of over 50 percent from 1980's figure of $22,886.

As median incomes have risen, so have the number of persons in poverty. Fifty-eight percent of San Jose households currently have incomes under the county median; 26 percent of San Jose households make 50 percent or less of the median income, meeting the HUD definition for very low income households (City of San Jose 1991a, 3). The rise in median income concealed a polarization of the Santa Clara County labor market, an expanding market for both highly paid professional workers and low-paid, low-skilled workers. The latter are often employed as contingency workers with few or no benefits and are forced to live in the poorest communities of the county. According to a study conducted by the Homeless Overview Study Task Force, "Many of the jobs created in Santa Clara County are in the service sector. Currently, these jobs pay between $6 and $10 per hour. On the average, assembler jobs pay less than $8 per hour . . . Affordable housing, either to rent or own, in Santa Clara County for persons earning less than $12 per hour is practically non-existent" (Homeless Overview Study Task Force 1989, 39). The City of San Jose understands this problem and acknowledges that these trends can lead to disparities, but emphasizes the expansion of high-paying professional and technical positions, believing that services, wholesale trade, and manufacturing will continue to expand and that San Jose will continue on an upward growth curve. Anticipating a growth in high-technology services and products and the importance of research facilities and administration, the City of San Jose's (1991b, 39–40) General Plan is to seek development that will encourage "the administrative headquarters and research and development functions, with expansion of fabrication and assembly operations occurring in other regions."

Sales, clerical, administrative support, and service employment were expected to grow by 25.1 percent between 1988 and 1993. These positions make up at least 57.5 percent of all employment in the Santa Clara County area. While professional, manager, and administrator jobs were predicted to grow 22.2 percent during the same time period, they accounted for only 36 percent of the workforce (City of San Jose 1991a, 25). Given the economic difficulties precipitated by the cutbacks in the defense industry, combined with an extended recession, these projections will undoubtedly be lower than expected. It is clear that support services, while growing slower than professional and managerial positions, constitute the largest increase in numbers of employed. Hence, it is crucial to take into account the wages in this sector to establish affordable housing. According to conversations with the Association of Bay Area Governments (ABAG), a regional planning agency, between 1990 and the year 2000, Santa Clara County is expected to grow by 53,000 jobs. Of these, the largest growth rate will be in the service sector, where 62.9 percent of all new positions will pay less than $24,457 a year. For those working in technical, sales, administration, or service positions, either full-time or part-time, residing in San Jose will continue to be difficult due to the lack of reasonably priced, affordable housing. The minimum wage increased only 37 percent between 1980 and 1988, rent costs increased by 100 percent (Homeless Overview Study Task Force 1989, iv).

Polarized Topographies: Housing, Race, Redevelopment

The rapid expansion of service employment, combined with the shortage of affordable housing, generates problems of housing equity that are magnified by redevelopment plans that privilege one class of employee over another. The privileging of housing for professionals, managers, and specialty occupations over housing for lower-paid workers distorts the housing market, resulting in lower-paid workers moving to the periphery of the city, where housing costs are lower, or into marginal areas of the city close to industry. In addition, privileging the "business class" has created an overbuilt downtown area, wasting both human and material capital. The overbuilding of offices and other commercial projects by San Jose developers during the 1980s was an attempt to attract professionals, take advantage of tax code changes and increase development profits. However, as was the case for Chicago, this resulted in high office vacancy rates (18.9 percent) in the 1990s (City of San Jose 1990).

During the 1970s and early 1980s, the rapid growth of surrounding suburbs and the construction by developers of several large regional shopping malls less than five miles away drained much of the family retail business out of the downtown area. One of the main concerns in San Jose's urban redevelopment, therefore, was to construct a downtown that would attract high-income professionals and large, well-known department stores. A major department store chain was eagerly sought to "anchor" the downtown and thereby catalyze downtown redevelopment.[21]

San Jose, previously known only for canneries, agriculture, the Rosicrucian Museum, and the Winchester Mystery House, in the 1980s became a target for expensive redevelopment policies designed to "rescue" a depleted downtown and put San Jose "on the map." These policies were embodied in projects like the Hilton and Fairmont Hotels, the McHenry Convention Center, the Guadalupe River Park Project, the Children's Museum, the Technology Museum, the Performing Arts Center, the Sharks' hockey stadium, and a host of other commercial and public projects that produced a boom in land values in the downtown areas,[22] raising rents and property taxes, raising housing resale values,[23] reducing the affordability of housing in the downtown area, and generating overcrowded housing conditions.

One result of the decline in housing affordability is an increase in overcrowded households. Fifteen percent of all households and 12.5 percent of all renter households in San Jose are overcrowded. Overcrowding has doubled since the 1980 figure of 6.8 percent (City of San Jose 1991b, 19), largely due to the rapidly escalating cost of housing. With housing vacancy rates contracting from 5.6 percent in 1975 to 3.5 percent in 1990, and median rent for a two-bedroom apartment expanding from $350/month in 1980 to $700/month in 1988, it is not surprising that 33 percent of all households are paying over 30 percent of their income for housing (Homeless Overview Study Task Force 1989, iv; City of San Jose 1991a, 10; City of San Jose 1991b, 13).

In 1988, 84 percent of very low income renters[24] paid more than 30 percent of their income on rent (City of San Jose 1988, 8). The fair-market rent of a two-bedroom unit now stands at $954/month. (City of San Jose 1993, 10). The availability of lower-rent units[25] decreased from 33 percent of total housing units in 1980 to 15 percent of all housing units in 1987 (City of San Jose 1988, 11).[26]

The need for low-cost housing is acknowledged by the city of San Jose (1988). In 1988 the final report of the Mayor's Task Force on Housing admitted, "The supply of affordable housing in most cities, including San Jose, has not matched demand" (2), explaining that low tax yields and high land and development costs combined with costly service demands have restricted housing construction. "There is a critical need for decent, affordable housing for low and very low income families and individuals, especially large families, single parents, the disabled and the homeless" (3). The City also acknowledged that "if supply does not meet demand, purchase prices and rents will increase, possibly beyond the affordability of many households" (15).

While the recommendations of the Mayor's Task Force on Housing included "increasing the supply of affordable housing, preserving the housing stock, and reducing the cost of developing affordable housing," the actual numbers that are recommended fall far short of the Association of Bay Area Government's (ABAG) calculations. According to my calculations,[27] the City of San Jose, while attempting to increase its housing production rate, still maintains a housing deficit of 7,349 very low income units. These are units that are destined for households making 50 percent and below of the city's median income. While the City of San Jose and Santa Clara County are doing better during the 1990s than in previous periods in housing the poor, the prior record is making it difficult to catch up during a period of economic hard times. As a recent update to San Jose's Comprehensive Housing Affordability Strategy states, "while there are enough units to house every existing household (excluding those who are currently homeless), what exists is generally not affordable to those making less than 50% of the median [income]" (City of San Jose 1993, 17).

Very low income households constitute 47 percent of downtown Council District 3 households, the downtown area redevelopment zone, and 45 percent of Council District 5 households just east of the downtown.[28] Both districts are heavily populated by poor Latino households, with Latinos comprising 52.6 percent of the population in Council District 3, and 57 percent of the population in Council District 5 (City of San Jose 1991a). Race therefore becomes an important ingredient, in addition to class, for assessing the impact of urban redevelopment strategies. The effect of many urban redevelopment plans, as we have seen in the case of Chicago, is the displacement of people of color. However, although race is a key issue, it is not necessarily an intentional focus of redevelopment strategies. On the other hand, to the degree that those who are poor are racial minorities within the inner cities, redevelopment cannot ignore the issue of race no matter what planners or developers may say. In fact, the homeless in San Jose who were interviewed as part of this study overwhelming mentioned race as an issue in homelessness, directly impacted by redevelopment.

The privileging of redevelopment plans that attract increased numbers of white middle-income residents to gentrified downtown areas has often meant the displacement of poorer segments of the population that are predominantly people of color. In District 3, gentrification policies are most evident in the downtown area. In the surrounding neighborhoods and suburban areas to the south and south-west, which are predominantly white, exclusionary policies are prac-ticed to keep out unwanted service-dependent populations (Dear and Wolch 1987, 156–164). Hence, poorer Latinos, African Americans, and Asians living downtown are being squeezed between a gentrifing down-town, which is becoming increasingly white, and surrounding, mostly middle-class neighborhoods, which work through community groups and associations to bar the construction of low-income housing that could benefit the poor. What this means in many cities is that poor nonwhite segments of the population are increasingly pushed from downtown areas to low-income neighborhoods surrounding the city center. In Philadelphia, for example, which undertook extensive down-town redevelopment, nonwhites dropped from 23 percent of the popu-lation in the center of the city in 1950 to 10 percent of the population by 1980 (Adams et al. 1991, 119). This process may be repeating itself in San Jose.

Small, family-owned retail businesses catering to the needs of the downtown working poor and middle classes, such as used book stores, shoe repair shops, and hardware stores, are gradually being replaced by larger chain franchises, fast-food and expensive restaurants, boutique shops, chain bookstores and franchised nightclubs. Small social spaces running on a shoestring budget, like independent bookstores, have been forced to close as rents have increased. Small independent theaters are increasingly threatened by large conglomerate chain theaters that can support the high overhead needed to operate in the business district.

The above economic developments and the steamroller politics of redevelopment have threatened both the economic livelihood and the social networks of poor neighborhoods. Ethnic communities slated for redevelopment in neighborhood business districts outside the down-town are shortchanged in funding. Money is funneled into the central business district in the form of large projects in the hopes of generating quick capital to pay off the redevelopment agency's $470 million debt, a debt built on the shaky premise of continued economic growth within the city.[29] Many households within these poor communities, and many households within working-class communities throughout San Jose, are already living in precarious conditions and are at severe risk of becoming homeless.

Changing San Jose Visions

A business-centered activist urban regime (Stone, Orr, and Imbroscio 1991, 229; Trounstine and Christensen 1982; Elkin 1985) best typifies the organization of actors setting the policy agenda for San Jose. At particular times, however, the regime may be at odds with other political players such as state agencies, county agencies, or the local regional planning agencies. This business-oriented urban regime crystallized in 1982 around a group of local business leaders, politicians, and community persons involved with finance capital and real estate called the Downtown Working Review Committee (DWRC). The DWRC convened in 1988, headed by Susan Hammer, the present mayor, and Frank Fiscalini, a current city council member, in an effort to set redevelopment policy for the next twenty years. The result was the implementation and promotion of the *Downtown 2010: Strategy Plan* (City of San Jose 1992b). The vision of the DWRC divided the city into "core" and "frame" boundary areas (map 3.4). The 480 acre downtown "core" area is considered the "primary employment center in the region" (finance, insurance, government offices, convention, hotel and other service industries) surrounded by a 2,400 acre "frame" area comprised of diverse neighborhoods (single family homes and apartments, convenience stores and other commercial facilities) (City of San Jose 1992a, 4). The "core" is bounded by Interstate 280 to the south, Julian Street to the north, Fourth Street to the east, and State Route 87 to the west.

Primary redevelopment activity was targeted in the downtown or core area, also known as the "central incentive zone." Attendant to this vision was the use of extensive redevelopment to mold the downtown business district into an upscale package. Projecting a "new image" that would attract and hold new business investment was San Jose's primary focus. A draft of *Downtown 2010: Strategy Plan* states this explicitly:

> Over the next 20 years, the development can lead to a concentration of urban activities and project a new image for San Jose. New offices, hotels, and civic facilities will further strengthen the role of San Jose as the capital of Silicon Valley and create more jobs. (City of San Jose 1992a, 4)

Downtown redevelopment was perceived as a way to both boost employment and attract "safe" middle- and upper-income citizens. The question of employment composition and wages, however, is rarely addressed by redevelopment agencies. City boosters like to portray their city as a major regional center, able to compete and attract well-

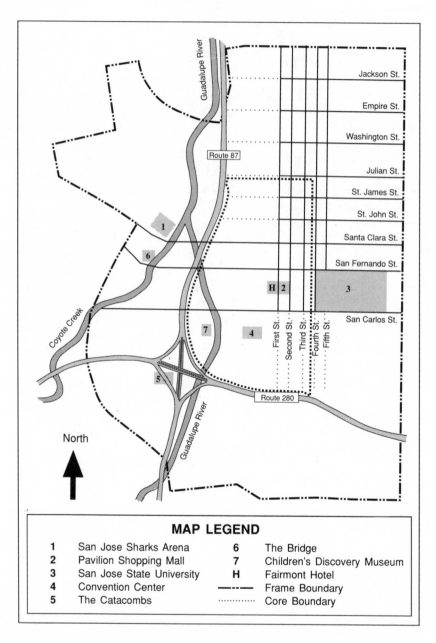

Jackson St.

Empire St.

Washington St.

Route 87

Julian St.

St. James St.

St. John St.

Santa Clara St.

San Fernando St.

H 2

3

San Carlos St.

First St.
Second St.
Third St.
Fourth St.
Fifth St.

7

4

5

Route 280

Guadalupe River

Coyote Creek

Guadalupe River

North

MAP LEGEND

1	San Jose Sharks Arena	6	The Bridge
2	Pavilion Shopping Mall	7	Children's Discovery Museum
3	San Jose State University	H	Fairmont Hotel
4	Convention Center	---·---	Frame Boundary
5	The Catacombs	············	Core Boundary

Map 3.4 *San Jose Downtown*

paying occupations, producing the "golden egg" of an increased tax base to fund new city services. In the eyes of the DWRC, downtown San Jose is destined to become a major corporate center:

> Corporate office headquarters sites will take advantage of amenities such as the Guadalupe River, the Convention Center, the Pavilion Shops, and public parks. Attracting corporate headquarters, especially for high-technology companies, is an important goal because it emphasizes Downtown as the capital of Silicon Valley. (City of San Jose 1992a, 19)

It is worth quoting the words of Frank Taylor, executive director of the San Jose Redevelopment Agency, for what they reveal about both present and future plans for San Jose initiated by the DWRC:

> In 1982, the original Downtown Working Review Committee (DWRC) pledged to rebuild San Jose's core. They envisioned a resurgent Downtown San Jose with first class hotels, entertainment facilities and a community arena. They looked to Downtown San Jose to become the regional financial center as well as continue and enhance the presence of the performing arts. Today, a stroll along Paseo de San Antonio reveals the achievement of many of the original Downtown Plan's goals. Parks, arcades, fountains, events and festivals in the park now attract people to the Downtown. Office towers, the San Jose McEnery Convention Center, restaurants to satisfy every taste and an active night life characterize San Jose in 1990. A variety of museums for children and adults along with performing art theaters complete the urban experience. This revitalized heart has drawn residents and patrons back into the center of their city to celebrate the diversity of our community's heritage. (City of San Jose 1990, 2)

What is interesting about Mr. Taylor's comments, and indeed the policies of the DWRC, is the exclusion of the very poor from playing a legitimate role in rebuilding downtown. This exclusion of the poor and disaffected from public discourse, tinged with unspoken racial assumptions that wealthier patrons deserve downtown, is compatible with exclusionary policies that force poor people, particularly African Americans and Latinos, to the periphery of the city. Extensive public improvements and millions of dollars in construction loans have been granted to downtown developers. In defending itself against charges of ignoring the poor, the Redevelopment Agency maintains that it spent $71 million on homeless shelters and on very low- to moderate-income housing, and that it is pledging $84 million over the next five years (City of San Jose 1992b). However, a sizable percentage of these projects will be for politically "safe" senior housing.[30] The major business-oriented redevelopment projects that have most affected the actions of local poor and homeless communities are the Guadalupe River Park Project, the campaign for the now-failed Giant's baseball stadium, and the construction of the 20,000-seat Community Arena (for the San Jose Sharks).

New Pleasure Spaces: The Guadalupe River Park Project and the Downtown Plan

The Guadalupe River is a narrow, slow-moving river that runs for three miles through the heart of downtown San Jose. The banks of the river and its tributaries, such as Coyote Creek, have provided marginal living space for over 250 homeless persons for many years. A natural feature previously neglected by the city, Guadalupe River has become the major focus for urban redevelopment, for bringing "nature" back into the city. Waxing eloquent about the proposed Guadalupe River Park, San Jose's Redevelopment Agency stated in its public brochure:

> The Guadalupe River flood control project and park will provide 3-miles of open space for jogging, bike riding and picnicking. Care is being taken to preserve and reinstate the native plants and animal life along the banks of the river. (City of San Jose 1992b)

In the Downtown 2010 plan, the uses to which Guadalupe Park are to be put are quite clear as are the social classes to which such uses are intended to appeal:

> Running three miles along both riverbanks, Guadalupe River Park will be a place where people come to walk by the river's edge, jog on well-maintained trails, or have a leisurely picnic. They will be able to enjoy city-style sights and sounds, a visit to the planned Technology Center Museum perhaps, or people-watching along the park's plazas and fountains. They also will find quiet retreats. Within Guadalupe River Park will be places where urban back-

Figure 3.12 *One of approximately 100 homeless camping sites counted along the Guadalupe River and Coyote Creek area in downtown San Jose.*

drop disappears, leaving only the serenity of rustling trees and gurgling water. (City of San Jose 1992b, 54).

The total cost allocated for Guadalupe River Park is $135 million for flood control and $70 million for the park itself (City of San Jose 1991b, 54). This urban pastoral vision directly conflicts with the survival of many of the area's local homeless residents, many of whom live in the bushes along the Guadalupe River (fig. 3.12). This clash between vision and present reality will provide the basis for our examining, in the next chapter, how the Student-Homeless Alliance (SHA) became involved in direct action against the city.

In addition to the Guadalupe River Park Project, the Redevelopment Agency has also promoted the development of the Fairmont Hotel (550 rooms), the De Anza Hotel renovation (98 rooms), and the Hilton (355 rooms), with a goal of increasing hotel room numbers to 3,200 by the year 2010. The agency justifies the extensive public funding of private hotel businesses by claiming that the public must assist private investment until a strong commercial/retail base is firmly established within the city (City of San Jose 1992a, 23–24). The down-town plan calls for 3.9 million gross square feet of new office space, 850 additional hotel rooms, 3,600 new dwelling units, and 400,000 gross square feet of new retail space.

Attracting public support for large sports complexes is another avenue of redevelopment. The proposal for a $140 million publicly funded stadium as a home for the San Francisco Giants was defeated twice in two citywide elections. This instance of city financial boosterism is just another example of the "build them and they will come" school of urban planning typical of the 1980s. Seventy percent of sports sta-diums are publicly funded (Euchner 1993, 6). When city projects cannot remain solvent, they are most often bailed out by the public, as Goodman (1979) demonstrates in his analysis of city competition for regional de-velopment dollars through the construction of sports stadiums. Attempt-ing to attract an out-of-town team, such as the San Francisco Giants, was perhaps more palatable to local city officials than to the public—which, however, made allowances for the San Jose Sharks, a local team. While the multiplier effect on local economies is often trumpeted as the reason for constructing sports stadiums, there is little evidence that money gen-erated by such stadiums remains in the city where the stadium is located (Euchner 1993, 70). In addition, the economic booms that such stadiums promise to local cities are often marginal at best. As Rosentraub et. al. (1994) illustrate, in a case study of Indianapolis sports stadium develop-ment, public funds invested in a sports stadium could be better spent if invested in other economic projects more directly beneficial to a city's population and not just to private investors. Stadiums are inefficient economic catalysts for downtown redevelopment.[31]

Exclusive Redevelopment: Dispersing the Poor

The redevelopment of downtown San Jose is accompanied by the spatial dispersement of the poor. This is clearly reflected in the city's policies toward the development of SROs, shelters, and low-income housing. Funded proposals are to be executed only in areas outside of downtown District 3 and District 5 to the east. The exclusion of funded proposals from District 3 and District 5 in 1989 was relaxed in 1995 allowing limited development within these areas, but still discouraging SROs, shelters, and low-income houing in the core area of the city. This urban policy ignores links between poor communities, employment sites, and social services. Spatial dispersement without subsequent employment opportunities or decentralized social services penalizes the poor for occupying land desired by wealthier classes and disrupts already established social networks.

The redevelopment agency envisions new multifamily housing construction, in the form of six housing clusters, ranging from apartments to condominiums, to be built in the downtown area. However, the percentage of units in each income category is heavily weighted toward upper-income populations (6 percent low-income, 9 percent medium-income, and 85 percent high-income) (City of San Jose 1992a, 6). The intent of the city council and the Redevelopment Agency is to privilege construction for upper-income groups. For poorer households, displaced from the Guadalupe/Auzerais and Convention Center redevelopment areas, $4 million dollars of housing fund money was set aside by the city council to relocate families away from the downtown redevelopment area (City of San Jose 1988, 32). Dispersion is further facilitated by the construction of the downtown light-rail transit system. The San Jose Housing Task Force recommended the "development of a policy which disperses new facilities along arterial streets and LRT stations throughout the City" (City of San Jose 1989, 7). The city's position in regard to new construction of non-traditional housing is this:

> No additional SRO units or other types of non-traditional housing be approved in the downtown or the Frame area, except those needed to replace the Terry Hotel and any other SRO units that may be need to be removed in the future. These should be on arterial streets or near LRT stations to facilitate access to jobs and services. (City of San Jose 1989, 7)

New SRO facilities and low-income units are to be distributed along main transit corridors and away from the downtown area. This position is codified in Implementation j-6 of *Downtown 2010: Strategy Plan* (City of San Jose 1992a, 12). This policy of strict exclusion of SROs from the downtown area was relaxed with the recent repeal of Implementation Measure j-6 in 1995, even though SRO housing is still discouraged in the core area. According to the city of San Jose, "it is the policy of the City to locate new SROs throughout the City, excluding Council Districts 3 and 5" (City of San Jose 1992a, 12). It is acknowledged that 4,000 additional SRO units will be required downtown by the year 2000 to handle the housing needs of the very poor. After the Terry Hotel was destroyed in 1989 to make way for the Performing Arts Center, San Jose stipulated that replacement SRO units must be provided in the general area.[32]

In 1988 it was acknowledged by the city that SRO units were invaluable for housing the city's poorest populations. It is also true that the numbers of available SROs have been radically reduced. According to the city's Task Force on Housing, "Since 1950, through fire, demolition of unsafe buildings, and removal for redevelopment, roughly 1,200 SRO units have been lost . . ." (City of San Jose 1988, 20). The city also acknowledges that "no new construction of this housing type has occurred in the last 20 years" (City of San Jose 1989, 5). San Jose did take limited steps to rectify this situation, although new SRO construction remains outside of the core area of redevelopment. 534 hotel-type SRO units remain in District 3 out of a current total of 1,737 guesthouse, hotel and residential service units (City of San Jose 1995, 16). Many new SRO units which are available are the result of building conversions not new facilities. The current problem with SRO housing is affordability. Standard hotels and motels are too expensive for low-income people. In San Jose, only 160 SRO units were available for $350 to $600 a month in 1988, and even these are very expensive for those who work only on an occasional basis or receive small disability checks. The rest of the units (1,509) were renting at $600 month and above. The greatest concentration of these units are in District 3.

Spatial dispersion is not confined to SRO units or low-income housing but is also applied to nontraditional housing such as shelters. The City Team Rescue Mission, one of several former safe havens for homeless in the downtown area, occupied a corner of highly valued downtown real estate. Located close to needed social service agencies, the mission provided a 32-bed sleeping quarter on a first-come, first-served basis. In 1990, the city council voted to move the mission to a larger facility, with a greater bed capacity, outside of the core and frame area of the redevelopment zone into the city's peripheral industrial area. This action, as part of Implementation Measure c-2 (City of San Jose 1992a, 11), was foreshadowed by the DWRC vision of a "clean" downtown. To encourage the relocation of the Mission to Council District 4, the city offered a new facility, which included a 12-month transitional program and expanded space for 100 beds. In addition, the Salvation Army, formally located in the downtown area, was relocated to Council District 7 in an attempt to reduce to size of the service-dependent population in the downtown area.

San Jose has stated its commitment to constructing a multiservice center similar to that built in downtown San Diego while researching sites outside of the downtown area. While a downtown multi-service center for homeless was proposed by the city supported advisory group,

Help House the Homeless, the only project which has been funded ($1.95 million), if not scheduled with a definite construction deadline, is the Reception Center. The Center is to be built two miles south of the downtown area in a mixed industrial-residential area. The City's funds were used by the Emergency Housing Consortium to purchase an industrial office building that would serve as a year-round facility to replace the National Guard Armory which will be closed to the homeless after the winter of 1997. This dispersion of service-dependent populations throughout the city, while appearing aesthetically pleasing, puts an extra hardship on those already in crisis. The distance homeless persons have to travel to find services is increased, and as a consequence many are tempted to sleep in the streets rather than continuously travel back and forth. One Mission resident noted in an interview that many of the beds were not being used because of the distance homeless residents have to travel to reach the facility. This, at a time when shelter facilities were near capacity.[33]

According to the city's Task Force on Housing, between 1985 and 1990 there existed only 300 beds for San Jose's homeless population located in the downtown core and frame area.[34] These numbers will decrease in the downtown area as facilities are moved outside the core and frame areas. Emergency shelters located in Council District 3 (Julian Street Inn, Montgomery Street, Manor House, Commercial House, and Emergency Housing) are all subject to relocation in the future, making way for future redevelopment projects.

With an increase in the size of the local homeless population, San Jose responded by expanding police patrols and creating a special police division that will be discussed in the next chapter. Surveillance of the local homeless population expanded throughout the downtown area. Homeless found sleeping in the Guadalupe River, under bridges, or in parks after hours are now routinely arrested, given tickets, and charged with trespass violations. In addition to forcing the abject poor into industrial/commercial districts, away from middle-class shoppers, this now adds the penalty of arrest for returning to one's prior sleeping site.

In the examples discussed above, spatial dispersion from downtown areas and concentration in controllable institutional shelters remain the underlying features of how Chicago, San Jose, and indeed many other cities are coping with a post-Fordist economy and increasing homelessness. The production of officially defined pleasure and refuse spaces is contingent upon the spatial dispersion and concentration of poor populations and the privileging of wealthier, employed segments of society. In this manner city development is not development for all citizens, but only for those who know their proper place, those who are part of the market economy. To be homeless in the new hypermodern city is to be both "no-place" and to be forced into a refuse place.

In San Jose, redevelopment has had the impact of dispersing shelters, services, and the homeless from downtown sites to industrial areas. In Chicago, the homeless are routinely dispersed from Lower Wacker Drive in the downtown Loop and subject to further pressures to move out of newly gentrified areas to abandoned factory locations and public housing. The development of the South Loop and Near West Side in Chicago means that greater numbers of poor African Americans and Latinos will be excluded from living near the city center. Homeless huts and shanty towns are routinely dismantled and the residents scattered, sometimes into public housing, sometimes into temporary shelters, sometimes just back to the streets. Attempts by the homeless themselves to erect housing, however shoddy, are met with hostility and derision. Patterns of redevelopment, while containing local and regional variations, still assume the same patterns of dispersing the poor to the periphery of the city and concentrating them in definable places of institutional control, from shelters to low-income housing complexes. How these actions are actually accomplished at the micro level, and resisted, will be detailed in the next chapter on authoritative strategies and homeless containment.

CHAPTER 4

Authoritative Strategies, Borders, and Homeless Containment

Resistance became a rejection of the human subject reformulated as a docile object when spontaneity is repressed for efficiency and productivity, in compliance with the grammar of capitalist domination. (McLaren 1989, 195)

City redevelopment agencies seek to create urban spaces acceptable to consumers and office workers. This often involves removing unwanted visual sights that may detract from consumption, or celebrating token instances of such sites as "local color." The dispersion of the poor from downtown areas and their concentration in housing projects, shelters, and other semi-institutional arrangements creates borders between the privileged and the nonprivileged, acting to contain unwanted visual sights. Homeless persons continually violate these borders by confronting consumers—sometimes as "beggars," at other times simply by a difference in physical appearances, and at other times by simply sleeping "out of place."

Land development, seeking the "higher and better use" of property, means protecting city land from elements that planners, business owners, and property developers believe will lower land values. What are unwanted visually, or are perceived as lowering property values, are the people, buildings, signs, clothing, and social actions that communicate "poor" and "unruly" to those who frequent downtown establishments and offices.

Local businesses in downtown areas routinely complain that homeless people disrupt their ability to conduct commerce, and shoppers complain of being harassed for donations. Pressure from shoppers and property owners is exerted at community and city council meetings, often erupting in spontaneous protests against locating facilities for the poor in a particular neighborhood or near a particular businesses (the "not-in-my-backyard" response). City council members who come from wealthier and propertied sectors of the community are generally sympathetic to such pleas. However, responses to the "presence" of the very poor and homeless vary depending upon the resources of the city and the state and the political sympathies of their perceived constituencies. City actions that marginalize the poor are expressed in the rhetoric of redevelopment and charity. This rhetoric often reduces complex race, class, and gender issues to engineering considerations and health concerns. Redevelopment involves authoritative strategies that contain the actions of homeless families and individuals. These authoritative strategies are successful insofar as they disperse and/or concentrate populations of the very poor to enable policing of the boundaries between the homeless and the nonhomeless.

In this chapter I examine the different strategies practiced by those in positions of authority, either consciously or unconsciously, in efforts to contain homeless actions, drawing upon data from San Jose, Chicago, and other cities. I will also examine the homeless responses to such actions in San Jose and Chicago. The Student-Homeless Alliance and Chicago's "Tranquility City" are discussed in detail in chapters 5 and 6.

First I will define authoritative strategies and tactical resistances and their combinatory possibilities, giving illustrations of each, and then I will conclude with a section on shelters and surveillance, since the rejection or frequenting of shelters is the most common feature of the lives of those I worked with. While authoritative strategies may be consciously planned and carried out through local police work, unconscious strategies may be implemented through the routine practices of city officials and local private interests. Examples of these strategies will be discussed for Chicago, San Jose, and other cities.

In defining authoritative strategies I do not want to give the impression that such actions are the product of a conspiracy against the poor. The enforcement of a "proper" use of social-physical space does not depend on organized conspiracies to maintain social boundaries. The contest over what is a "proper," use of space and to what degree different social-physical spaces are to be concentrated and separated is the domain of political strategy and tactics. To ensure control over the definition and use of a place as "proper" city authorities must employ strategies (de Certeau 1984, 36) that link their institutional power to a specific urban space. Control over place is not given, not a systemic oppression or definition, but rather a strategic oppression depending, according to Lefebvre (1976a, 28), on the actions of individuals acting on behalf of institutional interests within well-defined spatial and temporal boundaries.[1] City council decisions concerning the dispersion of the poor, the relocation of shelters, and the establishment of redevelopment agendas are commonly guided by redevelopment "visions" but they are not unified by a single plan in practice; they are a result of complex negotiations between factions of property owners, county and state officials, activists, and others, and depend upon the relative political strengths of each.

Decision making is dynamic, not static, subject to public pressures and counterpressures at critical junctions.[2] For these reasons city authoritative strategies can be contested, negotiated, disrupted, or abolished at all levels of society through what de Certeau (1984, 34–38) termed "tactics." Authoritative strategies are employed to establish a place as "proper," as a place within which understandable and controllable things will happen.[3] A "proper" place is a place where social events occur that are understandable to authoritative decision makers. Conversely, to be "out of control" or "out of place" is to not be in a "proper" place. As bodies considered "out of place" by housed society, the homeless are subject to the continual gaze of authority to ensure that their actions will not violate "proper" social boundaries. On the other hand, tactics as a vehicle for the dispossessed depend upon temporal features such as "seizing the moment," since the dispossessed lack control and ownership over place. Tactics may include ways to avoid the gaze of authority by keeping out of sight or to refuse homeless stigmatization by "seizing the moment" and squatting in abandoned buildings.

Opposition to authoritative strategies begins with small local actions, as "small acts of cunning" (Staples 1994), that often mock the powerful (Scott 1990) and counter expected behaviors accorded to one's stigma. Homeless persons may go out of their way to act in accordance with mainstream expectations of middle-class comportment, defying stereotypes of homeless "deviancy." Or people living on the stréet might move in the opposite direction, rejecting as much as possible middle-class expectations in favor of redefining homelessness.

Rosenthal (1994, 1989) and Cress (1990) demonstrated how homeless populations often acted in accord with mainstream norms as a resistance to strategies of authority designed to marginalize them, strategies that depend on a particular construction of homeless persons as "deviant," as the "other." On the other hand, Wagner (1993; Wagner and Cohen 1991) has demonstrated how homeless encampment members *tactical resistance* in Portland, Maine, developed alternative definitions of family and work to resist their marginalization. In addition, Snow, Baker, and Anderson (1989) demonstrated that socially defined criminal behaviors are often positive, adaptive strategies for those who have to live on the streets and lack the material resources to hide their actions behind closed doors.

The construction of novel street identities is another form of resistance to homeless stigmatization (Snow and Anderson 1987). The creation of public theatrical performances (Burnham 1987) and poetry readings, the organization of homeless unions and cultural productions (Paschke and Volpendesta 1991; Wallis 1991), and the occupation of boarded-up houses and public squares by homeless families and individuals demonstrate significant levels of cultural and political opposition to authoritative strategies designed to render "them" as the "problem."

Authoritative strategies are anchored in hierarchies of power resulting from inequalities in social, cultural, economic, and political resources. Opposition to them does not necessarily develop along consciously reasoned, well-thought-out lines of action; it usually emerges out of the simple necessity of survival within a particular local situation. For those rendered "out of place," just being in a place not sanctioned by power is to resist authoritative strategies. Existence is resistance.[4] As homeless individuals and families wander across policed social borders, established within the physical confines of the cityscape, across lines separating public from private functions, middle class from lower class, proper from improper behavior, disruptions are generated, and those very borders are called into question. The freedom to move between pleasure, refuse, and functional spaces generates problems for authorities who desire to contain or disperse those homeless willing to cross boundaries. The potential for these violations to accumulate, to become conscious and thereby political, calls forth responses from city officials to establish order, to maintain the "proper" use of social-physical space, and to ensure that homeless people are in their "proper" place—in refuse or functional spaces.

Street and shelter survival call forth tactics that can overcome the inconsistencies and ambiguities inherent in the implementation of authoritative strategies. The practices of surviving on the street in both urban and suburban areas conflict with the lifestyles of "housed" persons, and hence with state institutions developed to protect and regulate the property of housed persons. Local governments and private businesses attempt to mute this conflict by strategically managing given definitions of social-physical space and behavior. Dominant strategies of authority for managing the unruly, the homeless, include, but are not limited to: exclusions, displacement of conflicts, assimilation of populations and leaders, and repression.

Exclusions I define as actions that exclude populations from particular physical areas, discourses, narratives, and any given means of communication. *Repression* I define as forcible removal, punishment, or harassment for occupying space or communicating in ways not sanctioned by authority. These two practices appear to be the most common strategies exercised upon "out of place" persons. *Displacements* I define as strategic actions that relocate the causes of conflict from one source to another source that is perceived by authority as less threatening to their interests. *Assimilation* I define as the absorption of protest without change and or the redefinition of social-physical space to favor authoritative interests. One example of assimilation is the use of negotiating tactics designed to bring homeless groups into a political process that will ensure their marginalization from the decision-making process, from real power. Another form of assimilation is the granting of special privileges to selected homeless individuals rather than to homeless groups or collectives. Of course, these analytical distinctions should not be taken in isolation. Most often they appear simultaneously, although in varying combinations and degrees of strength.

All four of these managerial strategies conducted by public officials include their tactical counterparts—resistances by the homeless. The interplay between strategies and tactical resistances may be viewed within a larger framework of struggles over urban physical and social space around the United States. Public officials and private developers seek to control the uses of public and private resources, to maintain the boundaries of what are considered by mainstream society to be public or private, the "proper" use of space. These struggles mean battles over cultural as well as physical space. This can be accomplished by the effective deployment of authoritative strategies. To assist in interpretation, I have divided up the various manifestations of authoritative strategies, also titled "strategic practices," and tactical resistances into a typology—a simple categorization of a complex network of strategies and resistances operating upon, within, and between the homeless communities studied. The same typology can be applied to examining how strategies and resistances operate within city decision making. However, I shall leave that for another time.

The complexity of these interrelationships is illustrated in the matrix in table 4.1.

Table 4.1

Matrix of Authoritative Strategies and Tactical Resistances

	STRATEGIC PRACTICES (SP)	TACTICAL RESISTANCE (TR)
Exclusions (EX)	SPEX	TREX
Assimilations (AS)	SPAS	TRAS
Repressions (RE)	SPRE	TRRE
Displacements (DI)	SPDI	TRDI

The four authoritative strategies (exclusion, assimilation, repression, and displacement) and tactical resistances form the larger set of actions within which homeless and official identities are developed, since these actions are practiced not just on the homeless, but between the homeless, between the homeless and city officials, and between city officials themselves. Strategic use of exclusion practices by city officials may be met with tactical exclusion of city officials by homeless groups; homeless groups may refuse to meet with city officials. City decision makers and homeless groups must also contend with strategic and tactical exclusions practiced within their respective groups, although I will not be addressing this here.

By the continual *repositioning* of strategies and tactical resistances, internally between factions of city organizations or homeless groups, or between city and homeless groups, historical relationships are generated that create the conditions for either trust or mistrust, for degrees of social solidarity. How these relationships are negotiated, I believe, determines the success or failure of a given policy or group goal as well as the construction of subjectivity for both homeless protesters and city officials.

Institutional, Cultural, and Market Exclusions

Practices of exclusions can be divided into institutional exclusions (shelters, social services), exclusions due to past records, political exclusions, market exclusions, exclusions based on difference, exclusions from private/public spaces, and exclusions predicated upon gang intimidation. Shelter exclusions were perhaps the most visible and aroused the most intense reactions from homeless members in Chicago and San Jose.

Exclusions by Chicago and San Jose politicians were taken for granted among the homeless encampment members I studied. One

Chicago encampment member mentioned, "How many times do you actually see an alderman on TV talking about homelessness?" As media coverage of Chicago's homeless encampments expanded, many homeless residents assumed a more confident stance, realizing that for the first time many were now being heard. In contrast to this is the degree to which stereotypical perceptions of race, class, and heterosexuality color the treatment of homeless individuals. A Chicago homeless man who had worked with one of Chicago's advocate organizations mentioned being socially excluded, marginalized from others, by the obvious differences between himself and the public. He attributed much of this behavior to stereotypical responses generated from fears and misconceptions about AIDS. Dick explained:

> I have three counts against me. I'm black for one thing. I'm unemployed . . . and I'm gay. Those are three things that I have to deal with on a regular basis. Once they find out that you're gay the first thing is, "You got AIDS, don't touch me!" They just don't treat you like they would an average citizen. But who's your average citizen?

Dick commented on the continual surveillance and offhand comments by local police about his appearance, which were also strategic practices of repression. Some Chicago homeless encampment members believed that exclusion based on gang violence on the South Side was a principal factor in forcing many men to go to the streets. According to one homeless man:

> If you walk up to a gang member and say, "I'm gonna kick your ass." And then you turn around and kick his ass then six more guys are gonna be after you. You ain't got no choice but to leave or else you're dead. That's why a lot of people are homeless now. A lot of them cannot go back to the South Side because they opened their big mouth.

But perhaps the most pointed exclusion was also the most subtle. Market exclusion, based on a combination of low wages or unemployment and high rents, is one of the main reasons why many of Chicago's homeless ended up in the streets. With declining incomes and increasing rents, many of the near-poor cannot maintain their households. The absence of well-paid manufacturing jobs makes it difficult to keep up with the cost of living. John, a Chicago encampment member, explained:

I remember the time whites [got] $15 an hour jobs. The lowest whites I knew would go $10 an hour . . . I got whites now working side by side with me for four and a quarter. They ready to jump out the goddamn window! Commit hari-kari! They ain't even homeless—their woman's baggin' them up. They got a good woman with a good job but they ain't pullin' what they used to pullin'. I'm a black man and I'm homeless and I'm by myself. I could never get married with four and a quarter. Think about it. Four and a quarter! Do you know how much money that is? I am making $7,500 a year! Just think ten or fifteen years ago $20,000 a year was something. Now you need 45 or 50.

Tactical resistances to these exclusions were many and varied. Organizing, forming separate encampments away from the shelters, developing a sense of community, withdrawal from social contact, and creative use of public/private spaces were mentioned by homeless encampment members as methods of coping with strategic practices of exclusion. The simple presence of Chicago's homeless huts served to make the issue of homelessness visible, and the visibility generated tactical resistance to the official strategy of exclusion and assimilation. While the City of Chicago currently assists 77 shelters, numerous social services and food programs, the huts nevertheless served as a reminder that homeless people do not necessarily stay in their place. According to Tom, a hut resident:

The huts made the homeless issue visible. Not only to the people in the community but to the people who were riding the trains everyday back and forth. They noticed the huts because we made it clear to them. But to put people in shelters and say that you don't have a problem with homelessness, I think the city should get its priorities together.

Aside from resisting official exclusion, the Chicago hut encampments provided a micro community in which participants could share a certain amount of security, something that was perceived to be in short supply within the shelter system. Decisions were made collectively, tactics reviewed and security established through mutual aid. Tom from Tranquility City commented:

I got off of my black ass every morning and I tried to go do something. I came home in the evenings and ___ and them, if they were there, they would watch my hut. If ___ had some important business to do and I didn't have to work then I'd stay and watch his hut. We learned how to protect each other . . .We stuck together. As a group we stuck together because we had nobody else. We ate better than Pacific Garden Missions would feed you or Sousa House or Cooper's Place or Olive Branch because we had the Fulton Market. We'd sit up there and roast the meat. We were eating better outside than in the shelter.

By establishing a micro community, Tranquility City attracted support from other institutions, churches, students, neighbors, and community activists who shared their time and resources. Able to lock their huts during the day, many Chicago encampment residents felt their possessions were safer in the huts than in any shelter. The ability to lock one's door and to retreat into the safety of the hut provided a much needed sense of privacy for many, a place where one could safely reflect on their situation. In San Jose, SHA students and community members often brought food and clothing to San Jose's Guadalupe River encampments. When housing takeovers commenced, local churches donated furniture and heavy appliances.

In response to the issues of racial exclusion and homelessness, those Chicago homeless interviewed overwhelmingly mentioned that race was not an issue. The consensus was that if you were homeless and excluded, it didn't matter what color your skin was, you were still homeless. On the other hand, the highly charged atmosphere of race in Chicago might create conditions in which discussion about race and homelessness is itself a problem. According to John:

> You can be black or white. Your nationality doesn't have any affect on being homeless. If you're homeless you're homeless. You can be a homeless person and you don't have any running water and I don't have any running water you're a white boy and you can get greasy too if you ain't got no water for your face. It don't make no difference. *both suffer, no differences.*

This was not the perception in San Jose. Race was discussed as a very important factor in one's treatment by city officials and the public at large. In addition, race was mentioned by the San Jose homeless as important in their relationships with each other. In Chicago most homeless men are African American; in San Jose, African Americans constitute only about one-third of the homeless. However, this is disproportionate to their low numbers in Santa Clara County. One man described being African American and being homeless as placing one in "double jeopardy":

> It's like double jeopardy. You have two strikes against you right there. We already have certain problems in society with race and then people have an attitude against you about being homeless. They have an attitude against you of being a black person and being a homeless person combined so it's double.

This status of being in "double jeopardy" was reemphasized by another SHA homeless member who talked about police attitudes toward African American homeless persons:

> Yes. This is taking it back to the police. The first thing they say is, "Excuse me, where are you going?" and I say, "I'm taking the bus home." He says, "What do you have in the bag?" and I say, "Excuse me, but these are my personal belongings" and he made a smart comment like, "This nigger wants some trouble." That's exactly what he said. The first thing I said when he said that was, "Excuse me officer, but that was not called for." That was the same night I was arrested and they threw those bogus charges on me.

Most of the homeless in both Chicago and San Jose say that these types of behavior are not typical of all members of authority groups. However, there is a widespread perception that, while police departments may officially disapprove of such behavior by police officers, they tolerate individual cases of abuse.

Racial problems occurred on occasion within the homeless community of San Jose. While I was researching San Jose's homeless encampments, one incident happened that illustrates some of the racial antagonisms that exist on the street. One of the street encampments under a local freeway took in a white youth who professed neo-Nazi sympathies. He was accepted as long as he kept his beliefs to himself. However, when the police forced the encampment to disperse, encampment members went to stay in the local National Guard Armory overnight. While there the white youth used racial slurs against one of the groups of African American males living in the shelters. This prompted a brief scuffle, in which some of the other encampment members were forced to intervene, keeping both sides apart. The next day the white youth was banished from the encampment, which had returned to its former place under the freeway overpass.

Local homeless people's organization of protests and participation with other advocacy groups proved to be a powerful antidote to strategic practices of official exclusion, in addition to establishing encampments. The homeless who described participating in protests made a point of explaining how their meeting with the governor of Illinois was itself an empowering act. Alan, a Homeless on the Move for Equality (H.O.M.E.) activist, commented:

> The least powerful persons in this state have met the most powerful person in the state. That's what shocked a lot of people that homeless people can go in there and speak to the governor. A lot of people spent fifty or sixty thousand dollars in his campaign and can't go in there and see him any time they want to. All we got to do is sit out there and protest and the next day we seen the governor.

Finally, many forms of tactical resistances are utilized in negotiating public spaces, particularly functional spaces. This is especially true for libraries, airports, bus stations, and even hospitals. One hut dweller sat in the pharmacy section of a hospital, avoiding the security guards; another sat on the chairs at the airport acting as if they were waiting for someone. In those instances "keeping up appearances" became an essential prop in conveying respectability to the security guards. Some collected baggage carts at O'Hare airport for money; others used the restroom facilities for cleaning up and privacy. Occupying abandoned buildings became another tactic for securing living space. According to John:

> A person who has no place to stay has no respect for any property at all. Especially if he knows he's been violated. When I'm downtown and I see a building with boards up I'll break my way in there 'cause I know nobody gonna come in there on me.

One homeless activist mentioned that to make the public aware of homelessness you must personalize the issue through the local media. Encampment and homeless activist members in Chicago and San Jose blamed the media for promoting stereotyped images of the homeless as "bums" and "winos," but they also acknowledged that the media could be a vehicle through which a better image of the homeless could be generated. In discussing how people become numb to statistical figures and mass destruction, Max mentioned that if someone close to you suffers, you pay attention: "When someone says Uncle Pete was one of those people, all of a sudden it's a real thing. So we want to turn homeless people into Uncle Petes."

Homeless Social and Cultural Assimilations

Strategic practices of assimilation occupy a quite different social space than exclusions, and are met with somewhat different resistances. Insofar as they enforce a passive subjectivity, shelters reinforce homeless assimilation into a status commensurate with their race, class, and gender position, compared to the status positions of dominant elites. Advocates would often unwittingly adopt a similar perspective. Both shelters and advocate strategies will be discussed in more detail at the end of this chapter.

The strengthening of property values as a result of accumulating material goods constituted another practice of assimilation. Individualism and individual success, as opposed to collective success, was encouraged with the passing out of individual leases giving Chicago's hut dwellers their own apartments. Power now resided in individual control over a limited social space, versus the collective control exerted within the homeless encampment. While securing public housing was an improvement over their prior conditions, the dimensions of collective solidarity, as a vehicle for attacking individual isolation, were ignored by city officials. Mainstream individualistic values were reasserted as formerly homeless members went their separate ways. Owning something, retaining a lease, gave the encampment members a new stake in dealing with conflict situations. This is reflected in John's comments after he had secured a lease from the Chicago Housing Authority to replace the hut in which he was living:

> If you piss me off I'm gonna go get the police. I ain't gonna bust your head. I'm gonna get the police and file a complaint against you. I'm gonna lock you up . . . I didn't have nothing. Now I have something. I have a lease.

Finally, one strategic practice that worked to assimilate homeless members was the initial acceptance of encampments by Chicago officials. Statements made by Chicago's Mayor Daley to the effect that he had no problem with the homeless staying at the encampment site assisted in bringing the encampment under the confines of legitimate authority. By the following July, however, the mayor reversed himself,

saying the encampments had to be dismantled. Such partial assimilations are reflected in litigation that sets aside areas of the city for
"homeless" camps. The former Justiceville encampment in Los Angeles
and the rulings in Miami, Florida (*Pottinger at al. v. City of Miami*
1992), allowing for camping within specific areas, have served to "contain" homeless camps within definable, controllable areas.

Street and Store: Exclusions and Repressions

Repression and exclusion are the most visible levels of control over the
homeless, involving physical force, arrests, police sweeps of encampment sites, extensive surveillance and documentation of homeless camp
locations, and the general control of public and private space through
intimidation. These strategies have also encountered the most extensive
resistance from homeless individuals. Police harassment is both constant and unrelenting when homeless people are found in areas of the
city deemed improper by the authorities.

Arrest patterns show distinct variations between housed and
unhoused persons. In Fischer's (1992) Baltimore study comparing arrest
records of homeless and housed persons, most homeless arrests were
for disorderly conduct and violation of park and liquor laws. In Atlanta,
Georgia, an examination of arrest records from May through August
1993 revealed that of the 24,960 charges filed, 1,727 were against
homeless persons (Task Force for the Homeless 1995). New city ordinances included violations for "remaining or crossing a public parking
lot, panhandling, and lying down on public park benches." Violation
of these ordinances constituted 11 percent of all the homeless arrests
during the above period. Only 1 percent of housed persons were
arrested for these violations.

Police officers often make numerous sweeps before major downtown conventions. According to a report of the Atlanta Task Force for
the Homeless (1995) "of the 367 homeless individuals arrested in May
1993, 54 were arrested in the days prior to the COMIDEX computer
show, which brought more than 60,000 conventioneers and business
travelers to downtown Atlanta" (3). The effect of these arbitrary arrests
and sweeps is to further criminalize an already destitute population and
stigmatize them with prison terms. Those not taken in by shelters will
be taken in by local jails.

Given the urban spatial divisions outlined previously, it is all too
clear that the role of the police is in fact to "contain" (Snow and
Anderson 1993, 98–102; Aulette and Aulette 1987; Barak 1992, 80–84).

In carrying out this activity, the police are often perceived as having ambiguous intentions, sometimes helping, sometimes hurting. Being removed from public places in "sweeps," being arrested for camping, extensive surveillance upon entering stores, and being stopped for questioning are considered common features of street life. Indeed, a typical example of police practices against the homeless is the "sweeps" of Grant Park and Lower Wacker Drive conducted during the week prior to the opening of the World Cup soccer tournament in Chicago (Wilson 1994). Homeless persons were dispersed, their belongings and shanties taken away by sanitation workers. While sweeps happen every few weeks along Lower Wacker Drive, the sweeps were much more extensive just before the World Cup, according to the homeless themselves; some arrests were captured on film by a visiting Berlin television news crew.

In a 1991 report issued by the National Law Center on Homelessness and Poverty (National Law Center on Homelessness and Poverty 1994), antihomeless actions were divided into five groups, actions that work to both repress and exclude homeless persons from a given area. Their survey of 49 cities indicated, with the exception of 7 cities who adopted alternate approaches, that 62 percent of cities enacted or enforced antipanhandling ordinances, 26 percent enacted or enforced public place restrictions, 24 percent conducted police sweeps like those outlined above, 24 percent selectively enforced laws, and 21 percent enacted or enforced restrictions on service providers. Antipanhandling ordinances are being adopted by many cities attempting to cope with their "homeless problem." For many homeless who find that day labor produces insufficient income, panhandling may be the only way to provide needed goods. As a result, those homeless who do panhandle risk criminalization. With the repression of homeless activities arises the next procedure, which is forced exclusions from specific areas of the city, notably areas associated with consumption. Panhandling laws may be enforced sporadically in order to drive homeless individuals out of view of paying customers. In the absence of a coherent national policy on housing the poor, cities are forcing their poor to move out of town or into controlled shelters. Some examples of these provided by the National Law Center on Homelessness and Poverty (1994) are Cleveland, where police "drive homeless people from the downtown areas to remote industrial areas . . . leaving them there," and San Francisco, which conducted neighborhood sweeps, passed the antihomeless law Measure J prohibiting loitering within fifty feet of an ATM machine, and selectively enforced laws leading to "between 11,000 and 25,000 citations in a little over a year" (iii).

San Francisco's Matrix program, combining sweeps with enforce-ment of nuisance laws, routed those homeless who slept in the Civic Center Plaza and was used to arrest members of Food Not Bombs who had attemped, without a permit, to feed the homeless. Over 350 Food Not Bomb volunteers were arrested for distributing free food in San Francisco between September 1993 and September 1994. In Santa Cruz, California, the passing of an anticamping ordinance was followed by more stringent measures controlling access to public space. Under City of Santa Cruz Ordinance No. 94-09, Municipal Code Sections 9.50.010, 9.50.012, and 9.50.020 made it a crime to occupy a portion of the public way so as to obstruct the flow of pedestrians and or vehicles. Sitting on lawns or lying down in certain areas of Santa Cruz is also prohibited, except for persons watching a parade, sitting on benches, or sitting due to a disability or medical emergency.

In April 1995, a bitterly contested suit over Santa Ana, California's, sweeping anticamping ordinance was ruled upon by the California Supreme Court. In a 6-1 ruling supporting the city of Santa Ana the *Tobe* decision now criminalizes the use of "a sleeping bag or blanket (sleeping/camping paraphernalia) or the storage of personal effects on public sidewalks, streets, parking lots, and government malls within the city of Santa Ana" (Wylie 1995, 1). In a city containing only 322 shelter beds for a homeless population of over 3,000, such rulings have the intended effect of criminalizing homelessness and abolishing any demo-cratic use of public space. Violators of Santa Ana's ruling are subject to six months in jail and substantial fines.

The overt regulation of public space and the exclusion of home-less families and individuals from areas of the city considered "tourist areas" or commercial districts works to banish the very poor from the view of those persons who are tired of viewing poverty every day. The assimilations created by setting up special camping areas for the home-less are offset by the repressions and exclusions practiced by city officials in other areas of the city. One set of strategic practices pushes the homeless out of areas of concern for redevelopers and local gov-ernment officials while another set of practices concentrates them into controllable areas where they may be assimilated, or at the very least controlled.

When legal means fail to move homeless persons from areas where they are not desired, other methods are employed. In an attempt to move homeless persons into shelters, where many do not want to be for fear for their own safety, New York City instituted a special police team consisting of thirty-six plainclothes officers and supervisors who work the streets in an effort to persuade the homeless to seek shelter (Dugger 1994). However, the motives of the police are clearly suspect. In a series of crimes committed in Central Park in July 1994, homeless women were the victims. However, the generic category of all homeless persons as "criminals" was typecast in the sentiments expressed by Captain William Bayer, the commanding officer of the Central Park precinct: "The answer is, we have to cut off the head of the enemy and the enemy is the homeless . . . They are the predators" (Dugger 1994). Captain Bayer later apologized for his remarks, but his sentiments echo the attempt to criminalize the homeless by local politicians and homeowners.

While there are predatory individuals among the homeless, constructing an ideology of criminalizing homelessness and poverty acts to produce overgeneralizations and reinforce stereotypes of the homeless as the dangerous element, the foreign "other." The spreading of a moral panic over homelessness and criminality contributes to an atmosphere of violence on the streets. On 5 August 1995, Joseph Gould, a homeless man who sold Chicago's homeless paper *Streetwise* for a living, was shot in the head at point-blank range by an off-duty police officer, Gregory Becker, at 12:30 a.m., after Becker "rejected Gould's offer to wash the windows of his car" (Bennett 1995, 5). Officer Becker then drove away with his female companion and was apprehended only after he was traced through his license plate number. The area where Gould washed windows is populated by studio art galleries, loft conversions, and trendy restaurants; it is an area that is rapidly gentrifying, a pleasure space. While this was a highly unusual case, milder forms of random street violence are experienced by the homeless on a weekly basis.[5]

San Jose formed a special police detail, the Street Crimes Division, responsible for interacting with the homeless on a regular basis. It is estimated that the Street Crimes Division spends 25 percent of its time policing the homeless, patrolling areas where the homeless are known to sleep. This division has compiled a list of the sleeping locations of homeless persons—creeks, buildings, railroad tracks, cars, foothills, woods, bus areas, underpasses, and city parks—and has received the most complaints from the local homeless population (Homeless Overview Study Task Force 1989, 72). Those caught sleeping in unauthorized locations are subject to arrest.

The shape of things to come may be evident in the privatization of patrols as evidenced in the allegations made against the Grand Central Partnership Social Services Corporation in New York City. The Partnership, which hires homeless men to work for it, has secured contracts throughout much of downtown Manhattan to the tune of $1.6 million (Lambert 1995a). While offering social services and hot meals, the Partnership has been accused of creating a "goon" squad of formerly homeless men who beat up other homeless found in undesirable areas of New York City, forcing them to move on. Chase Manhattan, the client with the largest number of Partnership employees, hired the outreach services to patrol its forty-seven Manhattan branch offices. The role of these guards was to clear any vestibules of the homeless. On 5 July 1995, the Department of Housing and Urban Development terminated a $547,000 grant to the Grand Central Partnership upon concluding that there was "substantial evidence" that homeless persons had been brutalized and harassed by Partnership workers (Lambert 1995b).

These exclusions and repressions of the destitute are not new; they can be traced back to the passage of the Elizabethan Poor Laws in the sixteenth century (Simon 1992, 637; Snow and Anderson 1993, 10-11). Authorities within local governments were appointed to look after the poor and were given the power of raising taxes to pay for their services. Vagrancy laws, passed in earlier times, served as the penalizing component of the Poor Laws and continue to this day in a somewhat different form, but with the same intended effect.

Rather than punishing people for crimes they *commit*, the regulation of poor bodies served to punish the poor and homeless for what they *might* do. As Snow and Anderson (1992) comment, the purpose of the police is to contain the homeless: "containment is a mode of response that seeks to minimize the threat they pose to the sense of public order by curtailing their mobility or ecological range and by reducing their public visibility" (100). The strategies for doing this are exclusions and repressions. Police practices, combined with legal codes passed to assuage public fears, work to severely restrict the use of both public and private space by homeless persons. Overt regulation of sidewalks, beaches, and creeks, as in Santa Cruz, California, Key West, Florida, and other places, combines with the enforcement of trespass, loitering, and vagrancy laws (Stoner 1995) to shape the everyday life of homeless persons. This requires police to choose enforcement over social peacekeeping, further dividing local communities (Kleinig 1993).

According to those homeless interviewed in Chicago and San Jose, robbery and assaults upon and between the homeless were frequent occurrences on the streets, often leading homeless hut dwellers to demarcate what areas of the city were safe and which ones were not. In discussing safety and public parks, Tom commented:

As far as the parks are concerned, it was very unsafe. Because you have people walking around at all hours of the night. Were talking about people who walk and stand over you while your sleeping, check you pockets, make sure that if you had any money, they would steal your shoes, or they would just rob you. Cold-blooded robbery.

In addition to watching out for authorities homeless persons must also watch out for each other.

For most of the Chicago homeless encampment participants, the police were described as more of a help than a hinderance. Many commented on off-duty police and security guards who brought food and clothing to the encampments. In addition, it was claimed by encampment dwellers, fire department personnel turned on a hydrant, adjacent to the encampment to enable them to have fresh water. Chicago's police actions are in contrast with San Jose's police, where frequent ticketing for sleeping in the Guadalupe River is now the order of the day. In San Jose, the police were perceived by the homeless less as a means of ensuring public safety maintaining everyday repression, often with a racial aspect.

Differences in police treatment between Chicago and San Jose may be due to several factors. In Chicago, many of the homeless knew members of the local police force, having gone to school with some of them. Compared to San Jose, the homeless in Chicago, while concentrating in particular areas of the city, tend to be more widely dispersed than homeless in San Jose. Also the Chicago hut dwellers were in a remote location out of view of the public except for frequent suburban trains that passed by their huts. However, the police regularly acted to disperse the homeless sleeping on Lower Wacker Drive, under the downtown Loop.

In San Jose most of the visible homeless are concentrated in the downtown central business district, an area subjected to intense redevelopment pressure. Extensive sweeps of San Jose's Guadalupe River and the use of horse patrols throughout the downtown area generated a negative atmosphere between San Jose's homeless and San Jose police. The police, perceived in the past as relatively benign, were now perceived as a threat, assisting the city in moving the homeless out of the downtown redevelopment area. Homeless individuals who had previously slept on the steps of the Santa Clara County courthouse, leaving before the morning opening time, described how they are now routinely roused and sent on their way by the local police. Those found sleeping in the local riverbed near the no-trespassing signs are given tickets for trespassing. Restrictions were tightened as the San Jose city council voted to begin expanding their downtown redevelopment projects. According to Frank from the San Jose encampments:

We can tell all kinds of stories of San Jose PD infringing on people's rights, going along the Guadalupe River destroying property and simply harassing people in the downtown area or whenever they get the opportunity. We feel that we're being targeted by San Jose PD. No question about it in my mind. Whether it's conscious or unconscious . . . there's definitely an effort by the city police to move us out of the downtown area at all costs.

Ill treatment by San Jose Police, of both the local homeless population and the Latino community, brought vocal calls from the community for a civilian police review board in 1992. Organized homeless individuals joined in with Latino groups in joint protests. Actions included testifying before city council meetings and finally the occupation of the city council chambers, resulting in the fleeing of the mayor and council members. Several protestors were arrested in the melee, but charges were later dropped.

Chicago's and San Jose's homeless understood that while many police appeared to be sympathetic toward their plight, there were a few "bad apples" who were best avoided. These were individuals, often known by name, who went out of their way to make life difficult for those living on the streets. Their actions, often ambiguous, resulted in a deepening mistrust of authority by the homeless. According to Tom, when asked how the police treat homeless persons:

They harass homeless people. Throw them in jail for nothing. Especially in the summertime. In the wintertime you can't get them to take you to jail. Its cold outside. Its like the two go hand in hand. They're out to hinder you more than to help you.

In Chicago, one informant mentioned that the police "read" gestures and would often subject homeless individuals to frequent stops or identity checks. This was especially true when someone, perceived by the police to be homeless, was observed entering a retail store. According to Bill:

For instance, like at White Hen Pantry on Van Buren in Greek Town. I used to go in there to get coffee or something. That place . . . that's where the police hang out. If they see you walking in, and before you know it, you walk down the street, and the police pull you over.

Extensive surveillance by store managers, clerks, security guards, and police is common according to the homeless in Chicago and San Jose. Unlike other store patrons, homeless individuals are acutely aware that they are being singled out for special attention. This selective treatment reinforces the stigma attached to being homeless. Dick commented on the inordinate attention paid to himself and a friend as they entered a store in Chicago, attention that masked a deeper stigmatization equating homelessness with criminal behavior:

> When they opened that new toy store, FAO Schwartz, and immediately when my friend and me walked in the door, "Can I help you?" but they didn't stop nobody else. And then this guy followed us around the store, so that was uncomfortable. In the shelters . . .those guys I don't know where they come from or who the hell they think they are but they treat homeless people like shit.

Not having a home makes resistance to the gaze of others all but impossible, privacy impossible to accomplish. A San Jose SHA homeless member commented on surveillance and stores and the power of the gaze:

> A: Oh, in stores they watch you. They watch you because they know you used to live on the streets. They watch you to make sure you're not rippin' off the store or something. It's like you're at a prison. You walk in a store and they're right there watching you. Like you're stealing something and you're not.

> Q: So, you're like under constant surveillance then?

> A: Yeah, and inside my home I'm not. When I'm here I can say what I want to say.

> Q: It sounds like a part of being home is not being watched.

> A: That's it. When you've got your own place nobody watches you.

Resisting these forms of strategic repressive and exclusionary practices is difficult but not impossible. Litigation has been a common form of resistance (Blasi 1987; Simon 1992; Barak 1992, 145-72; Blau 1992, 93-102; Stoner 1995). While successful at contesting unfair social welfare practices, warehousing, arbitrary roundups, and other forms of gross abuse, such litigation remains incomplete without the participation of the homeless themselves. That participation has taken a variety of forms, from establishing direct action organizations, such as the Community for Creative Non-Violence (Hombs and Snyder 1983), the Coalition for the Homeless, the Union of the Homeless, Up and Out of Poverty, and numerous local organizations (Yeich 1994, 29–63) like the Homeless Peoples Association established by the homeless of Santa Barbara, California, in 1982–83 (Rosenthal 1994, 96). But again, these are predominantly organizational responses, often led by those with greater access to resources. Sometimes homeless people have formed their own organizations, such as the Union of the Homeless, but forming coalitions with those who have greater access to resources has been a strategy that has helped homeless-run organizations survive.

For the destitute, resistance is difficult in the best of times. Direct actions in the form of squatting, tent cities, protests, hunger fasts, and other activities designed to draw public attention to the problem have been frequent and widespread. The most visible struggles have been in Thompkins Square Park in New York City (Wallis 1991), and Portland, Maine (Wagner 1993). However, resistance might not take such overt forms. As Scott (1990, 1985) demonstrates, its forms are often varied and diverse, from direct action to telling jokes and using invented private languages. Tactical resistance to repression that I observed in Chicago and San Jose took the forms of negotiating with authority, developing increased public visibility and strategic alliances with other groups, avoidance (the most common response), developing new knowledge, and acting "crazy" to create distance between oneself and authority figures. As might be expected, of these actions, avoidance was the most frequently employed by the homeless.

Homeless persons, as persons "out of place," are subjected to the inquiring gaze of authority—surveillance is a common feature of homeless daily life. Surveillance by police, passersby, store clerks, welfare workers, and others. In coping with these overt forms of surveillance, one-third of those homeless I talked with in the SHA listed various tactics of assimilation, politeness, or "passing" as ways to deflect surveillance. Blending in with the housed population became a general tactic for surviving on the streets. But the majority of SHA homeless members chose tactics like seclusion, avoidance, hiding, or leaving the area to deal with police presence and overt forms of surveillance. This was also typical of the Chicago hut dwellers. In San Jose, the intermingling of students with homeless encampment members had the effect of blunting police surveillance tactics. As long as the SHA was on the street, many of the homeless SHA members felt the police would treat them with more respect. In recounting one incident where students were involved, a SHA homeless member commented about the effect of the SHA on police behavior:

> They helped a lot because the cops never came down and both-
> ered us after that, when we started that. They never bothered us.
> I remember one time the cops came down and Jim and Suzie was
> there and they (police) said something to me and I got up and
> said, "Do you know what? You just take yourself and go back up
> the hill because this is our domain. We're the cops down here.
> We don't need you—go!" And the cops said, "We can't do that
> ma'am. We're supposed to tell you guys to move out." I said, "I'm
> not moving until I get my place to live. When I get it then I'll
> move. Until then I ain't movin'." And the cops didn't like it so a
> sergeant came down and he said, "What's wrong?" I said they're
> down here telling us that we have to move and this and that and
> I'm not moving until I get my place from the Guadalupe sweep.
> He goes, "Hey, you guys—go up the hill now! Leave these people
> alone." They left.

Interestingly, student SHA members overwhelmingly listed active ways of coping with surveillance—from confrontation to counter-surveillance—as opposed to homeless members' preference for assimilation, hiding, or leaving an area. This is not surprising, because the danger is much greater for the homeless than for students. One tactic that proved very effective was to reverse the gaze by developing countersurveillance of the police through employing videocameras and still cameras. The use of legal tactics and video cameras to document homeless conditions and confrontations with police was mentioned by one student:

> We have the law and we need to help each other and document
> injustices and brutalities committed against the homeless people.
> Those things have to be documented. We have video cameras
> where we can record brutalities or some actions that brutalize a
> human person. That is a way we can fight back—by documenting
> these things and by exposing them to people here in San Jose
> and by exposing them to the powers that be. We can fight back
> in that way.

Moving from one location to another was the most frequent tactic used by both San Jose and Chicago homeless to avoid police patrols.[6] When asked to move their encampments, members of San Jose's homeless community would move their tents and belongings across an unused freeway, damaged in the October 1989 earthquake, to another overpass out of sight of the police. When discovered they would repeat the action, moving to the opposite side. Moving might happen as often as once a day or once a week, depending on the locale and frequency of police patrols. This type of passive resistance to repression appeared to be the least dangerous tactic for the homeless. The constant cat-and-mouse game played between the local police and San Jose's encampment members was discussed by the members themselves in science fiction terms. Young encampment members referred to themselves in terms connoting rebellion and marginality. More will be said about this in later chapters.

The conversion of deprivation into rebellion was another way new identities were constructed, contesting normative images of family, community, and work in favor of more combative and apocalyptic imagery. That is, family identities were formed through the combative imagery generated out of the real deprivation suffered by homeless. However, this conversion appeared situational for most of the homeless studied, not extending beyond their immediate life situation. Most SHA members, which included some encampment participants, viewed this overly romanticized image of deprivation-as-rebellion as superficial and unrealistic. This might be more a reflection of age, however, since the SHA had middle-aged, senior, and young people involved in its organization, some from shelters, others from street encampments.

As the SHA moved in the direction of housing takeovers, the increased risk of arrest created new subjective barriers that had to be overcome. Confronting and overcoming their fear during the housing occupations assisted many of San Jose's homeless in building a new awareness of a large collective project. This also occurred with the development of Chicago's hut encampments. Jack, a homeless SHA member, commented:

> We do really far-fetched things sometimes. Like an extreme example is taking over a house, which is a major extreme thing. I was involved with it but that was an extreme risk . . . [yet] I feel now that I could face the media or anybody with no fear.

To lose one's fear is a first step in the development of collective mobilization. However, this means confronting the very real danger of facing authority directly.

Avoidance and concealment were more common, as safe tactics that depended upon knowing specialized street rules, knowing when and where to find a place out of public view. While it was acknowledged that public parks were okay during the day, the night was a time when one should "just stay off the streets." According to one homeless San Jose encampment member, concealment in the brush under freeways, along riverbanks, or adjacent to city parks, was one tactic used to evade police searches:

> What we did is we went and we'd find a secluded area and we'd find different means of getting there so that no one could really follow our footsteps and track us down to where we are because if they did they could get us out of there. So we kept hid as well as possible. Even our tents we tried to get them to the colors where it would match the environment so that we could hide.

In Chicago, one encampment member avoided police surveillance, while returning to his hut, by going around a corner near the encampment and doubling back, confusing cruising patrol cars. A more active tactic was to negotiate with the local police, to have a respectful attitude for them and oneself. Alex commented:

> You have to talk with them. Have a respectful conversation with them and make them understand. If your in an area where they are getting complaints about you then the best thing you could do is to keep from arguing. You try to negotiate with 'em. Tell them why you are there. You get to know them . . . You get to know his name, and you give him your name because he might be helpful to you. You try to make they get an understanding why your not in the shelters . . . make them understand that.

This tactic has its risks. A homeless person may have a warrant out for his or her arrest and negotiating is subject to the whims of police patrols. This is especially the case in the legal gray area of semilegal encampments. Official sanctions can always be taken away at the last minute. In response to this ambiguity of official responses, tactical resistance by homeless groups may include increased public visibility to both buy time and convey to authorities the power of organized community connections. Buying time and clarifying ambiguous authoritative demands also operates at the intimate personal level. Dick, a San Jose encampment member, advised that if you are getting conflicting messages from the police, you should just stand there:

You don't know what way is right to say anything to them. They ask you a question and when you're getting ready to answer the question they tell you to shut up. When they pull you over just stand there and let the people around you see that you're not the one causing no disturbance. Make the people around there wonder, "Well, why is he treating him like that? He's just standing there. He's doing everything they're saying." So that raises eyebrows.

When personal resistance fails, public visibility may be sought by creating a spectacle, either as an individual or as a group. Tom explained that the wide base of support for their homeless encampments, in Chicago and the suburbs, was a product of their visibility. The huts were located less than fifty feet from the suburban Metra rail tracks, in plain view of suburban train commuters. The actual physical placement of the huts helped to build visibility as an issue for both the mayor of Chicago and the homeless residents themselves.

Finally, "acting crazy" can provide a certain degree of safety when confronted with hostile authority in either shelters or from police on the streets. According to Alan:

If [shelter personal and other homeless] think you're crazy then they'll leave you alone. A lot of police won't bother you either if they think you're crazy. They'll just leave you alone . . . Police will walk up to me and say, "Sir, who are you talking to?" I'll say, "I'm talking to my brother right here. Officer, please don't step on him now. I'm standing here talking now." The officer would say, "Were you swinging at me?" and I would say, "No, I was trying to tell him to shut up." The police just walked on away. They would say, "Man, you're crazy!" and I would say, "No, I'm just talking to my cousin." They left me alone.

Political and Media Displacements

The last category of authoritative strategic practice, displacement, works to redirect public and private attention away from the causes of social problems toward their effects. Displacement may occur at the official level by pointing to one set of "causes" while distracting attention away from the authentic causes. One example of displacement occurred when Chicago's Mayor Daley said that the Tranquility City huts had to be removed for health reasons at a time when the huts were receiving extensive local media coverage. According to Bill, an encampment member, "Mayor Daley said he wanted all those tore down because there was no running water and stuff like that. For years people in the South lived without bathrooms and in outhouses or whatever, so what's the difference?" The difference, of course, is that the hut dwellers had become widely visible, an embarrassment to the city's failing shelter policies.

Criminalizing the homeless (Barak 1992, 80–96; Barak and Bohm 1989) is another strategic practice of displacement. This works by displacing considerations of inequitable power, privilege, and wealth, and replacing them with considerations of individual behavior, labeled as "deviant" by those in power (Snow, Baker, and Anderson 1989, 98–101). Both local police and shelter staff will displace considerations of power and privilege into the practices of distinguishing between who is deserving and who is not, who are violating the rules, who are not. Concern for "proper" attitudes and correct behavior replaces a broader political or cultural agenda.[7] Stereotypical attitudes that equate homelessness with criminal behavior may be reproduced in police reactions to homeless individuals. Harold, one of the Chicago encampment members, mentioned an example of these stereotypes in an incident that happened to him while staying at Chicago's O'Hare airport:

> They make racial slurs or stereotypical slurs concerning homelessness that they're all kinds of bums and say bad things about you and everything. Even at like O'Hare airport a lady happened to leave her luggage on a cart and she went into a little gift shop or something like that and the police tell them, "Don't leave the luggage there, those guys are homeless and they'll steal it." And that was wrong. I stayed out at O'Hare for about nine months or so and I actually saw employees taking the luggage, bags, pocketbooks, different things.

In fact, a year after this interview was conducted, twenty-one employed baggage and security personal were later caught in an airport sting operation and arrested for stealing passengers' luggage. Such incidents might be limited to a particular local site; but broader forms of displacement occur, most often with the construction of media representations of the homeless.

Chicago and San Jose's homeless claim that mainstream media portrays the homeless as "bums," "crazy people," and victims, and not as real, complex individuals with their own sense of agency. Tom commented:

They're drunkards. They're bums. They're no good. They're alcoholics. They're mentally crazy. They're lazy people. This is all I've
been hearing in my ten year span of homelessness. They don't
want anything, if they wanted anything they would go out and get
a job. All they want is to stay out on the street and beg for change
so they could go out and get drunk. All they want to do is get a
fix. That's their (the public's) general idea of homeless people.

In fact many media images of the homeless go out of their way to tell
personal stories, related to "human interest" slots on local news docu-
mentaries. However, these personal stories reproduce the individuality
of homelessness at the expense of the contextual, structural considerations that generate the conditions for homelessness in the first place.
In the reproduction of individual human interest stories, collective efforts by homeless people, which go beyond assimilation and or established mainstream notions of work, family, and community, are simply
excluded from media discourse.

The images of mental disability and substance abuse associated
with early Skid Row inhabitants found their way into contemporary
representations of homelessness. Popular movies, such as *The Fisher
King*, present the homeless as deranged, if somewhat likeable. Others,
such as *Down and Out in Beverly Hills*, use homelessness as a vehicle
for teaching the wealthy about charity. Even the action genre has used
homelessness as a metaphor for class and race conflict. In the movie
Hard Target, directed by John Woo and starring Jean-Claude Van Damme,
homeless veterans are presented as human targets in hunts arranged by
a group of wealthy white businessmen. Class associations of rich versus
poor, elites versus the rabble, are clearly conveyed by one of the
businessmen: "It has always been the privilege of the few to hunt the
many." Van Damme, portraying a homeless veteran who works at day
labor on the New Orleans docks, successfully fights back and wins
against his opponents after one of his homeless friends is murdered by
the group. Interestingly, in the film a large homeless squatter camp
occupies the space of the Piazza d'Italia, which was designed in the
1980s by postmodern architect Charles Moore as a site for community
activities. This site and the homeless street mission "frame" homelessness
as caught between the monetary pretensions of the 1980s and the
accelerating poverty of the 1990s. In *Surviving the Game*, rap artist Ice-
T plays another homeless person who is being hunted by wealthy
hunters, each of whom pay $50,000 for the privilege of killing another

human being. Ice-T's character, although presented as suffering a prior personal tragedy, is clever at outwitting his adversaries. In both of these action movies, homeless persons are presented as both victims and heros; both movies portray homeless people as having a sense of defiant active agency.

In *The Saint of Fort Washington,* Danny Glover and Matt Dillon star as two homeless men attempting to survive on the streets of New York City. While using the "buddy movie" format, the film also uses images of mental disabilities to create a sympathetic character. However, the film does accurately portray the harsh life in some of New York's largest shelters and goes farther than most films in portraying homeless people as real persons, not fictional stereotypes. However, even in this film it is clear that the main characters are acceptable images of the "deserving poor."

To make homeless people acceptable to the public, advocates have also played with representations of the homeless as the "deserving poor." This fragmentation of the poor into deserving and undeserving displaces concern for social inequality, property, privilege, and community diversity into acceptable issues of individual compassion, moral behavior, and charity. According to Max, a homeless advocate:

> The advocacy community has to bear some of the blame. We play that game. For the last couple of years or so we've really been playing up families and children. Well, at least these people don't really deserve to be out there but the single male, now, that's different to me.

New constructions of the homeless as victims are mixed with older popular notions of "tramps," "vagrants," "bums," and "bag ladies," in which appearance is equated with one's value. When homeless groups or individuals have attempted to assert their rights, to protest, such compassion fades, and the homeless, like many poor people when they assert their rights, are labeled as "undeserving," even criminalized.

The popular association of homeless people with dirty clothes, offensive smells, and torn clothing is reproduced in popular media portrayals of the homeless. The power of such images is reflected in the fact that homelessness is used as a trope for being "outside" of mainstream society. The image of homelessness associated with dirty clothing and matted hair can be used as a disguise for those wishing to escape "mainstream" society. This was the image of homelessness presented in the movie *F/X* where the hero escapes from his pursuers underground and conceals his identity by disguising himself as a street person. In fact, such images of the homeless are representative of only a small fraction of the population, most often those with severe mental disabilities.

The degree to which these images still pervade Hollywood was revealed in the attempt to cast extras for the film *Curly Sue*, shot on location in Chicago. The movie director put out a call for homeless people to act in the movie as themselves, which apparently was not good enough to satisfy the director's aesthetic sense. According to Harold, another homeless advocate, himself formerly homeless:

> They wanted us to like ... come to the studio, or to the site where they're shooting the movie Curly Sue about homeless people, and [said] ... "Don't comb your hair, do not shave your face, don't wash your face, don't come shaven or groomed or nothing like that. Let your hair get nappy and dirty. Don't brush your teeth and have this stench on you. Take your clothes and lay them in the street and let cars roll on them and everything so you can have that grime and grease into them so that you can really look like a homeless people." I thought that was so terrible. I said, "Now, what the hell!"

The firm supplying extras for the movie simply saw this as good business. Mark Ridge, co-owner of Holzer, Roche, and Ridge Casting, Inc., a Chicago-based company, commented: "This is a movie ... When the director asks for street people and bag people, he wants a certain look" (Zorn 1991, 1). In fact most of the homeless involved in the Chicago encampments and in San Jose's SHA were indistinguishable from a housed person on the street. Chicago's and San Jose's homeless were careful about their appearance, showing other people that not all homeless people are dirty, offensive, or raggedly clothed. Disciplining one's personal hygiene and dress was a common motif for "passing" as someone who was not homeless. According to Alan, "There's a lot of people out on the streets who hate looking dirty. I know some people who wash their clothes in the park. A lot of people ride up and down the trains all night long and you'll never know they're homeless."

In mainstream film entertainment, settings evoking *film noir* are used as tropes for despair and misery. These settings are often inhabited by the mythical homeless person or the drunk in the alley. In these dysutopic spaces, represented in films like *Bladerunner, Terminator, Batman,* and a host of other *film noir* settings, marginality is conveyed through the intersection of bleak environments combined with stereo-typical images of homelessness or impoverishment. The homeless body becomes the signifier for the proletarian city. MacCannell (1993) points out the contradictory character of *film noir* spaces and representations of homelessness:

> who could possibly want to save this abject, filthy, dangerous space, except as a kind of fictional forbidden territory habitable only by heros, villains and fools? This space was created to serve as a place from which to flee, or to enter only as a matter of courage beyond reason . . . this space defines the imaginary bound-aries of human misery. Yet the fact remains that the abject interior spaces of *film noir*, originally, a nostalgic bourgeois phantasm of gamey or "real" subproletarian existence, could, if preserved, serve as a sheltering haven for the homeless. (282)

And indeed it has, as we have seen with the dispersion of homeless shelters in the real city to marginal economic commercial and industrial districts, the landscapes of the new *films noir*. In examining how homeless men respond to mainstream Hollywood films, John Fiske (1991) notes that in a shelter his accomplice studied, men watching the movie *Die Hard* cheered whenever the police were being defeated and turned off the movie before the ending when the police triumphed. At the point in the first part of the film when the corporate CEO is taken and shot, the homeless men cheered. Aligning themselves "univocally with the terrorists," Fiske maintains, these homeless men "generated considerable pleasure in imaginatively aligning themselves with the weaker side of each violent conflict. As the movie progressed and the hero became more closely identified with the police outside, so they progressively lost interest in him" (Fiske 1991, 456).

While not changing their material conditions, this audience re-sponse can work to solidify a cultural consciousness that recognizes and contests the dominant social inequalities in society, in particular the class conflicts portrayed often implicitly in cops-and-robbers genre movies. The displacement and assimilation of class conflict into the concern for order is turned on its head by those so affected through socially produced political and economic inequalities. Of course, as Kellner (1995) points out, borrowing from the work of Stuart Hall, there are different forms of resistance, not all of which lead to forms of liberation. "Unredemptive male violence" can be celebrated as easily as resistance that truly does contest the social order. For instance, while those homeless men in the shelter may recognize class boundaries and contest them, they also reaffirm patriarchal gender boundaries. Resistance to authority does not necessarily translate into affirmation of solidarity and reason.

Another form of cultural capital that conveys to the public "normalized" images of the homeless is cartoons. The domination of stereotypical images of the homeless can be viewed in editorial cartoons in which cartoonists use leveling, sharpening, and assimilation techniques to develop an image of their subjects. In Penner and Penner's (1989) analysis of a sampling of cartoons from the *San Francisco Chronicle* and *Examiner,* and the *Daily Californian* from the University of California at Berkeley, from September 1988 through May 1989, what were most typical were standard images of homelessness going back to the Skid Row period of American history. Images of physical illness and disability associated with homelessness were absent, as were images that conveyed the diversity of homeless families and individuals. "This highly heterogeneous population is over represented as consisting of middle-aged male alcoholics, and only some of their problems are depicted" (Penner and Penner 1989, 105).

News coverage is perhaps the most direct environment for conveying homeless stereotypes. Local news coverage of homeless situations and protests focus on "human interest" rather than issues of land-use planning and displacement. When local governments are practicing a strategy of repression and exclusion, local media often cooperate through the "framing" of news stories about the homeless as public health problems.

Criticism of these frames are rare indeed. Perhaps the most complete analysis of how mainstream news media "frame" homeless persons is provided by Campbell and Reeves (1989) in their article on the Joyce Brown story. Campbell and Reeves examine three conventional network news narratives and a "60 Minutes" story covering the plight of Joyce Brown, a mentally disabled homeless woman on the streets of New York City. Joyce Brown became the subject of media scrutiny when she was picked up from the street and committed to psychiatric care without her consent. This precipitated a clash of lawyers and psychiatrists over the rights of homeless persons within public settings. Campbell and Reeves identify the language of reporting about homeless persons as language that separates "us" from "them." "We" have common sense, "they" do not. In commenting on Dan Rather's report for CBS, Campbell and Reeves (1989) look at the way Rather's language "locates the homeless in the realm of the 'other,' the 'not us' 'the': 'We call them the homeless. They call the streets their home" (27). The continuing combination of camera shots and narrative used by the other major networks all contribute to the increased distance and displacement of homeless concerns from middle-class citizens, and this distance occurs within, as Campbell and Reeves term it, a hierarchy of discourse in which claims of expertise are given greater weight than considerations of homeless agency. The reporting of the Joyce Brown story quite simply illustrates the displacement of race, gender, and class issues into personal tales of pathology and despair combined with the resolution of dramatized class conflict "by celebrating, not condemning, the social order" (39). This "normalizing" of the status quo works to reinforce a viewpoint according to which those who advance in society do so by use of their own talents and those who do not advance are merely displaying the evidence of personal failure.

When San Jose proceeded with its redevelopment plans for the Guadalupe River area, stories conflating crime and public health, linking homelessness with drug dealing, began to circulate in the weeks preceding the city council decision to vote for park funding. During June 1990, news reports circulated in the major press about the dangers of drug dealing along the Guadalupe River and the adjacent Coyote Creek area. Homeless encampments were "framed" as a health problem and dispersion was framed as the solution. In a statement made to the press the day of the vote for proceeding with the Guadalupe River Park Project, the city manager of San Jose said, "When you go down there and you see feces and when you hear the people are using the [river] water for bathing and even for drinking, people are going to get sick" (Cassidy 1990a, 1A). The city denied any harassment, claiming that "they simply want to clean up a health hazard that has been allowed to fester for years" (Cassidy, 1990a, 1B). The decrease of homeless persons from 200 in April to 75 at the time of the Guadalupe Park vote one month later was explained by the city as resulting from increased police activity in response to drug use in the area. However, the following editorial from the *San Jose Mercury News* best indicates the dual purpose for this police activity:

> The presence in the area of a large homeless population has resulted in serious health and law enforcement problems for surrounding downtown neighborhoods, and that would be an impediment to the imminent development of the Guadalupe River Park. (Cassidy, 1990b, 6B)

While acknowledging that the homeless were in the way of redevelop-

ment, the dominant "frame" remained "serious health and law enforcement problems." The misunderstanding of homelessness as simply a
problem of mental health was quite evident in San Jose's leaders.
According to then mayor Tom McEnery (1994), "the general cliched
image of the homeless man babbling to himself insanely is correct . . . the
root of the problem" (40). In mid June, massive police sweeps of the
riverbed areas were conducted. According to some of the encampment
members, these sweeps coincided with the burning and confiscation of
homeless possessions and shanty structures by unknown assailants. The
general consensus among the homeless I talked to was that the burning
of squatter camps and the confiscation of personal possessions were
carried out by the local police. However, this could not be verified. A
general eviction of the local homeless encampments commenced after
the initial fires.

Further media stories linked drug use and homelessness in the
public mind. The following is a typical framing of and rationalization
for the police sweeps: "Along the banks of the Guadalupe River, two
scourges of the 90's—"crack" cocaine and homelessness—are colliding
head-on and spilling an urban nightmare on to a once-quiet downtown
neighborhood" (Cassidy 1990d). However, what was not reported was
that the homeless were often victims of nonhomeless crack dealers who
did business in the river area and perceived the homeless as an ob-
stacle. The moral panic generated by the use of health and substance-
abuse categories collapsed drug dealing into homelessness, labeling all
who did not fit mainstream class standards of decorum with criminal
intent. In the words of then mayor Tom McEnery, "Frankly, we're not
going to allow encampments in this city—we've spent millions of dollars
on housing and other programs" (Hazle 1990, 3B).

Further associations of criminality and homelessness may be invoked by juxtaposing narratives of crime, panhandling, and homelessness.
Not all homeless people panhandle, and not all panhandlers are homeless. To give an example that is representative of struggles happening
in communities across the United States, the Evanston, Illinois, Police
Department released a report that identified most local panhandlers as
"not primarily concerned about improving themselves through available
social services . . .The vast majority have criminal records" (Clorfene
1994, 1). Although the police report attempted to distinguish between
the homeless (the truly deserving) and the panhandler (the unworthy),
in reality many of Evanston's homeless do in fact blend in with the
local street population, making the distinction academic in the eyes of
the public. As Art Newman of the First Ward commented, "The panhandler is not a guy on the street with a patch over his eye. People with

criminal records are hanging around downtown" (Clorfene 1994, 1). What is also not discussed is the fact that the majority of downtown Evanston shoppers are white and the majority of homeless and panhandlers are African Americans. In this instance, issues of poverty, race, and deprivation are displaced onto the twin tropes of homelessness and panhandling.

By criminalizing panhandling, homeless persons, and, by extension, poor African Americans, are also criminalized simply by association. One can be homeless, be respectable, not panhandle, and not appear in the downtown area near shops, or one can be a panhandler, a criminal, and risk arrest. What is lost here is the fact that some homeless people do panhandle. Also ignored are the larger issues of how to address race and social inequality. Instead, there is moral exhortation to self-improvement simultaneous with spatial exclusion. It may be true that those who panhandle do use the money for drugs or alcohol; the question is, so what? The assumption that one can eliminate such activity simply by banishing it from the public realm is merely a disguise for displacing the problems of poverty to other parts of the city and to other realms of public discourse.

In still another example of the association of homelessness with criminality, a story appeared in the New York Times on 31 August 1994 titled "13 Deaths by Heroin Prompt Investigation in Manhattan" (Holloway 1994). The front-page story reported the deaths of drug users in New York City from a particularly powerful blend of heroin and linked homelessness with drug use via association with the settings where the bodies were discovered. Even though homeless people had nothing to do with these deaths, and the victims were not homeless, the homeless were invoked in discussions about the site in the second paragraph. According to Holloway (1994), the reporter, "The area, dense with ferns, pine scrubs and abandoned tires, is frequented by homeless people, some passers-by said today" (A1).

It is difficult to resist these practices of strategic displacement. Ability to access media is limited by the lack of money, power, and contacts. Homeless demonstrations are framed through the lens of stereotypes. The question of who speaks for the homeless and how they speak are crucial in combatting stereotypes. In San Jose, the initial media coverage of SHA protests would always exclude any talk by the homeless themselves in favor of an articulate student or community activist as spokesperson, even after homeless activists had been extensively interviewed by local camera crews. Differences in articulateness between homeless persons and their advocates often meant that the advocates were presented on television and the homeless excluded. In the case of SHA this changed over a six-month period as demonstrations increased in frequency. Nightly news media banners and titles were changed, along with the language used to describe the group ("homeless protesters" became "homeless advocates") and finally, more interviews with the homeless participants were included. The key was the media's increased familiarity with the SHA. This created new opportunities for the homeless to break old stereotypes.

In resisting displacement strategies, homeless persons risk individual assimilation at the expense of collective advancement. The degree to which homeless encampment participants and activists shared a common vision for change is questionable. The stronger a common vision, the more likely individual assimilation will be supplanted by collective organizing. While city officials sought to displace land-use issues in favor of individualized social welfare, the homeless looked at their physical surroundings in a collective fashion, asking how more housing could be built through the rehabilitation of abandoned factories. Chicago's and San Jose's homeless understood that land use, not simply social welfare, could be a vehicle for attacking homelessness. Land is not simply a commodity, but a place, a location for living. As Tim commented:

> For instance, the other day I passed this place, it was just this big golf course here with all this land. And on this golf course was no more than about ten or fifteen people. This is land I'm talking about. Straight land. I mean acres and acres of land. Just for a fucking golf course. I said to myself, "Gee, do you know how many houses you can put here?"

Finally, struggles between the SHA and city officials in San Jose, and the hut encampments and city officials in Chicago, worked to unite advocates and homeless participants, generating a degree of collective empowerment for the duration of the organizations and encampments. In Chicago, continuous discussions were conducted among encampment members during the height of negotiations with the city, often rejecting the help of advocates in favor of direct negotiations between the city and the homeless. When the encampments were finally dismantled, a high degree of solidarity existed for those who moved into the housing projects. Communication, performed through face-to-face contact, was now accomplished through an extensive network of notes, occasional visits, and street meetings. In San Jose, while demonstrations would come and go, many of the homeless who would periodically drop in and out of SHA would remain in contact through the local street network, informed through soup kitchens and shelter participants of local happenings.

Shelters and Surveillance: Exclusion, Assimilation, and Containment

National Guard Armories were the first places used to shelter the newly expanding ranks of the very poor during the 1980s. The traditional mission facilities and the Salvation Army could not handle the increasingly larger numbers of dispossessed people now moving onto the streets. Armories provided some measure of support. Large, impersonal, and lacking services, the armories functioned as emergency housing to stem an evergrowing problem. In 1981, New York City opened up the Flushing Armory in Queens and the Twenty-second Regiment Armory in Manhattan (Fogelson 1989, 230). This pattern was followed by large cities across the country, leading to a revival of the term *warehousing the poor*. Armories that had originally been built to contain the poor after the 1877 railroad strike were now functioning as places to literally contain the very poor. By the mid 1980s smaller shelters were developed as services expanded and facilities for the very poor mushroomed into a burgeoning segment of the nonprofit sector. With nowhere to go, homeless persons gravitated to large and impersonal armories, small shelters when room was available, friends' or relatives' places, or the street. Shelters provided one vehicle for assimilation of the very poor into the new social-physical landscape of the hypermodern city.

Exclusion from and assimilation into shelters constitutes a major part of homeless people's lives. Even though many of those associated with the SHA used shelters from time to time, some living in them for extended periods, there was a great deal of ambiguity as to how well they performed their role of helping the homeless. Shelters provided a warm bed, hot food, and a shower in exchange for following a set of rules that were arbitrarily enforced and rigid schedules. For Chicago's hut dwellers and for those homeless associated with the first and second set of SHA encampments, these requirements were too much to follow except where absolutely necessary. Bill, a Chicago hut dweller, compared his experience in shelters to a jail:

> Nobody should have to stay in a shelter. They don't treat you right. It's like being in jail. They don't want to hear nothing you got to say and they don't really care about you. It's a job to them.

For most of them it's just a job. Sometimes I've seen them treat people really bad. The police found a guy in an alley one day and they brought him to a shelter. He had blood all over himself and he was in really bad shape. I know for a fact that day they had clothes and stuff and a place where you could shower. But they turned him away because he didn't have a card or something. He didn't even come to stay! He just wanted to shower and get some clean clothes.

Staying in shelters was highly problematic for Tranquility City and SHA residents. Many of the squatters had spent time in the shelter system. As members of a community considered to have what Goffman (1962) referred to as "spoiled identities," homeless individuals have to cope with various types of "degradation ceremonies" (Garfinkel 1956) in order to use shelter services. The purpose of these degradation ceremonies, aside from conveying a lowered social status, is to separate out the deserving from the undeserving homeless. Those who obey are deserving. Those who do not are undeserving. An extension of this arrangement within the professions is what Estroff (1985) terms "medicalizing the margins." Whether or not one is deemed to be deserving of attention is dependent upon one's being perceived as "ill." Evidence of "illness" is produced through disorderly appearance or behavior. Homeless who do not appear ill or disorderly might be labeled "undeserving". In addition, as Katz (1989) points out, because of societal perceptions of women as nurturers and mothers, homeless families receive more public sympathy and the status of being deserving, compared to young single males, who are labeled as being recalcitrant. Claiming the status of being deserving often means undergoing extensive screening for drug or alcohol use, whether or not one engages in its consumption, limiting the hours spent at the shelter, obeying curfew limits, sleeping in cramped quarters with others who may rob you, dealing with abuse from security guards, and other behaviors that impinge upon one's sense of dignity, respect, and freedom. Homeless individuals cope by resorting to various tactics "alternating between resistance and manipulation, accommodation and avoidance" (Wagner 1993, 98). Quite often, as pointed out by Robertson (1991), nonprofessional service providers are unable to furnish the necessary level of care to the homeless community. This may account for why many of the squatters perceived some shelters as better than others.

Shelters were perceived by both the Chicago encampment members and SHA members as warehousing the poor, a throwback to the nineteenth-century poorhouse (Fabricant 1987). Shelters, as "total institutions" (Stark 1994; Keigher 1992; Gounis 1992; Loseke 1992) run by nonprofit agencies, function in the third sector, an area where networks of power, what Foucault (1991a) called "governmentality," are extended beyond the State.[8] As a by-product of the "politics of compassion" (Hoch and Slayton 1989, 208), shelter development acted to contain the poor, localizing the homeless within definable and controllable borders.

This policy of "shelterization," while rejecting the neoconservative model of blaming the victim, reproduced external networks of domination and power through excessive rules, regulations, and procedures designed to effect the smooth operation of the institution. The containment of the destitute acted to assimilate the poor on the terms of the shelter provider. The other side of this relationship was shelter exclusion. Containment, assimilation, and then exclusion for those who misbehave are the dominant strategies of social control in the shelter setting. These relationships occur within a set of models that treat the homeless as either a soul to be saved or a body to be repaired. Shelters as caretaker organizations swing between a medical and a salvationist model, embracing treatment-oriented ideologies (Snow and Anderson 1993, 88), which discourage collective empowerment in favor of individual self-oriented success, or a simple caretaker response. Most shelters, according to Snow and Anderson (1993, 78), give either an "accommodative" response, a form of charity designed to merely maintain the homeless in their present status, or a "restorative" response designed to change the individual to conform to institutionalized status inequalities. The latter is most typical of shelters that use either the medical or the salvationist model.

Gounis (1992, 691) demonstrated that the way a shelter operates is often responsible for a resident's loss of community ties, often mistaken for disaffiliation. The inconsistency (or rigidity) of rule enforcement discourages autonomous self-directed behavior on the part of the homeless who use shelter facilities. Loseke's (1992) account of a battered woman's shelter demonstrated how shelter staff would routinely construct homeless behavior as a result of the staff's perception of the woman as suffering the consequences of "wife abuse." When a woman did not conform to the collective representation of being abused, "these women lost their membership in the battered woman social collectivity" (144). The consequences of this socially constructed division between deserving and undeserving homeless women were quite clear in the exclusions that followed. According to Loseke, "clients who criticized workers' interventions, rules or interpretations, clients presenting themselves as angry and defiant, clients who were constructed as strong and independent women lost worker support and organizational assistance" (145).

These forms of assimilation create a passive subjectivity on the part of the homeless, a passivity further encouraged by the ways advocacy and research are practiced (Wagner 1993, 4–10). The dominant perception among the homeless men that I studied in Chicago and San Jose was that private nonprofit shelters wanted to assimilate you into their facilities for the organization's own financial gain. According to Tom:

> Shelters . . . they hinder [you], because the shelters is, like you know, as long as you were there, you supply them with your social security number, you are supplying them with money. They weren't encouraging you to get out of there, they were really allowing you to be homeless.

Shelters were perceived as places of only last resort, dangerous for one's body as well as one's self-respect. The apparently arbitrary nature of shelter rules is perceived by squatters as abusive. One Chicago hut dweller talked with me about how such a simple act as having a sandwich could have you barred from a shelter even on extremely cold days. Sometimes the rules are enforced, other times they are not. This arbitrariness leads to abuse of power between shelter staff and homeless persons.

As institutions of social control, shelters often impose a disciplinary agenda coded in extensive rules combined with attempts to maximize use of the limited resources at hand. Often short of help and money, underfunded shelters find themselves caught between a "moral agenda" to reform the individual and the need to maintain order within the shelter. The keeping of order may be entrusted to nonprofessionals, often previously homeless individuals, who may abuse their new found authority. The squatters talked much about how homeless individuals are "talked down to" by security guards. Tim commented:

> I went to the shelter over here, Sousa House, Me and Wayne. They had this off-duty guy there who worked for Cook County jail and anytime he would just come in there and this guy would talk just as nasty. He would say, "If you don't stand in line, you can get the hell out of here!" He would threaten people. He had a mixed crowd. You have some people that love to have that power, that authority telling you what to do. But if a man ever

tells me what to do then I'm out of here. And I have been to a lot of shelters. Even the staff try to tell me that I have to take an alcohol blood test. I don't have to take the test, I don't drink. Then I have to come to you and ask you for a pair of jeans because I have to go to work and you say "I'm busy right now, come back around four or five hours later." Why are you abusing your power when you can help me? The shelters only do one thing. They're concerned about one thing—their payroll and their staff . . .These are people that love authority. To have power over other people. To dominate you and to abuse you. They talk to you like they want to and you can't say nothing in return and if you do you're out of here.

Another dominant perception of the Chicago hut dwellers was that shelters were controlled by gangs, where "gangs" were equated with "criminals." This became a problem when disability checks were passed out, as some gang members would attempt to extort money from the weaker homeless men. How much of this was fantasy and how much was reality was difficult to ascertain. Some of the homeless did mention that the problem had been corrected; others were not convinced. Stories gathered from those living on the streets of Chicago's Lower Wacker Drive mirrored these concerns (Zorn 1994). Quite often those using shelters are afraid of other homeless persons in the shelter who may have mental or drug disabilities. Stories of intimidation and harassment were common for both Chicago hut dwellers and San Jose SHA homeless members, although the SHA members usually ascribed this to the larger shelters such as the National Guard Armory. According to a squatter, "Out here you don't have to do nothing to nobody. They'll [people in shelters] get you for no reason at all. If you don't fit in they'll get you. The gangs get you." The inability to defend oneself in the face of predatory behavior pushed many of the squatters out of the shelters and into the camps. According to Tim, "You never know when the next guy next to you would go off. If you protected yourself from this person you were barred from the mission and this guy would stay. So it was like your hands was tied. So that was my main reason for getting out of the mission. I was tired of that plus I was tired of not being able to work when I had to." Smaller shelters were given higher marks, as were ones that were well organized and clean.

On the other hand, one Chicago hut dweller commented that one chooses to be in a shelter. "If you don't like it you ain't gotta be there. It ain't like if you was in jail. It ain't like they makin' you be there."

He remarked that one has to be a man and stand up for himself. The situation of dire poverty accentuates this split between the desire to "be like a man," which is translated as seeking autonomy and self-respect through independence, and the necessity to be a shelter dependent, a part of the "people warehouse."

Shelter rules were also perceived to inhibit working jobs with late hours. The inability to stay up late prohibits night employment, and the early morning rush to the showers means getting up at daybreak in freezing cold weather. According to Tamara, one of the only African American female Chicago hut dwellers:

> They depress you more than anything. If you're going to bed at night you gotta be in by nine and then you have to be out at five thirty in the morning and it's ten below zero. It's cold and you got nowhere to go. And it's on first come first serve basis. If they fill up then you don't get in at all. As soon as you take your shower and go to sleep it seems like it's time for you to get out again.

There is also a recognition by SHA homeless members and Chicago hut dwellers that shelters are inadequately funded and lack the programs necessary to assist in long-term stability. This was reflected in comments about inadequate food and unsanitary conditions. Some Chicago hut dwellers mentioned getting lice in shelters that did not change blankets frequently. However, squatters and SHA members praised shelters that had instituted extensive programs. Shelter "warehouses" were avoided whenever possible.

What homeless persons perceived as minor infractions of the rules (for example, drinking) shelter staff perceive as evidence of "moral disorder," behavior subject to punishment. Issues of respect, being treated with dignity, and having the freedom to make one's own decisions separated those who used shelters extensively from those who lived on the streets, according to the squatters. It was an issue of having personal control over one's surroundings. What shelter providers treat as a minor inconvenience, following certain rules, the Chicago squatters perceived as a major attack on their self-respect. Tim, a Chicago hut dweller, commented on the difference between those living in shelters and those living on the streets:

> the people in the mission always have their hand out. They want you to abide by their rules and regulations. This is for homeless people. Homeless people got rules and regulations. Why should

I do that when I can have all the freedom in the street to do what I want to do? I can feed myself. I can take care of myself. I been doing this all my life and they can do it, too. These are people who want dependability. They like handouts and stuff like that.

The structure of authority within the shelters and the disadvantage of being on the streets relative to being in the shelter makes issues of respect a prime site for daily resentment. The inability to control the shelter setting makes it difficult to determine how one should act. One of the Chicago squatters mentioned how resentful he felt at always having to take a breath test for alcohol when he didn't drink. He was resentful at having to use the same apparatus that other shelter people had to use. It would mean placing himself in the same position as those who use the shelters—that is, to lose his self-respect. Every attempt to satisfy a human need—whether securing clothes or finding a bed for the night—is met, from the squatter's perspective, with degrading procedures and extended waits that communicate the homeless individual's worthlessness. To remain in this situation is to accept the condition of one's own degradation. The consequences of this loss of worthiness, which Goffman observed in *Asylums* (1961), is not only depression, but also a weakened ability to formulate goals and plan strategies for survival. Homelessness is not simply being without a home, but also involves a way of acting that communicates to others one's worthlessness. According to one Chicago hut resident:

Some people act like they're homeless. You see, when you lose your respect you might as well just lay down and die. All I got left now is my respect. Nobody gonna' take that from me. Nobody else. Some people have lost all of their dignity and respect. I sympathize with these people and I'm just glad I'm not like that. I'm different from most of the homeless people. You see some people, like the people who lived on the street are more private and secure people and they know how to act and their different from the ones that go to the shelters. Because they're always looking for handouts and they can just scream and holler and this and that.

Insofar as shelter providers are dispensing charity instead of "social justice," they are perceived by squatters as "poverty pimps," as part of a shelter industry. Rather than act as a base for organizing around issues of social justice, such as housing, employment, and health care, shelters serve a custodial function, the modern day poorhouse for those unable to compete in the marketplace. Because they are beholden to their benefactors, usually through city grants and charitable contributions, shelters have a limited ability to be more political. The fear of reduced contributions is everpresent. Shelters are a poor substitute for adequate housing, in particular a poor substitute for single-room-occupancy housing.

The homeless I talked with also mentioned exclusions from the system of social services. This was especially the case in San Jose, where many SHA homeless members commented on the "run-around" they received in applying for benefits. Waiting and searching for the appropriate office or agency consumed vast amounts of time, complicating planned schedules when day shelters would serve free meals, when one had to be at a particular place at a certain time. Trying to access services meant managing a very complex set of time demands with limited resources at best.

For many homeless, using social services in general, and applying for Supplemental Security Income (SSI) in particular, involved a humiliating process of waiting and searching. According to Rich, "trying to get on welfare you get the run-around. Trying to get what is righteously yours—your unemployment. We've got a guy right here now today that has been getting the run-around for a couple of months from his rightful pay." Social service workers act to displace considerations of need into technical considerations of eligibility. Technical considerations, which work to cement social distance between social welfare agents and the homeless, are accompanied by practices that overtly discourage homeless people from participating in the programs (Wright and Vermund forthcoming; Spencer 1994). Service agencies resort to what Spencer and McKinney (1995) call "agency raps" and "self-help raps," each designed through negotiations with those asking for services to produce accounts that can justify denial of services. Homeless exclusions are concealed beneath the rhetoric of rule constraints. Local homeless people have to spend time locating the appropriate agency and may wait for hours to get a referral. According to Tom, "its a big run around." Most of the homeless, in both San Jose and Chicago, were poorly connected to the social service system, either rejecting the extensive paperwork and humiliation involved, and or sanctioned off the rolls by missing appointments, not showing up for labor, and other causes defined as "bad" behavior by social welfare agencies. Instead, they chose to take their chances with day labor, panhandling, or hustling up jobs.

The struggles between exclusions and assimilations within the shelter and social service system were also extended to the advocate

community by many homeless. While recognizing that "doing demonstrations" helps discipline the body, as one participant inferred, the
overwhelming response was of being neglected and or used by homeless advocacy groups. Most often, advocate groups would all be lumped
together with little distinction made between types of advocacy or the
purposes of the advocate.

In San Jose, the mayor's response to homelessness was to initiate
a group called Help House the Homeless (HHH), composed of city
officials, nonprofit shelter providers, and police. While appearing to
share the same goals of ending homelessness, the conflicting purposes
produced by different occupational positions and roles—whether police, church providers, or city managers—worked against homeless
solidarity. The police were instructed by city council members to enforce the law against trespass in areas where the homeless formerly
slept, church directors wanted to house the homeless with charitable
intentions but not come into conflict with the police, and shelter staff
wanted the homeless to come to their facilities without considering
why many homeless wanted to stay on the streets. With so many
divergent interests, it was difficult for this group to reach a consensus
on any substantial changes that could assist the homeless. HHH also
provided a vehicle to assimilate local homeless leaders, as tokens, into
a predictable relationship with the city. Jim, an African American homeless man discovered by city officials, was singled out by the city,
housed, and given job opportunities, plus the facilities to establish his
own homeless newspaper. While commendable as an individual act,
the assistance rendered Jim was not forthcoming for the remainder of
San Jose's homeless. While San Jose officials trumpeted Jim as a local
success story, plans were carried out for the dispersion of the remaining homeless from the downtown Central Business District. Jim was
reluctant to take any position that would antagonize city authority.

The SHA recognized this form of assimilation and while attending
HHH meetings kept a respectful distance. The homeless in San Jose
and Chicago decried being given lower-status roles in advocacy groups,
not being taken seriously, and the seemingly endless battles over "turf"
by homeless advocates. The ambiguity with which many of the homeless joined protests not organized by themselves reflected their own,
often accurate, perceptions of low status within advocacy organizations.
As Max mentioned, "I see a lot of groups that kind of give homeless
people the lower roles in activism or what not that are not that hopped
up about homeless people themselves leading the fight." On the one
hand, advocacy groups are recognized as important for gaining a voice,

for resisting exclusion; on the other, they are perceived as being more concerned with their own agendas than that of homeless individuals. According to Alan, "Most of them don't even talk to homeless people. They're not empowering the homeless people. They're empowering the foundation that they're getting their money from." A popular perception in Chicago's Tranquility City encampment was that the generosity of the Mad Housers of Atlanta, a group of students, planners, architects, artists, and activists who originally built the Chicago huts, was limited to constructing the huts and did not extended to "real" solidarity with the homeless—i.e., spending lots of time in the camps or understanding the complex social networks that were created there. When the city of Chicago began to dismantle the huts, the Mad Housers stepped in to negotiate on behalf of the homeless, not understanding that most of the homeless participants wanted to do their own negotiating. These mistakes could have been avoided by closer contact between the Mad Housers and the encampment members.

Tactical resistance to the assimilations by advocates included critiquing advocates and organizing by and for the homeless themselves. For many of the homeless in Chicago and San Jose, holding local protests at the state capital and "making noise" were not sufficient to achieve social change. Feeling used as "props," many of the homeless developed a critique of the groups who were supposedly there to assist them. The concern was that advocacy groups not only relegated the homeless to lower-status positions of power within the organization but also suppressed the possibility of more militant action by the homeless themselves. The homeless I studied preferred action over negotiations. For many homeless, city policies change slowly due to the integration of advocacy groups within dominant systems of power. Tom commented:

> I mean . . . you have a lot of advocacy groups for the homeless. They say they are "for" the homeless. Their major concern is collecting a check every two week so that they could get paid. There are no feelings involved. There's little help received. I think that as long as we're homeless they have a job. That's one reason I want to erase the homeless issue. I'm tired of poverty pimps.

I have attempted to outline in a comparative fashion the local networks of power, composed of strategic practices and tactical resistances, within which homeless identities in San Jose and Chicago were constructed, struggles constantly being negotiated at the boundaries between pleasure, refuse, and functional spaces. This rather bleak social topography of differentiated despair is interwoven through the social-physical spaces of the city. A person who is homeless and on the street carries a different map than does the person who has a place to go at night. In the next chapter I will examine the mid-range context of these networks of power operating through the specific, local histories of both Chicago's hut city encampments (Tranquility City) and the birth and development of the Student-Homeless Alliance (SHA) in San Jose. The networks of power and resistance that served to structure homeless conceptions of what is possible also provided the milieu from which successful political actions were initiated by and on behalf of the homeless in Chicago and San Jose.

CHAPTER 5

Homeless Mobilizations
and Spatial Resistances

*In this large city that we have, this beautiful city . . . we
have a lot of wealth here, you know. And right in the
midst of it, right below the city, up under the city, a lot of
poverty . . . Yeah, you have two cities in one . . . I think of
that often. You know . . . we created a sub-city here.*
(Taylor, homeless resident of Chicago's "Tranquility City")

*If you're gonna say you're gonna help the homeless—you
keep going back. Once you get that bridge of friendship
then that bridge can take you to another bridge. Then you
get more and more people.* (Susan, homeless resident of
the "Bridge")

Authoritative strategies practiced by city officials that both contain
and disperse homeless persons, and homeless resistance to such
strategies, generate social forces that lock the participants into struggles
over the "proper" use and definitions of urban space, whether refuse,
functional, or pleasure spaces. The different political, economic, and
cultural interests of city officials and homeless individuals ensure that
any actions that are taken to privilege either city officials or the
homeless will themselves create new conditions, new social forces,
that will in turn give rise to new authoritative strategies and new
forms of resistance. However, given the limited resources of the very
poor, these struggles are decidedly one-sided. As long as homeless
families and homeless individuals remain isolated or connected only
with minimal social networks and limited political skills the dynamics
of power outlined in previous chapters will marginalize, render invisible, the very poor.

Authoritative strategies, however, may be blunted by the development of broad coalitions or alliances between collective groups. When
such coalitions or alliances act, they act within specific spatial contexts
of structured possibilities for change. Not every change is possible, no

matter how much it may be desired. Not every social or physical space leads to conditions of contestation. Moving from individual to collective resistance involves more than just forming alliances or developing coalitions; it also requires "having" the power to act within a given topography. Although individual actions are the dominant mode of resistance for the homeless, collective resistance is possible simply through the collective experience embodied in sharing the streets together, in being out of place from housed society. However, this presumes that the multiplicity of ways in which different homeless populations interpret their street experience can be unified around a central theme. That theme can be the very fact of their "homelessness," of being out of place and without a place to call home. Understanding that street experiences can be shared can bridge differences, a very difficult step. To be homeless and out of place is a state that calls into question how a place, a space, is to be treated. The very meaning of urban space as structured authoritative power, embodied literally in concrete, is called into question by those who use it for purposes that were not intended by planners and politicians. The development of alliances—between universities, homeless encampments, community groups—involves not simply the expansion of social networks, but also the connecting of multiple ways of using urban space, uses that can contest the local political intent of such spaces and build bridges between different homeless experiences. A riverbed becomes something more than a geological formation or a future urban park when those homeless who have lived within its confines are suddenly allied with institutions of higher learning, walking their halls, visiting their classrooms, or meeting with local churches and community groups.

The authoritative strategies that regulate the separation and concentration of space depend upon the legitimated separation of groups from each other in order to maintain a particular vision of spatial usage. When these strategies are confronted with a potential alliance which calls into question the original distinctions of such space, distinctions generated by the zoning plans and development dreams that shape a downtown, potentials for a different use of space are formed. Acting on this new potential, indeed, is the basis for new forms of collective resistance.

In chapter 4 we examined the relationships between authoritative strategies and the myriad forms of resistance developed by the homeless I studied in San Jose and Chicago. In this chapter I will examine the development of initial alliances and coalitions for the San Jose Student Homeless Alliance (SHA) and Chicago's Tranquility City, in addition to the perceptions of leadership and role involvement by the homeless themselves in these new groups. Examining the authoritative strategies of city officials found in downtown redevelopment plans is inadequate without also discussing the historical manner in which these contesting groups also developed. Future actions and the potential for future actions are shaped by what occurs in a group's early stages of development, in the initial formation of homeless organizations and alliances with outside institutions and or community groups. Hence, I wish to focus here on the early formation of SHA and Tranquility City with an eye toward their later successes.

In the two cases studied here, differences can be observed in the ways the two groups acquired and utilized outside support. In addition, asking what the leadership role of the homeless is in these groups, and in other advocacy organizations, is crucial in understanding the potential for collective mobilization within a specific spatial setting. The SHA represented a coalition of students, homeless persons, and community activists connected directly to the San Jose State University community. The ability of the university community to provide resources, students, and organizational skills established a different dynamic, and hence a different potential for action, compared to homeless groups initiated primarily through community organizations or by the homeless themselves. Tranquility City, by contrast, was established with the support of a segment of Chicago's art community, homeless advocates, and homeless persons, and not specifically students.

The SHA and Tranquility City can provide insights into two distinct approaches to homeless collective mobilization and to different understandings of the "proper" use of the urban landscape. SHA struggles ranged from defending homeless encampments from arbitrary police sweeps to challenging the very context of city redevelopment policies. Tranquility City participants directly challenged the authoritative strategies outlined previously by simply attempting to hold on to the space they occupied, and when that failed to demand concessions from authorities. Both of these cases developed not simply from acquiring outside resources, but from developing distinct and different modes of organization and decision making.

Insofar as homeless subjectivities are influenced by the practical struggles between city officials and the homeless, it is safe to say that changes in the types or strengths of strategies or tactical resistances will also produce changes in homeless subjectivities. Agency is not fixed but continually created in the dynamic between action and reflection. The possibilities for release from the deprivation of homelessness are, of course, both constrained and encouraged by dominant cultural, economic, and political relationships of social inequality—inequalities of race, class, and gender that privilege one class, one race, one gender over another.

The emergence of collective homeless encampments and politically inspired homeless groups is a testimony to the fluidity with which homeless subjectivities can change given the "right" circumstance, the "right" opportunity to cross borders. Homeless collective mobilizations can lead to the assertion of different definitions of the "proper" use of urban space, in addition to personal gain. We shall explore this issues more closely in the next chapter.

The University and Homeless Mobilization: The Student-Homeless Alliance

That universities can be the site for student involvement with local homeless communities is well established. Levine (1992) documents how students from the University of Massachusetts at Lowell assisted the local homeless community. University assistance was based upon the Campus Compact model, a community service model originating out of the Campus Outreach Organizing League (COOL) founded in 1984. Campus Compact is an organization of approximately 250 college and university presidents. Their objective is to create a program that links service learning to curriculum issues, delivers community services through student involvement, and publicizes those activities for each campus. By 1991–92, 74 academic institutions affiliated with Campus Compact had developed housing/homeless programs (Levine 1992, 530). One of these, the Bay Area Homelessness Program, based at the San Francisco State University campus, played a crucial role in the initial development of the SHA by sponsoring a grant for homeless outreach, offered through the Department of Social Work at San Jose State University. This grant allowed the SHA to set up a regular soup kitchen and pay for phone bills and other costs incurred in working with the local street population.

The degree of involvement and intensity of critique brought to such involvement are critical in establishing the boundaries for student involvement with local homeless communities and for convincing local homeless persons that students are serious about changing the condition of homelessness. Creating a soup kitchen and feeding the hungry, while admirable, do not address systemic causes or lead to wider political involvement of homeless individuals. However, they can be a means to achieve a much larger goal of organizing the unorganized.

Service with critical reflections, informed about politics and economics, is essential in understanding the relationship between students and homeless persons.

The role of the university is also called into question. According to Levine (1992), universities can act as arbiter "by remaining beyond local politics and power struggles" (536). Sometimes they can and sometimes they can't. These differences in interest must be articulated and not simply assumed. Levine is correct in pointing out how the university can provide models for bringing different segments of the community together. The question of whether that will achieve change is the issue. However, the project that emerged at San Jose State University was, unlike those models of service-learning that attempt to remain nonpolitical and charitable, unique in combining service, research, and militant political activism.

Aside from the large numbers of students available for community service, the physical location of San Jose State University, in the heart of downtown San Jose guaranteed that urban problems would not be mere academic topics of the classroom, but would often be found wandering through campus. Situated three city blocks from the Guadalupe River, San Jose State University provided easy access for students who wished to explore the benefits and problems of urban redevelopment. Unfortunately, most of the over 23,000 students are commuters from outlying parts of Santa Clara County. Lacking a central student community made it difficult for students to have any sustained contact with San Jose's downtown homeless. Much of the housing surrounding the campus was previously occupied by students, until the mid 1960s when it was sold by the University; now many of the units are facilities for service-dependent populations. Therefore a well-designed service-learning program that encouraged sustained contact with the very poor provided a much needed bridge for closing the gap between middle-class students and very poor homeless persons. Students who chose to do sustained work with the homeless were able to take advantage of the opportunity provided by the service-learning program or could volunteer without making long trips downtown. In exchange, the influx of university resources into the homeless community provided a much needed boost for those homeless who were willing to act, to challenge the dominant stereotypes. Hence, we cannot consider homeless actions without also talking about student actions. Each was vital for the actions of the other.

Active community resistance to city plans had occurred for years in San Jose, including the organizing of protests around the destruction of the Terry Hotel, an SRO structure in downtown San Jose, and neighborhood organizing against gentrification in outlying areas. But the emergence of a politically conscious and organized homeless group can be dated beginning in June 1990, when the city of San Jose decided to disperse approximately 250 homeless street people living along the banks of the Guadalupe River. This dispersion met with resistance from a newly developed alliance between students affiliated with Stanford University and San Jose State University and the local homeless population, an association that had been nurtured by students' voluntary commitments. In the fall of 1990 these involvements were intensified when students enrolled in San Jose State University's University Studies 157 (Community Concepts) began to research and develop various projects associated with the newly developed relationship between local homeless street encampments and students. Built upon ideas derived from the *Wingspread Special Report* on service-learning, funded by the Johnson Foundation, University Studies 157 worked to involve faculty from different departments with each other and with students on projects related to community service.

The resistance that emerged over the Guadalupe River dislocation entered a new phase upon the public release of a critical study of San Jose's redevelopment policies, a critique developed by University of California Berkeley students. With the new focus on city council decisions, redevelopment agency budgets, and city armory shutdowns, homeless activists began to attend city council meetings, intrude in city offices, and engage in other defiant activities often considered "out of place." These widespread resistance activities culminated in a series of building takeovers during the fall of 1992 in conjunction with the Up and Out of Poverty Campaign, a campaign conducted nationwide to occupy abandoned houses for homeless persons. This active integration of students and homeless persons, politically informed, and using academic resources to research city policies, moved the group from individual charity to social justice. How these developments transpired and their beginnings are crucial for understanding the ways social space and social action can be redefined by the very groups most affected by city policy.

At the opening of 1990 many homeless people had formed encampments in the local riverbed of San Jose. An estimated 250 homeless individuals made the banks of the Guadalupe River their home. Others could be found sleeping in doorways, or under bushes in the local parks. They remained disorganized politically, even though street networks remained quite extensive. In the spring of 1990 students from

Stanford University began delivering bags of food to homeless persons sleeping in downtown San Jose's McHenry Park. Inspired by a student who taught weight lifting at Stanford and was active in assisting local shelters and soup kitchens in Palo Alto, and who now was "discovering" the homeless who lived on the streets of San Jose, Stanford students volunteered to assist the homeless in McHenry Park once a week, bringing food and clothing. In return, the homeless assisted by the students would be taken to Stanford University where they would give talks to classes and discuss conditions of homelessness with student groups. These frequent "meetings in the park" were critical in establishing the first basis for trust, and hence entry into San Jose's homeless communities.

In March, the students were encouraged by the homeless living in McHenry Park to visit other camps located nearby. In particular, the "Bridge" encampment was discovered by one of the students on a routine patrol of the area and became the new focus for the Stanford students, in addition to the visits to McHenry Park. The "Bridge," at the intersection of Coyote Creek and San Fernando Street (see map 3.4) was a minicommunity of eight to ten people who were well connected with the surrounding neighborhood, often using a local market for communicating messages and receiving checks. I shall discuss more of the specifics of the "Bridge" in chapter 6. The "Bridge" gave the students an entry point to a semi-stable homeless encampment, unlike those who slept in downtown McHenry Park, who were often moving around from night to night. The four identified street encampments scattered over a five-block radius around McHenry Park were constantly changing as a result of police pressure, unlike the "Bridge," which remained relatively stable in both numbers and types of people who stayed there. The social relationship of solidarity that revealed itself in the "Bridge" encampment allowed for the growth of collective bonds between the students and the homeless, whereas the relationships between the students and the homeless in McHenry Park were more anonymous and instrumental. Only one, or at most two, people from the periphery camps visited Stanford at any one time to present their story, but the "Bridge" often sent a minimum of two and sometimes more to present their stories. The functioning of the "Bridge" as a family was one of the key characteristics that allowed for homeless placemaking and for the possibility of collective mobilization. "Bridge" encampment members measured trust by the consistency and intensity with which those who said they would help—community activists, students, other homeless—followed through on their stated commitments.

Did the advocates do what they said they were going to do, and did they appear at a site on a consistent basis? Consistency allowed for the construction of trust, which in turn allowed admission into the wider social networks of the local homeless population.

By June 1990 students from San Jose State University and Stanford University were assisting the scattered encampments on a regular basis. In early June workers from the city of San Jose walked the Guadalupe River informing the local homeless that they had to leave in two weeks. One week later "No Trespassing" signs were erected up and down the length of the river. News reports increased fear within the homeless community over what would be done to them and for them. Several homeless camps were set on fire by unknown assailants. Santa Clara County's Human Relations Commission established a site adjacent to the riverbed to process homeless applications for housing and services. At the conclusion of the riverbed sweeps, according to county officials, 179 individuals and families were located into apartments. However, the effort was perceived by the homeless as too little, too late, and disorganized. While indeed some individuals did receive benefits, many did not and left with the impression that the effort was more a way to placate the public than to truly help them.

In an effort to stop the sweeps, the local Legal Aid office filed legal action against the city of San Jose and Santa Clara County, charging that the city's relocation plan was inadequate under Welfare Code 17000. The suit charged that mentally ill disabled persons were being housed in Julian Street Inn, a local shelter, causing an overload of their facilities, instead of being given adequate housing and that after a ten-day stay no follow-up was conducted for those who had been denied benefits. It was further charged that there was no provision for due process since there was no mechanism to address complaints about the process beyond the ten-day application period. A temporary restraining order was issued, but overturned in court. The sweeps continued. In this tense atmosphere, students who had been active with the "Bridge" helped camp residents through the application process. However, only two, the main leaders of the camp, received Section 8 housing vouchers; the rest received nothing and returned to their camp. In a short time Susan, one of the "Bridge" members, moved into her apartment about two miles south of the downtown area, as the "Bridge" began to break up. Susan's eight-year stay on the streets had at least temporarily come to an end. Individual members drifted off, many farther south toward Willow Creek, or deeper into the bushes to hide from the police. Those who stayed behind risked police harassment and arrest.

Much of the motivation for conducting the sweeps of the river was to lower the visibility of the homeless camps along the river, a visibility intensified by the appearance of squatter shacks and jerry-rigged lean-tos. Using military metaphors, then Mayor Tom McEnery (1994) talked about the Guadalupe sweeps as "Time for the D day assault" and as "the few successful strategic attacks against homelessness" (43–44). This treatment of the homeless as enemy is not suprising when we consider that the visibility of homelessness is more of a problem for city governments than legitimate attempts to end homelessness. City power is conveyed through the visual orderliness of its streets. Out-of-place persons do not contribute to a sense of order. They arouse the antipathy and fear of consumers and office workers. Visibility is about demonstrating control over public and private spaces. Making the homeless "invisible" is a key requirement for city governments in order to please their housed constituencies. Clearly, for the city of San Jose, loss of public support for homeless institutions coincided with the appearance that homelessness was out of control. This was clearly the reason stated by McEnery: The problem of homelessness was really about the public perceiving "the problem to be out of city hall's control" (43). One is expected to be either in a shelter, in place, or in a legitimate housing unit. Lowering homeless visibility therefore becomes a key method of gathering public support. When asked why the homeless had not reappeared in large numbers after the Guadalupe River sweeps, one police officer who had coordinated the removal stated:

> It's certainly a matter of survival . . . If somebody throws a sleeping bag under a tree, it's much less likely that they'll be detected than if they throw up a tent with a sliding glass door. (Cassidy 1990c)

Waiting for their benefits, "Bridge" residents remained in their camp through the middle of July; several remained into September. On the Fourth of July, the two main leaders of the "Bridge" accompanied students to Santa Cruz, California, to attend a rally by homeless and housing activist groups to protest Santa Cruz's proposed anticamping city ordinance. This was the first time that members of the "Bridge" had spoken publicly before a large crowd, as opposed to a small group of students. This pivotal event cemented a bond between the students and several of the homeless, leading to the birth of a new group, the Peninsula Homeless Action Project (PHAP). At this stage the group was "located" at Stanford University, often with meetings of twenty-five or more students and homeless. However, over time student interest at Stanford began to wane as committed students graduated or drifted away. With the decline of interest at Stanford, new interest was generated by students and community activists in San Jose. The name was then changed to the South Bay Homeless Action Project (SHAP) to reflect the new location of the group.

During the time PHAP was functioning, a soup kitchen was started that served dinner to approximately 130 people every two weeks through a local downtown shelter, the Cecil White Center. This activity was key in recruiting new homeless members to the group and in providing street information. In addition, it provided a common meeting ground, and "neutral" terrain, for students and homeless individuals to meet with minimal risk. At this stage students and homeless were now circulating between McHenry Park, the Cecil White Center, and the "Bridge." PHAP assisted other shelters and food services in Palo Alto through August and worked with local churches in Los Altos and Mountain View. The movement to San Jose was initiated, in part, because one of the student leaders began regular attendance at San Jose State University. However, other reasons were the unwillingness of the Stanford group to move beyond a "charity" model to one of individual empowerment, providing services, and direct political action. Many students just did not have the time or willingness to extend their commitments, and most of the homeless PHAP was working with at this point were in San Jose.

By the fall of 1990, students from San Jose State University's University Studies 157 course had begun to work directly with those homeless individuals involved with SHAP. Susan, the formerly homeless "Bridge" leader, became further involved with the students. She began to come on campus, often bringing other homeless people she knew, to speak to the students and to help in the collective meetings. Forming work teams to tackle soup kitchen work, legal advocacy, outreach, media, and health care/housing, San Jose State students developed specific projects that contributed to the expansion of the SHAP group. As students and homeless group members conducted outreach throughout McHenry Park, they would befriend members of the homeless community, often bringing them to campus for the weekly meetings. Beginning students were always accompanied by a "veteran" student who had worked in the older group, PHAP.

By the end of September, a proposal was made to San Jose State University's School of Social Work to fund a biweekly soup kitchen. With the grant money, a soup kitchen was established involving both the students and the homeless serving food together, building bridges to the local homeless community. At this stage advocacy was accomplished on an individual basis according to each homeless person's circumstances. With the exception of the July Fourth rally, collective advocacy did not develop until homeless and student members united around their own platform. This began tentatively with homeless SHAP members speaking at the Bay Area Homelessness Conference in December, speaking as a group to San Jose State Students three days later, speaking at a fund-raiser in February 1991, and finally speaking with a powerful voice at city council hearings in May 1991.

Given the changing nature of the local street population, student projects would quite often have to radically change in midstream. A sense of constant crisis pervaded our working environment. During the project one homeless man, Gerald, who we had worked closely with and who elected to stay under the "Bridge" risking arrest, died of a heart seizure related to his drinking. According to street informants, another man who had lived under the "Bridge" was arrested for manslaughter after an altercation with another homeless man, in which the other person fell off the concrete platform under the bridge, breaking his neck.

In September students from the University Studies 157 class witnessed an interaction between local police and some of the homeless they had worked with. One homeless man was spotted in the back of a patrol car, blood streaming down his face; another was handcuffed by police parked above the "Bridge" camp. The students responded by taking notes on what was happening and meeting with a nearby resident who knew the homeless men. This incident had a profound effect, shaking some of the students' view of the police and engaging still others in thinking about their involvement with the project. In a later incident, group members were informed that one of the members of another encampment, a young man around 21, had been beaten up and threatened with a pistol by a local group of neighborhood "toughs" after they had slashed his tent. This undercurrent of violence and deprivation took its toll on many of the students, necessitating much discussion and emotional support, often creating polarizations with the group and bringing out inner tensions. However, the students remained with the project and realized afterward the importance of flexibility. One student who previously described himself as a "frat boy," who stated that all homeless were "bums" or "alcoholics," during the course of the semester turned around completely, developing an identification with the homeless population and expressing anger at those who did not understand their plight. However, after working with the group for five months he returned to his prior habits, reintegrating with fraternity life, although not with the same attitudes. Three days after the students witnessed the arrest of one of the homeless people they had worked with, they and a small group of the "Bridge" people confronted the mayoral candidate at a forum on the San Jose State campus, asking question about police practices and the homeless. In this instance, the homeless spoke out forcefully, accompanied by the students. The mayoral candidate expressed her sympathy for the plight of the homeless. At this stage in the group's practical work, charity issues dominated social justice issues. Yet the stage was set for more advanced work as members of the local homeless community were emboldened to go onto the San Jose State campus, a terrain from which they frequently had been removed in the past by security. Simultaneously, student attitudes were changing given the witnessing of street events and the increasing familiarity with the local homeless street population. This familiarity produced the effect of either drawing students further into a more committed involvement or the reverse, having them pull out of the group all together. The intensity of the emotions aroused in this type of work polarized the work environment, leading to many arguments and much discussion between the homeless and the students.

In September the "Bridge" population declined as a result of police pressure, and the group began looking for other sites. A second site was discovered, as a result of talking with those who came to the soup kitchen, under an offramp of a downtown freeway that had been disabled by the 1989 Loma Prieto earthquake (fig. 5.1).

This encampment was really several encampments set close together, inhabited by five to fourteen people varying in age from eighteen to those in their mid forties. Most were in their early twenties. I will discuss more of the details of this camp in the next chapter. SHAP began to visit the encampments once, sometimes three times, a week, researching the population and assisting them. Camp residents in turn would attend campus meetings and make suggestions about direction for the group. As students began working with this set of encampments, bringing food, clothes, and listening, many were moved to act beyond their initial motivations for taking the class. During November three students slept overnight in the camps and familiarized themselves with the residents on a first-name basis. Without being asked to, another student spent $250 of her own money to get medical attention for a puppy that was the pet of one of the homeless youth. In return, encampment members appeared on the San Jose State University cam-

Figure 5.1 *Homeless encampment near the catacombs, San Jose.*

pus speaking to scheduled classes about their condition and what could be done about it. They would often confide in the students about their problems, and the students often confided with them about their problems. The border-crossing between these two diverse populations was fraught with a sense of danger, excitement, and learning. As news coverage of these meetings expanded, more student interest was generated, attracting more students, community activists and other homeless persons; many now entered the group from local shelters.

By December 1990, the integration of students, homeless members, and community activists through SHAP had produced a group that could speak out forcefully to diverse crowds. Speaking engagements ranged from local churches to the Bay Area Homelessness Conference held at the University of California at Berkeley, at which over ten homeless SHAP members spoke and presented their own panel. In addition, a dozen homeless SHAP members organized a panel on homelessness, with student assistance, presenting to students at San Jose State University and to an official of Santa Clara County's Human Relations Commission. At semester's end, many of the students who had taken the University Studies 157 course left. However, the projects they completed while in the course, such as fund-raising and soup kitchen setup, contributed to the stabilization of the group. During

Spring 1991, SHAP changed its name to the Student-Homeless Alliance (SHA) upon recommendation by the homeless. At this point homeless encampment members and new shelter arrivals were fully integrated into the group, often attending student-led protests over the Gulf War and over tuition hikes.

In April, SHA was recognized as a formal student/community organization, and with local news coverage from the San Jose Mercury News, fifteen new members joined the group. During this period, organizing efforts began to shift from street encampments, which were rapidly disappearing due to police pressure, to local shelters, soup kitchens, and the National Guard Armory. Many student veterans of the group knew people in the encampments, the shelters and the Armory. They often acted as negotiators between the different groups when problems arose.

May was a turning point for SHA. Official confrontation with the city of San Jose began with the release of a report, developed by University of California Berkeley students, analyzing the city's redevelopment, housing, and homeless policies. Data gathered from the Association of Bay Area Governments critical of the city's lack of affordable housing prevented the study from being easily dismissed. In defending the city's housing policy, San Jose's Mayor Susan Hammer stated in a letter to the author dated 13 June 1991, "As I said, your study presents some excellent information. I agree with much of what you say. However, I must take exception to the report's conclusion that the City 'is more interested in getting rid of its low-income residents, than in providing affordable housing for them.' " In defense of San Jose's policies toward the homeless, the mayor pointed out that the city council had created the Department of Housing in 1988 and provided funding for a Homeless Coordinator. The report released at a press conference outside city hall was accompanied by over forty homeless persons, students, and community activists, who presented their case to the local and regional press and then marched upstairs into the mayor's office unannounced, presenting the report to her staff for consideration. This was the first time many of the homeless had been in the mayor's office.

As Benford (1992, 38, 43) points out, "scripting" and "staging" of events are very important for generating large media coverage. This was no less true in the press conference and invasion of the mayor's office by the SHA. At this event media cameras focused on the students and community activists while neglecting the homeless. In later actions, this was blunted by a strategy of having all definable spokespersons for the group dress the same and follow the media around when they conducted interviews. Over time homeless voices were added to the chorus of media attention, and the label given to participants changed from *protestors* to *homeless advocates*, a more respectable definition. The introduction of the Redevelopment Critique allowed for a change in the way the SHA approached City Hall. Issues of police abuse against the homeless were reframed as part of a much larger problem having to do with the city of San Jose's priorities as expressed through their redevelopment plans.

Scripts, "as a set of directions that define the scene, identify actors, and outline expected behavior" (Benford 1992, 38), are built upon action "frames, that provide a collective definition of the situation" (Snow, Rochford, Worden, and Benford 1986; Snow and Benford 1988). For the SHA, the release of the Redevelopment Critique was a powerful tool that redefined the problems of homelessness in San Jose, reframing the debate over homelessness by connecting homelessness to the policy of city development. With recommended solutions and rationales, the Redevelopment Critique pointed to a definable antagonist: city council and redeveloper interests. Responsible redevelopment, not rampant redevelopment, was the call. Effectively, the mayor was targeted as pushing development agendas that excluded the city's poor in favor of real estate interests. One protestor carried a placard reading, "Don't Hammer the Homeless." The scripting of demonstrations occurred in front of San Jose's city hall and extended into the inner chambers, where during city council meetings SHA members would line the back wall with their placards held up for all to see. Homeless voices, silent before, now spoke loudly and clearly.

The nervousness of San Jose's City Hall was evident in one event which is noteworthy. A local task force, Help House the Homeless, invited members of SHA to speak about San Jose's redevelopment issues and the displacement of homeless persons at their monthly meeting. One of the University of California Berkeley students who had participated in assembling the report presented the arguments at the meeting along with homeless members of SHA. Also present were San Jose city officials, who proceeded to attack the student's report. The criticism was so intense that it discouraged the student from presenting the findings of the group at the next city council meeting. However, another San Jose State University student secured a copy of the study, mastered it, and presented the findings at the city's next vote on the redevelopment budget. At the end of June protests had escalated to marches and more overt demonstrations in front of City Hall, targeting specifically the city's redevelopment policies for privileging the wealthy over the poor. When the city council scheduled a vote on the new redevelopment budget, SHA packed the city chambers with more than sixty demonstrators. As a result of that protest, one council member telephoned SHA, set up a morning breakfast with the students, community advocates, and homeless leaders of the SHA, and informed the group that the mayor was going to unveil her plans for a proposed Giant's baseball stadium that very afternoon. The reframing of the redevelopment issue provided an opportunity for one city council member, who may have had another agenda of his own, to give legitimacy to SHA concerns. The press conference to announce the proposed Giant's baseball stadium on Zanker Road now included vocal homeless demonstrators from local shelters and community advocates standing not more than twenty feet from the conference and captured well by regional San Francisco Bay Area media outlets (fig. 5.2).

In these actions we see a critical transition from a group empowering individuals to perform individual acts of charity to one linked to issues of political and social power, to social justice for the poor. Homelessness solutions were "reframed" from simple local defensive actions designed to reduce police harassment of bridge encampments

Figure 5.2 *The Student-Homeless Alliance protests San Jose's proposal to build a baseball stadium for the San Francisco Giants.*

to an attack on San Jose's downtown redevelopment policy. It remained to be seen how long the group would last or what new forms it might assume with these new changes. Over the next fourteen months the group was able to initiate fourteen demonstrations and marches, twenty community outreach meetings, eleven media and letter writing events, and several major housing occupations. However, the consequence of this shift in focus was less immediate work on the street, such as serving food, and more "political" work on protests and demonstrations. The SHA's militancy was a logical development from the increased integration of students, homeless persons, and community activists, combined with a new understanding, a "reframing," of city redevelopment policy. As city intransigence increased, so did SHA militancy. In April 1992, fourteen SHA members, students, and homeless were arrested at the steps of City Hall protesting the closure of the National Guard Armory and the San Jose's unwillingness to house those displaced. In late April, SHA marched with community leaders to protest the Rodney King verdict, meeting with the chief of police and representatives from the African American and Chicano community. Working with Latino organizations SHA helped to found the Direct Action Alliance (DAA) involving homeless persons and community leaders and began to work closely with MECHA, a Chicano student group at San Jose State.

In May, SHA's first housing occupation occurred with the takeover of the abandoned rectory at the old St. Joseph's School in downtown San Jose, a previous site of food distribution to the homeless. After almost a week of occupation, one member was arrested and the house was shut down by police. A chain-link fence was erected around the property and guards were posted full-time. This was followed by the erection of several "tent cities," one at City Hall and another on the steps of the Fairmont Hotel, next to the McHenry Convention Center. By fall, St. Joseph's School and Rectory had been leveled to make a parking lot for the nearby Sharks hockey stadium.

In October, homeless and community support for SHA seemed to dwindle. Without tangible successes the strategy of confronting the city was at risk of losing many of the homeless who had joined early on. A success was needed. On Thanksgiving 1992 five houses were occupied along River Street, near the downtown Redevelopment Agency and adjacent to the Guadalupe River. Over fifty people were involved in the action. After nine arrests were made, SHA returned the next day and reoccupied two of the houses with about twenty-five members, but left shortly before police arrived (Anderson 1992). There was extensive regional media coverage of the event. Six of those arrested were sentenced to twenty-five hours of community service and carried out their service by renovating another nearby house as a temporary shelter. This house, one of the six owned by the Santa Clara Valley Water District, was given the green light for renovation and housed six ex-homeless persons for the next two years (Gelhaus 1994). A small success was achieved. However, the loss of a faculty advisor and the low commitment of new students altered the dynamics of the group once again, leading SHA to finally break with the university and reestablish itself in the community as the Community-Homeless Alliance (CHA). Several homeless individuals and community activists broke with the group to form their own organization, Voice of the Homeless. Many of the original group of homeless, with the group since the beginning, left between August 1992 and July 1993. Some simply disappeared, others left the area. SHA had lasted well over three years, far beyond the original expectations of group members.

Community Groups and Homeless Mobilization: Tranquility City

In Chicago, homeless mobilization took a different form. Active for years, the Coalition for the Homeless (CCH) took an active position in opposing the removal of homeless persons from Chicago's O'Hare airport in 1990. With the support of CCH a small number of the more than two hundred homeless residents of the airport formed their own group called Homeless On the Move for Equality (HOME). Organizing and convening with street people on Lower Wacker Drive, in the shelter system, and in industrial areas of the West Side, HOME members worked to register homeless people to vote and to become collectively empowered. Members were recruited by CCH for various campaigns for more low-income housing and to curb the abuse of homeless persons by local officials. HOME and CCH members became key supporters of those who settled into the Chicago hut encampments.

Starting in September 1991, a local art gallery, the Randolph Street Gallery, ran a series of forums entitled "Counter-Proposals: Adaptive Approaches to a Built Environment." One group invited to appear and conduct workshops was the Mad Housers of Atlanta. The Mad Housers, composed of volunteer architects, planners, and community activists, provided one model for shelter, gaining a reputation for direct action by constructing over two hundred huts for the homeless around the city of Atlanta. Through connections at the Randolph Street Gallery, the Mad

Housers were placed in contact with HOME and CCH. Throughout the month of October 1991 debates between the Mad Housers, interested homeless persons, community activists, artists, and members of CCH and HOME occurred at the Randolph Street Gallery around the issue of where to locate the first huts and what purpose they would serve.

For the Mad Housers, as indeed for many of the advocates, the construction of huts was viewed as a way of making visible the plight of Chicago's homeless. For the homeless it was a way of securing some minimal housing. However, many of the homeless who attended the meetings were willing to engage in symbolic politics, encouraging the placing of huts were they would be visible. In addition, the Mad Housers attempted to dovetail their efforts with those of CCH, which at the time was conducting a campaign to force the creation of affordable housing at Presidential Towers. Initial plans suggested placing the huts at the entrance to the Towers, for symbolic effect. Other ideas included placing the huts in wealthier North Side neighborhoods to make a point about Chicago's lack of affordable housing. All of these were ultimately rejected as causing problems for the homeless population itself. Finally, it was decided to locate the "huts" where some of the street people were already sleeping—near the Fulton Street markets, on Chicago Milwaukee Corporation property adjacent to the suburban Metra railway lines. This decision was prompted, in part, by the fact that a local graphic artist, when walking the railroads near his home, spotted homeless squatters living in an abandoned warehouse near the Fulton markets and befriended them, inviting them to meetings with the Mad Housers at the art gallery. It was decided that homeless individuals who attended the meetings on a regular basis would receive the first huts.

The actual design workshop, where the first huts were built, was conducted on 31 October followed by transport and erection of the first huts under the Halsted Bridge, on the Near West Side. The first huts, given to two middle-aged homeless men who slept under the docks next to a warehouse they named "Pallet City," prompted the construction of more huts, as word filtered out through the shelter system and the streets (fig. 5.3). The number of huts grew rapidly. The site was named "Tranquility City" by one of its inhabitants, for "it's natural surroundings." From November 1991 to June 1992 "Tranquility City," this moderate-size squatter camp of twenty-two 6-×-8-×-8-foot plywood "huts," was counted as home by approximately fifty homeless persons for varying lengths of time.

Figure 5.3 *Two huts in Tranquility City.*

Only two of the identified hut dwellers worked, in either day-labor or part-time low-paying jobs; others collected SSI or engaged in "shadow work," usually collecting cans. Prior to becoming homeless, the hut dwellers had worked at primarily blue-collar jobs: construction, sandblasting, machinist, cab driving, cook, forklift driver, telecommunication sales (part-time), and day labor. Most of the squatters received small benefits—SSI, food stamps, or General Assistance—which helped them get by from month to month. Prior work tended to be unstable and episodic, with work periods ranging from a low of 1 month to 13 years. Interestingly, with the exception of one person from Africa, all of their fathers had working-class occupations (railroad worker, cargo ship worker, truckdriver, construction, bartender, and farmer). The hut dwellers' mothers worked in the home as housewives, except for three (factory worker, waitress, teacher in Africa). With the exception of several African American females, one white, and two Latinos, all squatters were middle-aged African American males with a median age of forty-three, precisely the group most affected by the downtown's loss of low-wage, union, manufacturing jobs in Chicago. These were working-class men who had experienced a radical rate of downward mobility.

A February article in the Chicago *Sun-Times* (Smith 1992) about the Mad Housers and the encampment gave "Tranquility City" a high public profile. At this time, one of the coldest months of the year, the city of Chicago gave tacit permission for their presence. According to spokeswoman Avis La Velle: "We haven't had any complaints from property owners—and without complaints, the mayor sees no reason to tear them down" (Smith 1992, 4). In addition, Metra rail, the owner of the property upon which the huts were located, gave their okay to the settlement. According to Wayne, one of the homeless residents, "Metra had wrote the mayor. Metra and then Old Milwaukee, the owner of the property, sent a letter to the mayor's office and he came down and okayed it to us in person."

During this period, members of HOME patrolled Lower Wacker Drive talking to local street people about the huts and the alternative to the shelters as well as recruiting homeless individuals to vote. Other homeless individuals not affiliated with HOME would meet with the Mad Housers and go to the shelters to spread the word about the huts. In the discussions between the Mad Housers, community activists, and members of the local homeless population it was emphasized that the huts were not a solution, but rather a way of making a symbolic statement about homelessness. The Mad Housers understood their role as that of builders—to provide temporary housing, to conduct guerrilla architecture. The homeless residents were of a more diverse mind, perceiving the building of the huts as both a symbolic gesture, a protest, and a way to stabilize their own lives, a place of security and privacy. Many of them had been homeless for over six months, some as long as ten years; they had a high degree of street knowledge. This contradiction in intent, I believe, came to fruition in the final struggles over "Tranquility City" after the encampments were condemned by the city of Chicago.

With the onset of spring weather the city had a change of heart. According to the mayor's spokesperson, "The Mayor has decided that it is not in the best interest of the city to allow these structures" (Smith 1992). Citing problems of lack of running water, sanitary facilities, and electricity, the city was eager to dispose of the huts, even though no complaints had been filed. As Commissioner Dan Weil commented, "It is clear they're not safe. They don't have permits. They don't have plumbing. They don't meet the code. They're coming down . . . If those huts were allowed to exist, then why should anyone have to obtain a permit for anything?" (Smith 1992b). These reasons caused much indignation in the local homeless community, who believed that Mayor Daley's decision had been precipitated by their visibility combined with support from commuting suburbanites and community activists and a proposed redevelopment plan for the area. Speculation abounded in the papers about a proposal to build a new "urban Ravinia" and casino near the huts' location. According to Robert Wiggs, executive director of the West Central Association, a group representing property owners in the area, "we might call it a type of necessary displacement" (Smith 1992c). Any connection between developers' interests and the dismantling of the huts was denied by the city. It was clear that other areas of the Near West Side occupied by shelters were also feeling the squeeze of gentrification. While the city said that it had no plans to close any of the shelters in the area, local businesspeople and incoming neighbors were disturbed by the presence of large numbers of homeless in the area (Stein 1992).

It should be said that the huts—which were well ventilated and well insulated and had a sleeping loft, window, storage space, and an internal stove that doubled as a range and a heater—kept the squatters warm in subfreezing weather and provided security and privacy (there were locks on all of the doors). Showers were taken at a local shelter, and running water was taken from a fire hydrant that a city worker had turned on for the squatters. The huts were clearly visible during the winter months from the luxury apartment windows of nearby Presidential Towers. According to Wayne,

> and you could add, they were clearly visible from the Metra trains. Yeah, because they started slowing them down, even stopping them, and the conductors would show everybody where there're at. 'Cause a lot of people did see them, and they would be standing up in the windows looking for them. And that's when they started slowing the trains down, so they could show them exactly where they were at.

With notice that their huts were being dismantled, the squatters organized a campaign to bring public attention to the plight of the homeless throughout Chicago. Encampment members mobilized community support, involving several local churches, activist groups, universities, and local volunteers. Human Services Commissioner Daniel Alvarez began negotiations with the squatters and promised that "there would be no bulldozers" (Thorton 1992). Instead the huts were lifted onto flatbed trucks and taken away.

The Chicago Christian Industrial League, one of many shelters offering overnight and transitional housing, referred to the problem as one of lack of information—the "homeless don't know how to access the system"—and encouraged them to come into the shelter system rather than be on the streets. The squatters themselves had other ideas. These ideas included rehabilitating abandoned buildings and moving into apartments, but not moving to a shelter. Shelter providers often perceive squatters as recalcitrant, as not wanting to follow the rules against alcohol or be in at certain hours and leave early in the morning. Unfortunately this disciplinary agenda of social control outlined in the previous chapter conflicts with the squatter's desire for privacy, autonomy, and freedom, the ability to come and go when he or she pleases, and the security of being able to lock up one's possessions.

During negotiations with the city, the Mad Housers were often given a high-profile role that occasionally clashed with the squatters themselves. However, both groups were united against the city's efforts to displace the squatters. The Mad Housers were joined by the Architects, Designers, and Planners for Social Responsibility, HOME, and CCH, as well as some local churches from the South Side of Chicago. As negotiations progressed between the city and the Mad Housers, attempts were made to cut deals for the squatters. The squatters were offered public housing as replacement housing. The attempt by the city to negotiate with the Mad Housers as opposed to the squatters brought sharp reactions from the homeless. The squatters were determined to negotiate with the city on their own terms. One homelesss resident of Tranquility City confirmed this, explaining:

> That came about when the Mad Housers themselves went down to City Hall and tried to have a meeting with Commissioner Alvarez. We knew something like that was going to happen because of the conflict with _____ tell'n the other guys "we could tell them for ourselves." All of us are together. This is what I was telling them. And everybody had to say what they want, where they want to live, and all that. But, we didn't want nobody from the Mad Housers. We made that clear from the jump street—we was going to do our own negotiating. We told them we wanted you to be around for the support, that was the main thing.

This precipitated a refusal on the part of some of the squatters to tour the Chicago Housing Authority housing offered by the city as an alternative to the huts. Eventually this was resolved, with the city opening negotiations directly with the squatters. While promising not to take away any of the huts during negotiations, the city confiscated seven huts on 10 June and relocated their residents in various public housing projects. The squatters wanted the huts to remain to house other home-less street people after they moved into new dwellings, but to no avail. Said Human Services Commissioner Daniel Alvarez, "I don't know what they are complaining about. We said we weren't going to bulldoze those huts. And we're not. But after relocating these people, what's the use of having those wood boxes there? We are simply trying to clear the area of debris" (Smith 1992d). In response, Wayne exclaimed, "Come on! I mean, clear the area of debris? All that time we was down there we cleaned up more than the city did. I mean, we had people comin' down there trying to dump on our property, so we had to run'em off. We had the city streetsweeper came down there and dump some stuff . . . [the huts] those were our cribs." As a result of negotia-tions with the city, all of the homeless living in the encampment received apartments in Chicago's public housing projects, apartments that normally take years to receive. Homeless squatters were dispersed and relocated to Lathrop Homes, Rockwell Gardens, Washington Park Homes, and the Wicker Park Apartments, according to their preference. The remaining huts in the visible area were carted off.

As the Tranquility City squatters dispersed into Chicago's public housing, some organized further, establishing their own social move-ment organization—the People's Campaign for Jobs, Housing, and Food. They have continued to search out other homeless persons to encour-age them to take an apartment in public housing. Because they have little access to telephones, they keep lines of communication open by leaving messages and talking to neighbors.

On Thanksgiving 1992, one of the main leaders of the camp, Dwayne Snyder, was found dead outside the Harold Washington Li-brary downtown, reportedly from liver failure. The fact that he was left lying on the sidewalk, still alive, after being discovered in freezing weather and not taken to the hospital for several hours precipitated an angry reaction from the homeless community. A small memorial service was conducted in December at Chicago's Daley Plaza, and a procession went to the site of Dwayne's death and placed flowers there. A similar ritual was conducted by *Streetwise* for Joseph Gould, the homeless vendor killed by an off-duty police officer two years later. Former homeless persons, students, community members, and those still living in shelters joined in as the group of several hundred made their way from the plaza to the library. The students, community members, and homeless who had worked with Dwayne felt his loss most bitterly, because he had just started working again at his old job and now had a place to live in public housing. When he was found on the street, though, his pocket identification contained the address of a local shelter. The following summer former hut dwellers scheduled a Labor Day reunion of supporters and former members of Tranquility City. Over two dozen people celebrated "Remember: Tranquility City."

What began as a protest against the lack of affordable housing became a method of building community, involving homeless individuals, artists, and community activists. Active protests by the homeless generated real material gains, contributing to the formation of an organization called the People's Campaign for Jobs, Housing, and Food and disputing the concept of disaffiliation, often discussed in relationship to the very poor. Tranquility City, far from being an aberration, illustrated the creative capacities of those marginalized by the lack of affordable housing and decent employment. Similar to Wagner's "Politicos" (Wagner 1993; Wagner and Cohen 1991), many of the hut dwellers exhibited a high degree of political consciousness and the capacity for sustained organizational work, some having participated in the early civil rights movement, another with the Black Panther Party. I shall discuss this more in depth in the next chapter.

What squatters gain by organizing encampments, and why encampments are "chosen" as opposed to shelters, are questions that speak to the desire for community, autonomy, and privacy. The social space Tranquility City occupied placed it at the center of the controversy over the meaning of public space and the role of the unhoused. The resistance of those who lived in the encampments to their dispersion by the city of Chicago would not have been possible without the prior establishment of social networks throughout the community.

The SHA and Tranquility City represented different paths for empowering the homeless. These paths involved real relations of power between the homeless participants and the other actors within associated groups, either community activists, students, church groups, or the art community. These relations of power were reflected in attitudes toward what were perceived as the group's leaders and how included the homeless themselves were in the decision-making process as both groups went through various transitions. In Tranquility City there was one level of decision making between the Mad Housers and the hut dwellers, another within the encampments themselves, and still another between the hut dwellers and the city of Chicago. These levels were being constantly renegotiated by the actors involved, as revealed earlier. The slow accumulation of resources and networks within both groups was accompanied by changes in the participants themselves. More of this will be discussed in the next chapter. Roles often shifted from passive onlooker to active participant, and sometimes the reverse, as struggles ensued over group control and topographical control, over the literal physical topography of the camps, and over the relationship between such camps and shelters and city council decisions.

Avenues of recruitment for the SHA and Tranquility City varied quite widely. Half of the SHA participants mentioned that they decided to become involved with the group when they were informed about it by other homeless friends or when they saw other homeless people taking action. For the homeless in the SHA, the charitable acts of students, while appreciated, were less important factors in their involvement. However, those actions did establish regular and sustained contact between community activists, students, and the homeless, and they carved out a social space within which the homeless could observe the active involvement of other homeless and students without having to immediately commit themselves. Clearly, homeless social networks were critical in recruitment. The street "grapevine," observed in the soup kitchens, provided a source for information on which shelters to avoid, police actions in the area, which groups to join, which to avoid, and which soup kitchens were operating. Students involved with the homeless in the SHA became involved for roughly similar reasons, except that about half the students became involved for political or personal reasons and took their own initiative, whereas homeless participants were attracted when persuaded by homeless friends.

Tranquility City residents came into contact through various means, some through direct contact with the arts community on the North Side of Chicago, others through the actions of HOME and CCH, still others through the shelter system. Many who came into the camps arrived after being informed about the huts by other homeless men who had stayed in the huts. Several homeless men sleeping on Lower Wacker Drive in the downtown Loop area found out about the hut encampments through the patrols of HOME members and or through the local shelters and became involved. Again, as with the SHA, street networks were critical in recruitment and in sustaining the viability of the camps. Often when somebody would move out of their hut, or plan to move out, they would inform someone in the shelters who would take their place. When overlaps occurred, two people at a time occupied a hut.

Questions of leadership and authority emerged in issues of whether or not those making decisions for the group listened to others and whether or not the decisions made about actions to be taken were initiated internally or from outside the camps or groups. Questions of listening will be taken up in the next chapter. In the SHA, struggles occasionally emerged between the students and the homeless as to what actions should be taken in particular situations, such as police disruptions of a camp, a building takeover, or a demonstration. Usually the students deferred to the homeless. Although several students were key leaders in the group and often made tactical decisions about demonstration locations and logistics, only two of the homeless participants in the SHA stated that they thought the SHA's president, a student, made all the decisions for the group. The majority of homeless participants believed that it was "the group" or "everyone" who made the decisions about what actions needed to be taken. Occasionally a homeless person or student would complain about nonhomeless members making decisions for the group, but this was clearly a minority opinion. Student responses to the leadership question were almost identical with those of the homeless. In Tranquility City, homeless hut dwellers made their decisions about the camps collectively, even though day-to-day decisions were made on an individual basis. The main problems in the Chicago camps were between the Mad Housers and the hut dwellers, arising from negotiations with the city. However, many of these differences were resolved in discussions. Some hut dwellers who lived farther away from the main cluster of huts perceived several of the men in the main huts as the "group leaders" and complained because they didn't receive the best items that were brought down to the huts by community groups. These were the same people who identified with the Mad Housers and followed their lead during negotiations while the camps under the Halsted Bridge stuck to an independent line. Hence, the Mad Housers's first attempt to maintain control over the huts they had built contributed to destablizing the "community" of camp dwellers. Even so, most of these differences were resolved through patient discussion and in the dynamic of the huts' being dismantled by the city. For their part, those who lived in the huts under the Halsted Bridge would complain that hut dwellers who lived farther away who just wanted something for themselves and didn't care about the larger issues.

The SHA and Tranquility City lasted for only a short time. However, I believe that these brief experiments in homeless collective empowerment demonstrate the ability to collectively mobilize what was thought to be an isolated, alienated, disaffiliated, and passive population often framed as "victims." The fact that the participants refused these frames speaks to the ability of the very poor to throw their bodies against the machinery of their own oppression—to find liberation in collective action. How this occurred will be explored in the next chapter.

CHAPTER 6

Homeless Placemaking, Collective Identity, and Collective Action

They really pay attention to you, then. Just walking around on the street ain't gonna do it. You've got to build a foundation out there like we did. Then they start noticing you . . .You've got to really come together and act like you really want something. (Tom, homeless resident of "Tranquility City")

Historically, African-American people believed that the construction of a homeplace, however, fragile and tenuous (the slave hut, the wooden shack), had a radical political dimension. Despite the brutal reality of racial apartheid, of domination, one's homeplace was the one site where one could freely confront the issue of humanization, where one could resist. (hooks 1990, 42)

Building foundations to get noticed, the building of place as resistance to authoritative strategies of power, illustrates the importance of placemaking, of homebuilding, in the development of collective action, and indeed collective identity. bell hooks's observations about strategies of African American survival can be easily applied to the dispossessed population of homeless men and women, regardless of race, who find themselves having to establish a homebase outside of housed mainstream society. In our culture, homelessness equates with the historical position of many African Americans—marginalized, excluded, repressed, and dominated by mainstream representations of race, class, and gender. Solidarity, "sticking together," in the face of such violence remained essential for survival. Developing solidarity, organization, and militant action, indeed, characterized the development of San Jose's multicultural SHA. In contrast, the struggles to sustain Tranquility City on Chicago's Near West Side, to maintain a new homeplace, constituted a form of defensive protest, a protest to force the city to house the homeless in decent apartments. The SHA and Tranquility City witnessed the emergence of homeless placemaking, nurtured in temporary "safe" zones, dramatizing the importance of social-physical space in the development of collective identities and actions. For the SHA, the university provided a temporary safe haven to nurture new collective identities and new types of collective action. For Tranquility City residents, the location of the huts on Metra railway property in a remote site next to abandoned buildings, social attachments to surrounding communities, and the support of a neighboring art gallery provided the camps with a temporary safe zone.

These were conflicts that "happened somewhere," where the social-physical dimensions of space provided the means through which such struggles could be defined and carried out. The concentration of so many huts in one spot provided visual evidence to all who rode by on local commuter trains of the city of Chicago's inability to deal with homelessness. For the homeless, they provided a safe haven in which residents looked after one another. If the huts had been scattered in widely dispersed locations, they would not have given visible testimony to the contestation over power—over what was "proper" behavior or what were the proper locations for homeless persons to dwell in—and collective identities would have been more difficult to establish. The conflict between versions of what was a "proper" place for a given activity, whether it occurred on the pleasure spaces of North Michigan Avenue in Chicago or the refuse spaces of abandoned industrial areas, infused the visible political conflicts outlined in chapter 5.

Attempts to curb police actions against SHA-affiliated homeless encampments in San Jose, when occurring at the camp site itself, were quite different from attempts to curb police actions by speaking to the mayor, demonstrating in front of city hall, or being arrested for disrupting city council meetings. What is or is not possible can often be judged from the degree of power one has in making visible the underlying intentions of those who have the power to control situations. Out of sight, out of mind. But to make the transition from contesting power at a remote site, free from the public gaze, to contesting it at a site where the public gaze is the main focus requires quite a large change in homeless residents, students, community activists, and other supporters. Three actions defined these changes: the establishment or demarcation of a place with a particular "proper" identity (homeless placemaking), the generation of new collective identities among homeless group residents, and collective action as a group that presents demands.

Homeless placemaking occurs when homeless persons redefine the meaning of social-physical space and then act on those redefinitions. As we have pointed out earlier, social-physical space is not merely the backdrop for collective actions but an integral aspect of how identity is constructed, of how homeless participants understand their situation. The sudden occupation of a stretch of pavement in a public place, the construction of a shack on an industrial site, may be carried out without the conscious intent to redefine the meaning of that space. However, the very act of creating a place to sleep, of survival itself, contributes to the redefinition of that space, especially in the eyes of authorities who wish to maintain a "proper" version of space as one in which those activities should not and will not be allowed.

Bodies have to be put somewhere, and often, from the perspective of city officials, homeless bodies occupy "improper" places. While individual homeless persons may remain unaware that they are redefining space by their very presence in specific locations, others, namely city personnel, will often rudely remind them that they are "out of place." Since there are many ways social-physical space can mean something, fixing that meaning becomes an object for both homeless persons who use that space and authorities who attempt to stop them from doing so. The constant negotiation and renegotiation over these meanings work to produce individual and collective identities. Susan and the San Jose "Bridge" people redefined their space not simply as "an area under a bridge," a bridge over troubled waters, but as a home. But this was not simply an "individual" home, but a "collective" home with embedded meanings of family and community. This was also true for the other encampments studied. In all these cases social-physical spaces were redefined by their occupants. Their identities, both collective and individual, were deeply connected to the ability to replace authoritative meanings of social-physical space with their own meanings. And it was precisely this redefinition that came into conflict with both San Jose's desire to create an urban park and Chicago's desire to rid the city of an expanding number of squatter huts. The struggle over redefining spatial meanings is the definition of "control": Who is going to control this site?

The ability to contest a site, a result of the redefinition of spatial meanings by homeless participants, was made possible by the *proximity* of homeless persons to the site. The cities of San Jose and Chicago, on the other hand, depended upon their agents, the police and city workers, to establish proximity through either patrols or periodic cleanups of homeless camps to enforce authoritative definitions of what that site meant. However, such agents could not occupy the contested spaces as frequently as the homeless could, so they had problems enforcing authoritative notions of "proper " use of the space. By increasing the severity of penalties for occupying the space, such as trespass regulations in San Jose, cities may hope to extend their power of redefining space by attaching sanctions to those willing to violate their definitions. The imposition of legal sanctions against "improper" uses of space also ensures that when occasional police patrols do move through an area, their authority will be respected by the homeless. In the absence of such "respect," physical force is considered a legitimate option. As long as the Mad Houser huts did not attract too much media attention, Chicago authorities were content to let them go about their business in a remote part of the city. However, as the visibility of the huts increased, due to the influx of greater numbers of homeless and expanded media coverage, control over this remote refuse space was called into question. The second form of spatial control as outlined in previous chapters was the attempt to concentrate homeless populations in shelters where social control could more effectively be implemented on a regular and systematic basis—where proximity could be established by the authoritative implementation of rules, regulations, and codes of conduct.

Homeless places that contest dominant spatial meanings are by no means secure; they are subject to constant challenge by authorities and by homeless participants themselves, who often may have widely different definitions of what a place should be. Defending a created place, an important component of what Wagner (1993) calls a "subculture of resistance," is decidedly difficult. Strategies of authority can be quite effective in reinforcing dominant hegemonic meanings of social-physical space. On the other hand, tactical resistances by the homeless can sometimes thwart such strategies. The development of a collective identity by homeless persons as "family" (and in some cases, especially among the young, as "rebels") works to resist authoritative strategies designed to keep them in their "proper" place. This was true for the homeless encampments in San Jose as well as in Chicago. The actual physical terrain of placemaking combined with ongoing political battles over San Jose's police practices worked to cement solidarity among homeless persons, at least for a short time. Collective identity did not emerge in a vacuum, but rather from the ability to redefine oneself in relationship to contested meanings of social-physical space. Therefore, homeless placemaking is critical in establishing the foundation for collective action.

Discussions of collective identity (Friedman and McAdam 1992; Gamson 1991; Gamson 1992, 57; Hunt 1991; Hunt and Benford 1994; Melucci 1985, 1988, 1989; Pizzorno 1978; Taylor and Whittier 1992) have expanded over the years with the development of identity politics and the New Social Movements. Culture, consciousness, and human agency remained marginalized in the early models of social movements, most often associated with either relative-deprivation or resource-mobilization theory. However, as Cohen (1985) demonstrates, even in the New Social Movements literature, where culture and identity are recognized as very important, strategic considerations common to resource-mobilization theories are often dissociated from issues of identity. Understanding the significance of homeless protests (Barak 1992, 135–42; Cress 1990; Yeich 1994; Stolarski 1988; Fabricant and Kelly 1986; Cohen and Wagner 1992; Wallis 1991, 208–16), homeless affinity groups, and the collective gains they secure, requires the reintegration of culture and consciousness with reference not only to collective identity and collective action, but also to models of strategy and resistance, often found in resource-mobilization theory.

In the past, issues of identity, culture, and activism focused on specific events, encounters, or acts of protests, and on the development of well coordinated social movement organizations. Resource-mobilization theory, the social movement perspective popular during the 1970s and into the 1980s, analyzed social movements of the poor from the rational-actor viewpoint, examining social movement organizations (SMOs), social movement institutions (SMIs), elite recruitment and access to resources (McCarthy and Zald 1977; Oberschall 1973; Gamson 1975; Tilley 1978). This overconcentration of attention on SMOs, as Wagner and Cohen (1991) correctly point out, acted to "obscure the obvious fact that the gains of social movements, at least for the poor and other disenfranchised people, should accrue to participants and their class, not to an organizational activity" (545). Framing resource-mobilization research in terms of rational self-interested motivations also ignored the emotional and psychic gains developed from newly emergent collective identities, focusing instead on political successes or failures, on goal-oriented behavior steered by elites. The messiness of culture and consciousness was subsumed under models of individual, utilitarian, and rational action, as can be seen in the early work of Mancur Olson (1965), a rationality predicated upon "the experiences of nineteenth-century, white Western, middle-class men" (Ferree 1992, 41; Hartsock 1983; Jaggar 1989). The split between mind and body, the ruling desire to discipline the body as an outside "thing" by force of will, meant that emotions, and the identities constructed from these emotions, remained foreign, something to be tamed, the "wild." Human agency collapsed, in this historical sense, into conquest, domination, and bodily alienation. Those associated with the "wild"—women, people of color, and, in our case, homeless bodies—existed as threats to social order. They needed to understand their place, to be in the correct place produced for them by their owners, controllers, possessors. To be "out of place" was to be no-place, to be nobody, or conversely to be on the margins and thereby a threat. Subordination and social order were equated with rationality. This model of one-dimensional rationality, often implicit in resource-mobilization theory, imported from rational choice theory, has been critiqued by a combination of resource-mobilization and New Social Movements theorists, with mixed results (Ferree 1992; Ferree and Miller 1985; Fireman and Gamson 1979; Klandermans 1988; Pizzorno 1986, 1978). Interestingly, New Social Movements research, focusing as it did upon culture and identity politics, attempted to address issues that were missing from previous social movement debates. However, such theory still remained mired in similar rationalist models of investigation that privileged largely middle-class protest movements and neglected movements of the poor, of "poor" bodies, of spontaneous eruptions of the "unwashed masses." This could be easily attributed to the preoccupation with the presence of visible protests commonplace among antinuclear, gay and lesbian, women's, and ecology movements— a preoccupation with visible protests at the expense of less-visible protests. A step had been made in examining people marginalized historically within the dominant society, but only a step. This step failed to make the class connection, as Eder (1993) points out. The subordination of class to identity politics rendered the poor, and in our case the homeless, "invisible" once again.

Alberto Melucci (1985, 1988, 1989) and Alain Touraine (1981, 1985), the first set of European writers to frame New Social Movements theory, challenged the earlier relative-deprivation and resource-mobilization models of the 1970s by expanding the concept of collective identity, connecting it to collection action. Melucci's and Touraine's research, helpful in recasting the social movement debates, still remained focused on predominantly middle-class-based social movements. The poor were excluded from analysis.

Historically, mainstream American models of social movements, privileging political and organizational goals, neglected the fact that identity formation itself may be a legitimate goal. William Gamson (1992), although himself a resource-mobilization theorist, did understand the problem of privileging the rational achievement of protest goals as the way to measure success. Gamson pointed out that collective identity is itself "a cultural achievement in its own right, regardless of its contribution to the achievement of political and organizational goals" (57). This is important to keep in mind when examining camp organizations and the gains achieved by the SHA and Tranquility City residents.

What does Melucci (1989) mean by collective identity and how can it help us to understand the actions of the SHA and Tranquility City inhabitants? Melucci defined collective identity as, "an interactive and shared definition produced by several interacting individuals who are concerned with the orientations of their actions as well as the field of opportunities and constraints in which these actions take place" (34). This process clearly is continually negotiated. Human agency is not subordinated to autonomous processes or structures, but viewed as intertwined with "opportunities and constraints." The key word in Melucci's definition is *shared*. For Melucci (1985), " 'shared' means constructed and negotiated through a repeated process of 'activation' of social relationships connecting the actors" (793). What is not explained in Melucci's model is the role, purpose, function, or point of social-physical space in this process of sharing, in the process of forming collective identities. Space, as we have seen from our discussion in earlier chapters, is reduced to "environment," something that is outside of human agency, something that is distinct from the body. This reduction makes it difficult to understand the importance of homeless placemaking, and particularly the importance of homeless placemaking to emerging collective identities. Melucci's concepts are valuable, revealing the importance of *submerged networks* of social relationships that exist prior to the formation of SMOs. The relationships established between students and homeless persons in San Jose and between the homeless and their supporters in Tranquility City provided the necessary networks for the development of trust and solidarity, enabling the formation of collective identities bound to particular places. Complex negotiations between SHA student and homeless members were present not only at meetings, but informally on the streets and in the encampments, "constructing an action system" of possibilities, a "collective identity" (Melucci 1988, 342).

Existing before their professionalization into SMOs, social networks are "composed of a multiplicity of groups that are dispersed, fragmented and submerged in everyday life, and which act as cultural laboratories" (Melucci 1989, 60). The use of street networks, the circulation

of students between the university and encampment sites, the circulation of homeless camp dwellers between shelters, camps, and the
university, all pointed to a giant "cultural laboratory" in which new
cultural codes about space, place, and homelessness could be created
and tested. It was only after a year and half of these circulations that
the submerged networks of social relations crystallized into visible
protests at the steps of San Jose's City Hall. Tranquility City residents
built their community much quicker since many of the social networks
had been established in prior shelter and street contacts. An expanded
network developed over the nine-month period of Tranquility City's
existence; it included persons in the huts, on the streets of Lower
Wacker Drive, in several community churches and art galleries, at local
universities, and in local solidarity groups. The spidery web of social
networks extended across the city and into the suburbs well before
visible actions appeared on the nightly news.

However, developing submerged networks of friends and associates is insufficient to generate the necessary solidarity to engage in
collective actions. As Gamson (1992) points out, "preexisting friendships
are helpful in recruitment, no doubt, but unless the continuing relationships among activists have some of the qualities of a primary social
support network, it seems hard to imagine that participants will develop
organizational solidarity" (62). This development of a primary support
network was evident in the development of the local site, or "family," in
San Jose and Chicago and in the emergent political organizations that
nurtured such "family" identities. Essential to this development was the
establishment of recruitment strategies and networks (Melucci 1989, 31)
by the SHA and Tranquility City residents. Recruitment strategies for
Tranquility City residents involved talking with fellow homeless at local
shelters and on Lower Wacker Drive, and using street networks to get
out the word about hut availability. For the SHA, recruitment networks
were established through the university, via presentations in classrooms
and at campus events, in local soup kitchens where newly recruited
homeless persons would serve food alongside the students, at community and advocacy organization meetings, and in supportive local shelters. A very effective recruitment tactic used by SHA student activists was
the use of video recordings of SHA protests combined with the visual
coverage provided by local media in sympathetic shelters. Several homeless men became involved with the SHA after watching those videos,
videos that provided dramatic proof of the efficacy of direct action.

Melucci (1989) refers to the developed locations of submerged
networks as "mini-movement areas." However, his concept of social-

physical space remains static and inadequate. The establishment of social support networks and the creation of solidarity have to happen somewhere. That somewhere is critical in defining the potentials for collective action and indeed for collective identity. We know that people "define themselves as collective actors by means of a variety of negotiated interactions" (32). The question of how these negotiations occur and the context for their discussion is important in determining the success of any movement. For example, after the first housing takeover by the SHA—the occupation of the former rectory of the St. Joseph's School in downtown San Jose—the students and some of the homeless began discussing taking over another downtown building. These discussions generated tensions but occurred in the shelters and at the university, a safe place for discussions. This first SHA housing takeover lasted three days and ended with one of the homeless members being arrested. While the students and a few homeless individuals wanted to take over another, nearby building, the homeless members of the SHA backed out of the action at the last minute. The tensions this produced were negotiated through discussion between the students and the homeless, using the university as a "safe" area. The SHA provided the social space within which these differences could be negotiated, and the university provided the physical space, removed from the street, to mediate discussion.

Melucci makes an important point in asking the question of how the process of negotiating develops. As he explains, "Individuals construct their goals and make choices and decisions within a perceived environment. Here the concept of expectations is fundamental in analyzing the link between actors and their environment" (32). The problem with this argument, however, is that Melucci still reduces the complexity of social-physical space to that of "environment," to an arena in which the individual body remains separate, detached from the world around it, mediated only through "social networks," although with "expectations." This ignores how collective identity is constructed through the interrelationships between bodies and social-physical spaces. To put this another way: There is no outside, environment, or space, nor inside body or mind, only social relationships composed of the integration of bodies and social-physical spaces within a fragmented and contested landscape. The "expectations" we generate are consequences of these integrated social relationships, which often remain invisible to those who have them. That we ignore this integration of bodies and social-physical space is one of the reasons why it is difficult to see the importance of homeless placemaking in the development of new collective identities and, indeed, the authoritative strategies of power in the production of hierarchial spatial forms. Bartholomew and Mayer (1992), in their critique of Melucci's concept of identity formation, recognize this neglect: "it is only in a context of domination that one has to fight for . . . the recognition of difference, as it is suppressed or devalued by dominance. The claim to difference is a claim to the 'space' to be different, which presupposes that space has heretofore been denied" (151).

Creating "safe" spaces in which to gather is essential, not only for SMOs but for local affinity groups and indeed loose collections of individuals who gather together for a common purpose. It is not as if we have homeless placemaking, and that leads to collective identities. Homeless placemaking is one side of the development of collective identity, and collective identity is the other side of homeless placemaking. Understanding the integration of placemaking and collective identity leads to understanding the importance of the formation of collective places, spaces given a particular social meaning by a group. Of course, then the question becomes what type of collective identity are we talking about. I will leave that for later in the chapter when we examine what the participants say themselves.

Melucci's mini-movement areas are mirrored in the concept of micro mobilization (Gamson 1992, 71; Gamson, Fireman and Rytina 1982; McAdam 1988). According to McAdam (1988), "a micro-mobilization context can be defined as that small group setting in which processes of collective attribution are combined with rudimentary forms of organization to produce mobilization by collective actors" (134–35). While McAdam, along with Melucci and others, still conceives of social-physical space as a "setting," or "context," as a backdrop to "processes," he does contribute to a refocusing on the ways in which early networks can support collective action in the future, a perspective compatible with Melucci's submerged networks. Refocusing on the smaller levels of engagement, group dynamics and face-to-face encounters, which often remain below the surface of analyses that examine only spectacular protests, would assist in understanding how collective action develops. Still it should be said that micro mobilization, as the examination of small social networks within a spatial "context," ignores the manner in which such networks are intertwined throughout social-physical space. However, by examining the specifics of "encounters" (Gamson 1982)— in our case, Tranquility City and SHA social relationships and the everyday life of homeless encampments rather then simply protest actions—we can learn about the process of developing collective identities within particular social-physical spaces. These relationships are interwoven throughout social-physical space, indistinguishable from the phenomenon of collective identity, a created social "place." Knowing how homeless residents establish sites, family and community, their social relationships, and their perceptions of leadership, knowing how they organize everyday life and perceive their gains from their collective actions gives us a glimpse into what it means to be a member of the SHA or Tranquility City.

This level of analysis reveals the role of social-physical space in the support and development of collective identity. The importance of social-physical spaces to the development of collective identity is well illustrated in the role the African American church played during the civil rights era (Morris 1984; McAdam 1986, 1988), in the role of the shops and restaurants of Telegraph Avenue to the developing student movement at the University of California at Berkeley during the 1960s, and in the role of local churches and support groups meeting in individual houses for the Central American solidarity movement during the 1980s, to name just a few. Homeless placemaking, the establishment of encampments, and the production of relationships within particular spatial configurations (church meeting rooms, university classrooms, soup kitchen eating areas, etc.) are critical in determining the realistic basis for collective action. The seizure of abandoned buildings in the case of the SHA and the occupation of "empty" property in the case of Tranquility City were ways to carve out "safe" places from which further actions could be taken. But such actions were preceded by a long period in which homeless placemaking changed and altered along with group perceptions of collective identity, of place, "family," and community.

Collective identity is not uniform, but varies from situation to situation, from place to place. And yet the groups—SHA and Tranquility City—still remained the primary focus of attention for those homeless residents when called upon to act. Individuals generally did not act on their own, but often acted to either support or momentarily reject an established collective identity in favor of a new collective identity. This process of formation was accentuated by the involvement of students from San Jose State University and Stanford, in addition to those students from Loyola University who visited with the inhabitants of Tranquility City. Their presence, and indeed the growing presence of community activists, church members, and others, expanded the definition of what community was, altering the homeless placemaking that had occurred. SHA homeless members would often call SHA students asking for information or requesting assistance, and students would frequently visit encampments and work with homeless SHA members in shelters. A new collective identity different from that established within the isolated encampments formed from the ongoing political struggles over the attempt by the city of San Jose to control the diverse communities of homeless street encampments. The same process was observed in the final struggles over the Tranquility City camps.

The integration between homeless placemaking and collective identity formation makes it possible to develop forms of action that move from individual actions, most often associated with a radical utilitarian individualism, to collective actions in which the group "family" becomes the prime referent. Such an identity is fragile at best, subject to tremendous pressure to return to individual forms of action that are compatible with dominant authoritative social institutions (such as welfare offices, police, and city services). Such collective actions and collective identities remain strategic, subject to reversal at any time. For the SHA, brief periods of collective identity were maintained through the exercise of militant political action, housing takeovers, and protests, but because these actions did not have sufficient victories, collective identities deteriorated rapidly, in part because of the daily forced survival schedules of the homeless. Not having a secure "place" made organizing difficult. In this climate, shelter rules and police practices served to break up formations not only of physical bodies, segmenting and cataloging them according to "medical" models of pathology, of "deserving" and "undeserving," but also fractured emergent forms of collective identity. However, in shelters that were supportive of homeless collective struggles, such collective identities could be maintained. The dispersion of homeless services, shelters, and other social institutions common to poor people, combined with a rigid enforcement of rule behavior, create large demands upon the time and energy of the homeless, making it more difficult for them to maintain collective identities. As we saw in earlier chapters, spatial dispersions are a classic method of city social control. In the case of the SHA, sometimes homeless participants could not make meetings because they had to be at a shelter to receive their meals at a given time, at other times they had to go across the city for some piece of information they needed. This pattern was also common with Tranquility City residents. After the destruction of the camps, members were scattered to various public housing projects, a choice they made themselves, but a choice that was structured by the fact that the huts were being removed. The networks established through the homeless placemaking in the camps were disrupted as older social networks reasserted themselves. Most of the hut dwellers moved to the Chicago Housing Authority's Lathrop Apartments. Others moved into more remote projects. In this new topography, collective identities were difficult to maintain. Individuals were spatially isolated from each other. Several returned to the streets. Even so, many of the core group members of Tranquility City struggled to maintain contact by visiting each other, often leaving messages under each other's doors if they weren't home, and expanding their political work with other homeless and formerly homeless persons. It remains a question how long this can be sustained.

Resistant Heterotopias: Site and Community

Hut dwellers in Chicago and "Bridge" encampment members in San Jose occupied *resistant heterotopias* in a hierarchial network of social-physical spaces. The hut-dwelling communities were places where one could experience protection against external authority and power, if only momentarily. Existing in what to the housed community were functional/refuse spaces, members of San Jose's and Chicago's encampments were able to create spaces where they were accepted, places where, as one homeless man commented, "one could think." In looking out for each other, homeless members attempted to craft a power that could limit assaults on their camps by the police, hostile neighbors, or each other. The image the homeless had of shelters as public, unsafe, unsanitary, and degrading contrasted sharply with hut dwellers' perceptions of Tranquility City. Residents talked about how they could establish privacy, autonomy, and respect within the hut encampments. By contrast, shelter operation and ideology is perceived as being focused on individual clinical treatment, if there is any treatment at all. The stigma carried by the label *homeless*, connoting people with spoiled identities needing to be "helped," deterred the encouragement of resistant collective identities. The collective identities encouraged by shelters are based most often upon a medical-therapeutic model in which homeless persons must defer to authority in order to "return to society." In the camps, resistant collective identities were perceived as positive, a way of strengthening one's own individuality through the development of "family" bonds. Going off by oneself or retreating with one's own agenda, while tolerated, were perceived as just another symptom of authoritative power, of having "bad habits." This was the case in the attitudes the residents of Tranquility City has toward panhandlers. We shall discuss this a little later. The respect garnished from collective support and collective identity paid off in a newfound respect for many of the homeless who occupied the camps. As Wayne, a Tranquility City squatter, exclaimed:

> because we got respect there [in the encampment], see. We got respect from the Metra police, the city police. We got respect from the community business people. They helped us out. They supported what we was doing. When people seen the way we was keeping the whole area clean, I mean we didn't have to be out there on the railroad tracks chopping weeds down, they got people that do that, they get paid for that. We was doing that, was cleaning up the whole area.

Living in the huts was never perceived as a final solution to homelessness by Tranquility City residents, but they saw it as a vehicle to gain concessions for themselves and others and to maintain respect without falling into the shelter system. As Jim, a Tranquility City resident, explained:

> Like I say, it's a temporary measure with the huts. The huts were not designed to be permanent residence, just temporary residence. Just temporary residence for individuals as a stepping stone to sort of help get their life . . . started. They have some independence of their own. You don't have that feeling when you're in a shelter because you're still working with a system. It's a system that helps keep you depending on that system instead of your own independence.

Resistance by establishing encampments and by being involved with activist networks appeared as adaptive survival strategies and also an "escape" from bourgeois sensibilities of the subject, both adaptive and defiant. Many in the Chicago and San Jose encampments identified themselves as "heros" undertaking forced deprivation on behalf of all the other homeless, whom they perceived as less able to take care of themselves. When faced with limited choices, homeless squatters adopted identities that increased their self-respect. These forms of "identity work," identified by Snow and Anderson (1987), may assume a wide variety of appearances, from grandiose beliefs to exaggerated stories. Distancing talk, where individuals distance themselves from imposed roles and associations, dominated the SHA group. In the encampments, homeless individuals distanced themselves from others based on others' behaviors—whether they "panhandled," "got drunk," used drugs, and so on. This "association distancing" (Snow and Anderson 1987, 1349) was widespread throughout the camps. For example, in showing me where Chicago hut dwellers procured fresh water, Jim spotted another homeless man pushing a cart toward us. Jim exclaimed, "This guy is transient. Yeah, like I said before, way before the huts was built down here this was like a haven down here for homeless people to travel back and forth to the scrap yards." Institutional distancing was also common in the homeless rejection of shelters, as we have seen in previous chapters. Distancing oneself from shelter staff and other homeless persons worked to counter the negative labels one had been given due to one's status position. It became another tactic to resist the degradation ceremonies performed by the organization of the shelter social-physical space. Of course, one could also assume that some individuals maintained a social distance even before they became homeless. Role embracement appeared in Chicago and San Jose with encampment members who identified themselves as rebels, while associational embracement was exhibited in the many statements made by those who said that they wanted to remain on the streets to protect others. What is interesting is the way such identity work underwent change through the process of collective action. Associational distancing became far less prevalent during struggles with city hall. In petitioning and protesting city hall, prior homeless identities, what I term *nomadic identities*, were engaged by city council members and by the homeless themselves. City officials framed homeless identities based upon their understanding of prior homeless use of social-physical space, and indeed the homeless themselves defined their identities based on these prior occupations of social-physical space. At each level of increased militancy, from opposing police practices in the camps to protesting in front of City Hall to militant housing takeovers, new reconstructions of collective identities were necessary, producing an erosion of imposed nomadic identities. The final housing takeovers for the SHA, along River Street, involved a higher degree of risk than previous occupations, a new form of collective identity and a literal occupation of a new social-physical space, an occupation that threatened old nomadic identities, and indeed old forms of associational distancing, associated with the constantly moving encampments and the labeling of homelessness by authorities. To take a fixed position, a house, was to assert active power, not just passive acceptance and adaptation, not survival but affirmation. In the act of seizing a house, homeless participants shed their identities as nomad in exchange for that of "housed" person. They moved from "homeless" to "poor." At the same time one could say that the participants were strategically assimilated into the ranks of those who occupy housed space, connected to the market. One could also say that the overt defiance of authority and the limited success that brought reinforced a resistant heterotopia. SHA and Tranquility City participants learned that organized, active, and collective mobilization could lead to practical and emotional results. They learned that disruption could sustain group solidarity as well as break it up and that struggling collectively could achieve results in the end. Adopting not the polite mainstream strategies of petition, but the disruptive and occupying strategies of those who have little to lose, they reaffirmed their other identities as "houseless but not homeless." The success of San Jose's housing occupation served to reinforce the possibility for further involvement and further transformations in subjectivity. The police were compelled to overreact in the house arrests at River Street in 1992, in part due to this refusal of homeless identities as simply "nomadic," or what police define as "transient." The new "housed" collective identities of some SHA members, outside of traditional market mechanisms, the seizure of abandoned buildings under the windows of San Jose's redevelopment agency, did not conform to the notion that homeless people should be in their proper place, either camps where they could be dispersed or shelters where they could be controlled. They were now somewhere else, in their own place. The reassertion of a new "housed" identity came into direct conflict with the hierarchical power of property and the market, which stipulates that you cannot occupy a space unless it is owned or rented by you. Authoritative strategies of exclusion had been refused. The Chicago encampments, in the short time they lasted, generated a different subjectivity for their participants, a subjectivity removed from that inspired by the spaces of Lower Wacker Drive or the local shelters. Authoritative strategies of exclusions were countered by tactical resistances of inclusion. With the dismantling of the huts and the scattering of the encampment dwellers into public housing, the new subjective changes were subject to reversals. However, in some cases collective identities, while changing, were also strengthened, for those who continued to organize in public housing.

The "Bridge"

The perception and formation of a "family" or community and the interpretation of a particular site as safe, attractive, and convenient for reaching other needed services were two of the main characteristics of the San Jose and Chicago resistant heterotopias. In the first "Bridge" encampment in San Jose, two Native American families, one with children, and four former veterans, plus several single men, lived in separate concrete partitions, elevated five feet above the creek bed, susceptible to flooding during the rainy season. The complex social networks formed between the residents of the "Bridge" and the local community were revealed by the ongoing relationships among the local Delmas Market, a block away, the immediate neighborhood, and the downtown shelters, which acted as occasional places for sleeping and showers. Social networks within poor housed communities tend to be locally based (Jeffers 1967; Martin and Martin 1978; Shimkin, Shimkin, and Frate 1978; Stack 1974; Zollar 1985), and this was true of the "Bridge" residents, although for many homeless, such networks may extend much farther than housed persons because they have to keep on the move. The stability of an encampment may determine the locality of such networks. Susan received her General Assistance checks at a nearby friend's house, still another "Bridge" member had a brother living two blocks away whom he would regularly visit. Homeless members of the SHA talked about forming friends, learning to trust those "who treated you right," waiting to see if those who might come to visit returned or were consistent in doing what they said they were going to do. Sharing with each other whatever resources they could find, "Bridge" members were fond of talking about their camp as a "family." Susan, considered the "grandmother" of the camp, said, "Underneath there is like a home. There are people who really cared. We all worked together as a family and I think that's the main thing." The question that arose for the SHA was how to reproduce the sense of "family" outside of the bridge site. Aside from looking after the other members of the camp, Susan would make sure that the one epileptic member in the camp took his medicine. Social rules were acted upon and limitations set on what was and what was not acceptable behavior. Members of the camp worked in the daytime, bringing home limited earnings that were shared with the others of the camp. Marginal work marked the "Bridge" members. Scavenging and day labor were the only apparent options for securing money legitimately. One camp member worked at sorting newspapers for the *San Jose Mercury News* early in the morning, another would scavenge for aluminum cans all day, turning them in for money in the late afternoon. This latter job was rather hazardous because shopping carts, often removed from supermarkets by customers, would be used to transport the cans. Several homeless men mentioned that police had confiscated their cans and their carts under suspicion that they had stolen the carts from the local supermarket. Panhandling was frowned upon, and indeed I encountered few instances of it while working with the "Bridge" people. Panhandling was perceived by these homeless as something other homeless may do, but not the "Bridge" people, although they were not adverse to accepting handouts. "Bridge" residents conceived of their site as "home," a place from which they went forth every day and worked. According to one resident, "We just do our thing down here . . . The cops call us trolls, but we work and make an honest living. Old Ernie, he's got a bottle in his hand but he gets up at 4:30 [a.m.] and does his work. You can't tell me that rich people don't come home from work and do the exact same thing—they just don't do it under a bridge, and they don't take care of each other the way we do."

The organization of site space was influential in reproducing norms of middle-class behavior. Private spaces were carved out of the concrete niches under the bridge. Rules about where you could go and when you could enter another's area were enforced; when spaces were violated, often a confrontation would develop that had to be settled by the senior members of the group. Community was generated by the enforcement of respect for each other's personal space and through exchange of goods, which contributed to group solidarity. Enforcement was established by those perceived by the members as the most capable, with the most endurance and access to resources. These were the family members of the "Bridge" and in particular the senior members of those families. These behaviors bore a striking resemblance to the "swapping" recorded by Stack (1974), the streetcorner behaviors observed by Liebow (1967) and Anderson (1990, 1978), and the solidarity observed by Wagner (1993). Susan, a member of the "Bridge," described how social life operated through the organization of social-physical space:

> Do what you can for them and they'll do what they can for you. They go out and work and they bring in whatever they could. We go to a dumpster, get steak, wash it off, cook it, and make stew or whatever. On our bridge we had a rope that went from each dorm all the way across. We hung curtains and stuff up. And if anybody wanted to see us we told them to say "knock, knock." If we weren't busy we'd say "come in." If we were busy we'd say "stay away." We all had our privacy that way. If we had to go to the bathroom, we'd go down to the train depot or we'd go down where there was no water and everybody watched out for everybody around them there. Everybody took turns doing everything.

Of the five camps identified in the area near McHenry Park, the "Bridge" had the most stable social organization, with solid social networks in the surrounding neighborhood. The pull of the "Bridge" community was powerful enough to give Susan second thoughts about staying in her new apartment. Both the former members of the "Bridge" and San Jose State students, working closely with Susan, discouraged her from returning to the bridge site, supporting her in her new place by preparing dinners and visiting regularly, as they had done in the camp. According to one of the homeless members of the "Bridge," "I'm very proud and I look up to ___. She's dealt with a lot . . . she was talking about going back under the bridge and I said, 'No. You're gettin' older and you need to be in a warm sheltered house.' She took the advice." Susan, in turn, commented on how her move into her own apartment acted to change her views about responsibility and indeed her notion of a space to call her own. She remarked that student involvement, concern, and support helped her to make the transition from street living to apartment living. It was not enough to have either the resources or the emotional support; Susan felt that the integration of the two assisted in the changes she felt were necessary for her life. As she explained:

> They turned me all the way around. Before, I just didn't care about nothing when I lived under the bridge. I did whatever I wanted to. But, when I got involved with ____ and ____ I turned all the way around. I love my house and I love it being my place. Now if I was out there I'd be saying, "Hey, I don't like my place so I'm gonna stay out here and forget it. I don't have to pay no bills, no nothing." But now I love where I'm at and I've got the responsibility to be back where I used to be a long time ago— paying my bills and getting the stuff fixed up in my house.

Susan's eight-year stay on the streets had come to an end.

Clearly the pull of a created community, of "family," is powerful for anybody. The "Bridge" demonstrated that even in the most dire of circumstances, elaborate social networks, rules, and codes of behavior will form, bringing people into close contact with each other. When the "Bridge" was dissolved, from intense police pressure, the community persisted through street contacts and greetings at local soup kitchens. Such memories die hard. The addition of student assistance at the camp magnified the sense of community, extending the reach of the "Bridge" beyond the immediate neighborhood into legal and educational institutions. Unlike other instances in which established institutions assist homeless persons in charitable circumstances, the "Bridge" residents reciprocated the attention they received by attending university meetings and events, broadening their community. At first the students had to physically go to the site and drive them to campus. However, after several meetings "Bridge" residents began to come to the campus on their own.

Police actions not only were effective in breaking up the encampments; they also had the unintended side effect of undermining the students' often naive belief in authority and order. This further cemented the students' closer identification with the homeless population, spurring many of the students to assist in ways they would not otherwise have done. For the students the "Bridge" community was a way to cross classes and races, to expand their political, social, and geographic sensibilities, since many now felt safer after actually spending time in areas they had been taught were unsafe. As the social-physical spaces of these refuse places were redefined in the students' interpretations of their experiences with the "Bridge" residents, so were student and homeless individual identities. For the homeless, their newly expanded community, now including students, gave them an opportunity to tell their stories and, like the students, cross class and race boundaries without fear, and especially to take a step into the forbidden territory of the university, a place where many homeless people were routinely excluded, escorted out by campus police. This pattern was repeated in all of the camps studied by the SHA. An interesting side note: When SHA homeless members would visit the campus, they would often assume the body comportment of students, sitting straight in their desks, lined up neatly, and raising their hands to ask questions.

The Catacombs

After the dissolution of the "Bridge," SHA homeless and student members discovered a second camp. This camp, located next to San Jose's light rail tracks and under the intersections of five major freeways exhibited a greater complexity in social-physical space and social interactions than the "Bridge." The site of the second encampment, the "catacombs," existed on the border of San Jose's redevelopment zone, the edge of the proposed Guadalupe River Urban Park. The closure of a major freeway overpass, damaged with severe cracks from the Loma Prieta earthquake, combined with an area fenced off from the housed community, gave this site the marginal status of refuse space. One could enter the site through a hole cut in a neighborhood fence or by hiking southwest of the downtown and across both the light rail tracks and the Guadalupe River. The landscape was dotted with weeds, ice plant vegetation, occasional trees and thick brush, packed dirt, and debris. Upon entering through the hole in the chain-link fence, one traversed a brush-filled lot with scattered trees, walked up onto and over a closed freeway on-ramp, itself suffering from wide fissures and broken pavement, and walked down under another vacant overpass to the camp site. Not visible to the general public, the camp was visible to occasional police patrols and highway crews that patrolled the abandoned freeway section. The unfinished freeway remained vacant to the north and south, a large expanse of empty concrete spreading into the distance. The steady hum of traffic running east and west on the remaining freeways filtered down to the camp. Freeway columns standing like sentinels under a filigree of concrete overpasses, with automobiles and trucks roaring by above, formed a dense topography marked by homeless campfires. Smoke often drifted up to and above the raised freeways. Sleeping in donated tents, homeless camp members organized their site with great attention to detail, placing their tents around a central fire pit used to cook food. A latrine was dug about a hundred yards away behind a column; scrap metal and cans were neatly piled in rows along one wall of the overpass for processing. When police would arrive, camp members would simply pack up their belongings and move to another site in the area, out of sight of police patrols.

Diversified in religion, politics, age, and race, the catacombs camp embodied many extreme tendencies and a volatile dynamic that set it apart from smaller camps the SHA had examined. Often swelling to fourteen or more then rapidly shrinking to five, the camp was always in flux, partly in response to police pressure or economic opportunities. Racially the camp was composed of young white males and several females, with one regular African American male and several Latinos. The average age of camp members was approximately twenty-two; Tom, a member in his forties, fashioned himself as the group leader. Claiming he was a former special forces soldier, he talked about the encampment as a family, a family he would protect. The talk of "family" was similar to the "Bridge." Tom talked about how daily life should be organized, where tents should be put up, how money would be gathered (usually from collecting cans and scavenging copper wire). He perceived his role as looking after the younger members of the group. Tom's behavior, however, caused deep mistrust in other homeless not directly affiliated with the camp. The consensus from the streets was that Tom was using camp members for his own needs and was therefore somebody to be avoided. This was a big reason why many other homeless persons were reluctant to be involved with the SHA during this period. I was told that many homeless from the Armory would have nothing to do with Tom. On the other hand, when Tom would go to the Armory, he was not mistreated. He said the reason he didn't spend more time in the Amory was because they did not allow pets and he did not want to give away his dog.

Tom made frequent references to black magic and mentioned that he studied the occult, pulling me aside one day and claiming that he could make blue sparks jump between his fingers. Members of the group referred to him as "Satan." When asked why he embraced black magic, Tom mentioned an incident in which he was betrayed by somebody who identified themselves as a born-again Christian. He claimed he worked two weeks for this person and was never paid, that he was "ripped off," proving that Christians were not to be trusted. Black magic functioned for Tom as a surrogate identity; Tom was one of the few camp members who resembled Snow and Anderson's (1987, 1357) model of ideological embracement. Tom constructed an oppositional identity, resisting the appeals of the mainstream culture that surrounded him.

Most members of the catacombs camp were not religious, except for Alex, a disabled navy veteran and self-professed born-again Christian. At community meetings and at the university, Alex spoke for the group; Tom also spoke on occasion. However, camp dynamics were volatile, with constant power plays. When Tom was placed in the county jail for past warrants, a news story appeared about the camp in which Alex's religious votive candles featured prominently. Tom railed on about how the newspaper would show Christian symbols but not his black magic symbols. Shortly after Alex arrived in the camp, he said he became disturbed by Tom's attempts to control the other camp members and particularly by his black magic. Alex and another member of the group engineered a "coup" that isolated Tom. He was still living in the camp but now had little power over other camp members. According to Alex:

> When I got in the encampment there was basically one man running the encampment. The biggest problem that I had in the encampment was the man who was running it because of his satanic needs. He's a satanistic person ... So I knew then and there that I had to do something to stop that. And we did. I approached other people in the encampment and I told them it shouldn't be right that one person has authority because that's not

a democracy. It's a dictatorship, and that we should all decide as a group who we want as a leader. They agreed. They decided on not one leader but two leaders. Those two leaders being me and Larry and Tom was cut totally out of it.

I believe that this struggle between Tom and Alex was unknowingly assisted by the SHA (at the time called the SHAP). Alex was a great deal more articulate than Tom and would be placed in leadership roles within the SHA before Tom. This added to his status in the eyes of other camp members and contributed to a growing split between Tom's one-man rule and other camp members' desire for collective decision making.

Most camp members were men, but several women also lived there. Nancy was eighteen, Lucy was thirty-six. Lucy rarely stayed in the camp except to sleep; she managed a catering wagon during the day, arriving at work by 4 a.m., and did not participate in SHA meetings. She mentioned that she had had this job for fifteen years. Lucy used to stay around the corner from the encampment in her boys' father's sister's house, but because of a falling out she decided to take to the streets. When I met Lucy she had been on the streets for only a few months. Nancy allied herself with Dennis, her boyfriend at the time, also eighteen. Occasionally she would talk about her mother in San Francisco and the trips she and Dennis would take. When the SHAP was working in the encampment, she and Dennis had managed to hitchhike to Florida and back. Other members would often leave the encampment for weeks and even months at a time but eventually returned. At SHAP meetings, Tom, Alex, Nancy, Susan, and others from both the "Bridge" and the catacombs could be depended upon to show up.

Occasional crisis marked SHAP visits to the camps. For example, Linda, fourteen, appeared one day in the spring of 1991. Alex mentioned that she was running from her pimp, who was trying to find her. A runaway, she was taken in by the group and looked after. Because Linda was under age, no one in the camp or in the SHAP wanted to see her on the street. The SHAP assisted in finding shelter for her with a nearby church. Karen claimed that her parents abused her and tried to force their religious beliefs upon her. The SHAP attempted to negotiate with a local group that specialized in runaways. They sent one of their workers to the encampment to discuss Linda's situation. After that Linda disappeared with Nancy. Both, it turned out, went to a distant city to stay with Nancy's mother, during the spring of 1991. At this time the encampment was beginning to break up and people were moving in different directions, again in response to increased police patrols and the changing economic fortunes of several members of the camp. Tom was in jail, released, then jailed again for scavenging copper wire from a warehouse, and then escaped and was on the run. Alex had found work and moved into his own apartment. Dennis stayed with the SHAP and moved into a local shelter.

Social distinctions based on behavior were evident in the camp. Camp members took pride in the fact that they were such a diverse group and tolerated a wide range of behaviors. While some minor drug and alcohol use was evident in the encampment, it was also clear that these members as well as others on the streets differentiated encampments by categories such as "wet" (alcohol use), "dry" (no alcohol use), or "druggies," giving detailed descriptions and locations of other camps up and down the Guadalupe River. These social distinctions were played out in the catacombs as well. When some of the younger members of the group began using hard drugs, they were forced to relocate their tents about a football field length away. Excessive drug or alcohol use was discouraged, partly out of fear of the police, but also because it made camp dynamics difficult to control. This was evident in the problems with Bicycle Brandon, a man in his early thirties who would frequently appear drunk in public, bottle in hand, sometimes fighting with other camp members. He was known to all in the group, and the younger members would look after him, watching from a distance to make sure he was okay. He would often camp away from the rest of the group, and on occasion he was allowed to camp near them. In this manner the regulation of social-physical space was used as a mechanism for mediating group conflicts.

Relationships with the surrounding neighborhood, a poor Latino, community were mixed. Some residents would employ the camp members to take out their trash in exchange for a steady source of water, other residents looked suspiciously on the homeless camp members. The division within the housed community was severe enough that one neighbor expressed outrage that the homeless were stealing water from a fellow neighbor, until it was explained that the homeless had contracted to take the water in exchange for taking out her garbage. One group of young men from the neighborhood, coming from a house that local neighbors identified as a "problem," would occasionally sneak into the homeless camps. Once they slashed a tent. Another time they ripped up a homeless resident's tent, threw a rock at him, and pointed a small .22 caliber pistol at him. The man who was attacked claimed that the men who attacked him were looking for

someone else, a female member of the camp. Such incidents of violence were infrequent, but most disturbing. The catacombs were a
refuse space, a marginalized area that also served as a place for local
young people to drink beer and party, a zone outside of their neighborhood. When attempts were made to bring the housed community
and homeless community together, the homeless did not show. When
camp residents were asked about this, they said that they were too
afraid of identifying themselves to their neighbors. When other SHAP
members explained to the housed community what was happening, the
attacks ceased and the tension was defused.

In this type of social-physical space it is not surprising that collective identities would often be oppositional. Many members of the
camp referred to themselves as "runners," a name taken from the
science fiction film *Logan's Run* in which young people on the run
from death took up refuge outside the carefully controlled city center,
in the underground. The switching of identities between rebel and
victim was most profound. One moment somebody would be boasting
or telling stories about how they avoided the police or found a good
site to scavenge materials from, the next moment he or she would be
sadly speaking about abusive families and an unfeeling public. Collective identities of rebellion mixed uneasily with individual identities of
victimization. As camp members began to attend meetings with the
SHAP, their identities began to merge the defiant rebel image with that
of political activist, although most of the camp members still remained
suspicious of any organized political activity. Individual identities as
victims were dealt with either by befriending the homeless residents or
collectively through meetings, which many times took on the appearance of group therapy. Their concept of family now extended from the
camp to the SHAP (later to become the SHA) as well.

Like many families, camp members carried their own internal
conflicts into the SHA. These problems were often mediated on the
spot by the group's, listening, allowing someone to act out, acknowledging their feelings, and then getting on with business. Sometimes
problems could be resolved, sometimes not. However, it was the experience of being listened to that seemed to carry the greatest weight
for the homeless participants. Homeless newcomers to the SHAP, and
later at SHA meetings, would often speak loudly and talk on and on
about their condition while the group patiently waited for them to
finish. These testimonies would sometimes last up to two hours. Occasionally a newcomer would return to the group, sometimes not.
Functioning in part as group therapy and at other times as a political

organization planning strategy, the SHA was constantly negotiating emotions within the group. Whether or not the homeless participants or students felt listened to was an important factor in reproducing the solidarity of the group and in generating the micro conditions for the development of collective identity. Translating decision making and group involvement into collective action mobilized around specific goals required skill in listening to group members. Most of the homeless members of the SHA did claim they were listened to by other members of the group. However, several complained that sometimes they were and sometimes they weren't. These members had been recruited from a local shelter, although one who voiced complaints lived in the catacombs. The students by contrast all claimed they were listened to by others in the group, although some differentiated between the "leadership" and the group—the former were accused of not listening. The contrast between the students and homeless group participants is indicative of the status differences between both populations, even with the group acting as a mediator. The students clearly had more power than the homeless, as evidenced by the resources at their disposal. Interestingly, homeless members understood that their involvement in the SHA was limited to specific role positions, such as transportation person, activist, speaker, soldiers, with only two members mentioning advocates. Student members, however, described their involvement in terms related to assistance and service. Group roles appeared less defined for the student participants than for the homeless, who perceived themselves in clearly defined positions within the group.

Tranquility City

Site and community were important for Tranquility City inhabitants. The location of the huts was discussed fondly by homeless residents. Although more loosely knit than the SHA, the hut dwellers did have a decision-making structure clustered around those who had established their first huts under Halsted Bridge. Three of the homeless men living in these huts would often hold discussions with the other hut dwellers, and near the end of the encampment they were key players in negotiations with the city of Chicago. Tranquility City residents operated as a loose association. Differences existed between the scattered encampments, but when the city came to remove the huts, the hut dwellers were unified, depending upon their most knowledgeable or connected members, to bargain with the city.

The social-spatial configuration of this part of the Near West Side was a critical factor in locating the huts at this site. Close to day labor at the local Fulton Street fish markets, the site was ideal for providing easy access to many services. The markets for years had provided day labor for the unemployed and homeless. The site contained its own history as an area for the down and out. According to one hut dweller:

> this is the original area for a lot of homeless guys to come down to sleep, you know, cook their food, build bon fires. And before the Mad Housers came here, I mean, you had a little community itself that was established. It was a community of homeless people.

In addition, the location was visible to commuter trains, out of the way of most commercial activity, and in an urban pastoral setting. Tim, one of the first residents of Tranquility City, found sleeping next to "Pallet City," an abandoned warehouse adjacent to the hut sites, stated that he chose this spot to sleep over others because "It was a nice place, It was around trees and it was a beautiful area. It was scenic . . . It was safe . . . privacy, security, and safety." Others also commented on the quiet of the location, with the exception of the occasional Metra train to the suburbs. Another commented on the wide variety of birds that flew into the area. "We had quite a few different kind of birds over there, robins, woodpeckers, plenty of finches, they woke you up in the morning." Tim received his hut by attending the Mad Houser meetings after meeting a local graphic artist. Other hut dwellers drifted into the encampments through street contacts from Lower Wacker Drive and through local shelter contacts. With the approach of summer weather, some hut residents began to double up as shelters began to close. Those who received huts were obligated to attend the Mad Houser meetings at Randolph Street Gallery and assist in their construction at the site. In the beginning, HOME worked with several of the men at the site, drawing several more who were sleeping in Grant Park and under Lower Wacker Drive into meetings with the Mad Housers.

The site, bisected by the Metra suburban railway lines, presented contrasting close-up view of Chicago's Loop skyline; shiny glass office buildings gleamed in the distance. Abandoned brick factory buildings broken and boarded up rested nearby, smells drifting in from a nearby chocolate factory, and tall bushes, trees, and some wildlife, including many rabbits, crafted the landscape. As one hut dweller remarked:

> The most beautiful place I'd ever been in life. It was peaceful. We had every type of animal there. We had all types of animals including rats, woodpeckers, cats, dogs—we had all of them. I miss that place. I think about that place often.

Urban pastoral images were very strong in the hut dwellers' descriptions. Contrasting sharply with the hard, brutal world of concrete sidewalks and the environment of Lower Wacker Drive where many had slept in the past, the hut site evoked images of a previous era. Wayne connected not only the "peaceful" quality of the site, but also the relationship between that quality and what he perceived as a more leisurely and human pace of life, a pace reminiscent of another era:

> It's like peaceful, not a care in the world, nobody's bothering you, we listen to the radio, we listen to our gospel station, and you just kick back. And somebody walk up, and you ask them, "you want a cold drink?" . . . Come on sit down for a little while. It was something I haven't seen in a long time. I seen this done in the country when people would be walking down the road, for long walks to get somewhere.

For most of the hut dwellers, living in the shacks was a big step above sleeping in the shelters or on the concrete sidewalks of Lower Wacker Drive. The site location, combined with the presence of friends, convinced many from the shelters to join the hut dwellers. One hut dweller remarked that he was initially resistant to joining the camp after staying in the shelters. But what convinced him to join the hut dwellers was his desire for independence and the presence of his friends in the huts:

> It was better than the Mission and what have you. I was very hesitant about it at first because I didn't think . . . Well, who's going to break wood in the dead of winter to stay warm and all that. Once I went there with him one night. He was out breaking wood and getting the hut warm. I was still very hesitant, because it was very cold at that time and my feet were freezing. I don't know what made me go back, but I went back. When I went back I eventually got use to cooking on a wood burning stove and to me it felt a little bit more independence than standing in a long line to get into shelters, waiting for people to feed you, sleeping with 200 or so men.

The sense of peace, of a location where they could think and repair their lives, contrasted not only with the world of the shelters but also with the world of the public housing projects into which the hut dwellers were finally placed. Several of the former hut dwellers remarked about having to constantly watch their backs around the projects due to drug dealing and gang members. One remarked about the public housing project he was in:

> I hate this place. I hate to say that. I hate this place. I use to get off of work and just go to the store where we were by the railroad tracks. It didn't bother me to go to the store. I didn't have to look behind my back to see if there was anybody behind me that was going to rob me or hit me in the back of my head or something like that. It's like now when I'm over here, although you try not to give that feeling . . . you nervous, worried on what's around you. But it's a very uncomfortable feeling.

Privacy, the ability to lock one's door and have the freedom to not interact with other hut dwellers if one doesn't want to, was highly prized by the squatters. *Autonomy* and the *freedom* to come and go when one pleased was another quality that was highly valued. Many of the squatters worked at odd jobs requiring odd hours. However, the one factor that seemed consistent for all the squatters was the *desire for safety*. The shelters were believed to be unsafe, places where one could not be protected from predatory elements.

The rapid development of Tranquility City, what one squatter called a "subcity," depended upon the integration of the hut dwellers with the surrounding city community. As individuals they recognized their lack of power. However, the construction of eighteen huts in close proximity, combined with the extensive social networks established on the streets, through the shelters, and in the housed community, provided a locus for the establishment of collective identity and collective action. More than one squatter talked about fellow squatters as "family." A quality of family was staying in contact with each other. Squatters constantly kept in contact with each other. As John mentioned, "We would always keep in contact with each other, making sure that each other had what we needed, whether it be food, clothing, or what have you." Items brought into camp would be shared and swapping was commonplace:

> If I have a piece of pie, and I know that you're with me and I know that you're hungry. You're goin' to get half of that piece of pie. If I have a dollar and you're with me and I know that you have really been trying and I know you're trying to do something to obtain, you're going to get half of that 50 cents. It's called sharing.

This mutual support was perceived by the squatters not as a luxury but as necessary for their own survival. As one squatter said, "As a group we stuck together because we had nobody else." Conversation became a key point for communicating with each other, an arena in which one could be safe, unlike the shelters where one could say the "wrong" thing and set off a chain of events outside of one's control. Decisions were made collectively, although some newcomers would often exclude themselves, living on the farther edges of the camp. Those who chose to exclude themselves were still checked upon by the other hut dwellers periodically, and were left alone if they desired. Problems would be worked out collectively. According to Howard:

> If I was in my hut and I was having problems, like for example someone was talking about pouring gasoline on my hut. I started whistling for Jim and Jim will come and assist me along with the other sixteen or seventeen other brothers and we would deal with that problem right then and there.

Listening often occurred in group meetings. In the evening they would sit around a heater near each other's huts and discuss the issues of the day. According to Wayne:

> We had our little group sit downs. You know, nice day, get under the trees, sit down and discuss it. You know a lot of people would tell what happened to them. How they was doing, what they had, what they lost—and we even had some of the people crying while they was talking about it. And they would get up and want to go away, and we would tell them we support what you are doing. Man, you got friends here. You don't have to leave and be ashamed of crying, because everybody cries. We let them know we're there for you. We got to stick together.

This mutual support was critical in giving many of the men the confidence they needed to get through the day. Mutual aid also served as a mechanism through which all of those in the huts could acquire what they needed.

The proximity of the nearby markets on Lake Street provided discarded food in addition to occasional employment. When fire department personal turned on a local fire hydrant, the squatters could access fresh water to rinse and cook their food over woodburning stoves, which doubled as heaters in the winter. The ability to cook one's own food was important both to the squatters' self-image of independence and because it put distance between them and what they perceived as the institutional food of the shelters. As one squatter said:

> We ate better than Pacific Garden Missions would feed you or Sousa House or Cooper's Place or Olive Branch because we had the Fulton Market. We'd sit up there and roast the meat. We were eating better outside than in the shelter. I sat down one damn night and I cried.

With media coverage and word getting out about the encampment on the street, many people from the larger Chicago community became involved. This involvement was crucial to the establishment of Tranquility City as a community versus just a collection of individual huts. Using the surrounding site and community, the hut dwellers quickly expanded their net of contacts, gaining permission to post their flyers in the local surrounding bars, making contacts with local churches and community groups, and giving talks at local schools and colleges. They were being heard for the first time by city officials and community members. When they were in the shelters they were "nobodies." According to Wayne:

> We have all kind of people, we have different various homeless organizations, we have unions, you have people from the churches all different churches-Chicago Coalition for the Homeless, Illinois Coalition to End Homelessness, HOME, AFSCME, you have various different church groups Catholic, Lutheran, Baptist churches, various students from colleges that participate—Northwestern, Loyola, Columbia, Roosevelt, all kinds of college students participating.

Unlike homeless who have been tagged as disaffiliated, the squatters were quite conscious of mainstream norms and resources. For the squatters the recognition that others were concerned and actively took steps to assist fostered a larger sense of community that went beyond the small encampment. This sense of a larger community, a developing collective identity, combined with the struggles over retaining the huts, produced a greater understanding and political consciousness, an understanding that existed in weak form prior to the camp. For many of the squatters, these outside supporters who brought food, clothing, blankets, pots, pans, and conversation were not simply attempting to do good; in the squatters eyes, "they became a part of us." The generation of a larger sense of community continued in the work being done to house homeless people through the People's Campaign for Jobs, Housing, and Food operated by several of the men. This association underscores the necessity of integrating the gathering of resources, the strategic concerns of acquiring materials, with the cultural resources based around "identity." The integration of both are necessary to complete the development and maintenance of collective identity and collective action. As Tim put it:

> After we built the huts people started comin' in. We really got wrapped up into helping people then. We got totally wrapped up. We got so wrapped up that we came into the political arena with the mayor and governor and whoever else was involved. We started getting people into houses. You see us, we got houses today. And we got lots of people that we're still trying to get houses for.

The effect of this attention and of the cooperative relationships that characterized the camp inspired many squatters to ask questions such as "What do we want?" and to encourage each other to try to find work. Said John, "I think more or less what we did was motivate each other to help themselves." The movement of identities from those of individual personal survival to one of collective political protest for "all homeless people" was swift. After the mayor reneged on his promise to allow the huts to stay, the squatters were faced with the real prospect of ending up divided, back in the shelter system. This possibility forced most of them to act in unison, against the city's wishes. This "encounter," as Gamson, Fireman, and Rytina (1982) would define it, was sufficient to catalyze an emerging collective identity, organized around collective defensive actions. A strategy was formulated in order to deal with the city, and the proposal was acted upon by the squatters. According to Wayne, one of the squatter organizers:

> We decided to have a meeting and we decided, after the city was planning to—after the mayor wanted to renege on his promise, and so what we did, we all agreed in accord, that we would take our stance and not move until we get housing for not only the eighteen huts but as many homeless individual as we can and to make homeless issues an ongoing thing to get houses.

The effects of this type of resistance on public sentiment were not lost on the homeless squatters. They were well aware of the media publicity surrounding the decision to take down the huts and saw the city's actions as an opportunity for nonhomeless people to change their conceptions about the homeless. The countering of assertions of spoiled identity provided a particular power, a resistance against an authoritative strategy of exclusion, of marginalization. Hut dwellers would often speak at local schools and community meetings, refusing the labeling of the homeless as victims, as disaffiliated. Their visibility next to the Metra rails meant that sympathetic suburban contacts often supported their actions. As one camp member said, "We get a lot of support from people that live in the suburbs, you know. They used to call in when we had a little . . . I say, when the battles began, when we needed a support system, a support group from people . . . they called in from predominantly the suburb area and they was telling the mayor all of a sudden to leave us alone. Leave us alone, leave us be." They had to be listened to because they were able to enlist the support of more powerful others.

It is important to remember that Tranquility City was not completely unified or homogeneous. Factions emerged from internal group disputes that would require negotiating and reintegrating into the group. Many times these factions would emerge with the arrival of new squatters. New squatters, often from nearby shelters, would be allowed into the camp, resulting in a "doubling up." However, new squatters presented problems with maintaining the collective identity of the group that had developed in the encampments. In addition, those living in huts farther away from the first huts built in the area of "Pallet City" were more likely to feel on the "margins" of decision making and resource distribution. New recruits from the streets, usually those from Lower Wacker Drive, would often bring their problems with them, creating dilemmas for established hut dwellers. For example, some new hut dwellers attempted to panhandle near the sites of the original hut dwellers, causing friction within the group. As Wayne stated:

They [those living under Kedzie Bridge] wanted to come down on our end because of all the traffic . . . and panhandle down there. See, we didn't want to start that except'n money thing. We didn't. 'Cause we know people's going to come down there and try and manipulate one of us or all of us against each other with any kind of means to get us to fight among each other. And that's one way to do it. Because, if somebody comes on one end with all this money, and that happened on that end by the way, and give it to one individual and don't tell the other ones, and that person that gave it to them tells them to split it with everybody, and if they see this person again and they tell him, it could bring up problems . . . If you want to use money in that sense, don't give it to us, get something with it, things that we need. All of the guys were around and then they understood why we didn't want to panhandle and stuff.

The men in the original huts, under Halsted Bridge, understood that many of the men who were newly arrived carried with them habits formed from living on the streets, habits that had been necessary for their own survival and that died hard. However, the establishment of a community of huts with a collective identity, united against the attempts by the city of Chicago to displace them, was a powerful incentive for many to reexamine their identities. Wayne commented, "These guys didn't know no better because they were still in that rut. They were used to panhandling on Lower Wacker and that had to change. It took awhile for a lot of people to get used to their places. Some of the guys when they stepped in their doors were crying, like babies, they couldn't believe they actually had their own place finally." While differences in group behavior were often worked out in group discussion, factions did develop, most often over the distribution of goods. One squatter said in reference to perceived differences between his side of the camp and the initial huts, "I think they were different. They were on their own. They had their own ways." However, his absence much of the time from the camps contributed to his marginality within the newly created community. It is important to note that these squatters were more closely self-identified with the Mad Housers than were Tim, Wayne, or John at the first site. This point was brought out time and again during the interviews. This difference, as we discussed in chapter 5, stemmed from the conflicts between the Mad Housers, the squatter leaders, and the city during negotiations over what to do with the huts. The homeless men closely identified with the Mad Housers were placed in direct conflict with the other homeless men who wanted to deal with the city on their own terms. The perceived limited role of the Mad Housers as only builders of huts was resented by squatters not directly involved with the Mad Housers. Many of the squatters felt not only that the Mad Housers had abandoned them when the huts were built, rarely returning for visits, but that they took the initial lead in negotiating with the city of Chicago regarding the status of the huts. The squatters claiming ownership over the huts wanted to represent themselves. Some squatters wanted the Mad Housers to represent them to the city, the majority did not. The emerging collective identity of Tranquility City as a community overshadowed attempts by individual members to gain privileges through association with the Mad Housers. The city eventually shifted its negotiations to the squatters themselves when the squatters began to display a united front. As one of the squatters put it:

We were talking to various people, asking them what they want[ed]. We didn't say you are going to do this or else. We asked a question and the reply was they wanted to take a stance on this to get affordable housing. There were three people that . . . wanted the Mad Housers to represent them and we were dismayed at the time with their decision because we wanted to take a stance as a whole. United. But what we decide[d] to do was, since we had the majority of the people living in the hut; we decided to take a stance. We will work with that. We couldn't break nobody's arms an make them do what we wanted to. But eventually as the ball got rolling the Department of Human Services and the city and various other organizations such as Chicago Housing Authority started working with the hut people. These three individuals who wanted to go astray finally jumped on the band wagon and decided that we were making the right move. In that we managed to . . . instead of housing eighteen people we managed to house fifty-one.

Although the initial foray of the Mad Housers into the homeless community was met with enthusiasm, the lack of inclusion of hut dwellers on the Mad Houser board met with resentment from the hut dwellers. The underlying understanding of many of the squatters was that the Mad Housers wanted to help, but not get too close to actual homeless people. While it appears that the Mad Housers sought to generate public awareness over the issue of homelessness and to provide what they termed "guerrilla housing," this did not go far enough in the eyes of the squatters who managed to develop a larger sense of community out of their political action. The collective identity formed through the struggle to keep Tranquility City remained distant from the Mad Housers. For the squatters it was not enough to just build huts and expose the problem of homelessness. It was also necessary to generate a base for resistance, a base from which one could capture political attention.

As we have seen, the importance of site and community, of homeless placemaking, to the formation of collective identity is critical in establishing the basis for collective mobilization and action, as can be clearly seen in the examples outlined above. The resistant heterotopias of the encampments, the SHA, and Tranquility City highlight the need to understand the role of social-physical space in establishing "safe" areas, or "free spaces" (Evans and Boyte 1992), from which new collective identities can emerge and be tested against the forces of authoritative strategies designed to assimilate, exclude, repress, or displace marginalized populations. Another key issue that should be raised is to what degree the members of the SHA, the San Jose encampment members, or the residents of "Tranquility City" are different from other homeless men and women. How do their backgrounds predispose them to develop new collective identities centered around homeless placemaking?

SHA and Hut Dweller Differences
from Other Homeless Populations

Slightly less than half of the homeless members of the SHA had prior political involvements, such as registering voters, attending rallies, and working with local community groups. Group work ranged from working with a local peace social movement organization to, claimed one member, helping to organize a prison strike. While such self-reports are always suspect, there does appear to be a relationship between past political involvement and willingness to be involved in struggles for social change. The two non-SHA encampment members who indicated no prior political involvement also defined their situation in terms of individual problems. It appears that exposure to larger political battles creates the conditions from which one may redefine one's own problems in "social" as opposed to "individual" terms. The mixed political involvement of SHA homeless members contrasted with that of SHA students, most of whom had some experience with political work beyond the mainstream activities of registering voters or working on political campaigns. Student participants mentioned organizing protests against the Gulf War, environmental protests, human rights, and farm worker protests, and organizing with various leftist political organizations. In short, students who involved themselves in SHA on a long-term basis, as opposed to those who moved briefly through the organization, were the best and the brightest of what San Jose State University and Stanford University had to offer. Only one student listed no prior political experience. However, even she mentioned growing up in a family where politics of social justice were part of regular evening discussions. What was absolutely clear was the importance of these prior political involvements in establishing the preconditions for an emergent collective identity through group participation in the SHA.

Tranquility City residents were quite similar to San Jose's SHA homeless population, with the exception of race. The small core group that accomplished most of the negotiations with the city of Chicago were the ones who had the highest degree of past involvement with political work. Just about half the group had no prior political involvement. Past activities for the principal activists ranged from working with the Black Panther Party or the Young Democrats, marching with Martin Luther King, Jr., and canvassing for the Public Action Council on toxic wastes. However, in most recent times, most of the residents had either heard of or were directly involved with the Mad Housers, the Chicago Coalition for the Homeless (CCH), the Illinois Coalition for the Homeless, and Homeless on the Move for Equality (HOME). Several had spoken at CCH rallies. Those who had more political experience were defined by the other residents as the "leaders" of the camp. Most knew each other from prior experiences either on Lower Wacker Drive or in the local shelters. Several had attended demonstrations at the governor's office in Springfield. The less a resident was involved in past political activity, the more likely they would live farther from the initial cluster of huts. Social networks were the most developed for those who took the lead in negotiations with the city. It would be easy to conclude from this data that both the San Jose group and the Chicago group were exceptional and not generally representative of the homeless population at large. Perhaps this is the case. After all, it was the entrance into the SHA of a group of men from a local shelter, all of whom had prior ties with progressive organizations and radical politics, in particular the Communist Labor Party (CLP), that precipitated increased activity within the SHA. SHA activities became more focused, active, and militant. It was at this point that the *People's Tribune*, a newspaper with past associations with the CLP, became a frequent resource for both SHA and Tranquility City members, often covering homeless stories neglected in the mainstream press. It should be noted that the CLP agenda was never discussed or explicitly advocated in group meetings. SHA and Tranquility City residents were men and women who had embraced explanations of their problems outside the dominant frame of "homeless victim" or stereotypical "bum." All had convincing explanations for why homelessness existed. These particular homeless groups remained defiant and resistant to institutional social control, discouraging authoritative practices of assimilation or displacement, while blunting exclusion through practices designed to increase their visibility to the general public. A few in the SHA and Tranquility City were free riders, people who joined simply for having a roof over their heads, but the majority shared a common goal of securing housing for as many other people as they could help. When conflicts emerged in the SHA or Tranquility City, they often were over how these goals should be achieved. The fact that these new collective identities were difficult, if not impossible, to maintain after the residents had been forced into public housing or dispersed from their San Jose encampments, makes the initial formation of collective identities no less real, and a basis for future possibilities of identity changes, of political action, given the right timing and the right social-physical space. In the brief time they existed, these new forms of collective identity bonded the group participants together, allowing for concerted action, housing takeovers, and protests in the case of SHA, and resisting city demands for Tranquility City residents.

Collective and Individual Gains

In the end what was gained from the labor of the SHA and the Tranquility City residents? Clearly homeless placemaking, collective identity formation, and collective action proved to be one way of altering the status quo in the lives of the homeless who participated. All of those associated with the Chicago huts received places in public housing, however much they may have initially disliked the environment. The success of the SHA, however, was less obvious. Through militant housing takeovers, one house was ultimately secured for six homeless tenants, who remained in their house for over two years. No substantial changes in redevelopment law were initiated, however, and the process of excluding the homeless from the downtown area of San Jose continues. On the other hand, the alliances formed with segments of the local Latino community, and the vigilance in holding the city and county government responsible for their actions against the homeless have had some moderating effects on belligerent police practices. The material gains for the San Jose group were limited. This may be explained partly by the city's militant pursuit of redevelopment in San Jose's downtown area, as pointed out in chapter 3. In Chicago, on the other hand, a much larger city with greater distances between areas, there are more resources to work with, redevelopment is more localized, such as in the Loop or Near South Side, and many of the homeless know the police personally, some having gone to school with them. In Chicago, there are simply more places to hide and to camp without being detected. The consistent gains for all participants, students as well as homeless, were nonmaterial in the form of increased levels of respect, political awareness, and communication skills.

Emotional and social gains were noted by all homeless and student participants. All talked about a greater emotional uplift, a sense of hope, as a result of their involvement. A sense of direction and visibility was listed by some. A typical statement was this: "What I've gained is having people know who I am, which I really like. I am no longer invisible. I don't have to feel ashamed of being a failure because I know the situation was set up so that I fail." Another former SHA homeless member gained a sense of leadership, because he was held responsible for speaking at public gatherings:

> I gained a sense of leadership. An ability to represent myself and other people. I feel now that I could face the media or anybody with no fear. When I had first started I had a big fear of facing media and people in high places but now I've overcome my fear.

One SHA member said he was inspired to push himself, another overcame shyness, and still another "learned how to deal with diverse people." One mentioned being "politically empowered." All students listed emotional gains. The following quote from one of the San Jose State University students who joined SHA during the fall of 1990 semester is typical: "My experiences in the field have produced many changes in my attitude about the homeless. One fact that hit home was that homeless people are not all old. The people in the encampment were around my age and some were even younger. This fact made me take the issues more personally." Student involvement with homeless members of the SHA made the issue of homelessness concrete and thereby easier to understand. However, this knowledge comes with a price. One student said his involvement with the local street population via the SHA had led to increased family tensions, another lost faith in social change. But three noted improved personal skills. One student mentioned that working with the homeless transformed her knowledge. She became aware of how physical spaces of the city were used not only for transportation purposes, but also for housing:

> I never really thought about it but I do now when I drive over bridges . . . I look at bridges differently now. Even the word "bridge"

means something different. I used to think of it as a bridge over water and now I think of a bridge over people . . .When I hear bridge I think "shelter where people live."

The social gains achieved by student and homeless involvement in the SHA, while not principally material, were significant in preparing the ground for future mobilizations. Increased militancy over time resulted from both city resistance and from increasing levels of risk taking on the part of the students and homeless. Willingness to take increased risks—a sense of "empowerment"—was, I believe, a result of the creation of a new collective identity of the students and homeless as a "family" that could be trusted, even if such trust was limited. City policies of spatial dispersion actively worked against developing such trust. Homeless and student members as well as nonmembers shifted consciousness from purely individual achievement and personal gain to group achievement as their involvement intensified, as they engaged in homeless placemaking.

It is not clear from our sample whether or not collective action had been successful in changing the ideological understandings of society among SHA members. Such changes appeared evident from the start in the overt political responses of some homeless and student participants. However, there does appear some shift with SHA members who were more willing to express themselves and to speak out at political events. Attitudes toward authority hardened, moving from acceptance to a willingness to speak one's mind, but only when allied with a group that could offer some protection from reprisals. When given the opportunity, many SHA homeless members and nonmembers acted spontaneously, as witnessed by the "invasion" of City Hall and the brief occupation of the mayor's office during the second public SHA demonstration. Overcoming the fear and reality of repression at both the individual and the group level was necessary for collective action to occur.

The change in consciousness as a result of breaking down the barriers between "us" and "them," of recognizing the politically charged character of imposed cultural difference between students community activists and the homeless, is a key factor in social change, just as reinforcing a "us vs. them" mentality in the various homeless groups and the cities of Chicago and San Jose was necessary to generate the conditions for change. The new collective identities gave a context within which tactical resistances to authoritative strategies could be developed. For Piven and Cloward (1977), the belief in the legitimacy of current arrangements and ideology must be abandoned; members must believe that present conditions are not inevitable, that they can be changed, and they must develop a new sense of group identity before they can bring about active social change. These conditions were established in the SHA's approach, contributing to increased militancy through squatting actions. Ropers's (1988, 198–209) examination of "Justiceville," a homeless encampment in Los Angeles, demonstrated that these forms of active resistance often meet with moderate success; they are blunted by relying solely upon litigation strategies, documented by Ropers (1988, 189–198), Fabricant and Epstein (1984), and Blau (1992, 93–108) and commented upon by Wagner and Cohen (1991, 557). The problem with litigation, when practiced in isolation from direct action, is that "working for the homeless" takes precedence over "working with the homeless." It serves to maintain distance from a marginalized "Other," to maintain the social relations that reproduce systemic inequalities and to reinforce a lack of trust between advocates and the homeless. For SHA members, disruption through direct action was by far the most effective strategy for increasing group solidarity and expanding membership. This does not preclude litigation, but understands litigation as an integral part, a set of tools, within an overall system of actions. Wagner and Cohen (1991, 557) confirm this strategy in their study of "Tent City" in Portland, Maine, showing that a combination of legal and direct action work to produce substantial change.

Clearly the squatters expressed a sense of active agency and affiliation with established institutions. The conception of the homeless as a demobilized, helpless, and out-of-touch population found in the work of Roper (1988) and Rossi (1989) was not borne out in my experience. SHA and Tranquility City members showed only partial disaffiliation. Some were more detached and alienated than others. But as a whole, the social groups we examined demonstrated remarkable cohesiveness and social networking. Tent city inhabitants in Portland, Maine (Wagner and Cohen 1991; Wagner 1993), Santa Barbara's street population (Rosenthal 1989, 1994), Los Angeles's homeless youth squats (Ruddick 1990), and street people in Austin, Texas (Snow and Anderson 1993), show the same responses and activism as those in the SHA or Tranquility City. Indeed, not only were the squatters in Tranquility City affiliated with mainstream institutions, as indeed were many of the SHA's homeless, but they also demonstrated the self-organizational capacity to resist and negotiate for themselves over needed resources. Homeless communities often form subcultures of resistance, although not necessarily of their own choosing or as lasting as they might like.

The Chicago squatters mentioned material gains—securing apartments in public housing—but they also mentioned gains in a newfound belief in collective organizing as a way to achieve change. As Frank put it, "Some guys get together and you say, 'Look, if we can get together the politicians will listen.' But one person can't do too much. I was always a single type person and now if somebody comes to me and says, 'Hey, we can get together . . . ' I'll listen now." This ability to entertain the notion of collective action was inspired not simply by the material success of the hut encampments but also by the encampment's ability to bring authority, on their own terms, to their doorstep. Wayne commented:

> We're not bothering anybody, and were not on city property in the first place and we're not terrorizing the neighborhood or anything, and all of a sudden the City is like sending out the war party after us. And all the head leaders. Now what the hell is all the head leaders coming? The commissioner from Streets and Sands, the commissioner for Buildings and Codes, the supervisor of the park district. All of the head people, none of the understudies. That was definitely politics then, when we start see all of these people come down to a group of homeless people. Please! . . . Politically this was a big ass problem for [Mayor] Daley . . . He knew we meant what we said. He knew we weren't leaving without a fight. Anybody touch these huts can get ready for a physical confrontation.

In addition, an increase in self-respect was noted, but in particular many of the squatters felt a sense of power as others who had been in the shelter system began to view them as having access to power, as being able to help them find housing. This felt sense of power translated into a sense of collective responsibility for other homeless. Jim mentioned, "I feel like we're responsible to reach back and grab those that can't help themselves. Now I go some places and see some guys who knew that I was a part of the hut dwellers and the media thing and they say, 'Hey, Jim! Can I get a place? Tell me what to do.'" With the newfound attention and the willingness of the city to negotiate for the huts, Jim expressed his new sense of power by refusing to move for three additional days:

> I talked to the commissioner eye to eye. He and I had words, Daniel Alvarez from the city of Chicago Department of Human

Services. He came in with the contract that he wanted me to sign and I was the only hut dweller around there. I was really adhering to what he wanted and he was tired and wanted me to get together with the other guys who were already housed. So, he approached me and wanted me to sign a waiver that I was giving my hut to the city of Chicago to do whatever they wanted with it and I disagreed with that. And I told him to rewrite that because I felt that the hut was my property and I want to know where my hut is at. I may want to donate to whoever I want it donated to. He said he couldn't do that and I said I'm not leaving. I told him to get off my land! I had words like that and I knew it was hard for him to understand a person's basic needs, a person's own ability to know what he was dealing with, which was an emergency basis. It was something very personal and private and he just wanted me to throw it away. It was like this man . . . this . . . authority is not even listening to me. He wanted me to sign the papers and just get off the land and I wasn't goin' for that. I told him that sense he had that type of attitude that I was going to stay three more days. I told him I would give him the decision in three more days what I was gonna do with my hut. So we cost the city some money.

The ability to delay the city of Chicago for three days was in fact a real demonstration of power for those in the encampments, as was the SHA's practice of demonstrating in front of San Jose's City Hall and taking over abandoned buildings. In Tranquility City, some homeless residents described the encampment as "educational" with a wide variety of ethnic, racial, and religious groupings visiting the encampment to lend their support. The squatters thought that this helped to broaden their perspective. As Tim mentioned, "we learned new things. Sometimes people would come down there and give us certain issues to talk about. Not only did we talk about our needs but about everbody's." One member of the camp was able to secure his old job when his employer read about the encampment in the local newspaper. Mutual support was mentioned by all as one of the gains of the encampment. One squatter said that it taught him the "will to live." He said:

I was about ready to commit suicide. These guys told me there would be better days. They kept on trying and they told me not to worry about it and that something would happen. We got a place where we can hide and we got people that are helping us.

I gave up on the matter. But they told me don't give up and that's why I'm here.

Friendship, comradeship and a sense of solidarity were all mentioned as key benefits by the Chicago squatters. As a result of their organizing they were able to attract city attention, which further confirmed the viability of their collective identities and collective acton. One squatter said that after moving from a six-bedroom unit to a shelter to a hut he had a greater appreciation for living space. "I get respect for a home. I used to take it for granted. No more." What appears to have been gained, in addition to respect and feelings of self-worth, is a new faith in the possibility of organizing for change. The expansion of the possibilities for change resulted from the employment of disruptive, non-normative tactics through squatting. As Pivan and Cloward (1992, 1977) point out, for poor people who lack the resources of middle-class organizations, disruption may be the only way to precipitate change. This is not to refuse the effects of organized institutional approaches, as Roach and Roach (1978) seemed to think. It is not an either/or situation. It is merely a recognition of the abilities of different class segments to initiate social change and the differences between such segments in their approaches to collective action. The effects of such disruptions are not limited to established institutions, but directly affect the perception of future possibilities for change within poor populations. This hope for change, combined with the direct practical experience of squatting and developing organizational skills, seems to be one of the lasting benefits of the encampments. According to Jim, a Tranquility City resident:

> I've gained insight into this homeless issue. I understand it a little better than I did in the past based upon organizing ourselves with the group . . . I've learned that you can achieve a lot once you put your heads together toward a common goal. Any person trying to accomplish any kind of task alone is gonna be hard. Two heads are better than one. We achieved a lot because we came together and we spoke up for ourselves. And we asked ourselves what we want and how each other feel. We organized. And I know that I have learned a skill. And that skill is an organizational skill.

For a brief period Tranquility City and the SHA encampment became a mini-movement area in which a different way of living poor was experimented with; a possibility was created for the formation of a homeless community free of institutional shelter restraints. Within these mini-movement areas homeless residents were able to construct a collective identity centered around issues of social justice for other homeless individuals and collective action in helping each other acquire housing and needed services. Therefore collective gains were not simply individual gains but social gains, leading to new beliefs in the legitimacy of organizing. Homeless residents of Tranquility City never perceived their huts as the final solution to homelessness. Rather, the issue was about housing all of Chicago's homeless. As one man said, "We're not mad to try to live. We're trying to involve ourselves in a human event. Because we're looking out for more than over 60,000 people. You know, we're not just thinking about ourselves . . . we're thinking about the ones that can't even speak up for themselves."

CHAPTER 7

Conclusions

In the conclusions of any work it is customary to expand upon specific points raised within previous chapters and or come up with possible solutions, programs, plans, or courses of action. Clearly, the complexity of the issues I have just outlined prevent any singular comprehensive solution that can easily be summarized within a tight program. However, each of the previous chapter offers insights that, taken together, can indicate a direction for future research and just possibly a few political, economic, and cultural actions that could shake the foundations of everyday life.

Homelessness is an objective reality for many Americans, and indeed for many people in other countries. It is also a social construction that has functioned in policy circles by displacing attention away from social inequality, social-economic justice, and property relations. This has been accomplished through the academic segmentation of homeless bodies and in "speaking for the other." Rarely have the voices of the homeless—indeed, of the poor in general—been allowed to speak for themselves. And to a degree I have been guilty of that in this work. It is most difficult to integrate a theoretical perspective with a praxis that allows for the voices of those who have been silenced.

The emphasis on clarity, delivery, on performance and intelligibility, has driven the judgments of the legitimacy of "poor people's talk." Those who cannot routinely speak in the discourse expected by media reports, policy makers, or politicians find themselves simply excluded, ignored in favor of the "articulate" spokesperson, the "expert," or the stereotypical representative of "the poor." In addition, the boundary work accomplished between academic disciplines, between types of knowledge and their practice, works to prevent crossovers, to prevent the sliding of one discourse and knowledge into another; it is the debasement of poetic and somatic knowledge in favor of a rigid conceptual and normative knowledge that sacrifices the potential disruptive effects of utopic spaces for the false certainty of control and predictable outcomes. Following Hoch's (1990) suggestions, what is needed is an understanding of practical objectivity, not simply scientific objectivity. What is called for is the opening of widespread debates in all sectors of everyday life on the issues of social justice, social inequality, and the social organization of property and wealth. In particular, homelessness as a topic must be reexamined as not simply as an objective reality but as a trope of poverty and degradation within a functioning market economy that distinguishes others on the basis of dominant social imaginaries.

In chapter 1 I raised the question of the relationship among identity, social imaginaries, and social-physical space; of how the low status of homeless persons is generated from the dualisms created through the dominant social imaginaries in our society. Hence the status of homeless persons, constructed as it is through dualisms of deserving/undeserving, clean/dirty, moral/immoral, strong/degenerate, generates a "norm" for more-privileged segments of society—the norm of the "bottom of society." When these norms are reproduced through the organization of social-physical space, a ground is created from which social identities may be ascribed by the privileged who are not confined to such spaces. Since homeless identities are "fixed" in, on, and through the body in social-physical space, through the everyday practices of the body, it is also the body that offers a key to resisting particular identities. In the case of the SHA and Tranquility City, such resistance took many forms, but clearly the collective nature of bodies resisting together was one of the most powerful tools for challenging established identities.

It is clear from the writings of Castoriadis (1987) and Lefebvre (1991) that social imaginaries can work through spatial practices, representations of spaces, and representational spaces to both reproduce and challenge established notions of social-physical spaces and social identities. The abstract space imposed by engineers, planners, politicians, and police can be challenged by the construction of resistant heterotopias built upon a utopic space, the representational spaces embodied in social imaginaries of liberation. For a brief moment the SHA and the Chicago encampments offered utopic spaces for reimagining a different social identity for the homeless and very poor.

This theoretical framework may be very useful in furthering research into the types of imaginaries utilized by city planners, developers, and political figures and to contrast narratives collected from city officials with those collected from oppositional community organizations, homeless persons, political activists, and the like. In what manner does each group embody elements of the imaginary of freedom and liberation from the alienation of everyday life, and how does that imaginary operate in the fantasies of these different social groups? How much accord is granted imaginaries of the city that include *all* the citizens, not just those who are privileged? And how do these imaginaries manifest themselves at the policy level in such documents as the Comprehensive Housing Affordability Study (CHAS) reports, planning documents, and city council transcripts on specific "boundary" disputes involving privileged and nonprivileged populations?

These questions are given added weight within the concrete realm of the city proper, in the distinctions between inclusive and exclusive redevelopment. The social imaginary of what a modern American city should look like clearly excludes large numbers of citizens and produces a social-physical space of clear hierarchies of spatial and social worth. The dominance of exclusive redevelopment models can be opposed by calling for inclusive redevelopment that benefits all segments of the community and calls for the democratization of public space, an end to the corporate seizure of public places, and the extension of public rights to privately owned spaces that function as public spaces (such as shopping malls). This requires a nurturing of oppositional social imaginaries that would seek, in their manifestations, a model of city development based on joy and freedom for all citizens in which privileged, private access is replaced by public democratic economic development; such imaginaries directly oppose the imposition of abstract space by revolutionizing everyday life.

The "normal" generation of polarized topographies, whether they are the niche marketing categories of the latest fashions or the segmented and segregated social-physical spaces of pleasure, refuse, and functional spaces, can be subverted through the systematic and intentional collapsing of boundaries between segments. Homeless persons do this every day simply by being homeless and "out of place," but they do it from a position of weakness with few resources and little direction or intent, a by-product of situational deprivation. What is required is a systematic violation of boundaries, a revolutionary transgression of borders, with the goal of expanding joy and freedom for all and creating ecstatic, compassionate, and joyful social-physical spaces. These liberated zones or "free spaces" when multiplied and interlinked through widespread global communication networks will constitute a new everyday life, a utopic space from which the "old" social-physical spaces can be further eroded, their authority undermined.

At the pragmatic level the spreading of these polarized topographies may be blunted by the imposition of counter policies. To make a serious effort, not only to end homelessness, but also to end the deprivations of poverty, will require moving beyond the simpleminded tricks of job training or an expansion of shelter grants. The heart of privilege and property must itself come under attack from all sectors as counter to the development of a truly civilized society. This will require changes in employment, health care, housing, media, and education.

Challenging the Disappearance of Jobs, Housing, and Health Care

The disappearance of jobs as a result of technological changes, union busting, corporate downsizing, and outsourcing will require altering the relationship between the citizen and the employment market as Rifkin (1995) and Aronowitz and DiFazio (1994) point out. As Aronowitz and DiFazio remark, "there are simply not enough jobs of any kind with decent pay in relation to the actual—much less the potential—labor force, which has grown exponentially since 1970, and the long term tendencies in both manufacturing and in the services that point to the progressive displacement of labor, even during periods of economic growth" (300–1). The assumption by both liberals and conservatives that economic growth will mean more jobs for all, including those who are homeless, is a myth concealing the long-term trend toward a jobless future. Growth is occurring without proportionate job additions. Simply put, we can do more with less.

Americans who are still in the workforce are working longer hours with less pay (Schor 1992), while still others are underemployed struggling to get by in increasingly smaller wage checks with little if any health benefits. Fewer Americans than ever before have full-time, livable-wage jobs. Yet Wall Street is doing very well indeed. The jobs we have lost will not return. Homeless persons like other poor and working-class persons, are finding that their labor is simply not necessary any longer except in the most marginal service jobs. The chaos of the labor market is mirrored by the anarchy of the financial markets in which cyclical swings of bull and bear markets take on increased volatility as speculative investments replace long-term stable bond markets. Financial derivatives replace longer-term bonds in an attempt to make money faster over a shorter time period. The permanent structural change in job loss, however, does not have to be an occasion for despair, given the right set of social and political conditions.

To provide necessary job opportunities that pay a living wage in the midst of expanding part-time contract labor, several things can be done immediately. One, raise the minimum wage to the level where it can support a single parent working forty hours a week. This will require raising it above the almost comically low $4.25 hour to a little over $7 an hour to make it comparable to the worth of the minimum wage in 1967, the last time when the minimum wage was a true minimum wage. In 1993 it required a head of household earning $6.93 an hour on a full-time year-round work schedule to raise a family of four to the poverty level (Mishel and Bernstein 1994, 127). In 1979 those earning less than poverty wages constituted 4.1 percent of the workforce. By 1993 that number had increased to 26.9 percent. For the homeless I worked with, many of whom worked at marginal jobs, raising the minimum wage can make the difference between having enough to save for rent and not working at all.

The alternative to this could be presented simply as a guaranteed annual wage or a national guaranteed income available to everyone regardless of their socioeconomic status. Such an income would provide the basic nutrition, shelter, clothing, and recreational requirements. A national guaranteed income would force private businesses to compete on a realistic basis for worker labor and eliminate regressive management practices. In this "workers' market," employers, not workers, would be at the disadvantage. This will make technological labor-saving devices more attractive to businesses, as work in the form of labor begins to dwindle in favor of truly "free" time for all workers. This would also create incentives for schools to expand their arts programs as more and more people find the time to explore their previously creative sides in a noncoercive environment. In the past such lifestyle changes were only available to the "idle" rich. In this context welfare as we know it could be abolished in a dignified manner, while preserving the security of the poorest of the poor, provided national health care and free childcare were made available.

A second provision would be to mandate that overtime be paid at two to three times and a half rather than the current time and a half arrangement. The current arrangement gives corporations an incentive to cut their workforce and retain their remaining workers for extended hours because it is cheaper to work remaining workers harder than to train new workers.

A third and more radical provision would be to give preferential treatment in taxation policy and in the granting of government contracts to corporations that are worker owned and that operate on a collective democratic system of decision making. It has been proven that worker owned and operated companies, when they are not marginal companies to begin with, not only reduce work alienation but also are close to 30 percent more productive than non-worker-owned companies. The incentives for production are built into the nonalienating systems of management and in the ownership patterns of corporate assets. The formation of workers' collectives, cooperatives, and corporations could also be encouraged through labor educational programs and in contract negotiations with major corporations. Worker collectives, cooperatives, and corporations could be provided with starter resources and interlinks with other developing worker collectives, not only nationally but also internationally. Authoritarian systems of management could be penalized through the denial of government contracts and consumer boycotts.

Finally, as the European labor movement has advocated, a shorter work week would create new opportunities for job creation. There is nothing sacred about the 40-hour work week. Granting workers a 30-hour work week at 40 hours' pay would be one way to share democratically the productivity gains produced by new technology. According to Aronowitz and DiFazio (1994), "the thirty-hour week at no reduction in pay would crete new jobs only if overtime was eliminated for most categories of labor" (347). This has been accomplished in the most technically advanced sectors of the German economy as a result of a 1985 strike by the Metalworkers Union (IG Metal). German employers yielded to the demand for a 35-hour work week implemented over a five-year period in part because the use of highly productive technologies has maintained German productivity at a very high standard (347). The resultant increase in quality of life for all workers would improve productivity and morale and generate the conditions for increased expansion of cultural capital, not to mention providing more job slots overall.

The nonprofit sector has expanded rapidly, as Rifkin has pointed out, but I am not convinced that it can pick up the slack from the loss of jobs throughout the economy. Many nonprofit groups retain authoritarian systems of management and also run on shoestring budgets that make them unsuitable for stable employment. The key link here is stable employment. The capitalist fantasy of a completely mobile workforce, flexible and always willing to move, negates the needs of American families, of children, and of the community. It is more a fantasy of an individualistic Road Warrior/Mad Max than of a loving, nurturing community of care; it is a fantasy better suited to male adolescents than to adults who wish to create stable and loving communities.

A significant component of the above labor policy must also be how to manage sickness within our society. The current preoccupation with managed care schemes privileges large insurance companies, fragments health care delivery, and penalizes citizens at the expense of driving up health care costs. A simpler and more effective example is provided by the single-payer plan for a national health care, as in Canada. In making health care available to all, without the extensive paperwork, and as a universal right, corporations and worker collectives could save themselves the costs of paying for benefits by having the costs distributed throughout society. This would ensure that emergency rooms were not overburdened with patients who could not pay and would provide services on a more rational basis. In addition, many mentally ill homeless currently living on the streets would be able to secure effective treatment at state- and government-financed community mental health rehabilitation clinics according to the original intent of the initial deinstitutionalization of the mentally ill during the late 1960s.

While stabilizing the labor process and increasing low-cost and quality health care is essential, increasing the production of low-cost housing units that are truly affordable is necessary to eliminate homelessness. This includes the construction of new SRO units as well as low-cost apartments and single family homes. Large-scale homelessness made its appearance in the early 1980s as a result of the decline in workers' incomes, layoffs of blue-collar manufacturing workers, direct attacks on unions by the combined forces of private business and the U.S. government, inflated costs of housing relative to incomes, and the decline in the production of low-cost housing and single-room-occupancy units. Between 1970 and 1989 alone we saw a reduction of 4.1 million rental units for the poor (Timmer, Eitzen, and Talley 1994, 19). And, as I discussed in chapters 2 and 3, the decline of SRO housing in the central cities has meant the loss of units most likely to be inhabited by the very poor and occasionally homeless. The gentrification and displacements resulting from downtown redevelopment have directly contributed to these losses of rental units.

Following the National Low Income Housing Coalition's recommendation of an annual production target of 750,000 low-income units a year, combined with the preservation of public housing, strengthening landlord-tenant law to protect renters from unfair evictions, expanding the voucher program to give the poor greater access to market-rate housing units, providing relief for homeowners facing foreclosure, and expanding the stock of low-income SRO units nationally, would help end homelessness (Leavitt 1992, 31–32). The recent revision and ending of the Department of Housing and Urban Development's ruling of 1:1 replacement for public housing units that are torn down means a net decline in low-cost units at a time when public housing waiting lists are growing ever longer. The decline of the federal government's role in housing and the privatization of housing services has meant nothing short of disaster for the very poor and homeless. Only one-fifth of the poor in the United States live in government housing of any kind, an extremely low percentage compared to European countries. Urban public housing accounts for 40 percent of the housing stock in Europe compared to only 1.3 percent of the housing stock in the United States (Timmer, Eitzen, and Talley 1994, 23). The United States has the lowest rate of governmental assistance to the poor of any of the modern industrialized nations. And that percentage is shrinking as conservative ideologies expand to justify the new barbarism in pleas for more jails, more police officers, more security. The end result of this will be social breakdown and the disintegration of any social contract between social groups or classes. Given the current direction of policy and ideology, the desolation of the Mad Max/Road Warrior films is not too farfetched. Is it any wonder that larger and larger numbers of people are purchasing weapons and locking themselves behind closed doors? A society built on fear cannot sustain itself into the future.

Neither Chicago nor San Jose can produce the necessary numbers of low-income housing units without federal support. This support is hampered by both a conservative ideology and a conservative political approach that relies on market forces to supply the necessary housing for an expanding poor population. Increasingly charity is viewed as a substitute for real substantive policies. However, for cities like Chicago and San Jose to complain about the lack of federal aid while undertaking massive construction projects designed to attract upper-income patrons and multinational businesses reveals that the real agenda is to attract privileged homeowners while neutralizing poor opponents. It was precisely this dichotomy that privileged baseball stadiums, downtown hotels owned by out-of-town landlords, and unnecessary office construction through real estate speculation; the neglect of the need for low-income housing units integrated within the city (not simply segregated in outlying areas) revealed the city's development intentions.

Challenging City Redevelopment Strategies

As we have seen in the analysis of exclusive city redevelopment strategies, providing housing and jobs in and of themselves might not be enough. What is also required is to change the priorities of city and regional government, to discourage exclusive redevelopment plans, and to encourage inclusive redevelopment plans that treat all class and racial segments of a city equally. Clearly, changing redevelopment priorities will be difficult. Some planners have attempted to develop plans that work to democratize public space and expand opportunities for a city's poor population (Krumholz and Clavel 1994). The attempt by city planners such as Robert Mier in Chicago to implement a progressive planning agenda under the leadership of the Harold Washington administration ran into continuous oppositional forces in city government, which preferred the polarized topographies developing throughout Chicago. Different strategic resistances were encountered by Derek Shearer in Santa Monica, California, and Margaret Stracham in Portland, Maine, to name just a few equity planners. Changing city government agencies from within is difficult at best. The massive changes required for moving from exclusive to inclusive redevelopment will require both internal change and external pressure from organized coalitions of homeless squatters, housing activists, labor unions, human rights groups, and women's organizations applying pressure through media events, squatting actions (Welch 1992), litigation (Blasi and Preis 1992), and protests at shareholder meetings of real estate developers, who often line the pockets of local politicians prior to election time. The war to end homelessness and to gain dignity and justice for the poor must be waged on many fronts simultaneously and with any and every weapon available. The stakes are too high, the damage too great to those less privileged.

In Chicago and San Jose, gentrification and displacement continue under the guise of city redevelopment. Chicago's unwillingness to preserve the remaining SRO units in the South Loop area and San Jose's desire to disperse its poor and homeless from the downtown area speak to the need to rethink the manner in which redevelopment is conducted. Chicago could act to integrate the 20 percent set-asides for low-income, affordable housing immediately in the South Loop projects slated for upper-middle-class tenants rather than wait for an extended period of time after most of the poor, black, and Hispanic residents have been removed. San Jose could rescind its policy of no SROs in the downtown "core" area to provide low-cost decent housing for the city's poor and could discourage the placement of shelters in outlying, marginal areas of the city. Homeless persons deserve the same treatment as the privileged. However, in a cultural climate of fear and revulsion, accented by a dominant social imaginary that labels the homeless and very poor persons as the "degenerate" other, it is difficult for city officials, developers, police, business owners, and privileged segments of the housed community to understand that their own reactions to the very poor work to worsen the conditions of those living on the streets. Combatting this fear and revulsion, which equate homelessness with criminality, requires education of the general public and social mobilization by the homeless and their supporters.

The general issues of institutional, cultural, and market exclusions of the homeless discussed in the context of authoritative strategies and resistances reveal the difficulty of changing public perceptions and official city policies that equate redevelopment with an exclusionary vision of the city. Resistance practiced by the SHA and the members of Chicago's hut encampments to the exclusions, repressions, displacements, and assimilations of authority do indicate that such opposition can be mounted and that at least briefly perspectives can be changed. However, such actions must extend over a much broader range of issues, calling into question the very conceptualization of city space and city economic and social development by elected officials.

As we have seen, the altering of everyday social-physical space through collective action as we have seen, generates the conditions for a new political vision, a new vision of the city. To conceive of homelessness as simply a problem for the Department of Human Services or for charity ignores the role city officials, planners, and developers have in structuring city spaces that lead to the exclusion and repression of its poor. Few city officials understand homelessness as an issue of land use; most prefer the politically safe understanding of homelessness as a social welfare issue. It is not simply a question of building more housing, or even creating more jobs, although those are necessary, but it is a question of where these new housing units will be built and what type of jobs will be created. And that is directly related to land use, as I have pointed out. To think that homelessness can be contained by creating more shelter beds while diverting city funds into market-rate units, luxury housing, and expensive commercial development is to ignore the reality of a large number of our very poor constituencies. Shelters do not solve homelessness. Decent jobs, housing, and health care do.

For the remainder of this chapter I will discuss two issues related to education and collective mobilization. Challenging the dominant social imaginary within which city spaces are constructed will require moving beyond established images of the very poor and homeless to understand at a deep level the relationships among poverty, homelessness, and our imaginaries of race, class, and gender within a city-based market economy. The first issue I would like to briefly explore is the possibility of campus-based service-learning programs to challenge the dominant imaginary of charity in favor of an imaginary of social justice in assisting the poor. Second, since many service-learning programs discuss the advocacy of student empowerment or homeless empowerment, I conclude the book with a distinction between individual and collective empowerment, suggesting that collective empowerment is the more powerful tool in raising consciousness and changing policy.

Service-Learning: A Pedagogy to End Homelessness?

One possible step toward ending homelessness is the changing of public attitudes and the educating of young people toward a commitment to social change. Service-learning programs, as we discussed in chapter 5, can offer a vehicle for moving not only students, but also the general public, into a critical understanding of what is needed to stop the dispersion and containment of the very poor, to end homelessness. The Campus Compact model of service involvement is only one model; there are many more that I don't have time to explore. However, one must ask whether service-learning programs are sufficiently rigorous, critical, or active in challenging the polarized topographies that float across our cityscapes. What are the effects upon both students and homeless persons when they become mutually involved? These are difficult questions to answer. These questions speak to the nature of imagined politics.

What is the role and purpose of the university in developing service-learning programs? According to a spokesperson for the Campus Compact, that role is to educate students in "the exercise of civic responsibility by applying knowledge and skills to ameliorate a social situation" (quoted in Levine 1992, 529). However, neither civic responsibility nor amelioration are sufficiently defined. Instead we are left with the assumption that somehow by doing work in the community the student will be made a "better" citizen, that is, that he or she will be more involved in the community. The political presumption implied in this type of statement is the one learned from civics 101, that America is a democracy in which all have an equal voice if only people would participate; why they do not is rarely addressed. When lack of participation is addressed, it might be attributed to laziness, the allure of consumer culture, or ignorance, but rarely is the critique directed at the inequities of the political and economic system.

Hondagneu-Sotelo and Raskoff (1994) outline a number of problems that emerge in service-learning programs. Many students when they enter into a course that involves extensive work in the community have to struggle with "the tendency to reach unwarranted, often racist conclusions based on selective observations" (250). Most often this involves bringing to the experience common racial stereotypes mixed with individualistic assumptions about success. The second problem is the "white knight syndrome" in which students perceive their role as rescuing those they have worked with. Sensitized by the outrage they feel at the injustices they have observed, their first reaction is to want to rush in and fix the situation. In this case, no dialogue has been established between the students and those they want to help; rather the anger comes from realizing the differences in social power and wanting to reconcile that difference by taking action. Finally, the third problem is a detached, simple regurgitation of the lecture material, or giving the teacher what the student thinks he or she desires. Resolving these problems requires the engagement in dialogue between the student and teacher and between the students and the community participants with whom they work. However, such a dialogue must include not only a critical questioning of the student's own perspective, but also a critical questioning of the myriad forms of social inequality, of the supposedly "natural" operations of the capitalist market economy, that generate homelessness.

Service-learning programs, for the most part, remain oriented toward individual development, a cultivation of "private" sensibilities in attitudes of tolerance and charity toward the poor. A truly liberatory pedagogy that includes service-learning, however, would not stop here but move into the realm of political, economic, and cultural critique, asking the larger questions about the production and reproduction of social inequality and political privilege. As Harry Boyte understands in commenting upon the National Community Service Act, service-learning is useful for fighting against personal feelings of alienation privately but simply does not make the necessary political jumps to end this alienation socially (Levine 1992, 529). The public sphere is kept separate from the private realm of charity. As Boyte argues, today's young people are not disillusioned, they are angry at what they perceive as the inequalities in society and the declining opportunities for their own and other people's futures. One must ask whether service-learning programs are just another version of shelters for universities—designed to effectively "contain" real, legitimate anger and rage on the part of students? If they are, then are they not just another authoritative strategy of power, a strategy of displacement? This, of course, raises the question of "amelioration."

Setting up soup kitchens or spending nights on the streets to experience "homelessness" perhaps teaches students something about poverty; however, the depth of analysis the instructor brings to the experience can determine whether the witnessing of poverty is responded to with simple charity or steps on the way toward social justice. And how far does one pursue social justice in relationship, in dialogue, with those one serves? The assumption that one can be nonpolitical, or nonpartisan, in the conduct of service assumes that the making of economic and political decisions about other people's lives, in our case the homeless, is removed from considerations of power.

In a nationwide survey conducted by Phelan et al. (1995), with a sample of 1,507 adults, it was demonstrated that higher education increases student tolerance toward homeless persons but reinforces conservative economic views. While students were socialized into the "official culture" of equal opportunity and respect, they were also socialized into not supporting equal outcomes. That is, redistributive models of economic wealth are not accorded legitimate status within the "official culture," the dominant social imaginary, of the United States. Clearly then, higher education, as a host of authors have pointed out (Giroux 1983, 1988; Freire 1973, 1978; Mclaren 1986; Aronowitz and Giroux 1991; Bourdieu and Passeron 1977), is designed to reproduce dominant social imaginaries. A noncritical service-learning, then, is one more tool to effectively socialize students, to assimilate students into solutions that do not disturb capital investment or the smooth functioning of city governments.

Where one serves and who one serves will determine the type of critique that is necessary. In working with shelters or homeless advocacy groups, students need to have an academic component that transcends their immediate experience, to contextualize the experiences they have with homeless persons. There is a great deal of information available on the techniques of service-learning, the keeping of journals, the writing of papers, and the elaborate developmental models of student learning. However, what is needed is student understanding of city redevelopment processes, the role of real estate developers and gentrification and displacement issues, and how local communities understand student involvement, and, in particular, how involvements in some groups, shelters, or organizations can work against the people one is trying to assist. Part of the problem may be that service-learning courses have been connected directly with student services and granted primarily a psychological focus—student moral/emotional development (Delve, Mintz, and Stewart 1990). University ministry programs conduct service-learning around hunger and homeless from the religious perspective of service to the poor. Schools of Education may conduct literacy classes and involve students in local community organizations.

The problem is that each field, discipline, or organization approaches the service experience from the point of view of the student and their own discipline and rarely with a comprehensive analysis of the community's problems in the larger political and social sense. As in the realm of social-physical space, service knowledge remains homogenized, fragmented, and reproduced under a system of spatial hierarchies. A comprehensive analysis of city redevelopment policies, educational practices, health budgeting, and general policy orientations is difficult to achieve. One can give students a false sense that they are doing something meaningful if the larger picture is not included in their education.

In working with students and homeless members of the SHA, I used a great deal of material outlining the inequalities—social, cultural, economic, and political—that characterize American society. While this was an eye opener for the students, many of the homeless SHA members said they wanted to talk about solutions. Managing this disparity in knowledge was most difficult, but usually assisted through practical action. Without a critical approach coupled with concrete practice, those who are being assisted may also develop resentment toward those helping them. The problem of assistance may run into the difficulty of witnessing seemingly intractable social problems without the assistance of social, political, or economic theory that can provide the necessary insights into the relationship between the social problem in question and local assistance to reduce the problem.

Without a critical analysis of the social context for one's actions, solutions can easily slip back into a form of fatalism, and or volunteerism that effectively deflects political action. I realize that this might seem an overgeneralization. I don't mean to imply that all service-learning programs suffer from a lack of social or political context. However, if we are to develop a liberatory pedagogy, then service-learning must be coupled with a *systematic* understanding of the political and economic realities in our communities. To do less than this is to shortchange the students' experience, and to the degree that students also work in the community, it shortchanges the community's experience as well.

Direct service, as opposed to social justice programs and immersion experiences, seems to attract a great deal of student and faculty interest. The immersion experience, sometimes known as the "urban plunge," is often employed in service-learning courses that work with homeless persons. Students might spend a night in a shelter or walk the streets for twenty-four hours to get a sense of what life is like without a home. For the students I have worked with the urban-plunge approach played a distinctly ambivalent role in their learning. When asked about how they thought other students approached service-learning, in particular helping the homeless, about half of the SHA student members mentioned the problems of student fear and the need to overcome social distance. Other student SHA members mentioned that students were apathetic or interested only in charity. For example, one student SHA member remarked:

> My friends . . . it's like, "Oh, that's kind of cool." I don't think people differentiate between activism and liberalism in this area. When you say "I'm working with the Student Homeless Alliance" it's kind of already assumed that students come first and homeless come second, that students help the homeless out in kind of a charity fashion. It's almost the same reaction when you say, "I'm gonna go work in a retarded children's hospital." It's that same kind of liberal ideology. I think they kind of feel guilty themselves because they're like, "Oh, God, I've been meaning to do something like that for so long. I just don't have the time."

One student mentioned that SHA students tried to impose their own agenda on other students. This ambivalence toward other students reflects an understanding of the limitations of student involvement.

The SHA homeless members all responded positively to student involvement. One homeless man mentioned the high degree of student motivation and the emotional support the students offered. Another SHA homeless person pointed out that consistency was the key in building trust. One homeless member mentioned that students are in a particular position to initiate change:

> I think if it wasn't for them, the ones that are so deeply committed to this, homelessness would just keep growing and growing and growing. Of course, it's growing anyhow at the present time because of the economy but they're out there really bringing things to attention and there's no other organization that can because they get city and county funding. They're [other organizations are] bought off.

Another homeless member commented that students often approached the homeless as if they were "from a different planet." The issue of sincerity emerged time and again. Students were kept at a distance by some members of the homeless community until they proved themselves. The contradictory motivations for student involvement elicited mixed reactions from the homeless even though they all viewed students' involvement in a positive fashion. There was a gulf, however, between students and the homeless:

> My opinions of the students are some of them are really great and some get really stressed because of the pressure. And I believe its peer pressure because they're laughed at or picked on for working with the homeless by other students. And part of it is pressure that they feel because they are doing a lot of work and that the homeless are doing nothing. But really being homeless is bad enough to me . . . you are trying to survive everyday and its a lot of work. You don't know where your next meal is gonna come from. You don't know if you can get a shower that night because the showers might be full. You don't know if you're gonna have a place to sleep. The students don't have to worry about that. Most of the students have places to live. I haven't met too many students that are homeless.

University based service-learning programs have been helpful in bridging this gap between students and homeless populations. However, they can also be ineffective without critical reflections that systematically examine the race, gender, and class inequalities inherent in the United States. The expectation of urban-plunge programs is that exposure to "real" conditions of deprivation will expand the student's awareness of inequality. This "pretending to be homeless" was given a mixed reception by both student and homeless members of the SHA. When asked about the urban-plunge program, over half of the SHA students said that it was a good way to learn. One student said that it was better than talking to the homeless. Approximately one-third of the SHA students mentioned that it was not a good way to learn.

> Q: So, would you say it's probably a positive thing for them to do this kind of thing and pretend to be homeless?

> A: Yeah, if they've never had any other kind of experiences before. But for the homeless it's their life and for the students it's just a camping trip. There's really no way to break through that barrier of what it's like to be homeless. You can't do it.

This bitterness toward other students and frustration at their own inabilities also reflects the fact that SHA student participants were highly motivated to begin with, highly knowledgeable about politics, and had some form of activist background. In a situation like this, it was important to teach students tolerance for other students and homeless who are not in the same position or do not know the same things that they do. One student said that the connection between activism and homeless involvement is essential and was skeptical about "urban plunge" type programs:

> I don't think it is a good way to learn. I think a good way to learn is to actually get in the movement. When you pretend you're like an actor, you don't really feel it. You need to be out in the field as an activist. You will not feel what a homeless person really feels until you're homeless. There's no way you could feel it. Maybe you could have some kind of feeling but it's very difficult to feel it. You really have to be out there five days or a month without a shower.

Just exposing oneself to a new experience is no guarantee of understanding the meaning of that experience. "Learning by doing" is not a substitute for the demanding theoretical and critical analysis required to understand the social and political context of one's experience. However, the positive nature of exposing students to the conditions of poverty as a first step in realizing systemic inequality in America was clearly emphasized by another student:

> Undertaking the actions or activities of what they perceive that these people do . . . I think there is a breakthrough. I think there's a realization of what that role implies. When I went out and was homeless and did that and dressed up like a homeless person I was treated like a homeless person. For all practical purposes I was homeless. The motivation that brought me to the streets is a different question. Why did I go? The fact was that I was there. I was homeless. I lived in the street, I slept in the street, I was treated like a homeless person. I think the actual objective experience of being homeless has value. I think if we went and played the objective roles of prisoners and prison guards we would learn a lot from that. I don't think it's bad. I think it can be helpful but I don't think that's it, though. I think there's much more to it than that. I don't think we can go out and live in the street and say "wow, I live in the streets, isn't that neat?" It can be part of a learning experience because then you can empathize for a short time to some degree with the homeless.

A little less than half of the homeless SHA members said that an "urban plunge" type program would be a good way for students to learn about homelessness. However, a little more than one-third said that it was not a good idea, and two SHA homeless men said the students should simply talk with the homeless. The ambiguity reflected in the student sample repeated itself among the SHA homeless members. According to Tony, a homeless SHA member:

> A: I think it would probably be a good experience—a learning experience to get out there and meet with the people but I don't think that they could actually experience what it is like to be homeless.
>
> Q: Maybe you can explain what you mean by that.
>
> A: Being homeless, I guess, you're at the bottom or pretty damn close to it. When your down there your emotions are all down and if a student goes out there and participates with the homeless . . . back in the student's mind he knows, or she knows, that when this is over with he or she is going to go home. A homeless person is fully aware that he has no home.

Other homeless SHA members perceived the idea of pretending to be homeless as a "cute idea," or as a waste of time. Most of the homeless can tell quickly if one is homeless or not. One needs a reason for being on the streets, not simply a research project, in order to be accepted within homeless communities. However, homeless SHA members were understanding of the ambivalent nature of student involvement even if they were at times quite critical. A student, or for that matter anyone wishing to establish a relationship with someone living on the street, must have both sincerity and commitment. Never make promises you can't keep, and always be there when you say you're going to be there. According to one SHA homeless member:

> It depends on the student . . . how much they learn and what they do with it. ____ and _____, one of the big reasons I got hooked up with them is that they didn't pretend. I didn't see any pretensions with them. I saw them come down . . . they ate what we ate and they've come back time after time after time. It's not a joke with them. _____'s in that kitchen every Sunday, by herself sometimes, putting in some very long hours preparing a meal for

homeless people. Nobody's lifted a finger to help her. That's commitment right there. Yeah, I've been impressed with some students. Other students . . . ____ ____, do you remember ___? She was here for four or five meetings . . . she just disappeared.

The ambivalent responses outlined above indicate a conflict between accepting student assistance on the part of the homeless and students understanding the conditions of homelessness. The innate seriousness of homelessness places both students and homeless persons in a situation where their identities are challenged. Resolving the problems that emerge from this disruption requires extensive listening and an open dialogue. The problem with urban-plunge service programs or similar experimental experiences of poverty are related more to their limitations than to their intent. The problem is that they do not go far enough in integrating students in the struggles of the very poor. Class, race, and gender divisions are quite deep. Ameliorative strategies will not bridge this gap, originating as they do with a paternalistic approach to the very poor. However, linking the similarities of student and homeless identities, such as the relative marginal status of each, is fruitful ground for exploration. In recommending approaches to critical learning between the classroom and the streets, I urge all instructors to take the time to examine their city's housing and homeless policies, perhaps having students and some of the homeless analyze the city Comprehensive Housing Affordability Study CHAS reports and redevelopment plans. In addition, research should be undertaken to discover the labor market structure of a given region, the affordability of homes, and the cultural conflicts in a given city. This is only the barest of beginnings. For students to understand what homelessness means in relationship to poverty and social inequality, and to progress beyond the "charitable help" stage, requires that teachers, professors, and instructors make themselves familiar with the intricacies of city housing policy, city planning, and local labor markets.

Individual versus Collective Empowerment

Empowerment has become a greatly overused word representing anything that smacks of personal success or advancement. Individual empowerment is best represented by programs designed to teach personal motivational skills designed to make people employable, or to alter their behavior to make them acceptable to employers. Personal successes in the form of holding a full-time job and altering one's mannerisms to conform to middle-class norms are all involved in the notion of individual empowerment. Shelter workers spend a great deal of time working with the homeless in the hope that they will find an apartment and a job. Obviously, this type of success is to be applauded—but it is not sufficient. To understand empowerment as a method by which people gain control over their lives (Rappaport 1984, 3) is important but does not move awareness from the individual to the community. The vagueness of many definitions of empowerment make it difficult to develop the concept's analytical possibilities. Without an analysis of social inequality and differential social power, any awareness prompted by empowerment programs remained contained within a normative model of American society. Standard definitions of empowerment remain oriented toward technical and personal improvements, often reducing the term to a mere "process" of "adult learning and development" (Kieffer 1984, 9). For Kieffer (1984) empowerment means simply moving from a position as victim to one of "assertive and efficacious citizen" (32). This individualized success model of empowerment fails in not understanding the connection between individual failures and successes and social structural race, class, and gender positions.

As a model of individual empowerment, personal success stories may be useful, but if we wish to talk about eliminating homelessness we must develop an ethical system founded on social justice, not simply personal attainment. The conflation of these two aspects is precisely the work of ideology and the dominant social imagineries of possessive individualism. Irma Serrano-Garcia (1984) outlines these limitations quite explicitly in her description of a community development experience in Puerto Rico. In her analysis, empowerment appeared as just another ideological illusion masking the impact of cultural colonization by the United States. Community members involved gained personal control over their lives but did not gain any social understanding of the ethical concept of social justice.

The problem is not individual empowerment per se, but rather the displacement of any sense of collective empowerment in favor of socializing individuals into some mainstream "norm," thereby cutting off the possibility of dreaming the impossible, of developing alternative social imaginaries. An individual empowerment that accepts the status quo of ongoing social inequalities and celebrates the acquisition of individual property within a society of radical race, class, and gender oppression, reproduces that very inequality and oppression. To move beyond individual to collective empowerment means to challenge, not just individual behavior, but the social behavior of elites, to challenge the dominant relationships of land use and power. Collective empowerment, as I am using the term here, refers to the advancement of a group or class of individuals through collective action, in which collective identities are established, if only for a short time based upon a project that challenges established relationships of power, property, and space. The ability to engage in this form of empowerment was witnessed briefly in both Chicago and San Jose. For collective empowerment to be sustained, social-physical spaces must be carved out of everyday life and institutions created that reproduce collective notions of success rather than purely individual concepts of advancement.

Jennings's (1990) call for black empowerment understands that the solution is not to be found in a mere "access to the powerful," but rather in developing actual power within the black community. Any empowerment must focus on the interrelationships among race, class, and gender. In the homeless groups I investigated, many discussions were prompted over race, gender, and class issues, usually related to a specific incident of the day. Through these dialogues a sense of collective identity slowly emerged. According to Jennings, the purpose of black empowerment, and I would add collective empowerment, is to "strengthen the black community institutionally" (119). Public policies that guarantee only individual advancement or mobility within the status quo American system are not sufficient to meet the demands of the black community. In the last instance the object is not simply to redistribute resources from the privileged to the less privileged—it is to focus "on the control of land in black urban communities" (119). To accomplish this means to tackle the very issues of redevelopment and labor markets, issues far removed from individual empowerment.

The hidden normative concepts of individual empowerment may be critiqued using Foss and Larkin's (1986) concept of "disalienation" (89). Borrowing from Victor Turner's concept of antistructure and liminality, Foss and Larkin understand that disalienation means the rejection of alienated learning that reinforces the social order. Rituals that reinforce authoritative hierarchies are attacked and broken down; the result is "members of the more privileged sectors of the dissident subcultures begin defining these positions in terms provided by members of less privileged social categories thus radicalizing their consciousness" (89). This in fact was observed among many of the students involved with the street encampments in San Jose. Their understandings of everyday life and social-physical space underwent profound changes the longer they remained working with the population. The fostering of hope in change combined with a critical and strategic consciousness that rejects established hierarchies in favor of "disalienated" forms of existence is required before one can conceptualize a world of social justice. To reject a "disempowering" perspective is to teach a vision of possibility that moves beyond the Hobbesian view, "that whatever is not managed, watched, disciplined, or guarded by force of arms is dangerous; that society consists of selfish, isolated individuals who cannot be trusted" (97–98).

The cognitive praxis in which we develop a collective identity is critical in establishing an interpretative framework for strategic action. As Eyerman and Jamison (1991) explain, knowledge is "the broader cognitive praxis that informs all social activity" (49). Spatial and status hierarchies that separate students from homeless populations are challenged by the practical knowledge gained from student-homeless mobilizations. To the degree that these mobilizations move progressively from soup kitchen to protest and squatting activities, collective empowerment and collective identities may be nurtured. Student and homeless knowledge of social and physical spaces as well as attendant possibilities for action underwent a change with their mutual involvement in the SHA, as it did for students who worked with the Tranquility City huts. Many homeless members mentioned that what changed their minds about student involvement was the SHA's direct action, which produced results and required student self-sacrifice. These shifts in knowledge contributed to opening new debates among the homeless about what they could achieve, prompting several to develop new personal goals, another to organize his own "movement," and others to avoid the group altogether.

The problems of generalizing from the limited examples of Chicago and San Jose are apparent. However, I do think that these two case studies provide some opportunity for hope. Cases in which many homeless people have resisted their marginalization to survive and to develop a momentary glimpse of collective identity seem relatively rare from the studies conducted with homeless populations. But could it also be the way in which such studies have been conducted—that is, the manner in which those studied assume the perspective that the research implicitly communicates? Clearly this was a problem I considered in my own two case studies. However, the length of time I spent with both groups led me to believe that the changes I observed were genuine and could have a long-lasting positive impact.

To think and act beyond the dominant social imaginary of a given society is very difficult, often requiring the employment of resistant or counter imaginaries that are supported within oppositional social-physical spaces. For either someone who is homeless or a shelter provider to think and act beyond their socially proscribed roles is very difficult. The routine practices of daily life lock them into their views of each other, living worlds apart. We know that these constructed identities occur in and through social-physical space, so we can see that by altering, by freeing up, social-physical space—by creating what Sara Evans and Harry Boyte termed "free spaces"—shifting identities can be given fertile ground upon which to grow. The multifaceted nature of social-physical space, all of its race, class, and gender aspects, must be considered. It is not enough to simply have the physical shell of a building, a simple meeting area. After all this is social and physical space we are discussing. The social must also be given the necessary space for change, a true democratic space in which new liberatory social imaginaries may be dreamed.

Finding such a space is difficult at best in a society dominated by mass media communications and social relationships, in which the spectacle has been overruled by the simulation, if we are to believe Jean Baudrillard (1983). And yet, as Lefebvre (1991, 1976) points out, we are not left as only prisoners of someone else's dilemma. Utopic space is also present along with the domination of abstract space. It is the attempt to recover our vision, our ideal of what we would like our city spaces to look like, to be like, that we must focus on next. To learn how to dream again is to combat the technical forces that work to limit imagination, to channel, construct, and rule the possibility of envisioning other ways of organizing society, of organizing social-political space. To some degree, for perhaps a brief moment, both Tranquility City and the SHA found a utopic space in which all could come together as "family," producing a concern and imagining what could be in ways impossible through the dominant social imaginary, the dominant forms of social-physical space. For a brief moment those who were relegated to the outside could afford to dream.

Finally, in the rapidly expanding hypermodern urban spaces of today's city-suburbs, exclusive redevelopment has dominated, conforming to the primary social imaginaries of race, class, and gender, containing or dispersing the very poor, isolating "them" from wealthier sectors of the city. The integration of culture and economic city patterns can be particularly vicious, as Mike Davis (1990, 1992) has pointed out in such places as Los Angeles. Containment and dispersion seem to be the order to the day in coping with the very poor, minorities, and the homeless. However, the promise still remains, the vision of cities that are not exclusive, of developers and planning departments that do not practice exclusionary visions, that seek an inclusive vision of the city in which all are free to partake, and not limited by how much money you have in your pocket. A vision in which all classes and races are invited downtown, not just to buy, but to live together in a truly civil society. New spaces of representation must be developed and new representational spaces dreamed if the problems besetting us are going to be resolved. New economic priorities must be merged with cultural visions of diversity based on a sharing of power, both political and economic, a true democratizing of the economy and the political system.

What might some of these alternative social imaginaries and oppositional social-political spaces look like? We have already studied examples of two of them. There are many more dotted around the American landscape. Homeless squatting can provide rapid and effective housing as well as the needed space to create a resistant heterotopia. But squatter camps are no substitute for committed federal and state policies to ending poverty, hunger, and homelessness. While unfashionable in these conservative times, the promise still remains if we are willing to stand against the forces of predatory capital and possessive individualism, against that which reduces the human spirit to rationalized forms of technical efficiency. As we have seen, the contested landscape for struggles between the very poor and the wealthy are in the terrain of city politics affected directly by local, state, and national politics.

The brief formation of collective identities, facilitated by active struggle over homeless placemaking, opened up windows of opportunity for urban political work designed to reframe the debate of homelessness from one of individual pathology to one of land use. For example, the divisions created between the County Water District in San Jose and the city of San Jose produced an opening that precipitated the successful conclusion to SHA squatting of an abandoned house on River Street. The occupation of Metra railway land by Tranquility City residents temporarily blunted moves by the city of Chicago to remove them, since they had received permission from the railway to camp on the property. Working in between borders, in areas deemed refuse space or functional space for others, may often prove fruitful at generating the necessary time and space for developing new collective identities, a new forms of collective empowerment.

Electronic media, particularly computer networks, can contribute to homeless organizing and collective expression. For example, the establishment of Santa Monica's Public Electronic Network (PEN) by

Santa Monica's city council precipitated the development of the PEN Action Group, a group composed of both housed and homeless persons. PEN Action Group members, after knowing of the need for showers and lockers in order for homeless persons to seek employment, presented the city council with a proposal named SHWASHLOCK (SHowers, WASHing machines, LOCKers).

In July 1990 the Santa Monica city council granted $150,000 for the proposal, installing lockers and showers under the Santa Monica pier and opening public showers elsewhere (Rheingold 1993, 269; Rogers and Rogers 1995). Homeless members of the PEN Action Group lobbied for a job bank, resulting in the donation of a PEN terminal to a homeless drop-in center, staffed by graduate students who worked to produce job listings for the homeless. In addition, homeless persons have also responded to various city council development decisions, producing counterproposals of their own through the computer internet. When they do not communicate the stigma of homelessness, such proposals are often taken far more seriously.

Increasingly more very poor and homeless persons are accessing the internet, usually through public library or shelter computers. Although their numbers are hard to judge, it is safe to say that the numbers are quite low at the present, but growing. A computer electronic mail list set up by Dee Southard at the University of Oregon, and operated through Communications for a Sustainable Future at the University of Colorado (csf.colorado.edu), works to include homeless persons, shelter providers, and activists on a general homeless list. Oregon Public Networking and Eugene Free Networking are currently linking up nonprofit organizations free of charge and are assisting in-service providers in gaining internet access to social services.

While admittedly not a solution to the problem of poverty and homelessness, access to the internet can reduce isolation and assist the homeless in organizing and lobbying for more resources. In addition, increasing numbers of homeless newspapers are cropping up both nationally and internationally, sold by homeless members, and some are now linking with other papers in an international network, exchanging news stories and information developing an alternative source of news that places the voices of the homeless squarely into the public realm. These are only a few examples of how the internet can work to facilitate collective empowerment; the potential for much broader development remains.

Lastly, working with the media, in fact creating one's own media through securing cameras and video equipment, can prove an effective tool at mobilizing collective identities. As we discussed, the SHA made extensive use of videocamera work. Often demonstrations were filmed and the cuts then shown to shelter audiences with discussions afterward. This proved to be a powerful way to both show the legitimacy of the group and demonstrate real action. In addition, the side benefit of having cameras present around the encampments was the curbing of police abuse against the homeless. The third hidden benefit was the record that visual documents provided of the group's progress, a record the group could reexamine at a later time.

To call for the individual empowerment of the very poor and homeless in a new citizenship is merely to reintegrate their stigmatized status into a system that reproduces poverty and homelessness, locking out input from the margins. Collective empowerment must be the focus of the continuing struggle to end homelessness and achieve social justice. The celebration of democratic self-realization and self-management without the necessary public and cultural spaces that allow that to occur merely reinforces systemic inequities required by the reproduction of capital. In this context only the rhizomatic disruptions foreseen by Delueze and Guattari (1987) have a possibility, when allied with "internal" movements for change, of carving out "small spaces" for resistance. These "small spaces" and attendant local struggles through collective action are opposed at every step, and only with great effort can national and international linkups occur. Linking local struggles together on a global basis creates the possibility for real change.

San Jose's
Housing Shortage

In 1983, the Association of Bay Area Governments (ABAG), a regional planning association located in Oakland, California, estimated that San Jose would need to build a total of 49,556 units (ABAG, 1983, 14) between 1983 and 1990, including 9,911 very-low-income units (20 percent of the total), to provide enough affordable housing for those in all income brackets. If we add those units of very-low-income housing that could be built between 1980 and 1983 (4,248) to the 9,911 units proposed, the final total required for very-low-income units during the ten-year period 1980 to 1990 would be 14,158.

According to the city of San Jose, between 1980 and 1990, 40,298 units of all income levels were built, leaving a total deficit, according to ABAG standards, of 9,276 units. We must take into account that ABAG estimates are for a seven-year period and San Jose's record is for a ten-year period. Extending ABAG's estimated amount by three extra years will expand the need for housing during that ten-year span even further. If we use the city's housing fund spending ratio of 10 percent for very-low-income housing (City of San Jose 1991b, 86) during this ten-year period, only 4,030 very-low-income units would have been produced. This is less than half the necessary units required to satisfy the requirement for decent very-low-income housing. Using ABAG standards, San Jose produced a deficit of 10,128 very-low-income units between 1980 and 1990. This shortfall was attributed to "problems with the economy" (City of San Jose 1991b, 84). Critical of both city and county efforts, the Homeless Overview Study Task Force (1989, 44) stated that Santa Clara County and its incorporated cities together built only 1,800 low-income units between 1983 and 1988.

San Jose's Housing Task Force (City of San Jose 1988, 14) estimated that for the years 1989 through 1996, between 19,650 and 22,250 units, or 1,000 to 1,135 units for very-low-income residents, would need to be built to satisfy demand. If we include both new and rehabilitated very-low-income units, the numbers increase to between 1,154 and 3,078 units at an estimated cost of $46,163,000. These future estimates for low-income housing are grossly inadequate if we consider past deficits and use ABAG's standards. During approximately the same time period, 1988 to 1995, ABAG (1989, 31) estimated a perceived need of 37,633 units, of which 5,645, or 15 percent of the total, would be dedicated for low-income residents and 7,527 units, or 20 percent of the total, would be for very-low-income residents. In 1983 housing need was estimated based on potential demand. In 1989 housing needs were calculated on the basis of "alternative zoning," the number of units that could be built given a rezoning of particular areas.

According to the State of California (1992), between 1988 and 1992 the city of San Jose added 9,678 housing units of all income levels to its inventory. At the current formula of 60 percent spending (changed from 10 percent before 1989) for very-low-income units, 5,807 very-low-income units could be produced out of a total of 9,678 units between 1988 and 1992. The change in funding from 10 to 60 percent arose from recommendations made by the Mayor's Task Force on Housing in 1988 (City of San Jose 1988, 40). If production rates are maintained, by 1995 we could expect an additional 7,259 of very-low-income units for a total of 13,065 very-low-income units surpassing ABAG estimates of need for the period 1988 to 1995. However, In responding to ABAG's goals for the need of very-low-income and low-income units between 1988 and 1995 the city of San Jose explained that it issued or will issue only 7,498 building permits by 1995 for dwelling units of all income levels (1991a, Pg.86):

> The Department of City Planning estimates that between 33 percent and 50 percent of these units would be affordable to lower income households. However, an average production rate of 2,500 units/year indicates that only about 50 percent of ABAG's total 1995 dwelling unit goals for San Jose will be achieved.

At a 60 percent spending rate for very-low-income units that would be an increase of only 4,499 units by 1995. Including very-low-income units built between 1988 and 1992 (5,807) the total production of very-low-income units by the city would equal 10,305 units for the period 1988 through 1995.

Total need using ABAG's figures for very-low-income housing from 1980 through 1995 according to the above calculations would equal 21,685 units. Given the city's probable record of 4,030 between 1980 and 1990, plus 10,306 between 1988 and 1995, the total housing production for the city would equal 14,336 very-low-income units between 1980 and 1995. This leaves a total deficit of 7,349 very-low-income units for the citizens of San Jose.

Introduction: Out of Place

1. See Hombs 1992 for a review of the early developments in the homeless advocacy movement. Hombs analyzes the evolution of homeless advocacy by the type of advocacy, form, and effectiveness.

2. See Hoch and Slayton 1989, chapter 10, "The Politics of Entitlement," for an analysis. Recently Hopper and Baumohl (1994) and Hombs (1992) have examined the problems created by defining homelessness as simply an issue of inadequate housing, which reinforces the distinctions between undeserving and deserving poor, negating the issue of property and poverty.

3. Blasi (1994), using bibliometric analysis, examined the University of California MELVYL listings of 5,669,328 entries in 6,500 academic journals published between July 1989 and August 11, 1993. In a more recent search Blasi examined 539 entries, including 354 articles on homelessness.

4. As Collins (1989) observes, Glasglow (1981) excludes black women from his analysis of gender.

5. How this occurred can be partially explained by the position of the researchers themselves. Culture-of-poverty arguments and cultural-deficit arguments "emerged from white male intellectual communities and the approach taken reflects white male concerns" (Collins 1989, 86; see also Billingsley 1973). Collins (1989, 86) traces this problem to the absence of black women in the academy. The preoccupation of researchers with black male behavior can be traced to traditional white fears of racial disruptions. Increasingly black males and black females, not the inequalities that produce poverty, are perceived as a problem. Similarly, homeless behaviors are now viewed as an increasing problem, rather than the economic and political conditions that create homelessness. Concerns about social justice are displaced by fears of unruly behavior.

6. Snow, Anderson, and Koegel (1994) advocate a "language of biographic vulnerability" that works to socially contextualize statements by the homeless. Although this "extends our perception beyond the medical model so that we are sensitive to the broader array of biographic factors or experiences that can disadvantage some people more than others in competing for available affordable housing and other limited resources" (469), it still focuses attention upon the experience of individuals and not of homeless groups or collectives. It still remains within the rehabilitative model. While this is important, the links with structural change remain underdeveloped.

7. In those cases where homeless groups actively organized with political organizations, the response was swift and repressive. A good example of this was the dispersion of New York's Tompkins Square Park homeless and political activists in what has now come to be known as a "police riot." See Abu-lughod 1994.

8. The concept of mainstream integration underlying reform efforts ignored the ways "the homeless" formed their own communities, with their different ways of understanding family, power, and community.

9. For those field researchers working with homeless populations the question must always be asked, who is doing the speaking, for whom, or with whom? To ignore the researcher's own power, privilege, and status is untenable, just as it is untenable to speak "for" those who have less power.

10. European social theorists such as Giles Deleuze and Michel Foucault have adamantly refused, on indignant grounds, to engage in "speaking for others." However, as Spivak (1988) points out, they are still engaged in speaking through their silences, and that speaking is from a privileged position.

11. These disputes can be found most often at the border between science and religion. Many of the debates over a woman's right to choose and the viability of a fetus as "subject" reflect these types of border disputes.

12. One must call into question the ethics of Rossi's survey methodology. Rossi conducted his street survey in the early morning hours with plainclothes police officers accompanying survey takers, waking up homeless persons and offering them money for an extended interview. This type of overt intrusion, unwanted and unasked for, is a serious violation of homeless persons' social space, a kind of intrusion that happens far too often. As Snow and Anderson (1993) state, in commenting on how street survey work is accomplished, "Are not the hours between 10:00 p.m. and 8:00 a.m. generally regarded as a

period in which citizens are not to be disturbed unless the contact has been prearranged or there is an emergency? If so, then why are the homeless not extended the same courtesy domiciled residents take for granted?" (328). Rossi did not take into account that many homeless people are afraid of the police. It is speculated that fewer than 10 percent of those on the street admitted to being homeless (Ringham 1990, 112). In addition, homeless children, a substantial segment of the homeless population, were not included in Rossi's count. According to Sosin, Colson, and Grossman's (1988) 1986 study, homeless children make up close to 30 percent of the homeless population of Chicago, although most can be found in shelters.

13. Rossi, Sosin, and indeed Hoch remain connected to the world of policy development, of those interests removed from the immediate concern of the homeless as active agents. Even in the debates I have just outlined, these researchers still remain concerned with "speaking about and for," not "with or to," the homeless. This in part reflects the institutional position of academic researchers vis-à-vis the community and calls into question the relationship between academic research and community needs.

Chapter 1. Social-Physical Space, Social Imaginaries, and Homeless Identities

1. Middle-class comportment and respectability is associated historically with being affluent, white, and male (Young 1990, 136).

2. Hesse quotes Laclau's concept of the social imaginary, taken from *New Reflections of the Revolution of Our Time*: "The imaginary is a horizon: it is not one among other objects but an absolute limit which structures a field of intelligibility and is thus the condition of possibility for the emergence of any object" (Hesse 1993, 169). While effective at dissolving the supposed stability of dichotomous concepts embodied in social configurations of class, race, and gender, Laclau's notion of the imaginary remains hampered by postulating a division between history and space.

3. Social imaginary significations cannot be grasped directly, because they occupy the very basis for both the possibility of and the unification of the "real." Realist epistemologies cannot capture this concept, either, relying as they do on strictly observable and empirical categories, which themselves are products of the social imaginary. For example, functionalist theories—which pride themselves on discovering links among structural similarities of social phenomena, of functional

attributes applied to social practices—ignore how the very concept of functionality itself is a product of the social imaginary. The private fantasies that individuals produce, what Castoriadis terms "radical imaginaries," use significations that have been fashioned through the social imaginary of a particular historical time and place.

4. The counterpart to the social imaginary signification at the personal level is what Castoriadis terms "radical imagination." That fundamental phantasy is the first grasp of relationships among other significations, a new schema made manifest, that which acts to distinguish "inside" from "outside," one categorical schema from another, that which points to a future possibility of significant organization. Perhaps the term *vision* would be useful for talking about the radical imaginary, although the term remains very imprecise.

5. Acknowledging Michele Barrett's (1980) understanding that social-economic relations include gender, race, and various types of production, from mental to manual, Silverman uses a concept analogous to the social imaginary, called the "dominant fiction." For Silverman (1992), how one is oriented toward society, to the given mode of production, is "lived via the ideologies of gender, class, race, ethnicity, etc., ideologies which are always imbricated in crucial ways with the core elements of the dominant fiction" (34). Dominant fictions, then, comprise the stock from which popular culture narratives and images are drawn, often playing from socially constructed oppositional binaries—male/female, heterosexual/homosexual, clean/dirty, etc.

6. For political economists and some sociologists, space often remains "neutral" to larger economic or historical forces. However, social-physical space is not simply composed of fractions of political economy containing consumption, production, and exchange, but rather, space "itself must be considered as one element of the productive forces of society, especially through the operation of form and design" (Gottdiener 1985, 123). For Lefebvre, control over the spatial forms of a society is also control over the means of producing and reproducing that society. At question is not simply who owns and controls the means of production, but also who controls the material spatial forms that result from those means of production. Control over space means control over the ability for a given society to reproduce itself, its workers, managers, owners, and other class fractions of society, what Lefebvre would term "second nature," that produced design space of the town and the city.

7. In fact Lefebvre would maintain that the dominant tendency in modern capitalist society to fragment and parcel out space in accord

with the division of labor works as an ideology dependent upon conceptions of space as a passive container. Treating space "in itself" is a convenient way to avoid having to examine the specific contradictions that emerge from the production of space. According to Lefebvre (1991), "we come to think of spatiality, and so to fetishize space in a way reminiscent of the old fetishism" (90). In this fashion the old dualisms mentioned earlier are able to maintain their power.

8. Lefebvre is critical of Foucault's early work, especially *The Archeology of Knowledge* (1972), taking him to task for not clarifying what he means by "space," and for not explaining how he is able to bridge the gap between theory and practice, "between the space of the philosophers and the space of people who deal with material things" (Lefebvre 1991, 4). However, Foucault's later work, especially his notes on geography and his essays on power/knowledge attempt to grapple with Lefebvre's critique.

9. Giddens's theory of *time-space distanciation* and *structuration* is an attempt to anchor the micro relations found in isolated locales with their larger structural antecedents across time and space (Giddens 1981, 90), which means looking at the relationship between social life and social "system integration." Structuration means understanding "structure" through the rules and resources that are involved in reproducing a society. Institutions, for example, work through stabilized social relationships across time and space, grounded in set rules and procedures, codified in texts.

10. Using the time-geography concepts of Hagerstrand, Giddens also examines the positioning of the parameters of social action, extending Goffman's idea of "regionalization of encounters" by claiming that "locales," and the impact of regionalization on locales, are both the settings for social action and places where social actors understand and reproduce the meaning of their actions. Rowe and Wolch (1990), for example, look at the social networks established by homeless women in Los Angeles using Hagerstrand's model of time sequencing to plot the relationship between things that are done during the day and locales in which they are performed, connecting social space, time, and social networks. Rejecting Goffman's sole focus on micro-level interactions, Giddens attempts to integrate everyday behavior with that of broader social-historical developments.

11. Giddens (1984, 7) also specifies discursive consciousness and unconscious motives/cognition as vital for the operation of subjectivity. However, practical consciousness, which just remains out of conscious reach, is what Giddens most closely attaches to social structure. This

would, I believe, be compatible with Castoriadis's notion of the social imaginary working through individual subjects to reproduce the world in ways that are race, gender, and class charged.

12. However, the problem with relying upon a structuration theory that depends on routinization as a solution for a deep ontological insecurity (Giddens 1981, 36; 1984, 60–64), is the avoidance of breaks, ruptures, explosions of routines—the potential for change that is created by breaking customs, habits, and established rituals. Giddens's (1981) theory of structuration, concerned with "how social systems 'bind' time and space" (90), ignores or reduces the importance of social space as liberatory, or disruptive, focusing instead on the reproduction of structures of domination.

13. However, one should ask whether space and place were not also ruptured in *ancien regimes*, albeit not on the same scale. How would one explain the development of Greek city-states without the influence of wide-ranging traders and explorers gathering regional knowledge to be used locally? Rather than assume that modern life is characterized by a rupturing of space and place, it may be more accurate to say that the innovation of technical means to extend temporal and spatial features of action have intensified the ancient splitting of place, or locale, from space.

14. While Giddens makes a useful attempt to link global, regional, and local issues of space and time with micro events, his approach implicitly assumes that specific events, structures, and actions are associated with a unified concept of social structure and social space, rather than understanding them as products of struggle and conflict emerging out of a dynamic concept of space and place.

15. Spaces are areas labeled as "sites," which Foucault (1986, 23) defines as a relationship of proximity between different points. The vast multiplicity of sites may be divided into *utopian* sites, as "fundamentally unreal spaces," and *heterotopias*, or "counter-sites" that include real sites informed by utopian ideals, or what we might think of as counterimaginaries to the dominant social imaginary, a place to establish resistance to everyday life. However, Foucault's definition of utopian sites as "unreal," and heterotopias as "counter-sites," effectively demolishes the imaginary possibilities implicit in the term *utopia* in favor of a purely descriptive term, *heterotopia*, which simply describes the mainstream plurality of differences in spatial power.

16. This segregation of service-dependent shelter within a confined area of the inner city, the ghettoization of services, and or their displacement to the outer edges of cities, was ignored in debates

over land-use polices that could have arrested such practices of spatial isolation.

17. The imposition of technical planning schemas in a social system built upon an extensive social inequalities produces highly polarized topographies. These topographies, as areas or sites of radical wealth and income disparities shifting over time, contain select regions of environmental degradation and the wholesale containment or dispersal of the very poor. Local and regional conflicts often erupt along the borders of such topographies resulting in massive refugee flows. Movements of capital are accelerated by expanded communication and computer networks moving between different polarized topographies even as labor unions are weakened by restrictive national and local regulations. The flows of power and wealth produced by these typographies are large in scale allowing for extended developments, but, also precipitating larger numbers of community protests and micro-resistances.

18. For Lefebvre, the homogeneity of abstract space is not a given, a final fact, but rather the "goal," a goal often put to the test, I would claim, by such forces as community groups, organized homeless bodies, and homeowners. Abstract spaces appear to be homogeneous, but that doesn't mean that they are homogeneous. The carefully constructed hermetic look of modern hotel complexes may conceal ongoing labor struggles or community protests over displacement from that hotel's development. In discussing the apparent homogeneity of abstract space, Lefebvre understands that the appearance is illusionary, "that the space that homogenizes thus has nothing homogenous about it . . . it subsumes and unites scattered fragments or elements by force" (Lefebvre 1991, 308). It is the force that most often remains invisible.

19. For Lefebvre, the environmental and consumer movements were the most obvious actors in questioning the use of urban space, in attempting to reassert space as use value over space as a commodity (Lefebvre 1979, 291).

20. To cling to a strict correspondence theory of truth and a realist epistemology is merely to attempt to "fix" these fragmented and partial knowledges as "total" knowledges, to avoid the ultimate radical unknowability of that which forms the basis of knowledge.

21. Without assuming well-defined symbols, icons, causes or determinations, Castoriadis (1987) employs the term *magma* to talk about "not chaos but the mode of organization belonging to a non-ensemblist diversity, exemplified by society, the imaginary or the unconscious" (182). The specific social-historical nature of institutions therefore is informed by a people employing a particular "ensemblist-identitary" logic that

fixes and organizes the vast magma of significations available at any one time in the world. A more complete definition of magma is the following: "A magma is that from which one can extract (or in which one can construct) an indefinite number of ensemblist organizations but which can never be reconstituted (ideally) by a (finite or infinite) ensemblist composition of these organizations" (Castoriadis 1987, 343).

22. Semiotic codes are not simply the infinite regression of textual play. Gottdiener (1995), following Charles Peirce, calls them the "socio-semiotic," and they do have an objective referent, "even if that object is a constructed and reproducible element of fantasy . . . which exists as part of a text or material image" (24).

23. The recognition of multiple discursive formations in the production of identity is woven into the work of Ernesto Laclau (1990). Laclau correctly points to the play of discursive differences, to the "excesses of meaning," that any social system is surrounded with. But he fails to account for the ways phenomena like the social imaginary operate to create these differences, and not just any differences but very specific differences, fixed in material reality. What is left out is how power operates through the social imaginary, creating particular discursive formations, bodies, and social-physical spaces.

24. Separating out forms of cognitive knowing from the somatic, McLaren (1989, 191) coins the phrase *ritual knowledge*, for a type of ideological production that emerges as a result of investing in emotions and bodily knowledge. The significance of ritual knowledge is illustrated by McLaren's analysis of the differences between classroom knowledge and ritual knowledge, using as a context the earlier studies by Paul Willis, in *Learning to Labor*, (1981) of working-class student resistance to education. But Willis lacked the concept of the body that McLaren invokes, and hence he could not understand the different forms of contradictory knowledge that were at work except through a concept of "false" ideology. However, for McLaren (1989), "Bodily or ritual knowledge learned in the streets offers students a connectedness and relational context—a "lived meaning"—while negotiating their day-to-day existence" (193).

25. Nancy Hartsock (1990), using the concepts of Albert Memmi from *The Colonizer and the Colonized*, argues that a devalued "Other" emerges with the creation of the Kantian transcendental rational subject, a subject existing in a mythical realm beyond time and space. Edward Said's theory of Orientalism, in which the East is refracted through the Western lens of the exotic Other, also recognizes how

Western thought has traditionally dominated other discourses and bodies by reframing them as outside "normal" rational Western thought. See also Keller (1985), Lloyd (1984), Bordo (1986), and Di Stefano (1990).

26. See Iris Young (1990) for the analysis of oppression as a structural concept. Chapter 2 is especially helpful in articulating what Young calls the "five faces of oppression": exploitation, marginalization, cultural imperialism, violence, and powerlessness.

27. Krueger's poster designed for the April 1989 March on Washington to support legal abortion, birth control, and women's rights is illustrative of women artists working to deconstruct traditional images of gender. Like other women artists, Krueger understood the role of semiotics and sign production in the reproduction of sexuality and how the social creation of sexuality is radically influenced by the words we use and the images we see. Some other artists working in this context are Sherrie Levine, Louise Lawler, Silvia Kolbowski, Sarah Charlesworth, and Judith Barry.

28. Because our society contains many racial projects working at the institutional and everyday levels of life, racial "subjection" is a product of ideology (Omi and Winant 1994, 60).

29. A white supremacist imaginary is not simply about actions that lead to legal segregation of blacks and others; it is about the cultural segregation that results from privileging one particular set of constructed representations. Haymes (1995) outlines three ways white supremacy is expressed culturally. The first is a production of white stereotypes of blacks in which black culture is made "a marker for racial difference, so that whites are deracialized and blacks are racialized" (29). In the second, dialogue is discouraged and race is considered the problem of blacks, not whites. In the third, "the cultural authority of the white mainstream culture constructs blacks as either exotic or dangerous by sexualizing their racial physical characteristics" (29). Also see Bailey (1988), Gilman (1985), and Kovol (1984).

30. Quoted by Gooding-Williams (1993, 170).

31. Foucault, in *Discipline and Punish* (1979), outlines five ways a normalizing gaze is brought into play: differentiation, hierarchization, homogenization, exclusion, and comparison. I would maintain that the social imaginary operates through these "practices" to generate differences that are then perceived as "normal" by the population.

32. See Kristeva (1982) for an analysis of the fascination with and fear of abject horror in the *Power of Horror*. Young (1990) uses Kristeva to reveal how such abjection, while often unconscious, nevertheless

must be explained "socially and historically"—as a product, she would say, of social construction. I maintain that this social construction is in turn a product of the dominant social imaginary.

33. We must be careful not to "naturalize" such categories as did the early Chicago school of urban ecology, who considered "natural" distinctions of social-physical space to be functionally useful for maintaining social order. In such "naturalizing," the complex and often contentious nature of political negotiations, of power, is concealed beneath a normalizing perspective that privileges particular race, class, and gender positions. "Naturalizing" categorical distinctions is useful precisely because it conceals the unequal power relationships that go into their production. City professionals, planners, and politicians responsible for developing ever finer spatial and social categorical distinctions implicitly, if not explicitly, rely upon *correspondences* between developed categorizations or segmentations of populations and particular social-physical spatial configurations. Therefore an overly rigid, bureaucratic reliance upon this application of correspondence theory, even if it is unconscious, is useful to authorities. It provides a way to ignore the power relationships that can contest the dominant categorizations of people and social-physical space.

34. Harvey (1981) identifies three circuits of capital accumulation: the primary circuit, derived from Marx, involving the actual organization of production; the secondary circuit (the built environment); and the third circuit, which involves investing in reproducing labor power (science and technology—knowledge industries).

35. As Gottdiener (1985, 99) points out, Harvey's understanding of uneven development, as dependent upon devalorization of the built environment, undercuts the potential for uneven development as an explanation by reducing it to a functional result of devalorization. Allen Scott's understanding of uneven development, as discussed by Gottdiener, is a more productive explanation of uneven development; Scott presupposes, similar to Lefebvre, the contradictory nature of land value and the relatively uncoordinated nature of such land development (Gottdiener 1985, 101–2). Scott's (1980) concept of urban land nexus includes land development as one of many intersecting patterns of public and private decision making dependent upon the immediate context of city development. Unfortunately, Scott's theory suffers from the assumptions typical of mainstream location theory, relying upon concentric zone and central city concentration models that cannot explain the deconcentration currently happening within cities and suburban areas.

36. As Keith and Pile (1993) point out, Mike Davis's *City of Quartz* (1990) is a rare exception to this pattern so pervasive in the areas of cultural studies and in portions of sociological discourse on the city.

37. The volume of literature addressing the public/private debate is quite extensive. See Fraser 1988, Hanson and Pratt 1995, p. 94, Wilson 1991, Young 1990, p. 137, and Saegert 1980 for various perspectives examining a small sampling of these debates. In spatial imaginary terms, urban is equated with public and male, and suburbs equated with private and female. This persistent dualism further reproduces gendered spatial practices that isolate women and prevent men from coming to terms with domestic labor.

38. See Doreen Massey, specifically her work the *Spatial Divisions of Labor* (1984). Massey discovered that gender was a key factor in industrial relocation. In areas where industrial jobs declined, low-wage branch plants using high proportions of women laborers moved in, taking advantage of the traditional male breadwinner/female housemaker gender roles, and assumed that women without labor experience would be less receptive to union organizing (Hanson and Pratt 1995, 11).

39. In Worcester, Massachusetts, distances between home and work led to a decrease in geographic mobility for women. This is also reflected in the different gender compositions of jobs from one part of Worcester to another (Hanson and Pratt 1995, 25). Given the gendered spatial segregation of jobs, many women in Worcester who combined paid employment with domestic labor found themselves "trapped" in jobs close to home, decreasing the range of their job opportunities (Hanson and Pratt 1995, 155). According to Hanson and Pratt (1995), "the unevenness of the employment landscape, together with women's shorter work trips, means that a household's residential location on that landscape importantly defines women's access to jobs" (222). Since residential location is highly dependent upon class and gender relations, where women work will often be determined by where they live.

40. Linda McDowell (1991), in the tradition of feminist scholarship, notes that in most contemporary urban studies the focus on political economy at the expense of cultural issues related to gender and race "reflects the separation of the public and the private and its associated sexual division: where the former is the masculine public work of competition, individualism, legal rights, and waged work" (77). This separation is also reflected in the dualistic separation of production from reproduction. McDowell examines the relationship between

economic restructuring and the relationship between waged labor and unwaged labor in labor reproduction and concludes that struggles over child care, the provision of social services, and equal rights in the workplace ultimately affect women's ability to participate on an equal basis with men in the labor market. Such labor changes will also necessitate a change in spatial practices, the development of alternative social imaginaries.

Chapter 2. Redevelopment Visions, Social Imaginaries, Polarized Typographies

1. The literature on redevelopment and gentrification is quite large. Here are a few references for recent work on city development and redevelopment: Abu-lughod 1994; Beauregard 1989; Budd and Whimster 1992; Cummings 1988; Fainstein et al. 1986; Faintein 1994; Feagin and Parker 1990; Gottdiener and Pickvance 1991; Harvey 1989a; Logan and Swanstrom 1990; Mollenkopf 1983; Nyden and Wiewel 1991; Smith and Feagin 1987; Squires 1989; Stone and Sanders 1987.

2. Economies of makeshift are defined by "their strictly ad hoc character," increased mobility, a resort to public relief, charity, begging, and work in the underground economy (Hopper, Susser, and Conover 1985, 214). The assumption that the economy is divided into a dual labor market is problematic; in fact, the divisions of labor are much more complex. However, I agree with Mayer (1991) here when she claims that the growth of labor is occurring in "the advanced services and high-tech sector and the unregulated, labor-intensive sector" (109). While the objective growth of employment may be occurring in many areas, the resultant effect of labor market changes is to reduce growth to two polarized dimensions. One could ascribe this result to the decline of unionization common to the post-Fordist economy.

3. In New York City this has had the unfortunate effect of increasing competition for units in remaining SROs, with the result that SRO single tenants are displaced in favor of homeless families receiving state subsidies (Hopper, Susser, and Conover 1985, 202). See also Hoch and Slayton 1989 for Chicago data, and Kasinitz 1986 for general trends in SRO displacement.

4. This transformation from a Fordist to a post-Fordist economy (Mayer 1991) has expanded the relative difference in income levels between the top five percent of the population and the bottom fifty percent. The labor bargain with management established for over fifty years is now coming to an end. What the result will be, remains to be seen.

5. I use the term *polarized topographies* here in a manner similar to Savage and Warde's (1993, 86) use of the term *social polarisation* and from Chris Hamnett's (1984) use of the term *socio-tenurial polarisation.* Applied to Britain, socio-tenurial polarization is the "tendency for people with limited material resources to be increasingly concentrated in residualised public-sector housing" (Savage and Warde 1993, 87). However, I would like to broaden this definition to include both the dispersion and containment of the very poor and homeless in a manner similar to that conceived by Mike Davis (1990, 1992). Polarized topographies include a bifurcation of wages and housing costs, but also they include a cultural bifurcation expressed in geographic terms, often with border fights over the meaning of land use. Because, polarized topographies are generated through the expansion of social inequality, it is also clear that the uneven nature of that expansion will mean that such topographies are not stable but float temporally and geographically around a city, depending upon investment patterns and the flight of the very poor. One could say that polarized topographies are the dominant form of social-physical space in contemporary urban society, given form in the production and consumption of refuse, pleasure, and functional spaces.

6. In his study of Edmonton, Canada, Leo (1995) demonstrates how that city's economic fortunes were reversed after city officials accommodated developers. The outside forces, principally the surbanization of commercial and residential development, drew revenue and much-needed employment away from the city center. Developers promised a way for city officials to recover these losses, but failed to deliver on their promises. Economic decline was not inevitable, however. Rather, it was the failed regime politics within Edmonton's city government that led to the accommodations in the first place.

7. An example of this type of privately owned global development corporation is Olympia and York, with development portfolios in Europe, North America, Russia, and Japan. Responsible for developing Canary Wharf in England, Olympia and York has assets between $11 and $18 billion in 1990 (Crilley 1993, 128). Not simply involved in real estate development, Olympia and York has extensive controlling interests in Canadian energy production and distribution, in North American retailing and transportation, and other investments not directly related to land development. According to Crilley (1993), "O&Y is like a plague of locusts, settling on one city only to move on and devour the rich package of incentives that competing city growth coalitions feed it" (128).

8. In a measure to save state costs, cities might use incentive zoning to induce corporations to build miniparks in exchange for expanding their building space (Whyte 1988, 229–55).

9. Davis (1991, 10) critiques Logan and Molotch (1987) for their presumption of community solidarity. Community dynamics are much more complicated than Logan and Molotch imply, with many different coalitions and interests jockeying for power, often all at the same time.

10. However, as I have mentioned before, I do believe that the label *hypermodern* is more appropriate than either *postmodern* or *postindustrial* for the simple fact that such exclusions have been practiced in the past, as has the marketing of social-physical space. The difference, as I have mentioned, is the degree of intensity of such exclusions and commodifications. It is this degree of intensity that can generate extremely polarized topographies.

11. See Williams 1988 for a look at the way housed citizens made sense of their everyday landscape in the midst of stalled gentrification in a Washington, D.C., neighborhood. Renters used rhetoric of home to resist gentrification: "These renters too expressed their anger over the threat of displacement, in part through, efforts to align themselves with the qualities with which the home metaphor endows owners-settledness, commitment, connections, control" (75). Neighbors' refusing the siting of a shelter or low-income housing in a settled community illustrates the differences between housed citizens and homeless street people. The same process of refusal of the very poor and homeless is found in middle-class communities in the advancement of no-growth initiatives, barely disguising the attempt to exclude the poor from privileged neighborhoods.

12. In Harvey's analysis of the role of planning and the development of city spaces, rational calculation of gain is the most important variable. "The main thrust of the modern commitment to planning (whether at the state or corporate level) rests on the idea that certain forms of investment in the secondary and tertiary circuits are potentially productive" (Harvey 1981, 101). Budgetary and cost-benefit analyses are calculations performed to assure this fact.

13. See also Deutsche 1988 for a critical account of Battery Park City.

14. Savage and Warde (1993) identify four processes involved in gentrification, (1) the "resettlement and social concentration" of populations involving displacing one group for another of higher status, (2) the development of new services and newly designed aesthetic features in the built environment, (3) the coming together of individuals who

share a similar style in cultural consumption, and (4) the "economic reordering of property values" (80).

15. Much of this discourse was borrowed from the social sciences, which at the time held out the promise of developing more "scientific" ways of managing populations, conforming to the technocratic rationalism of the day (Jordan 1994).

16. The development of "naturalized" understandings of social-physical space by the early Chicago school of urban ecology worked in tandem with the newly developing city-planning schemes to rationalize given types of city forms. For example, in his 1929 essay, "The City as a Social Laboratory," in which he commented on Louis Wirth's *The Ghetto*, Robert Park notes that the Jewish ghetto studied by Wirth "has persisted . . . because it performed a social function, making it possible for two unassimilated peoples to live together, participating in a single economy, but preserving, at the same time, each its own racial and cultural integrity" (Park 1967, 9). Park views Wirth's study of the Ghetto as an example of the "natural history of an institution of Jewish life." For Park, as indeed for the urban ecologists in general, "the city is, in fact, a constellation of natural areas, each with its own characteristic milieu, and each performing its specific function in the urban community as a whole" (9–10).

In a 1926 essay entitled "Spatial Patterns and a Moral Order," Park claims, in commenting on Ernest Burgess paper of 1922, that the city is "a product of natural forces, extending its own boundaries more or less independently of the limits imposed upon it for political and administrative purposes" (Park 1967, 57). Refuting the notion that city growth is only a result of physical aggregation, Park states that transportation systems act to bring more people into the cities, inflating land values at the center and increasing the radius of speculation. Technological determinism replaced physical determinism. Both maintained functionalist distinctions and thereby preserved disciplinary control over land use. In Park's invocation of a mythical "moral order" in the community, the imposition of disciplinary control is naturalized, differentiated by the habits of specific social groups. Everything is in its proper place, and the relationships of power and privilege that gave rise to such relationships are ignored. That awareness had to wait until the birth of community sociology and the rise of the Marxian models in the 1960s. This tendency to naturalize land areas in functional domains relies upon psychology to describe, as Park would say, "not individuals, but attitudes." Therefore, bad attitudes would lead to bad behavior and dysfunctional arrangement of people's and spaces. One can easily see here an early version of contemporary blame-the-victim arguments used in developing contemporary homeless shelters and homeless policies of individual empowerment.

17. We have seen the problems of dualism in chapter 1, especially with regard to race and gender. Dualisms are inherently reductionistic and usually carry a "metaphor of dominance and submission. Such dualities reproduce hegemonic ideologies, stifle the imagination of resistance, and frequently reinforce a political conservatism" (Beauregard 1993, 218). On the other hand, people, including planners and developers, do use dualisms, to think about social-physical space, and, yes, they are about dominance and submission, centers and peripheries—such is the nature of everyday life under stratified systems of social inequality. To be aware of this is to look for ways such dualisms can be ruptured. One way is through the development of counter social imaginaries and appropriate social-physical spaces of everyday life to carry them through—this is the utopian impulse, the nature of dreams.

18. See Marcuse 1993, 1995, and the introduction to Mollenkopf and Castells's *Dual City* (1991) for a further critique of the "dual city model." Marcuse's invocation of the "quartered" city is a step in the right direction in understanding the great complexity of contemporary cities, which is often concealed by the use of the dual city model. However, even the "quartered" city model is a reduction that masks the fluid nature of social-physical space, the often rapidly changing nature of boundaries, and the complex nature of political maneuverings involved in redevelopment.

19. Duncan (1979) interprets marginal space to include "alleys, dumps, space under bridges, behind hedgerows, on the roof of buildings, and in other no man's lands such as around railroad yards, which are not considered worth the cost of patrolling" (27).

20. "The openness of open space is not a matter of how few buildings stand on it but whether it permits the freely chosen actions of its users" (Lynch and Hack, quoted in McDonogh 1993, 4).

21. As a result of "badly planned" deinstitutionalization procedures for the mentally ill during the early 1970s, discharged mental patients would frequently show up in public places. Acording to Hopper (1991), "it was not skid row but the metropolitan airport that can claim the distinction of being the site of early complaints about the wandering deranged" (157). However, contrary to many researchers who claim that homeless gathering in airports is a symptom of a deep "pathological disorder," Hopper maintains that the choice of an airport is a utilitarian one, not a symbolic one. Part of the reason has to do

with the suspension of established rules of social behavior, particularly behaviors that maintain distinctions between private and public spaces (162–63). Many people sleep in airports between flights, many carry bags and luggage. In such a functional space, it is easy to "pass" as a traveler.

22. As I noted in the introduction, Massey and Denton's (1993, 1989, 1988a, 1988b) argument is that racial segregation persists, as "hypersegregation," and continues to effect mobility patterns of black residents in patterns of mortgage discrimination, redlining, and a host of other spatial strategies that work to exclude blacks from white communities. However, critiquing the unit of analysis used by Massey and Denton, Maly and Nyden (forthcoming) assert that local community involvement can blunt the development of segregation within cities, a factor often obscured by the use of national and state data dependent upon a strictly quantitative methodology.

23. In a 1979 study of neighborhood revitalization in St. Louis, Tobin and Judd (1982) discovered the factors that prospective suburban neighbors rated as the most important for city redevelopment. They were "neighborhood appearance, type of neighbors, distance to work, racial make-up, and school quality" (Judd 1988, 400). Tobin and Judd (1982) concluded that these same people would move back into the city if they could be kept from having to interact with blacks and poor persons "both in their neighborhoods and in their schools" (778). Class and race segregation still seem to be main factors in influencing redevelopment in the 1990s.

24. See the material in chapter 4.

25. Citywalk, a sanitized version of downtown Los Angeles located next to Universal Studios, is a fabrication of "Mexican-American culture" that weakly simulates the original; it is intended to be palatable to non–Mexican American audiences who wish to "play it safe." This same process is also in effect in many other cities that have redevelopment projects that cater to a predominantly middle-class white audience with fantasies of the "other" as unsafe, dangerous, and dirty.

Chapter 3. Making Pleasure and Refuse

1. According to Ranney (1992) 79,744 jobs were lost in the Chicago area during the 1980s "as a result of plant closings or major layoffs by transnational corporate parents." Of these, 62 percent "involved corporate parents closing Chicago plants while expanding operations in other countries" (11). Electronics and primary metals were the largest

category and included companies such as Zenith, Sunbeam, General Electric, Wisconsin Steel, and U.S. Steel South Works.

2. The degree of racial segregation is evident. Of Chicago's 77 community areas, 31 contain majorities of African American, and 21 have concentrations of African Americans greater than 90 percent. These communities are concentrated on both the South and West Sides of Chicago.

3. Of the 18,781 clients who used the Department of Human Services during FY 1993, 8,329 used overnight shelters, 8,759 used transitional shelters, and 1,693 used the second stage shelters (City of Chicago 1994, 33). Chicago lists 77 year-round shelters, with only 4,600 beds. Of these, only 960 beds are listed for overnight emergency shelter.

In a report issued by the U.S. Conference of Mayors (1994), a survey of thirty major U.S. cities revealed a 13 percent average increase in requests for emergency shelter in 1993. Requests from homeless families increased 21 percent. San Juan, Los Angeles, and Charlotte, North Carolina, had the largest increases in requests. However, Chicago's level of requests remained low, with a zero percent increase in demands for emergency shelter, and a 2.5 percent increase in families requesting emergency shelter.

4. Homebase is a regional center for the development of homeless policy guidelines and programs, located in San Francisco, California. In a study of assistance and shelter approvals granted by Aid to Families with Dependent Children, it reported a total of 11,442 homeless people in family units for Santa Clara County during the fiscal year 1989–90. Assuming that homeless families constitute only 33 percent of the overall homeless population, the resulting total for Santa Clara County through 1989–90 would have been over 34,000 (Leary 1990). Figures for 1987 were reported by Homebase at around 13,000. Help House the Homeless, a nonprofit homeless advocacy group, estimated a countywide figure of 19,600 for the fiscal year 1987–88 (City of San Jose 1991a, 19). Current county estimates are placed at 30,000 homeless persons, with at least 18,000 of these residing in San Jose (City of San Jose 1993, 21–22). Preliminary reports from a countywide survey of shelter facilities indicated that for the fiscal year 1994-95, approximately 16,300 people experienced an episode of homelessness. A word of caution: Homeless estimates are unreliable due to the problematic nature of counting people who are frequently on the move. Many homeless do not use shelters or use their food services. The point to keep in mind is that regardless of the actual count of homelessness there are

"between 30,000 and 50,000 households who are at risk of becoming homeless" in San Jose alone (City of San Jose 1993, 19).

5. In addition, the decline of inexpensive movie houses makes it difficult for homeless individuals to sleep undisturbed during the day.

6. In struggles over the South Loop redevelopment, CCH has been assisted by numerous housing and community groups, including the Chicago Affordable Housing Coalition, the Statewide Housing Action Coalition, and Architects/Designers/Planners for Social Responsibility (ADPSR). In reaction to the city of Chicago's plans for the South Loop, the ADPSR, in coalition with community groups, developed *The South Loop Planning Process: The People's Working Plan* as an alternative that promoted community interests rather than corporate interests.

7. In 1993 the "Magnificent Mile" generated retail sales in excess of $1 billion—double the 1985 figure of $565 million, according to the Greater North Michigan Avenue Association (Podmolik 1995). The John Hancock Center sports a new exterior at a redevelopment cost of $22.5 million. Merchants associated with both urban and suburban locations are increasingly relocating to North Michigan Avenue, including Victoria's Secret, the Cheesecake Factory, the Ghiradelli Chocolate Factory, Eddie Bauer, and others. With 2.6 million square feet of retail space and demographics of 125,000 nearby workers and 22,000 living in the area of North Michigan Avenue, landlords can command rents of $450 a square foot for commercial space. In a very real sense, North Michigan is a cash cow for Chicago.

8. The newly refurbished Navy Pier, home of Chicago's Children's Museum, the Crystal Gardens, a Family Pavilion, and a 170,000-square-foot Festival Hall, cost more than $150 million of state money, which still wasn't sufficient to complete the project. (The new Navy Pier was designed by VOA and Benjamin Thompson Associates, the designers who built Faneuil Hall Marketplace in Boston and Harbor Place in Baltimore along with South Street Seaport in Manhattan.) Funding was supplemented by $26 million from interest on McCormick Place expansion bonds and $3.5 million from the National Park Service to produce a Gateway Park (Pick 1995, 19). Navy Pier juts out into Lake Michigan from the area known as Streeterville and promises to increase revenue for this area of the city.

9. The Loop is defined here as the area bounded by the Chicago River to the west and north, Michigan Avenue to the east, and Congress Street to the south. The Streeterville/North Michigan Avenue area is bounded by Lake Michigan to the east, Oak Street to the north, the Chicago River to the south, and Dearborn to the west. The West Loop

is bounded by Oak Street to the north, Congress Street to the south, Halsted Street to the west, and the Chicago River to the east. The West Loop area contains 2,346 housing units in Presidential Towers. The South Loop is bounded by Congress Street, to the north, Roosevelt to the south, Lake Michigan to the east, and Halsted to the west.

10. Percentages might not total 100 percent because farming, forestry, and fishing occupations were excluded from the chart but not from the calculations. Persons working in these occupations totaled 5,907 in 1990, an increase of 2,189.

11. In 1992 Sears Roebuck abandon its downtown Chicago building, Sears Tower, the tallest building in the world, clearing 38 out of 40 floors and moving 5,000 jobs to the suburbs northwest of the city (Laing 1996, 39).

12. Of course, one could say that you would move to an area of the city that has rents you can afford. But this is precisely my point. The lack of decent low-cost housing and low wages relative to prices in the region means that more people are competing for fewer resources in a much smaller area "that they can afford." Equity would involve not having to move far from where one works in order to find decent housing. While this principle often is applied to those who can pay, we rarely consider it for those who cannot pay.

13. Looking at the data by race, we note that non-Hispanic blacks make up 47 percent of very-low-income households, followed by Native Americans at 46 percent, Hispanics at 40 percent, and Asian and Pacific Islanders at 33 percent. Whites make up only 24 percent of very-low-income renters. Conversely, non-Hispanic whites make up 50 percent of households at 95 percent of the median family income, followed by Asians and Pacific Islanders at 39 percent (City of Chicago 1994, table 1A).

14. In an attempt to rectify the severe shortage of housing, the city of Chicago, under pressure from 260 institutions, churches, and community groups, initiated the Chicago Affordable Housing and Community Jobs Bill in 1993. This bill was supposed to implement tracking of new affordable units and generate funds for new construction. According to an initial report issued in 1994 by the Chicago Rehab Network, the city's Department of Housing (DOH) was 37 percent short of Mayor Daley's committed amounts of affordable housing (Chicago Rehab Network 1994). In addition, DOH intentionally overcounts by 25 percent, the number of units created and miscounts shelter "beds" as units.

15. There are only two automobile entrances to the development, one at Ninth Street and another at Fourteenth Street, and the entrances face out on to State Street.

16. According to the city of Chicago, the Near West Side lost 3,260 SRO units between 1973 and 1990, with only 476 units remaining. The downtown Loop lost 4,729 units during the same time period, with only 762 remaining. The Near South Side lost no units during this period and has 630 units; these are now threatened by the city's redevelopment plans. The Near North Side lost the most—3,584 units lost between 1973 and 1990—with only 1,705 units remaining (City of Chicago, 1994, 84).

17. When an area like the South Loop receives a TIF designation, increased revenues from property development are funneled into an allocation fund that pays off the bonds originally sold to the public and serves to stimulate further property development within the district. Such financing is designated only for the TIF area and cannot be used by other taxing bodies, such as the Chicago Board of Education, Cook County, or the city of Chicago. In order to receive a TIF designation, the city must declare the area "blighted." For this to occur a specified number of conditions out of fourteen must be met, such as vacant lots, deteriorated buildings, and broken sidewalks. The TIF area for Central Station met those criteria (City of Chicago 1990). In the short run the city loses money. But it is hoped that greater funds will be generated over time, by developing strategic areas of the city.

18. In a 1985 study analyzing seven possible sites for a domed sports stadium, the Near West Side location was rated as the least desirable. Residential displacement was listed as the primary reason (City of Chicago 1985).

19. See also Suttles 1990, pp. 168–71, for another view of the Presidential Towers development.

20. According to the Uniform Relocation Act of 1970, displaced residents were to be fairly compensated up to $4,250. According to Hoch and Slayton (1989), local officials "gave the residents a token payment of ten dollars each—regardless of need of eligibility" (185). This precipitated a lawsuit against the city (*Lacko v. City of Chicago*) in which Chicago was found in violation of federal guidelines and required to track down, where possible, the former tenants and compensate them fairly. The city was also ordered to complete a report on SRO losses and the housing needs of single, low-income households.

21. The city of San Jose has long stated that it wished to attract two major department stores to the downtown area (City of San Jose 1992a, 15). However, it is competing with two major regional shopping malls located within a five-mile radius of the downtown area. Valley Fair Mall to the west is a mile from the downtown area, and a second

mall, Eastridge Mall, located to the southeast, serves the residential suburbs to the south and east of the city.

22. "Land, in Santa Clara County, that sold for less than $100,000 per acre five years ago now sells for approximately ten times that amount" (Homeless Overview Study Task Force 1989, 41). For example a 5,500 square foot lot, containing a 2,000 square foot single family home, sold for $9,000 in 1979, but increased in price to $108,500 ten years later.

23. Median residential housing prices jumped from $97,000 in 1980 to $230,000 in 1990. One would need a yearly income of $75,000 to afford the average single-family home (paying 30 percent of one's income for housing). The problem is not one of qualifying income requirements, because interest rates have dropped, lowering the income requirements; rather, fewer houses are being built that are affordable for lower-income households (City of San Jose 1991b, 59).

24. N=35,375 persons.

25. Lower-rent units in this example are calculated at $500/month for 1987.

26. Households that could afford only the lower-rent units went from 13 percent of households in 1980 to 24 percent in 1987.

27. See the Appendix.

28. In District 3 and District 5, respectively, 19.8 and 14.6 percent of the population live below the poverty line. In District 7, immediately to the south of Highway 280, 10.1 percent of the population live below the poverty line. The remaining districts have about half this level of poverty. Districts 3,5, and 7 are clustered in and around the downtown area (City of San Jose 1991b, 21).

29. "Behind the appealing edifice is a leveraged house of cards that depends on inflation in commercial real estate prices to fund its accelerating cash needs . . . Every year since 1988, the agency has spent, on average, $50 million more than it takes in" (Stone-Norman and Vankin 1992, 10). To pay off its debt the redevelopment agency must make decisions of where to cut. It favors big projects like the former proposed $40 million project for the Giants baseball stadium that was defeated by the voters, the renovation of hotels, assistance of the Fairmont Hotel, and other projects focused on the central business district. What are shortchanged are the neighborhood business districts located in ethnic communities, redevelopment areas outside of the central business district. According to Stone-Norman and Vankin (1992, 10), only 2.6 percent of redevelopment capital expenditures were spent on these areas since the late 1970s.

30. "The Meadows," a senior project of 41 units, is one example. Compared to very-low-income housing and shelters, senior housing is a safe political choice for affordable housing.

31. See also Baade and Dye (1988), Baim (1992), Bale (1989), Johnson (1993), and Rosentraub and Swindell (1991) for additional material on the impact of sports stadium development on city economic redevelopment.

32. The City Council has now abolished the use of Districts as measures of exclusion for all affordable house in its Five-Year Housing Investment Plan (City of San Jose 1995), and instead is attempting to define smaller "impact areas." Three-hundred SRO units are on the planning board for inside the frame areas of the city, but not the core, but one can surmise that these units may, in fact, be replacement units for those destroyed in the downtown area. The city has asked that all negative references to SRO construction be abolished and that all city policy documents should ". . . redefine SROs as an important compoentnt of the affordable housing stock . . ." (personal communication, City of San Jose, Department of Housing, May 31, 1996).

33. "All of the emergency shelters in San Jose are continually running at or near capacity. Many now maintain waiting lists. Another 140 shelter beds for families with children, 600 shelter beds for single persons of both sexes, and 150 more beds for single males are needed County wide" (City of San Jose 1991a, 36)

34. The number of total shelter beds for the entire city of San Jose has grown from 440 in 1985 to 1,940 in 1989. This includes, transitional, year-round, seasonal, and SRO housing (Homeless Overview Study Task Force 1989, 19). The City of San Jose supported 504 permanent shelter beds, three-hundred-fifty seasonal beds, three-hundred transitional and three-hundred SROs for the fiscal year 1994–95 (personal communication, City of San Jose, Department of Housing, May 31, 1996).

Chapter 4. Authoratative Strategies, Borders, and Homeless Containment

1. There is no "social logic" or "total system" that can unite "the partial systems or subsystems" (Lefebvre 1976a, 28). The unity of subsystems is the object of strategy, even if not achieved in reality.

2. Lefebvre's definition of strategy is helpful here. He defines strategy as springing "from an interconnection of chances and necessities which are always particular ones: confrontations between diverse and unequal forces, split into two opposing camps . . . Many elements

play their part: the goals, interests, wills, and representations of the various factions involved in the struggle, and the conceptions of the leaders" (Lefebvre 1976a, p. 79).

3. "The 'proper' is a triumph of place over time" (de Certeau 1984, 36). It is the control over, and the division of, space that "makes possible a panoptic practice proceeding from a place whence the eye can transform foreign forces into objects that can be observed and measured, and thus control and 'include' them within its scope of vision" (de Certeau 1984, 36).

4. Often, disputes break down into defining either what is not resistance (e.g., simple adaptive survival behaviors) or what is resistance (e.g., conscious, rational, politically motivated and organized responses to oppression). This ignores the continuity between both positions, the "grey" areas, within which most everyday struggles are waged. The use of terms like *adaptive* or *survival* is a feature of class-conscious knowledge: the labeling of the unruly classes, of the drinkers, dopers, tramps, and other characters of the cityscape, by those entrusted to study them. Such terms serve to deny agency on the part of those studied, while emphasizing the agency of the researcher. The same holds for those who define resistance as linked to politically motivated ends. "Survival" could not possibly be linked with resistance in this scenario, since it is conceived as purely reactive, again not accounting for human agency.

5. In completing forty-four extended interviews and spending close to two years visiting with homeless residents who sleep on Lower Wacker Drive in the North Loop area of Chicago, I found that the demarcation of urban spaces into safe and unsafe areas was quite clear. Repeatedly I was warned by the homeless men I spent time with that they were not free go north across the Michigan Avenue bridge to the Streeterville area at night, lest they be harassed by police. The "tourist" areas were considered particularly bad in this respect. Apart from police conduct, homeless persons often must contend with arbitrary violence directed at them from passersby. It is clear that a cultural climate that stigmatizes homelessness contributes to the violence against the very poor. Lower Wacker Drive homeless men still talk about the person who drove around under Lower Wacker Drive several years ago shooting cardboard boxes with a crossbow. One homeless man was killed in those incidents. On 4 August 1995 a homeless man in New York City was burned to death by five youths, ages 12 to 19, for "fun," because "they were bored" (Krauss 1995). Such incidents happen nationally on an occasional basis.

6. In the San Jose encampments, patrols by local police were feared more than those by the state highway patrol. Encampment members were told that the property they were squatting on was the jurisdiction of the city of San Jose and not the state of California. As long as their site was kept clean and out of public view, encampment members appeared to have very few problems with state authorities. However, San Jose police routinely removed the encampments.

7. The shelter system distinguishes between "deserving" and "undeserving" homeless, dependent upon attitudes and willingness to obey shelter authority and regulations. Developing the ability to "get by" (present oneself as "deserving") was crucial in making sure one had a bed in the local shelter. Presenting a deferential attitude toward authority is difficult for many homeless men who have become substance abusers or who have emotional difficulties, but without it one may be considered a "problem" and be locked out of the shelter.

8. See Foucault's (1991a) work on governmentality, and Cruikshank's (1994) analysis of the War of Poverty, for examinations of how government operates through third sector institutions as "government, without government."

Abu-lughod, Janel L. 1994. *From urban village to East Village: The battle for New York's Lower East Side.* Cambridge: Blackwell.

Adams, Carolyn, D. Bartelt, D. Elesh, I. Goldstein, N. Kleniewski, and W. Yancey. 1991. *Philadelphia: Neighborhoods, division, and conflict in a postindustrial city.* Philadelphia: Temple University Press.

Adelson, Andrea. 1995. Entertainment steps up as a mall anchor. *New York Times,* 16 April, 22.

Ades, P. 1989. The unconstitutionality of "antihomeless" laws: Ordinances prohibiting sleeping in outdoor places as a violation of the right to travel. *California Law Review* 77:595–628.

Adorno, Theodore. 1973. *Negative dialectics.* New York: Continuum.

Alcoff, Linda. 1991. The problem of speaking for others. *Cultural Critique* 20:5–32.

Allen, J. Linn. 1995. Fun, fun, fun: Mega one-stop entertainment centers are new lure in city vs. suburbs battle. *Chicago Tribune,* 7 May, sec. N, 1, 7C.

———. 1996. Apartment squeeze pushing rents way up. *Chicago Tribune,* 26 March, 1, 16.

Amott, Teresa L., and Julie A. Matthaei. 1991. *Race, gender and work: A multicultural history of women in the United States.* Boston: South End Press.

Anderson, Elijah. 1978. *A place on the corner.* Chicago: University of Chicago Press.

———. 1990. *Streetwise: Race, class and change in an urban community.* Chicago: University of Chicago Press.

Anderson, Nels. 1923. *The hobo.* Chicago: University of Chicago Press.

Anderson, Nick. 1992. Protestors return to scene of homeless arrests. *San Jose Mercury News,* 30 November, 1.

Aronowitz, Stanley, and William DiFazio. 1994. *The jobless future: Sci-tech and the dogma of work.* Minneapolis: University of Minnesota Press.

Aronowitz, Stanley, and Henry A. Giroux. 1991. *Postmodern education: Politics, culture, and social criticism.* Minneapolis: University of Minnesota Press.

Association of Bay Area Governments (ABAG). 1983. *San Francisco Bay Area housing needs determinations.* Oakland, Calif.: Association of Bay Area Governments.

Auletta, Ken. 1982. *The underclass.* New York: Vintage.

Aulette, Judy, and Albert Aulette. 1987. Police harassment of the homeless: The political purpose of the criminalization of homelessness. *Humanity and Society* 11, no.2.

Baade, R. A., and R. F. Dye. 1988. Sports stadiums and area development: A critical review. *Economic Development Quarterly* 2, 265–75.

Bahr, Howard M., ed. 1970. *Disaffiliated man: Essays and bibliography on Skid Row, vagrancy, and outsiders.* Toronto: University of Toronto Press.

———. 1973. *Skid Row.* Oxford: Oxford University Press.

Bailey, Cameron. 1988. Nigger/lover: The thin sheen of race in "Something Wild." *Screen* 29, no. 4.

Baim, D. 1992. *The sports stadium and a municipal investment.* Westport, Conn.: Greenwood Press.

Baker, Susan G. 1994. Gender, ethnicity, and homelessness: Accounting for demographic diversity on the streets. *American Behavioral Scientist* 37, no. 4:476–504.

Bale, J. 1989. *Sports geography.* New York: E. & F. M. Spon.

Barak, Gregg. 1992. *Gimme shelter: A social history of homelessness in contemporary America.* New York: Praeger.

Barak, Gregg, and Robert E. Bohm. 1989. The crimes of the homeless or the crime of homelessness? On the dialectics of criminalization, decriminalization, and victimization. *Contemporary Crises: Law, Crime and Social Policy* 13, no. 3 (September).

Barrett, Michele. 1980. *Women's oppression today: Problems in Marxist feminist analysis.* London: Verso Press.

Bartholomew, Amy, and Margit Mayer. 1992. Nomads of the present: Melucci's contribution to "New Social Movement" theory. *Theory, Culture and Society* 9:141–59.

Bartkey, S. L. 1988. Foucault, femininity, and the modernization of patriarchal power. In *Feminism and Foucault: Reflections on resistance,* ed. I. Diamond and L. Quinby, 61–86. Boston: Northeastern University Press.

Baudrillad, Jean. 1983. *Simulations.* New York: Semiotext(e), Inc.

Baum, Alice S., and Donald W. Burnes. 1993. *A nation in denial: The truths about homelessness.* Boulder: Westview Press.

Baxter, Ellen, and Kim Hopper. 1981. *Private lives/public spaces: Homeless adults on the streets of New York City.* New York: Community Services Society of New York, Institute for Social Welfare Research.

Beauregard, Robert A. 1989. *Atop the urban hierarchy.* Totoaw, N.J.: Rowman & Littlefield.

———. 1991. Capital restructuring and the new built environment of global cities: New York and Los Angeles. *International Journal of Urban and Regional Research* 15, no. 1:90–105.

———. 1993. Descendants of ascendant cities and other urban dualities. *Journal of Urban Affairs* 15, no. 3:217–30.

Belcher, John R. 1992. Poverty, homelessness, and racial exclusion. *Journal of Sociology and Social Work* 19, no. 4:41–54.

Belcher, John R., and Fredrick A. DiBlasio. 1990. *Helping the homeless: Where do we go from here?* Lexington, Mass.: Lexington Books.

Benard, Michael M. 1988. When is a private space a public place? *Journal of Real Estate Development* 4, no. 2:70–72.

Benford, Robert D. 1992. Dramaturgy and social movements: The social construction and communication of power. *Sociological Inquiry* 62, no. 1:36–55.

Bennett, Brian. 1995. Slain man's mourners say homeless face rising ill will. *Chicago Tribune*, 5 August, Sec. 1, 5.

Bennett, Larry. 1990. *Fragments of cities: The new American downtowns and neighborhoods.* Columbus: Ohio State University Press.

Betancur, John J., Deborah E. Bennett, and Patricia A. Wright. 1991. Effective strategies for community economic development. In *Challenging uneven development: An urban agenda,* ed. Philip W. Nyden and Wim Wiewel, 194–224. New Brunswick, N.J.: Rutgers University Press.

Billingsley, A. 1973. Black families and white social science. In *The death of white sociology* ed. Joyce Ladner, 431–50. New York: Vintage.

Blasi, Gary L. 1987. Litigation on behalf of the homeless: Systematic approaches. *Washington University Journal of Urban and Contemporary Law* 31 (winter): 137–41.

———. 1990. Social policy and social science research on homelessness. *Journal of Social Issues* 46, no. 4:207–19.

———. 1994. And we are not seen: Ideological and political barriers to understanding homelessness. *American Behavioral Scientist* 37, no. 4:563–86.

Blasi, Gary L., and James Preis. 1992. Litigation on behalf of the homeless. In *Homelessness: A national perspective*, ed. Marjorie J.

Robertson and Milton Greenblatt, 309–22. New York: Plenum Press.

Blau, Joel. 1992. *The visible poor: Homelessness in the United States.* Oxford: Oxford University Press.

Bloch, Ernst. 1986. *The principle of hope*, vol. 1. Cambridge: MIT Press.

Bogue, Donald. 1963. *Skid Row in American cities.* Chicago: University of Chicago Press.

Bordo, S. 1986. The Cartesian masculinization of thought. *Signs* 11, no. 3:439–56

Bourdieu, Pierre. 1984. *Distinctions: A social critique of the judgement of taste.* Cambridge: Harvard University Press.

Bourdieu, Pierre and J. C. Passeron. 1977. *Reproduction in education, society, and culture.* Thousand Oaks, Calif.: Sage.

Boyer, Christine M. 1983. *Dreaming the rational city: The myth of American city planning.* Cambridge: MIT Press.

———. 1990. The return of aesthetics to city planning. In *Philosophical streets: New approaches to urbanism*, ed. Dennis Crow, 93–112. Washington, D.C.: Maisonneuve Press.

———. 1992. Cities for sale: Merchandising history at South Street Seaport. In *Variations on a theme park: The new American city and the end of public space*, ed. Michael Sorkin, 181–204. New York: Noonday Press.

———. 1995. The great frame-up: Fantastic appearances in contemporary spatial politics. In *Spatial practices*, ed. Helen Liggett and David C. Perry, 81–109. Thousand Oaks, Calif.: Sage.

Briggs, Rosland. 1995. Chicago title site sold to Zell. *Chicago Tribune*, 27 July, Sec. 3, 1.

Budd, Leslie, and Sam Whimster. 1992. *Global finance and urban living.* New York: Routledge Press.

Burnham, L. 1987. Hands across skid row. *Drama Review*, 32:126–50.

Burt, Martha, and Barbara Cohen. 1989. *America's homeless: Numbers, characteristics and programs that serve them.* Washington, D.C.: Urban Institute.

Butler, Judith. 1987. Variations on sex and gender: Beauvoir, Wittig and Foucault. In *Feminism as critique*, ed. Seyla Benhabib and Drucilla Cornell 128–42. Minneapolis: University of Minnesota Press.

———. 1993. Endangered/endangering: Schematic racism and white paranoia. In *Reading urban uprising*, ed. Robert Gooding-Williams, 15–22. New York: Routledge.

Campbell, Richard, and Jimmie L. Reeves. 1989. Covering the Joyce Brown story. *Critical Studies in Mass Communication* 6:21–42.

Cassidy, Mike. 1990a. Editorial. *San Jose Mercury News*, 12 June, 6B.

———. 1990b. River dwellers await S.J.'s sweep. *San Jose Mercury News*, 12 June, 1, 14A.

———. 1990c. River ouster's ripple effect. *San Jose Mercury News*, September 10, 1.

———. 1990d. River refugees scramble to find housing. *San Jose Mercury News*, 27 June, 12A.

Castells, Manuel. 1983. *The city and the grassroots: A cross-cultural theory of urban social movements.* Berkeley: University of California Press.

Castoriadis, Cornelius. 1987. *The imaginary institution of society.* Cambridge: MIT Press.

———. 1991. *Philosophy, politics, autonomy: Essays in political philosophy.* New York: Oxford University Press.

Chapkis, Wendy. 1986. *Beauty secrets: Women and the politics of appearance.* Boston: South End Press.

Chicago Coalition for the Homeless. 1994–95. South Loop campaign heats up. Chicago Coalition for the Homeless Quarterly Newsletter (winter).

Chicago Rehab Network. 1994. *The Chicago Rehab Network's progress report on Mayor Daley's 1994 affordable housing and community jobs commitments.* Chicago: Chicago Rehab Network.

City of Chicago. 1973. *Chicago 21: A plan for the central area communities.* Chicago: City of Chicago.

———. 1975. *South Loop New Town: Guideline for development.* Chicago: Department of Development and Planning.

———. 1985. *Analysis of potential sites for a domed sports stadium.* Report to the Mayor's Advisory Committee. Chicago: City of Chicago, City of Chicago, Department of Planning.

———. 1990. *Central Station area: Tax increment redevelopment project eligibility report.* Chicago: City of Chicago, Department of Planning.

———. 1994. *Comprehensive housing affordability strategy (CHAS).* Chicago: City of Chicago, Department of Housing.

City of San Jose. 1988. *Final report of the Mayor's Task Force on Housing.* vol. 1. 4 August, 1–52. San Jose, California.

———. 1989. Referral from the San Jose Housing Task Force. *SRO housing: Downtown Working Review Committee: Report and Recommendations.* Redevelopment Agency of the City of San Jose, California, 26 May.

———. 1990. *Annual Report,* 1–16. San Jose: Redevelopment Agency of the City of San Jose.

———. 1991a. *Comprehensive housing affordability strategy (CHAS).* Department of Housing.

———. 1991b. *Horizon 2000 General Plan: Housing Appendix.* Department of City Planning, City of San Jose, San Jose, California.

———. 1992a. *Downtown 2010: Strategy plan*, Draft. Redevelopment Agency of the City of San Jose, San Jose, California. April.

———. 1992b. The Redevelopment Agency of the City of San Jose public brochure. San Jose, California.

———. 1993. *Comprehensive housing affordability strategy (CHAS): 1993 Update*, vol. 1. Department of Housing, City of San Jose, San Jose, California.

———. 1995. *Five-Year Housing Investment Plan.* Department of Housing, City of San Jose, San Jose, California.

Clorfene, Bruce Eldon. 1994. Panhandlers have homes here. *Evanston Clarion*, 18 May, 1.

Cohen, Jean L. 1985. Strategy or identity: New theoretical paradigms and contemporary social movements. *Social Research* 52, no. 4:663–716.

Cohen, Marcia B., and David Wagner. 1992. Acting on their own behalf: Affiliation and political mobilization among homeless people. *Journal of Sociology and Social Welfare* 19, no. 4:21–40.

Collin, Robert W., and Daniel J. Barry. 1987. Homelessness: A post-industrial society faces a legislative dilemma. *Akron Law Review* 20:409–31.

Collins, Patricia H. 1989. The social construction of invisibility: Black women's poverty in social problems discourse. In *Perspectives on social problems*, vol. 1, ed. James A. Holstein and Gale Miller, 77–93. Greenwich: JAI Press.

———. 1990. *Black feminist thought: Knowledge, consciousness, and the politics of empowerment.* Boston: Unwin Hyman.

Coontz, Stephanie. 1992. *The way we never were: American families and the nostalgia trap.* New York: Basic Books.

Crawford, Margaret. 1992. The world in a shopping mall. In *Variations on a theme park: The new American city and the end of public space*, ed. Michael Sorkin, 3–30. New York: Noonday Press.

Cress, D. M. 1990. *"Lookout world, the meek are getting ready:" Implications of mobilization among the homeless.* Paper presented at the 1990 American Sociological Association conference, Washington, D.C.

Crilley, Darrel. 1993. Megastructures and urban change: Aesthetics, ideology and design. In *The restless urban landscape*, ed Paul L. Knox, 127–64. Englewood Cliffs, NJ: Prentice-Hall.

Cruikshank, Barbara. 1994. The will to empower: Technologies of citizenship and the war on poverty. *Socialist Review* 23, no. 4:29–56.

Cummings, Scott, ed. 1988. *Business elites and urban development.* Albany: State University of New York Press.

Cybriwsky, Roman. 1978. Social aspects of neighborhood change. *Annals of the Association of American Geographers* 68:17–33.

Davis, John E. 1991. *Contested ground.* Ithaca, N.Y.: Cornell University Press.

Davis, Mike. 1990. *City of quartz: Excavating the future in Los Angeles.* London: Verso Press.

———. 1992. Fortress Los Angeles: The militarization of urban space. In *Variations on a theme park: The new American city and the end of public space,* ed. Michael Sorkin, 154–80. New York: Noonday Press.

Davis, P. 1986. *Public-private partnerships: Improving urban life.* New York: Academy of Political Science.

Dear, Michael, and Jennifer Wolch. 1987. *Landscapes of despair: From deinstitutionalization to homelessness.* Princeton: Princeton University Press.

Dearborn Park Corporation. 1977. *Developer response to Environmental Security Report for South Loop New Town.* Report submitted to the Department of Development and Planning, City of Chicago, Illinois.

de Certeau, M. 1984. *The practice of everyday life.* Berkeley: University of California Press.

De Lauretis, Teresa. 1987. *Technologies of gender.* Bloomington: Indiana University Press.

Deleuze, Gilles, and Felix Guattari. 1987. *A thousand plateaus: Capitalism and schizophrenia.* Minneapolis: University of Minnesota Press.

Delve, Cecilia, Suzanne D. Mintz, and Greig Stewart. 1990. *Community service as values education.* San Francisco: Jossey-Bass.

Deutsche, Rosalyn. 1988. Uneven development: Public art in New York City. *October* 47:3–52.

———. 1990. Architecture of the evicted. *Strategies,* no. 3:160–83.

———. 1991. Alternative space. In *If you only lived here: The city in art, theory, and social activism,* ed. Brian Wallis. Seattle: Seattle Bay Press.

Deutsche, Rosalyn, and C. Ryan. 1984. The fine art of gentrification. *October* 31:91–111.

Di Stefano, Christine. 1990. Dilemmas of difference: Feminism, modernity, and postmodernism. In *Feminism/Postmodernism,* ed. Linda J. Nicholson, 63–82. New York: Routledge.

Dugger, Celia W. 1994. Police form new team to deal with homeless. *New York Times*, 18 August.

Duncan, James. 1979. Men without property: The tramp's classification and use of urban space. *Antipode* 11, no. 1:24–34.

Edelman, Murray. 1987. *Constructing the political spectacle*. Chicago: University of Chicago Press.

Eder, Klaus. 1993. *The new politics of class: Social movements and cultural dynamics in advanced societies*. London: Sage.

Elkin, Stephen L. 1985. Twentieth century urban regimes. *Journal of Urban Affairs* 7, no. 2:11–28.

Estroff, Susan E. 1985. Medicalizing the margins: On being disgraced, disordered, and deserving. *Psychosocial Rehabilitation Journal* 8:34–39.

Euchner, Charles C. 1993. *Playing the field: Why sports teams move and cities fight to keep them*. Baltimore: John Hopkins University Press.

Evans, Sara, and Harry C. Boyte. 1992. *Free spaces: The sources of democratic change in America*. Chicago: University of Chicago Press.

Eyerman, Ron and Andrew Jamison. 1991. *Social movements: A cognitive approach*. University Park, PA: Pennsylvania State University.

Fabricant, Michael. 1986. Creating survival services. *Administration in Social Work* 10, no. 3, (fall): 71–84.

———. 1987. The political economy of homelessness. *Catalyst* 6, no. 1:11–28.

Fabricant, Michael, and I. Epstein. 1984. Legal and welfare rights advocacy: Complementary approaches in organizing on behalf of the homeless. *Urban and Social Change Review* 17, no. 1:15–19.

Fabricant, Michael, and M. Kelly. 1986. No haven for the homeless in a heartless economy. *Radical America* 20, 23–34.

Fainstein, Susan S. 1994. *The city builders: Property, politics, and planning in London and New York*. Cambridge: Blackwell.

Fainstein, Susan S., Norman I. Fainstein, Richard Child, Dennis Judd, and Michael Peter Smith. 1986. *Restructuring the city*. New York: Longman Press.

Fainstein, Susan S., Ian Gordon, and Michael Harloe, eds. 1992. *Divided cities: New York and London in the contemporary world*. Cambridge: Blackwell Press.

Fanon, Franz. 1967. *Black skin, white masks*. New York: Grove Press.

Feagin, Joe R. 1986. Urban real estate speculation in the United States: Implications for social science and urban planning. In *Critical perspectives on housing*, ed. Rachel G. Bratt, Chester Hartman, and Ann Meyerson, 99–118. Philadelphia: Temple University Press.

Feagin, Joe R., and Robert Parker. 1990. *Building American cities: The urban real estate game.* Englewood Cliffs, N.J.: Prentice-Hall.

Ferree, Myra Marx. 1992. The political context of rationality: Rational choice theory and resource mobilization. In *Frontiers in social movement theory,* ed. Aldon D. Morris, and Carol McClurg Mueller, 29–52. New Haven: Yale University Press.

Ferree, Myra Marx, and Frederick Miller. 1985. Mobilization and meaning: Toward and integration of social psychological and resource perspectives on social movements. *Sociological Inquiry* 55, no. 1:38–61.

Fireman, Bruce, and William Gamson. 1979. Utilitarian logic in the resource mobilization perspective. In *The dynamics of social movements,* ed. Mayer Zald and John McCarthy. Cambridge, Mass.: Winthrop Press.

Fischer, Pamela J. 1992. The criminalization of homelessness. In *Homelessness: A national perspective,* ed. Marjorie J. Robertson and Milton Greenblatt, 57–66. New York: Plenum Press.

Fiske, John. 1991. For cultural interpretation: A study of the culture of homelessness. *Critical Studies in Mass Communication* 8, no. 4:455–74.

Fogelson, Robert M. 1989. *America's armories: Architecture, society and public order.* Cambridge: Harvard University Press.

Foss, Daniel A., and Ralph Larkin. 1986. *Beyond revolution: A new theory of social movements.* South Hadley, Mass.: Bergin & Garvey.

Foucault, Michel. 1972. *The archaeology of knowledge.* New York: Random House.

———. 1979. *Discipline and punish.* New York: Vintage Books.

———. 1980 *Power/knowledge: Selected interviews and other writings, 1972–1977.* New York: Pantheon Books.

———. 1986. Of other space. *Diacritics* (Spring):22–27

———. 1991a. Governmentality. In *The Foucault effect: Studies in governmentality,* ed. Graham Burcell, Colin Gordon, and Peter Miller, 87–104. Chicago: University of Chicago Press.

———. 1991b. Questions of method. In *The Foucault effect: Studies in governmentality,* ed. Graham Burcell, Colin Gordon, and Peter Miller, 73–86. Chicago: University of Chicago Press.

Fraser, Nancy. 1988. What's critical about critical theory? The case of Habermas and gender. In *Feminism as critique,* ed. Seyla Benhabib and Drucilla Cornell, 31–55. Minneapolis: University of Minnesota Press.

Frieden, Bernard J., and Lynn B. Sagalyn. 1989. *Downtown, Inc.: How America rebuilds cities.* Cambridge: MIT Press.

Friedman, Debra, and Doug McAdam. 1992. Collective identity and activism: Networks, choices, and the life of a social movement. In *Frontiers in social movement theory*, ed. Aldon D. Morris and Carol McClurg Mueller, 156–73. New Haven: Yale University Press.

Friere, Paulo. 1973. *Pedagogy of the oppressed.* New York: Seabury Press.

———. 1978. *Education for critical consciousness.* New York: Seabury Press.

Gallagher, Tom. 1995. Trespasser on Main St. (You!). *Nation*, 18 December, 787–90.

Gallup Organization. 1995. *Homeless but not helpless: A Los Angeles Mission report on what Americans believe about homeless people, their problems, and possible solutions.* Report prepared for the Los Angeles Mission, P.O. Box 5330, Los Angeles, Ca. 90055–0330.

Galster, George C. 1990. Racial steering by real estate agents: Mechanisms and motives. *Review of Black Political Economy* 19, no. 1:39–63.

Gammon, James, and George R. Grange. 1994. *Federal protection for Gospel rescue missions against unreasonable land use regulations.* Report prepared for the International Union of Gospel Missions, 1045 Swift, North Kansas City, Missouri, 64116.

Gamson, William J. 1975. *The strategy of social protest.* Homewood, Ill.: Dorsey Press.

———. 1991. Commitment and agency in social movements. *Sociological Forum* 6:27–50.

———. 1992. The social psychology of collective action. In *Frontiers in social movement theory*, ed. Aldon D. Morris and Carol McClurg Mueller, 53–76. New Haven: Yale University Press.

Gamson, William J., Bruce Fireman, and Steven Rytina. 1982. *Encounters with unjust authority.* Homewood, Ill.: Dorsey Press.

Gans, Herbert J. 1995. *The war against the poor: The underclass and antipoverty policy.* New York: Basic Books.

Garfinkel, Harold. 1956. Conditions of successful degradation ceremonies. *American Journal of Sociology* 61:240–44.

Gelhaus, Anne. 1994. Formerly homeless people find a haven on River Street. *San Jose City Times*, 5 January, 3.

Geoghegan, Vincent. 1987. *Utopianism and marxism.* New York: Methuen.

Giddens, Anthony. 1979. *Central problems in social theory: Action, structure and contradiction in social analysis.* Berkeley: University of California Press.

———. 1981. *A contemporary critique of historical materialism.* Berkeley: University of California Press.

———. 1984. *The constitution of society.* Berkeley: University of California.

———. 1990. *The consequences of modernity.* Stanford: Stanford University Press.

Gieryn, Thomas F. 1983. Boundary-work and the demarcation of science from non-science: Strains and interests in professional ideologies of scientists. *American Sociological Review* 48, no. 6 (December): 781–95.

Gilman, Sander L. 1985. *Difference and pathology: Stereotypes of sexuality, race, and madness.* Ithaca, N.Y.: Cornell University Press.

Giloth, Robert, and John Betancur. 1988. Where downtown meets neighborhood: Industrial displacement in Chicago, 1978–1987. *APA Journal* 54, no. 3:279–90.

Gilroy, Paul. 1991. *"There ain't no black in the Union Jack": The cultural politics of race and nation.* Chicago: University of Chicago Press.

Giroux, Henri. 1983. *Theory and resistance in education: A pedagogy for the opposition.* New York: Bergin & Garvey.

———. 1988. *Schooling and the struggle for public life.* Minneapolis: University of Minnesota Press.

Glasglow, David. 1981. *The black underclass.* New York: Vintage.

Goetz, Edward G. 1992. Land use and homeless policy in Los Angeles. *International Journal of Urban and Regional Research* 16, no. 4:540–54.

Goffman, Erving. 1959. *The presentation of self in everyday life.* New York: Doubleday Anchor Books.

———. 1961. *Asylums: Essays of the situation of mental patients and other inmates.* New York: Doubleday.

———. 1963. *Behavior in public places: Notes on the social organization of gatherings.* New York: Free Press.

Goldberg, David Theo. 1993a. "Polluting the body politic": Racist discourse and urban location. In *Racism, the city and the state,* ed. Malcolm Cross and Michael Keith, 45–60. New York: Routledge.

———. 1993b. *Racist culture: Philosophy and the politics of meaning.* Cambridge: Blackwell.

Golden, Stephanie. 1992. *The women outside: Meanings and myths of homelessness.* Berkeley: University of California Press.

Goldsmith, William W., and Edward J. Blakely. 1992. *Separate societies: Poverty and inequality in U.S. cities*. Philadelphia: Temple University Press.

Goode, Erich, and Nachman Ben-Hehuda. 1994. *Moral panics: The social construction of deviance*. Cambridge: Blackwell Press.

Gooding-Williams, Robert. 1993. "Look, a Negro!." In *Reading Rodney King: Reading urban uprising*, ed. Robert Gooding-Williams, 157–77. New York: Routledge.

Goodman, Robert. 1979. *The last entrepreneurs: America's regional wars for jobs and dollars*. Boston: South End Press.

Gottdiener, Mark. 1985. *The social production of urban space*. Austin: University of Texas Press.

———. 1995. *Postmodern semiotics: Material culture and the forms of postmodern life*. Cambridge: Blackwell.

Gottdiener, Mark, and Chris G. Pickvance, eds. 1991. *Urban life in transition*. Newbury Park, Calif.: Sage.

Gounis, Kostas. 1992. The manufacture of dependency: Shelterization revisited. *New England Journal of Public Policy* 8, no. 1:685–93.

Green, Bryan S. 1983. *Knowing the poor: A case study in textual reality construction*. London: Routledge and Kegan Paul.

Greenbaum, Susan D. 1993. Housing abandonment in inner-city black neighborhoods: A case study of the effects of the dual housing market. In *The cultural meaning of urban space*, ed. Robert Rotenberg and Gary McDonogh, 139–56. Westport: Bergin & Garvey.

Greenberg, M. R., F. J. Popper, and B. M. West. 1990. The TOADS: A new American urban epidemic. *Urban Affairs Quarterly* 25:435–54.

Hall, Peter. 1988. *Cities of tomorrow: An intellectual history of urban planning and design in the twentieth century*. New York: Basil Blackwell.

Hall, Stuart, Chas Critcher, Tony Jefferson, John Clarke, and Brian Roberts. 1978. *Policing the crisis: Mugging, the state, and law and order*. London: Macmillan.

Hamnett, C. 1984. Housing the two nations: Socio-tenurial polarization in England and Wales, 1961–1981. *Urban Studies* 21, no. 4:389–405.

Handler, Joel F. 1992. The modern pauper: The homeless in welfare history. In *Homelessness: A national perspective*, ed. Marjorie J. Robertson and Milton Greenblatt, 35–46. New York: Plenum Press.

Handler, Joel F., and Yeheskel Hasenfeld. 1991. *The moral construction of poverty: Welfare reform in America*. London: Sage.

Hanson, Susan, and Geraldine Pratt. 1995. *Gender, work, and space*. New York: Routledge.

Haraway, Donna. 1988. Situated knowledges: The science question in feminism and the privilege of partial perspective. *Feminist Studies* 14, no. 3:575–99.

Harris, Leonard. 1992. Agency and the concept of the underclass. In *The underclass question*, ed. Bill E. Lawson, 33–56. Philadelphia: Temple University.

Hartsock, Nancy. 1983. *Money, sex and power*. New York: Longman.

———. 1990. Foucault on power: A theory for women? In *Feminism/Postmodernism*, ed. Linda J. Nicholson, 157–75. New York: Routledge.

Harvey, David. 1973. *Social justice and the city*. Baltimore: John Hopkins University Press.

———. 1981. The urban process under capitalism: A framework for analysis. In *Urbanization and urban planning in capitalist society*, ed. Michael Dear and Allen J. Scott, 91–121. New York: Methuen.

———. 1989a. *The condition of postmodernity*. Cambridge: Blackwell.

———. 1989b. *The urban experience*. Baltimore: John Hopkins University Press.

Hayden, Dolores. 1981. *The grand domestic revolution: A history of feminist designs for American homes, neighborhoods and cities*. Cambridge: MIT Press.

———. 1984. *Redesigning the American dream: The future of housing, work, and family life*. New York: W. W. Norton.

Haymes, Stephan. 1995. *Race, culture and the city: A pedagogy for black urban struggle*. New York: State University of New York Press.

Hazle, Maline. 1990. Homeless program approved: San Jose to relocate camps from river. *San Jose Mercury News*, 13 June, 3B.

Healey, P. 1990. Understanding land and property development processes: Some key issues. In *Land and property development in a changing context*, ed. Patsy Healey and Rupert Nabarro, 3–14. Brookfield, VT: Ashgate.

Hesse, Barnor. 1993. Black to front and black again: Racialization through contested times and spaces. In *Place and the politics of identity*, ed. Michael Keith and Steve Pile, 162–82. New York: Routledge.

Himmelfarb, G. 1984. *The idea of poverty: England in the early industrial age*. New York: Knopf.

Hoch, Charles. 1990. The rhetoric of applied research: Studying homelessness in Chicago. *Journal of Applied Sociology* 7:7–23.

Hoch, Charles, and Robert. A. Slayton. 1989. *New homeless and old: Community and the Skid Row hotel.* Philadelphia: Temple University Press.

Holloway, Lynette. 1994. 13 deaths by heroin prompt investigation in Manhattan. *New York Times,* 31 August, A1.

Hombs, Mary E. 1992. Reversals of fortune: America's homeless poor and their advocates in the 1990s. *New Formations* (Summer): 109–25.

Hombs, Mary E., and Mitch Snyder. 1983. *Homeless in America: A forced march to nowhere.* Washington, D.C.: Community for Creative Non-Violence.

Homeless Overview Study Task Force. 1989. *Homelessness in Santa Clara County 1989: New faces and hidden costs.* Santa Clara County Board of Supervisors Inter-Governmental Council, Santa Clara County, 70 W. Hedding St., San Jose, California 95110.

Hondagneu-Sotelo, Pierrette, and Sally Raskoff. 1994. Community service-learning: Promises and problems. *Teaching Sociology* 22, no. 3:248–54.

hooks, bell. 1990. *Yearning: Race, gender, and cultural politics.* Boston: South End Press.

Hopper, Kim. 1981. *Private lives/public spaces.* New York: Community Service Society.

———. 1982. *One year later: The homeless poor in New York City.* New York: Community Service Society.

———. 1991. Symptoms, survival, and the redefinition of public space: A feasibility study of homeless people at a metropolitan airport. *Urban Anthropology* 20, no. 2:155–75.

———. 1995. *Margins within margins: Notes on homelessness among African American men.* Nathen Kline Institute, New York, New York. Unpublished manuscript.

Hopper, Kim and Jim Baumohl. 1994. Held in abeyance: Rethinking homelessness and advocacy. *American Behavioral Scientist* 37, no. 4, 522–52.

Hopper, Kim, and Jill Hamburg. 1986. The making of America's homeless: From Skid Row to new poor, 1945–1984. In *Critical perspectives on housing,* ed. Rachel G. Bratt, Chester Hartman, and Ann Meyerson, 12–40. Philadelphia: Temple University Press.

Hopper, Kim, Ezra Susser, and Sarah Conover. 1985. Economics of makeshift: Deindustrialization and homelessness in New York City. *Urban Anthropology* 14, no. 1:183–235.

Howard, Dick. 1977. *The Marxian legacy.* New York: Macmillan.

Hunt, Scott. 1991. *Constructing collective identity in a peace movement organization*. Ph.D. dissertation, University of Nebraska, Lincoln.

Hunt, Scott, and Robert Benford. 1994. Identity talk in the peace and justice movement. *Journal of Contemporary Ethnography* 22, no. 4:488–517.

Hunter, Albert. 1985. Private, parochial and public social orders: The problem of crime and incivility in urban communities. In *The challenge of social control: Citizenship and institution building in modern society—Essays in honor of Morris Janowitz*, ed. Gerald D. Suttles and Mayer N. Zald, 230–42. Norwood, N.J.: Ablex.

Hunter, Robert. 1912. *Poverty*. New York: Macmillan.

Jacobs, Jane. 1963. *The death and life of great American cities*. New York: Vintage Books.

Jaggar, Alison. 1989. Love and knowledge: Emotion in feminist epistemology. In *Gender/body/knowledge: Feminist reconstructions of being and knowing*, ed. Alison Jaggar and Susan Bordo, 145–71. New Brunswick: Rutgers University Press.

Jahiel, Rene I. 1987. The situation of homelessness. In *The homeless in contemporary society*, ed. Richard D. Bingham, Roy E. Green, and Sammis B. White, 99–118. Newbury Park, Calif.: Sage.

Jakle, John A., and David Wilson. 1992. *Derelict landscapes: The wasting of America's built environment*. Savage, Md.: Rowman & Littlefield.

Jarrett, Robin. 1992. A family case study: An examination of the underclass debate. In *Qualitative methods in family research*, ed. Jane F. Gilgun, Kerry Daly, and Gerald Handel, 172–97. Newbury Park, Calif.: Sage.

Jeffers, Camille. 1967. *Living poor: A participant observer study of choices and priorities*. Ann Arbor, Mich.: Ann Arbor Publishers.

Jencks, Christopher. 1994. *The homeless*. Cambridge: Harvard University Press.

Jennings, James. 1990. The politics of black empowerment in urban America: Reflections on race, class, and community. In *Dilemmas of activism: Class, community, and the politics of local mobilization*, ed. Joseph M. King and Prudance S. Posner, 113–36. Philadelphia: Temple University Press.

Johnson, A. T. 1993. *Minor league baseball and local economic development*. Urbana: University of Illinois Press.

Jordan, John M. 1994. *Machine-age ideology: Social engineering and American liberalism, 1911–1939*. Chapel Hill: University of North Carolina Press.

Judd, Dennis R. 1988. *The politics of American cities: Private power and public policy.* Boston: Scott, Foresman.

Kantor, Paul. 1993. The dual city as political choice. *Journal of Urban Affairs* 15, no. 3:231–44.

Kasinitz, P. 1986. Gentrification and homelessness: The single room occupant and the inner city revival. In *Housing the homeless,* ed. J. Erickson and C. Wilhelm, 241–52. New Brunswick: Center for Urban Policy Research.

Katz, Michael B. 1989. *The undeserving poor: From the war on poverty to the war on welfare.* New York: Pantheon Books.

Keigher, Sharon M. 1992. Rediscovering the asylum. *Journal of Sociology and Social Work* 19, no. 4:177–97.

Keith, Michael. 1993. From punishment to discipline? Racism, racialization and the policing of social control: Racism and the postmodern city. In *Racism, the city and the state,* ed. Malcolm Cross and Keith Pile, 193–209. New York: Routledge.

Keith, Michael, and Malcolm Cross. 1993. Racism and the postmodern city. In *Racism, the city and the state,* ed. Malcolm Cross and Keith Pile, 1–30. New York: Routledge.

Keith, Michael, and Steve Pile. 1993. Introduction part I: The politics of place. In *Place and the politics of identity,* ed. Michael Keith and Steve Pile, 1–21. New York: Routledge.

Keller, E. 1985. *Reflections on gender and science.* New Haven: Yale University Press.

Kellner, Douglas. 1995. *Media culture: Culture studies, identity and politics between the modern and the postmodern.* New York: Routledge.

Kelly, Edmond. 1908. *The elimination of the tramp.* New York: Putnam.

Kieffer, Charles H. 1984. Citizen empowerment: A developmental perspective. In *Studies in empowerment: Steps toward understanding and action,* ed. Julian Rappaport and Robert Hess, 9–36. New York: Hayworth Press.

Klandersmans, Bert. 1988. Mobilization into social movements: Synthesizing European and American approaches. In *From structure to action: Comparing social movement research across cultures.* International Social Movement Research, vol. 1, ed. Bert Klandersmans, Hanspeter Kriesi, and Sidney Tarrow. Greenwich: JAI Press.

Klein, Julie T. 1990. *Interdisciplinarity: History, theory, and practice.* Detroit: Wayne State University Press.

Kleinig, John. 1993. Policing the homeless: An ethical dilemma. *Journal of Social Distress and the Homeless* 2, no. 4 (October): 289–303.

Koegel, Paul, and M. Audrey Burnam. 1992. Problems in the assessment of mental illness among the homeless: An empirical approach. In *Homelessness: A national perspective*, ed. Marjorie J. Roberston and Milton Greenblatt, 77–100. New York: Plenum Press.

Kovol, Joel. 1984. *White racism: A psychohistory*. New York: Columbia University Press.

Krauss, Clifford. 1995. Five youths are held in the fiery death of a homeless man. *New York Times*, 4 August, A16.

Kristeva, Julia. 1982. *Powers of horror: An essay in abjection*. New York: Columbia University Press.

Krumholz, Norman, and Pierre Clavel. 1994. *Reinventing the cities: Equity planners tell their stories*. Philadelphia: Temple University Press.

Laclau, E. 1990. *New reflections on the revolution of our time*. London: Verso.

Laing, Jonathan R. 1996. Downtown blues: Technological and social changes cast a cloud over urban office buildings. *Barron's*, 25 March, 33–40.

Lambert, Bruce. 1995a. HUD pulls group's grant, saying it bullied homeless. *New York Times*, 8 July, A14.

———. 1995b. Indigents may be victims of outreach workers. *New York Times*, 14 April, B16.

Lang, Michael H. 1989. *Homelessness amid affluence: Structure and paradox in the American political economy*. New York: Praeger.

Langman, Lauren. 1992. Neon cages: Shopping for subjectivity. In *Lifestyle shopping: The subject of consumption*, ed. Rob Shields, 40–82. New York: Routledge.

Lash, Scott, and John Urry. 1987. *The end of organized capitalism*. Cambridge: Polity.

Latour, Bruno. 1987. *Science in action: How to follow scientists and engineers through society*. Cambridge: Harvard University Press.

Lawrence, Joseph B. 1990. *Creating jobs, creating workers: Economic development and employment in metropolitan Chicago*. Chicago: University of Illinois Press.

Lawson, Bill E., 1992. *The underclass question*. Philadelphia: Temple University Press.

Leary, Kevin. 1990. Startling Bay homeless study. *San Francisco Chronicle*, 14 November, A2.

Leavitt, Jacqueline. 1992. Homelessness and the housing crisis. In *Homelessness: A national perspective*, ed. Marjorie J. Robertson and Milton Greenblatt, 19–34. New York: Plenum Press.

Lefebvre, Henri. 1976a. Reflections on the politics of space. *Antipode* 8:30–37.

———. 1976b. *The survival of capitalism.* London: Allison & Busby.

———. 1979. Space: Social product and use value. In *Critical Sociology,* ed. J. W. Freiberg, 285–95. New York: Irvington.

———. 1990. *Everyday life in the modern world.* New Brunswick, N.J.: Transaction Press.

———. 1991. *The production of space.* Oxford: Blackwell.

Lemann, Nicholas. 1986. The origins of the underclass. *Atlantic,* part 1 (June): 31–55, part 2 (July): 54–68.

———. 1988. A culture of poverty created the black underclass. In *In poverty: Opposing viewpoints,* ed. D. Bender and B. Leone, 80–85. St. Paul, Minn.: Greenhaven.

Leo, Christopher. 1995. Global change and local politics: Economic decline and the local regime in Edmonton. *Journal of Urban Affairs* 17, no. 3:277–99.

Levin, Charles. 1987. Carnal knowledge of aesthetic states. In *Body invaders,* ed. Arthur Kroker and M. Kroker. New York: St. Martin's Press.

Levine, Mark D. 1992. Tents along the Merrimack: Homelessness and university-community cooperation. In *Homelessness: New England and beyond,* ed. Padraig O'Malley, 523–38. Amherst: University of Massachusetts.

Liebow, Elliot. 1967. *Tally's corner.* Boston: Little, Brown.

———. 1993. *Tell them who I am: The lives of homeless women.* New York: Free Press.

Liggett, Helen. 1995. City sights/sites of memories and dreams. In *Spatial practices,* ed. Helen Liggett and David C. Perry, 243–73. Thousand Oaks, Calif.: Sage.

Lloyd, G. 1984. *The man of reason: "Male" and "female" in Western philosophy.* Minneapolis: University of Minnesota Press.

Logan, John R. 1993. Cycles and trends in real estate. In *The restless urban landscape,* ed. Paul L. Knox, 35–54. Englewood Cliffs, N.J.: Prentice-Hall.

Logan, John R., and Harvey L. Molotch. 1987. *Urban fortunes.* Berkeley: University of California Press.

Logan, John R., and Todd Swanstrom, 1990. *Beyond the city limits.* Philadelphia: Temple University Press.

London, Rebecca, and Deborah Puntenney. 1993. *A profile of Chicago's poverty and related conditions.* Evanston, Ill.: Northwestern University, Center for Urban Affairs and Policy Research.

Loseke, Donileen R. 1992. *The battered woman and shelters: The social construction of wife abuse.* Albany: State University of New York Press.

Ludgin, Mary K. 1989. *Downtown development: Chicago, 1987–1990.* Department of Planning, City of Chicago, Chicago, Illinois.

MacCannell, Dean. 1993. Democracy's turn: On homeless noir. In *Shades of noir: A reader,* ed. Joan Copjec, 279–97. New York: Verso Press.

Mair, Andrew. 1986. The homeless and the post-industrial city. *Political Geography Quarterly* 5, no. 4:351–68.

Maly, Michael T., and Philip Nyden. Forthcoming. Racial and ethnic diversity in urban communities: Challenging the perceived inevitability of segregation. *American Journal of Sociology.*

Marcuse, Peter. 1988. Neutralizing homelessness. *Socialist Review* 18, no. 1:69–95.

———. 1989. Gentrification, homelessness, and the work process. *Housing Studies* 4:211–20.

———. 1993. What's so new about divided cities? *International Journal of Urban and Regional Research* 17, no. 3:333–65.

———. 1995. Not chaos, but walls: Postmodernism and the partitioned city. In *Postmodern cities and spaces,* ed. Sophie Watson and Katherine Gibson, 243–43. Cambridge: Blackwell Press.

Markoff, John. 1996. In Silicon Valley, halcyon days are back. *New York Times,* 15 January, C2.

Marks, Carole. 1989. Occasional workers and chronic want: A review of the truly disadvantaged. *Journal of Sociology and Social Welfare* 16, no. 4:57–69.

———. 1991. The urban underclass. *Annual Review of Sociology* 17:445–66.

Martin, Elmer, and Joanne Martin. 1978. *The black extended family.* Chicago: University of Chicago Press.

Martin, Emily. 1992. *The woman in the body: A cultural analysis of reproduction.* Boston: Beacon Press.

Martins, Rui Mario. 1982. The theory of social space in the work of Henri Lefebvre. In *Urban political economy and social theory,* ed. Ray Forrest et al., 160–85. London: Gower.

Massey, Doreen. 1984. *Spatial divisions of labor: Social structures and the geography of production.* New York: Methuen.

Massey, Douglas S., and Nancy A. Denton. 1988a. Residential segregation of blacks, Hispanics, and Asians by socioeconomic status and generation. *Social Science Quarterly* 69:797–817.

————. 1988b. Surbanization and segregation in U.S. metropolitan areas. *American Journal of Sociology* 94, no. 3:592–626.

————. 1989. Hypersegregation in U.S. metropolitan areas: Black and Hispanic segregation along five dimensions. *Demography* 3 (26 August): 373–91.

————. 1993. *American apartheid: Segregation and the making of the underclass.* Cambridge: Harvard University Press.

Mayer, Margit. 1991. Politics in the post-Fordist city. *Socialist Review* 21, no. 1:105–24.

McAdam, Doug. 1986. Recruitment to high-risk activism: The case of Freedom Summer. *American Journal of Sociology* 92 (July): 64–90.

————. 1988. Micromobilization contexts and recruitment to activism. In *International social movement research,* vol. 1, ed. Bert Klandermans, Hanspeter Kriesi, and Sidney Tarrow, 125–54. New York: JAI Press.

McCarthy, John D., and Mayer N. Zald. 1977. Resource mobilization and social movements. *American Journal of Sociology* 82, (May): 1212–41.

McCourt, Kathleen, and Gwendolyn Nyden 1990. *Promises made, promises broken . . . the crisis and challenge: Homeless families in Chicago.* A report prepared for and with the Chicago Institute on Urban Poverty and Travelers & Immigrants Aid, Chicago, Illinois.

McDonogh, Gary. 1993. The geography of emptiness. In *The cultural meaning of urban space,* ed. Robert Rotenberg and Gary McDonogh, 3–16. Westport: Bergin & Garvey.

McDowell, Linda. 1991. Restructuring production and reproduction: Some theoretical and empirical issues relating to gender, or women in Britain. In *Urban life in transition,* ed. M. Gottdiener and Chris G. Pickvance, 77–105. Newbury Park, Calif.: Sage.

McEnery, Tom. 1994. *The new city-state: Change and renewal in America's cities.* Niwot, Colo.: Roberts Rinehart.

McLaren, Peter L. 1986. *Schooling as a ritual performance: Towards a political economy of educational symbols and gestures.* New York: Routledge.

————. 1989. On ideology and education: Critical pedagogy and the cultural politics of resistance. In *Critical pedagogy, the state, and cultural struggle,* ed. Henry A. Giroux and Peter L. Mclaren, 174–202. Albany: State University of New York Press.

————. 1991. Schooling the postmodern body: Critical pedagogy and the politics of enfleshment. In *Postmodernism, feminism and cultural politics*, ed. Henry A. Giroux, 144–73. Albany: State University of New York Press.

———. 1993. Border disputes: Multicultural narrative, identity formation, and critical pedagogy in postmodern America. In *Naming, silence, lives: Personal narratives and the process of educational change*, ed. Daniel McLaughlin and William G. Tierney, 201–35. New York: Routledge.

McRoberts, Flynn. 1994. Protest right in Daley's back yard: Homeless marchers demand revisions in South Loop proposal. *Chicago Tribune*, 28 June, 1, 8.

Megill, A. 1985. *Prophets of extremity*. Berkeley: University of California Press.

Melucci, Alberto. 1985. The symbolic challenge of contemporary movements. *Social Research* 52:789–816.

———. 1988. Getting involved: Identity and mobilization in social movements. *International Social Movement Research* 1, 329–48.

———. 1989. *Nomads of the present: Social movements and individual needs in contemporary society*. Philadelphia: Temple University Press.

Merves, Esther S. 1992. Homeless women: Beyond the bag lady myth. In *Homelessness: A national perspective*, ed. Marjorie J. Robertson and Milton Greenblatt, 229–44. New York: Plenum Press.

Michaeli, Ethan. 1994. Homeless groups protest city's development plan. *Chicago Defender*, 28 June, 1.

Miller, Henry. 1991. *On the fringe: The dispossessed in America*. Lexington: Lexington Books.

Mishel, Lawrence, and Jared Bernstein. 1994. *The state of working America II*. Washington, D.C.: Economy Policy Institute.

Mitchell, D. 1994. Landscape and surplus value: The making of the ordinary in Brentwood, CA. *Environment and Planning D: Society and Space* 12:7–30.

Mollenkopf, John Hull. 1983. *The contested city*. Princeton: Princeton University Press.

Mollenkopf, John Hull, and Manuel Castells, eds. 1991. *Dual city: Restructuring New York*. New York: Russell Sage Foundation.

Morris, Aldon D. 1984. *The origins of the civil rights movement*. New York: Free Press.

Morris, Lydia. 1994. *Dangerous classes: The underclass and social citizenship*. New York: Routledge.

Moynihan, Daniel. 1965. *The Negro family*. Washington: U.S. Department of Labor.

Murray, Charles. 1984. *Losing ground.* New York: Oxford University Press.

Murray, Charles and Richard J. Herrnstein. 1994. *The Bell Curve: intelligence and class structure in American life.* New York: Free Press.

Murray, Matthew. 1995. Correction at Cabrini-Green: A sociospatial exercise of power. *Environment and Planning D: Society and Space* 13:311–27.

National Law Center on Homelessness and Poverty. 1994. *No homeless people allowed: A report on anti-homeless laws, litigation and alternatives in 49 United States cities.* A report by the National Law Center on Homelessness and Poverty, 918 F. Street, NW, Suite 412, Washington, D.C. 20004 (December).

Newman, Katherine S. 1992. Culture and structure in The Truly Disadvantaged. *City and Society: Journal of the Society for Urban Anthropology* 6, (June): 3–25.

Nyden, Philip W., and Wim Wiewel, eds. 1991. *Challenging uneven development: An urban agenda for the 1990s.* New Brunswick: Rutgers University Press.

Oberschall, Anthony. 1973. *Social conflict and social movements.* Englewood Cliffs, N.J.: Prentice Hall.

Olson, Mancur, Jr. 1965. *The logic of collective action.* Cambridge: Harvard University Press.

Omi, Michael, and Howard Winant. 1994. *Racial formation in the United States: From the 1960s to the 1990s,* 2d ed. New York: Routledge.

Park, Robert E. 1967. *On social control and collective behavior.* Chicago: University of Chicago Press.

Paschke, B., and D. Volpendesta. 1991. *Homeless not helpless.* Berkeley, Calif.: Canterbury Press.

Penner, Maurice, and Susan Penner. 1989. Visual ideologies of the street homeless: Comparing editorial cartoons to fieldwork observations. *Visual Sociology Review* 4, no. 2:99–106.

Perin, Constance. 1977. *Everything in its place: Social order and land use in America.* Princeton: Princeton University Press.

Phelan, Jo, Ann Stueve, Bruce G. Link, and Robert E. Moore. 1995. Education, social liberalism, and economic conservatism: Attitudes toward homeless people. *American Sociological Review* 60, no. 1:126–40.

Pick, Grant. 1995. Navy Pier's rebirth: Will the place live up to the promises? *Chicago Tribune Magazine,* 21 May, Sec. 10, 14–19.

Pivan, Francis Fox, and Richard Cloward. 1971. *Regulating the poor: the functions of public welfare.* New York: Pantheon Books.

———. 1977. *Poor people's movements: Why they succeed, how they fail.* New York: Vintage Books.

———. 1992. Normalizing collective protest. In *Frontiers in social movement theory*, ed. A. D. Morris and Carol McClurg Mueller, 301–25. New Haven: Yale University Press.

Pizzorno, Alessandro. 1978. Political exchange and collective identity in industrial conflict. In *The resurgence of class conflict in Western Europe since 1968*, vol. 2, ed. C. Crouch, A. Pizzorno. London: Macmillan.

———. 1986. Some other kind of otherness: A critique of rational choice theories. In *Development, democracy and the art of trespassing*, ed. A. Foxley, M. McPherson, and G. O'Donnel. Notre Dame, Ind.: University of Notre Dame Press.

Plotnicov, Leonard. 1991. Competition and cooperation in contemporary American urban development. *City and Society* 5, no. 2:103–19.

Podmolik, Mary Ellen. 1995. Boom on the "Mile." *Chicago Sun-Times*, 8 March, 59.

Pottinger et al. v. City of Miami, 810 F.Supp. 1551 (S.D., Fla. 1992).

Procacci, Giovanna. 1991. Social economy and the government of poverty. In *The Foucault effect: Studies in governmentality*, ed. Graham Burchell, Colin Gordon, and Peter Miller, 151–68. Chicago: University of Chicago Press.

Quadagno, Jill. 1994. *The color of welfare: How racism undermined the War on Poverty.* New York: Oxford University Press.

Rader, Victoria. 1986. *Signal through the flames: Mitch Snyder and America's homeless.* Kansas City: Sheed & Ward.

Ranney, David C. 1992. *Transnational investment and job loss: The case of Chicago.* Chicago: University of Illinois at Chicago, Center for Economic Development.

Rappaport, Julian. 1984. Studies in empowerment: Introduction to the issue. In *Studies in empowerment: Steps toward understanding and action*, ed. Julian Rappaport and Robert Hess, 1–8. New York: Hayworth Press.

Reardon, Patrick T. 1994. Street plan for Daley's area OKd. *Chicago Tribune*, 9 March. Sec. 2, 3.

———. 1995. Loop still has pull even as city jobs slip. *Chicago Tribune*, 12 April, 1, 13.

Rheingold, Howard. 1993. *The virtual community: Homesteading on the electronic frontier.* New York: Addison-Wesley.

Rifkin, Jeremy. 1995. *The end of work: The decline of the global labor force and the dawn of the post-market era.* New York: Putnam.

Ringham, Karen. 1990. *At risk of homelessness: The roles of income and rent.* New York: Praeger.

Roach, Jack L., and Janet K. Roach. 1978. Mobilizing the poor: Road to a dead end. *Social Problems* 26, no. 2, 160–71.

Robertson, M. 1991. Interpreting homelessness: The influence of professional and non-professional service providers. *Urban Anthropology* 20, no. 2:141–53.

Rogers, Phillip, and Pashcal Rogers. 1995. The public electronic network (PEN) and the homeless in Santa Monica. *Journal of Applied Communication Research* 23:26–43.

Ropers, Richard H. 1988. *The invisible homeless: A new urban ecology.* New York: Insight Books.

Rosenthal, Robert. 1989. *Worlds within worlds: The lives of homeless people in context.* Paper presented at the 1989 American Sociological Association conference, San Francisco.

———. 1991. Straighter from the source: Alternative methods of researching homelessness. *Urban Anthropology* 20, no. 2:109–26.

———. 1993. Skidding/coping/escaping: Constraint, agency, and gender in the lives of homeless "Skidders." In *Negotiating at the margins: The gendered discourses of power and resistance,* ed. Sue Fisher and Kathy Davis, 205–34. New Brunswick: Rutgers University Press.

———. 1994. *Homeless in paradise: A map of the terrain.* Philadelphia: Temple University Press.

Rosentraub, M. S., and D. W. Swindell. 1991. Just say no? The economic and political realities of a small city's investment in minor league baseball. *Economic Development Quarterly* 5:152–67.

Rosentraub, M. S., Swindell, D., Przybylski, M., and D. R. Mullins. 1994. Sport and downtown development strategy: If you build it, will jobs come? *Journal of Urban Affairs* 16:221–39.

Rossi, Peter. 1989. *Down and out in America: The origins of homelessness.* Chicago: University of Chicago.

———. 1991. Going along or getting it right? *Journal of Applied Sociology* 8:77–81.

Rossi, Peter, and James Wright. 1989. The urban homeless: A portrait of urban dislocation. *Annals* of the AAPPSS, (January): 132–42.

Roth, Dee, Beverly G. Toomey, and Richard J. First. 1992. Gender, racial, and age variations among homeless persons. In *Homelessness: A national perspective,* ed. Marjorie J. Roberston and Milton Greenblatt, 199–212. New York: Plenum Press.

Rousseau, A. M. 1981. *Shopping bag ladies: Homeless women speak about their lives.* New York: Pilgrim Press.

Rowe, Stacy, and Jennifer Wolch. 1990. Social networks in time and space: Homeless women in Skid Row, Los Angeles. *Annals of the Association of American Geographers* 80, no. 2:184–204.

Rubin, Barbara. 1979. Aesthetic ideology and urban design. *Annals of the Association of American Geographers* 69, no. 3:339–61.

Ruddick, Susan. 1990. Heterotopias of the homeless: Strategies and tactics of placemaking in Los Angeles. *Strategies* 3, no. 3:184–201.

———. 1995. *Young and homeless in Hollywood: Mapping social identities.* London: Routledge.

Rybczynski, Witold. 1993. The new downtowns. *Atlantic Monthly,* May, 98–106.

Saegert, Susan. 1980. Masculine cities and feminine suburbs: Polarized ideas, contradictory realities. In *Women and the American city,* ed. Catharine R. Stimpson et. al., 93–108. Chicago: University of Chicago Press.

Sassan, Saskia. 1990. Economic restructuring and the American city. *Annual Review of Sociology* 16:465–90.

———. 1991: *The global city: New York, London, Tokyo.* Princeton: Princeton University Press.

Savage, Mike, and Alan Warde. 1993. *Urban sociology, capitalism and modernity.* New York: Continuum.

Saxenian, A. 1981. *Silicon chips and spatial structure: The industrial basis of urbanization in Santa Clara County.* Working Paper 345. Berkeley: University of California, Institute of Urban and Regional Development.

———. 1983. The urban contradictions of Silicon Valley: Regional growth and the restructuring of the semiconductor industry. *International Journal of Urban and Regional Research* 7:237–62.

———. 1995. *Regional advantage: Culture and competition in Silicon Valley and Route 128.* Cambridge: Harvard University Press.

Schneider, J. W. 1985. Social problems theory: The constructionist view. *Annual Review of Sociology* 11:209–29.

Schor, Juliet B. 1992. *The overworked American: The unexpected decline of leisure.* New York: Basic Books.

Scott, Allen. 1980. *The urban land nexus and the state.* London: Pion.

Scott, James C. 1985. *Weapons of the weak: Everyday forms of peasant resistance.* New Haven: Yale University Press.

―――. 1990. *Domination and the arts of resistance: Hidden transcripts*. New Haven: Yale University Press.

Serrano-Garcia, Irma. 1984. The illusion of empowerment: Community development within a colonial context. In *Studies in empowerment: Steps toward understanding and action*, ed. Julian Rappaport and Robert Hess, 173–200. New York: Hayworth Press.

Shimkin, Demitri, Edith Shimkin, and Dennis A. Frate, eds. 1978. *The extended family in Black societies*. Chicago: Aldine.

Silverman, Kaja. 1992. *Male subjectivity at the margins*. New York: Routledge.

Simon, Harry. 1992. Towns without pity: A constitutional and historical analysis of official efforts to drive homeless persons from American cities. *Tulane Law Review* 66, no. 4:632–76.

Smith, Dorothy. 1979. A sociology for women. In *The prism of sex: Essays in the sociology of knowledge*, ed. Julia Sherman and Evelyn Torton Beck, 135–87. Madison: University of Wisconsin Press.

Smith, Michael Peter, and Joe R. Feagin, eds. 1987. *The capitalist city*. Cambridge: Blackwell.

Smith, Neil. 1992. New city, new frontier: The Lower East Side as wild, wild, West. In *Variations on a theme park: The new American city and the end of public space*, ed. Michael Sorkin, 61–93. New York: Noonday Press.

Smith, Neil, Betsy Duncan, and Laura Reid. 1994. From disinvestment to reinvestment: Mapping the urban "Frontier" in the Lower East Side. In *From urban village to East Village: The battle for New York's Lower East Side*, ed. Janel L. Abu-lughod, 149–68. Cambridge: Blackwell Press.

Smith, Neil, and Peter Williams, eds. 1986. *Gentrification and the city*. Boston: Allen & Unwin.

Smith, William. 1994. Towering problem: Title building owners seek help on vacancies. *Chicago Sun-Times*, 13 September, 43.

Smith, Zay N. 1992. Homeless huts draw support from City Hall to living room. *Chicago Sun-Times*, 5 February, 4.

―――. 1992a. City no longer tolerates homeless huts. *Chicago Sun-Times*, 21 May, 3, 77.

―――. 1992b. Daley decision hits homeless where they live. *Chicago Sun-Times*, 22 May, 4.

―――. 1992c. Huts periled by proposal for 'urban Ravinia.' *Chicago Sun-Times*, 4 June, 6.

―――. 1992d. City take 7 homeless huts. *Chicago Sun-Times*, 11 June, 5.

Snow, David A., and Leon Anderson. 1987. Identity work among the homeless: The verbal construction and avowal of personal identities. *American Journal of Sociology* 92:1336–71.

———. 1991. Researching the homeless: The characteristic features and virtues of the case study. In *A case for the case study*, ed. Joe Feagin et. al., 148–73. Chapel Hill: University of North Carolina Press.

———. 1993. *Down on their luck*. Berkeley: University of California Press.

Snow, David A., Leon Anderson, and Paul Koegel. 1994. Distorting tendencies in research on the homeless. *American Behavioral Scientist* 37, no. 4:461–75.

Snow, David A., Leon Anderson, and M. Martin. 1986. The myth of pervasive mental illness among the homeless. *Social Problems* 33:407–23.

Snow, David A., S. G. Baker, and Leon Anderson. 1989. Criminality and homeless men: An empirical assessment. *Social Problems* 36:532–49.

Snow, David A., and Robert D. Benford. 1988. Ideology, frame resonance and participant mobilization. *International Social Movement Research* 1:197–217.

Snow, David A., E. Burke Rochford, Jr., Steven Worden, and Robert D. Benford. 1986. Frame alignment processes, micromobilization, and movement participation. *American Sociological Review* 51:464–81.

Snow, David A., Robert D. Benford, and Leon Anderson. 1986. Fieldwork roles and informational yield: a comparison of alternate settings and roles. *Urban Life* 14:377–408.

Soja, Ed. 1989. *Postmodern geographies*. London: Verso.

Solesbury, William. 1990. Property development and urban regeneration. In *Land and property development in a changing context*, ed. Patsy Healey and Rupert Nabarro, 186–95. Brookfield, Vt.: Ashgate Publishing Co.

Sosin, Michael, Paul Colson, and Susan Grossman. 1988. *Homelessness in Chicago: Poverty and pathology, social institutions and social change*. Chicago: University of Chicago School of Social Service Administration.

Spain, Daphne. 1992. *Gendered spaces*. Chapel Hill: University of North Carolina Press.

Spector, M., and J. I. Kitsuse. 1977. *Constructing social problems*. Menlo Park, Calif.: Cummings.

Spencer, J. William. 1994. Homeless in River City: Client work in human service encounters. In *Perspectives on social problems*, vol. 6, ed. James A. Holstein and Gale Miller, 29–45. Greenwich: JAI Press.

Spencer, J. William, and Jennifer McKinney. 1995. The micropolitics of trouble in human service encounters with the homeless: The emergence and management of interactive problematics. Paper delivered at the meetings of the Midwest Sociological Society, Chicago.

Spilerman, Seymour. 1977. Careers, labor market structure and socioeconomic achievement. *American Journal of Sociology* 83:551–93.

Spivak, Gayatri C. 1988. Can the Subaltern speak? In *Marxism and the Interpretation of Culture*, ed. Cary Nelson and Lawrence Grossberg, 271–316. Chicago: University of Illinois Press.

Squires, Gregory D., ed. 1989. *Unequal partnerships: The political economy of urban redevelopment in postwar America*. New Brunswick, N.J.: Rutgers University Press.

———. 1991. Partnership and the pursuit of the private city. In *Urban life in transition*, ed. Mark Gottdiener and Chris G. Pickvance, 196–221. Newbury Park, Calif.: Sage.

Squires, Gregory D., Larry Bennett, Kathleen McCourt, and Philip Nyden. 1987. *Chicago: Race, class, and the response to urban decline*. Philadelphia: Temple University Press.

Stack, Carol. 1974. *All our kin: Strategies for survival in a Black community*. New York: Harper & Row.

Staples, William G. 1994. Small acts of cunning: Disciplinary practices in contemporary life. *Sociological Quarterly* 35, no. 4:645–64.

Stark, Louisa R. 1994. The shelter as "total institution": An organizational barrier to remedying homelessness. *American Behavioral Scientist* 37, no. 4:553–62.

State of California. 1992. *Report E-5*. Demographic Research Unit, California Department of Finance, Sacramento, California. April.

State of Illinois. 1992. *Occupational Projections 2000*. Illinois Department of Employment Security, Economic Information and Analysis Division, State of Illinois, Chicago.

Stein, Sharman. 1992. West Loop shelters feel pressure as gentrification knocks. *Chicago Tribune,* 23 November, Sec. 2, 1, 4.

Stern, M. 1984. The emergence of the homeless as a social problem. *Social Service Review* 58:291–301.

Sternlieb, George, and James W. Hughes. 1980. The 'Two-Cities' Phenomenon. In *America's housing: Prospects and problems*, ed. George Sternlieb and J. W. Hughes, 177–84. New Brunswick, NJ: Rutgers University Press.

Stolarski, Lynn. 1988. Right to shelter: History of the mobilization of the homeless as a model of voluntary action. *Journal of Voluntary Action Research* 17, no. 1:36–43.

Stone, Clarence N., Marion E. Orr, and David Imbroscio. 1991. The reshaping of urban leadership in U.S. cities: A regime analysis. In *Urban life in transition,* ed. M. Gottdiener and Chris G. Pickvance, 222–39. New York: Sage.

Stone, Clarence N., and Heywood Sanders, eds. 1987. *The politics of urban development.* Lawrence: University Press of Kansas.

Stone-Norman, Lisa, and Jonathan Vankin. 1992. Payback. *Metro* (San Jose, Calif.), 19–25 March, 10.

Stoner, Madeleine R. 1995. *The civil rights of homeless people: Law, social policy, and social work practice.* New York: Aldine.

Sutherland, Edwin H., and Harvey J. Locke. 1936. *Twenty-thousand homeless men: A study of unemployed men in the Chicago shelters.* Chicago: J. B. Lippincott.

Suttles, Gerald D. 1990. *The man-made city: The land-use confidence game in Chicago.* Chicago: University of Chicago Press.

Task Force for the Homeless. 1995. *The criminalization of poverty.* A report from the Task Force for the Homeless, 363 Georgia Avenue, SE, Atlanta, Geogria 30312-3027.

Taub, Richard D., G. Taylor, and Jan Dunham. 1984. *Paths of neighborhood change. Chicago:* University of Chicago.

Taylor, Verta, and Nancy Whittier. 1992. Collective identity in social movement communities: Lesbian feminist mobilization. In *Frontiers of social movement theory,* ed. Aldon D. Morris and Carol McMclug Mueller, 174–202. New Haven: Yale University Press.

Theodore, Nikolas C. 1991. *The geography of opportunity: The status of African Americans in the Chicago area economy.* Chicago: Chicago Urban League, Department of Research and Planning.

Thomas, K., and P. A. Wright. 1990. *An assessment of single room occupancy (SRO) hotels in the South Loop.* Technical Report 2-90. Chicago: Nathalie P. Voorhees Center for Neighborhood and Community Improvement.

Thorton, J. 1992. City searches for a compromise on eliminating homeless huts. *Chicago Tribune,* 27 May, 2.

Tilley, Charles. 1978. *From mobilization to revolution.* Reading, Mass.: Addison-Wesley.

Timmer, Doug. A. 1988. Homelessness as deviance: The ideology of the shelter. *Free Inquiry in Creative Sociology* 16 (November): 163–70.

Timmer, Doug A., Stanley Eitzen, and Kathryn D. Talley. 1994. *Paths to homelessness: Extreme poverty and the urban housing crisis.* Boulder, Colo.: Westview.

Tobin, Gary A., and Dennis R. Judd. 1982. Moving the suburbs to the city: Neighborhood revitalization and the "amenities bundle." *Social Science Quarterly* 63, no. 4:771–80.

Toth, Jennifer. 1993. *The mole people: Life in the tunnels beneath New York City.* Chicago: Chicago Review Press.

Touraine, Alain. 1981. *The voice and the eye: An analysis of social movements.* New York: Cambridge University Press.

———. 1985. An introduction to the study of social movements. *Social Research* 52:749–88.

Trancik, R. 1986. *Finding lost spaces: Theories of urban design.* New York: Van Nostrand Reinhold.

Trounstine, Philip J., and Terry Christensen. 1982. *Movers and shakers: The study of community power.* New York: St. Martin's Press.

Turner, B. 1984. *The body and society: Explorations in social theory.* Oxford: Basil Blackwell.

Underwood, Jackson. 1993. *The bridge people: Daily life in a camp of the homeless.* New York: University Press of America.

U.S. Conference of Mayors. 1994. *A status report on hunger and homelessness in America's cities: 1994, A 30-city survey.* U.S. Conference of Mayors, 1620 Eye Street, NW, Washington, DC 20006.

U.S. Department of Housing and Urban Development. 1984. *Report to the secretary on the homeless and emergency shelters.* Washington, D.C.: U.S. Department of Housing and Urban Development.

———. 1993. *American housing survey for the Chicago Metropolitan Area in 1991.* Current Housing Reports H170/91-22.

U.S. Department of Labor. 1991. *Occupational compensation survey, pay and benefits: Chicago, Illinois, Metropolitan Area.* Bureau of Labor Statistics. 3060-43.

van Vliet, William. 1989. The limits of social research. *Society* (May–June): 16–20.

Wagner, David. 1993. *Checkerboard square: Culture and resistance in a homeless community.* Boulder, Colo.: Westview.

Wagner, David, and Marcia B. Cohen. 1991. The power of the people: Homeless protestors in the aftermath of social movement participation. *Social Problems* 38:543–61.

Wallis, Brian, ed. 1991. *If you only lived here: The city in art, theory, and social activism, a project by Martha Rosler.* Seattle: Bay Press.

Watson, Sophie, and Helen Austerberry. 1986. *Housing and homelessness: A feminist perspective.* Boston: Routledge & Kegan Paul.

Weisman, Leslie Kanes. 1992. *Discrimination by design: A feminist critique of the man-made environment.* Chicago: University of Illinois Press.

Welch, Mary Beth. 1992. Homeless but not helpless: Squatters take care of themselves and each other. In *Homelessness: A national perspective,* ed. Marjorie J. Robertson and Milton Greenblatt, 323–38. New York: Plenum Press.

West, Cornel. 1992. Philosophy and the urban underclass. In *The underclass question,* ed. Bill E. Lawson, 191–204. Philadelphia: Temple University Press.

Whyte, William H. 1988. *The city: Rediscovering the center.* New York: Doubleday.

Wiewel, Wim. 1990. Industries, jobs, and economic development policy in metropolitan Chicago: An overview of the decade. In *Creating jobs, creating workers: economic development and employment in metropolitan Chicago,* ed. Lawrence B. Joseph, 27–58. Chicago: University of Illinois Press.

Williams, Brett. 1988. *Upscaling Downtown: Stalled gentrification in Washington, D.C.* Ithaca, N.Y.: Cornell University Press.

Willis, Paul. 1981. *Learning to labor: How working-class kids get working class jobs.* New York: Columbia University Press.

Wilson, Elizabeth. 1991. *The sphinx in the city: Urban life, the control of disorder, and women.* Berkeley: University of California Press.

Wilson, Terry. 1994. On eve of World Cup, city removes homeless. *Chicago Tribune,* 16 June, Sec. 2, 3.

Wilson, William J. 1978. *The declining significance of race.* Chicago: University of Chicago Press.

———. 1987. *The truly disadvantaged: The inner city, the underclass, and public policy.* Chicago: University of Chicago Press.

Winchester, H. P. M., and P. E. White. 1988. The location of marginalized groups in the inner city. *Environment and Planning D: Society and Space* 6:37–54.

Wines, Michael. 1994. Step up Folks! Check it Out! Nationhood! *New York Times,* 29 May, H1.

Wintermute, Wendy, and Charles Hicklin. 1991. The employment potential of Chicago's service industries. In *Challenging uneven development: An urban agenda for the 1990s,* ed. Philip W. Nyden and Wim Wiewel, 144–65. New Brunswick, N.J.: Rutgers University Press.

Wood, Edward M., Jr., Sidney N. Brower, and Margaret W. Latimer. 1966. Planners' people. *Journal of the American Institute of Planners* 32:228–34.

Woodstock Institute. 1993. *The 1991 community lending factbook.* Woodstock Institute, 407 South Dearborn, Chicago, Illinois 60605.

Wright, Barbara. 1992. *Market feasibility analysis for the St. James Hotel.* Nathalie P. Voorhees Neighborhood Program, Center for Urban Economic Development, University of Illinois at Chicago, Chicago, Illinois.

Wright, Gwendolyn. 1981. *Building the dream: A social history of housing in America.* New York: Pantheon Press.

Wright, Talmadge. 1995. Tranquility City: Self-organization, protest, and collective gains within a Chicago homeless encampment. In *Marginal spaces: Comparative urban and regional research* vol. 5, ed. Michael P. Smith, 37–68. New Brunswick: Transaction.

Wright, Talmadge and Anita Vermund. Forthcoming. Suburban homelessness and social space: Strategies of authority and local resistances. In *There's no place like home,* ed. Anna Lou Dehavenon. New York: Bergin & Garvey.

Wylie, Scott. 1995. California supreme court rules in Tobe anti-camping case. *Homeless reporter* (Shelter Partnership, 523 West Sixth Street, Suite 616, Los Angeles, California 90014) 11, no. 1:1, 10.

Yeich, Susan. 1994. *The politics of ending homelessness.* New York: University Press of America.

Young, Iris Marion. 1988. Impartiality and the civic public. In *Feminism as critique,* ed. Seyla Benhabib and Drucilla Cornell, 56–76. Minneapolis: University of Minnesota.

———. 1990. *Justice and the politics of difference.* Princeton: Princeton University Press.

Yudice, G. 1988. Marginality and the ethics of survival. In *Universal abandon?* ed. Andrew Ross. Minneapolis: University of Minnesota Press.

Zarembka, A. 1990. *The urban housing crisis.* New York: Greenwood Press.

Zollar, Ann C. 1985. *A member of the family: Strategies for black family continuity.* Chicago: Nelson-Hall.

Zorn, Eric. 1991. Homeless claim new movie is giving them a bum rap. *Chicago Tribune,* 8 January, Sec. 2, 1, 4.

———. 1994. Homeless shelters no place of refuge. *Chicago Tribune,* 20 January, Sec. 2, 1.

Zukin, Sharon. 1988. The postmodern debate over urban form. *Theory, Culture & Society* 5, no. 2–3:431–46.

INDEX

A

Abuse: alcohol, 20, 21, 276; domestic, 216; escaping, 65; police, 239; of power, 217; sexual, 65; substance, 18, 205, 211, 276

Action(s): affirmative, 66; border-maintenance, 58; collective, 10–11, 12, 253–297, 308; cultural systems of, 2; defensive, 254, 284; defiant, 230; deviant, 2; direct, 3, 199, 234, 242, 293, 320; disrespectful, 49; disruptive, 268; everyday, 38; future, 227; group, 3; human, 45, 50; individual, 60, 226, 257, 264; interpretations of, 2; legal, 293; local, 50, 181; meaning of, 331n10; militant, 223, 241, 253, 264, 289; mobilization of, 29; nonroutinized, 50; police, 254, 272; political, 234, 264, 290, 312; potential for, 227, 320; practical, 27, 312; preference for, 223; protest, 30; rational, 257; routinizing, 58; scripting, 238, 239; shared, 7; situated character of, 49; social, 50, 312, 331n10; squatting, 29, 307; staging, 238; strategic, 183; survival, 6; utilitarian, 257

Activism: acceptable, 30; community, 2, 3, 187; homeless, 29, 117, 157; housing, 307; political, 229, 277, 328n7; "respectable," 30; social, 21

Adams, Carolyn, 88, 89
Ades, P., 90
Adorno, Theodore, 61
Advocacy, 2, 17, 20, 28; collective, 235; groups, 189, 223; homeless, 29–30, 31; individual, 235; legal, 234; organizations, 260; self-interest in, 36
African American(s): demonization of, 25, 26; female heads of household, 13; male income levels, 13; marginalization of, 26, 121, 253; occupational concentrations, 131; police attitudes toward, 188; poverty rates, 118; proportion of homeless, 20, 119, 120
Agency: active, 6, 10–11, 15, 25, 206, 293; creating, 227; homeless, 210; human, 46, 257, 258, 259; issues of, 27; marginalization of, 257; passive, 6; raps, 221; sense of, 204; subjective, 59
Alcoff, Linda, 32
Alienation, 42, 45, 300; personal, 12; social, 40; understanding of, 41
Allen, J. Linn, 133
Alvarez, Daniel, 246, 248, 294–295
Amott, Teresa, 65
Anderson, Leon, 18, 27, 100, 181, 182, 191, 195, 204, 216, 266, 267, 274, 293
Anderson, Nels, 37

385

homeless, 3, 8; meaning of, 255;
mental health services, 18, 82;
micro, 186, 187; organizations, 56,
88, 137, 260, 311; "place" in, 92;
resistance, 75, 229; sense of, 186,
283, 284; solidarity, 340n8
Community for Creative Non-
Violence, 19, 199
Community-Homeless Alliance, 242
Community Redevelopment Agency
(Los Angeles), 113
Comprehensive Housing Affordability
Strategy, 96, 301, 317
Conflict: border, 104, 333n17;
boundary, 55, 99; class, 208;
cognitive, 64; creation of, 57;
disallowance of, 50; internal, 277;
land use, 95; mediating, 276;
negotiating, 47, 285; over bodies,
64; political, 254; social, 67, 108;
sociospatial, 55; spatial, 102;
substitution of dualism for, 115;
worker/capitalist, 97
Conover, Sara, 29, 81, 82
Consciousness: cultural, 208; discursive, 331n11; false, 60; image, 128;
marginalization of, 257; political,
230, 249, 283; practical, 70, 331n11;
reintegration of, 257; spatial, 108
Conservatism, 9
Containment, 8, 9, 38; authoritative
strategies in, 10–11; as goal, 19; of
the homeless, 179–224; in shelters,
40, 214–224; and social imaginaries,
78
Control: acceleration of, 55; centralization of, 84; collective, 190; contested, 97; of discourse, 26;
expanded forms of, 55; group, 250;
of homeless, 191–203; land, 319;
militarization of, 52; over bodies,
61; patriarchal, 79; of public space,
108; of racial differences, 112;
resistance to, 2, 289; social, 29, 73,

216, 217, 247, 256, 264, 289; spatial,
40, 180, 190, 256, 330n6; strategies
of, 72; topographical, 250
Coontz, Stephanie, 78
Corporations: downsizing in, 29, 128,
131, 302; images of, 76; and
incentive zoning, 340n8; multinational, 9, 51, 88, 95, 339n7; worker
owned, 303
Crawford, Margaret, 104
Cress, D. M., 181, 257
Crime, 6; as "blackness," 77; exploitation of, 77; and refuse space, 106
Cross, Malcolm, 77
Cultural: assimilation, 190–191;
assumptions, 25; capital, 15, 101,
117, 124, 125, 209; codes, 114, 260;
consciousness, 208; deficit, 327n5;
differences, 4, 54, 61, 292; diversity, 322; exclusion, 184–190;
hegemony, 47; identity, 75, 114;
inequalities, 98, 99, 182, 312;
laboratories, 259, 260; meanings,
68; oppositions, 182; power, 42;
productions, 182; relationships,
228; representations, 89; resources,
284; struggles, 101
Culture: marginalization of, 257;
marketing, 9; official, 311; panic,
77, 98; patriarchal, 63; of politics,
258; of poverty, 21, 25, 163, 327n5;
of redevelopment, 92–97; reintegration of, 257; transformation of, 92;
Western, 63
Cybriwsky, Roman, 92

D

Dallas (Texas), 128
Davis, Mike, 77, 84, 87, 97, 320–321
Daytona Beach (Florida), 113
Dear, Michael, 27, 29, 52, 53, 89
de Certeau, M., 55, 180, 181